The
Money
POWER

ProgRESSive

2016

The Money Power
(Two Books in One)
Empire of the City by Knuth
Pawns in the Game by Carr

Published by ProgressivePress.com, Dec. 12, 2012.
Updated March 31, 2016. All rights reserved.
ISBN 1-61577-121-2, EAN 978-1-61577-121-9
Length: 163,000 words, 318 pages.

Library of Congress Subject Area Classification:
World politics.
Illuminati.
Great Britain --Foreign relations.
United States --Foreign relations.
[LC classification: D445, D450]
Authors: Edwin Charles Knuth and William Guy Carr

BISAC Subject Area Codes
POL506000/SOC058000 Conspiracy
SOC038000   SOCIAL SCIENCE / Freemasonry
HIS037070   HISTORY / Modern / 20th Century

The Money Power contains two classic books on geopolitics, presenting the thesis that the wars and revolutions of modern times were not mere accidents of history, but have been engineered by an Anglophile finance oligarchy to perpetuate their balance of power over the world. They are the power behind the British throne and the American government. Behind a mask of liberal democracy, their method is subversion, destruction of the old world order, and the humiliation of all rival power centers.

The Money Power is about this power that controls world politics, behind the scenes and in full view, yet ultimately it is much closer to us than that. The power of money intimately impacts our very lives in every way. It is a relentless effort to determine every aspect of our family life, work and values, and monetize everything. If we consider any issue that faces us personally today, we can instantly see how the power of money dominates. This power beguiles us with the false satisfaction of consumer wants, the individual pursuit of pleasure over building character and society, and intense pressure to conform to its status symbols and world view. On the world stage, this power is a corrupt and cynical oligarchy that buys all the governments it can — with their own money.

Illustrations from http://www.peakprosperity.com/forum/coming-crash-usury-and-irrelevant-church/39369

The Money POWER

Two Classic Works
in One Volume:

Empire of the City

by Knuth

&

Pawns in the Game

by Carr

CONTENTS

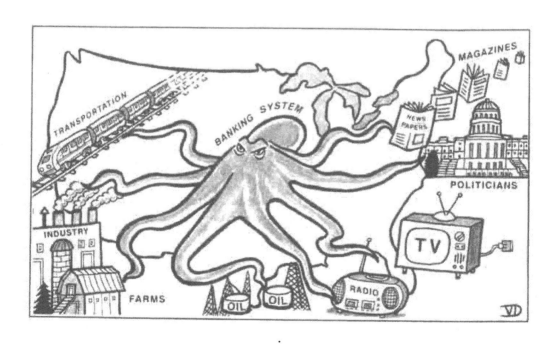

Where Angels Fear to Tread:
A Publisher's Note to the Combined Edition

It is hoped that presenting these two complementary classics together will afford readers greater insight into the identity and nature of those who really rule our world.

The authors of the two works agree on the essential argument: there is a great conspiracy to control the world, directed by an "international financial oligarchy" based on London, as well-organized as it is well-hidden: in plain view. Essentially materialistic, it treats mankind as subjects to be conditioned, as consumers of competing commodities and ideologies. Among the psychological tricks it uses is the ancient tactic of divide and conquer, the famous balance of power of the British empire. The unimaginable horrors of the 20th century are its handiwork, as the masses were incited and brainwashed to fight for opposing brands of materialism: Capitalism, Communism, Fascism, Zionism, all installed for one aim — to maintain world rule by a financial elite who would enmesh all the governments of the globe in bonds of debt.

Both authors served as young men in the Allied forces in the Great War — Knuth with the US Army, Carr with the Canadian Navy. Writing at the end of WW2, they believed both World Wars were planned, and that a Third World War, involving Bolshevism vs. Capitalism and Zionism vs. Islam, was next in the plan.

They were different in temperament. Carr still retained some sentimental attachment to the British empire. His approach is deeply imbued with Christianity, while Knuth, an engineer by profession, is more neutral in tone. Reading Carr today, some may be uncomfortable or unfamiliar with his Christian emphasis — yet this itself bears out one of his points. One is astonished to realize how much the influence of Christianity has waned over the last half century or so — a decline which he believed to be part of the conspiracy. He was considered as right-wing in his time, but the label has little meaning today, after the defeat of Communism, and a crop of new wars of aggression on Muslim nations, masked as "color revolutions," "freedom" and "liberation."

The very notion of Right and Left in politics refers merely to the two sides of the aisle in the Chamber of Deputies during the French Revolution. It is only another artificial fault line on which to play the game of divide and conquer. "Left" and "right" can't capture the many ways we can play out life's roles of rich or poor, generous or mean, innovative or old-fashioned. Regardless of our finances, we are all mortal; the only posterity we can hope for is a better life for our children. There is nothing right or left about that. No one wants their own children to be cannon fodder for any ideology. The supposed clumping of all attitudes under liberal or conservative poles becomes blurred and disappears upon inspection of real individuals.

The more one researches, the more one finds it to be no accident that revolutions large and small generally do not improve the lot of the common man, leftist romanticism and rhetoric notwithstanding. From the French Revolution to the destruction of Libya and Syria,[1] uprisings have been cynically instigated from the outside, as a means of

---

[1] For more on Syria please see my blog, http://www.progressivepress.com/blog/dirty-war-syria

overturning and subverting rival nations. This is delineated with a wealth of examples in our recently released book on the Strategy of Tension, terror and subversion in Europe, *Gladio: NATO's Dagger at the Heart of Europe*. It recounts how revolutionaries have been useful idiots, manipulated to frighten people away from "the left," so that policies and politicians with the people's interests at heart are undermined, and slavery to Corporatism is left to appear as the only safe alternative.

Venturing Where Angels Fear to Tread

Some people unfriendly to the thesis of a Money Power behind the scenes may suspect the term "international bankers" to be an "anti-Semitic" code word for "*THE* Jews." The anti-Semitic smear then becomes a convenient defense of the status quo, with the nations groaning under the debt slavery racket of unelected rulers, the money men. Anti-Semitism or Judeophobia is but a type of racism; as is Zionism too. While many oppose Zionism because they dislike racism, others may oppose it not out of sympathy for the Arabs, but out of race hatred for anything Jewish. This confusion paralyzes efforts to do anything about it. And this is why I venture to open and attempt to sort out this imbroglio, this slippery can of worms, although even to speak of "the Jewish Question" raises hackles.

Are Carr and Knuth writing about a British or a Jewish conspiracy? Their answers might agree: both, and neither: it's ultimately about money over man. Their approaches to the question are different, though, as may be glimpsed by an analysis of their vocabulary. Counting all forms of a word, I found the name "Jew" appears 370 times in Carr's book and only nine times in Knuth's. Carr also has "Christ" 150 times; "Lucifer" and "Satan" 50 times each, and "Illuminati" 138 times. Knuth has "Christ" only ten times, the Devil and the Illuminati not once.

Thus Knuth gives the impression of being agnostic about the link between Jewry and lending. To a certain extent, the difference may be one of style as well as substance — the name "Rothschild" appears about 70 times in each book! And Knuth's book is only half as long. Yet, as the subtitle implies, *Empire of the City* is directed foremost at London and the British. The root term "Brit" appears in Knuth twice as often (520 times) as in Carr. Thus, Rothschild may be understood as an agent of the Crown, and JP Morgan is his agent.

Knuth (a Danish surname) makes mention of "the fantastic doctrine of the racial superiority of the Anglo-Saxon and of his pre-ordained destiny to rule all the races of the earth." While the "chosen people complex" of the British may be less notorious than that of the Jews, it is no less real (indeed, of course, the sin of pride afflicts many peoples). Knuth lays blame for the past Century of War squarely with the Anglo-Saxons, quoting the Anglophile American adventurer Homer Lea, who wrote in 1912: "There can be no retention of present British sovereignty without the repression of the territorial and political expansion of other nations — a condition that must culminate in war." [2]

---

[2] Wikipedia: Educated in California, Lea is best known for his role as a close advisor who aided Sun Yat-sen in the 1911 overthrow of the Manchu dynasty. "Lea viewed American and British struggles for global competition and survival as part of a larger Anglo-Saxon social Darwinist contest between the 'survival of the fittest' races. He sought to make all English-speaking peoples

Although Knuth does note that "of the British nobility itself a large proportion is Jewish,"[3] he doesn't appear to believe the Jewish tail really wags the Anglo dog.

Knuth may be close to the agent view of Jewry in history. There was a symbiosis between Europe's rulers and their Jewish subjects, with monarchs offering protection to the moneylenders who could finance their wars. When times were bad, and the burden of usury could not be repaid, the people would rise up against the money-lenders instead of the monarch. Historically, Jews may have occupied an influential but ambiguous position — close to the seat of power, yet not the holders of absolute power.

Ambiguity has its uses. In the design of a conspiracy, attention must be given to the means of concealing it. One excellent method, which doubles as a divide-and-conquer tactic, is confusion and obfuscation. As in the proverbial good cop-bad cop routine, the US, the UK and Israel (and for good measure Saudi Arabia, the UK client and US petrodollar processor, too) carry on a charade in which they seem to be at odds, while working towards a common goal, of world empire. Knuth highlights the "secret agreement of 1897," an unwritten treaty binding the US to come to the aid of Britain in the hour of need, *while at all other times pretending to be neutral*. It worked. Had Germany known the US and UK were allies, she would never have let Sarajevo and the Austrians drag her into the Great War. This subterfuge sealed Germany's doom.

I put *Empire of the City* first because it is a short, concise work, as well as better avoiding the entanglements of the "anti-Semitic" label. However, we should not idly suppose Carr to be a Judeophobe. That would be underestimating the strength of his faith, which after all is rooted in the Old Testament of the Hebrews. Carr believes with all decent people that good and bad are be found in every ethnic group. (Tolerance doesn't mean pretending we are all identical, of course; if we were, we would have no need of it.) He repeats that most Jews (and Freemasons) are good citizens, who have the burden of blame foisted on them for the deeds of the few "moneylenders" among them. Yet Carr does draw for many of his ideas on books like *The Palestine Plot* or Capt. Ramsay's *The Nameless War*, which are written in an extremely anti-Jewish tone, whatever their merits may be as factual compendia.

The interesting thing about Carr is how he hammers away at an amazing insight into the conspiracy's divide-and-conquer methods. The conspiracy is not Zionist *per se*, but operates by setting Jews and Gentiles against each other — Zionists against "anti-Semites."[4]

---

see that they were in a global competition for supremacy against the Teutonic, Slavic, and Asian races. He believed that once awakened, they would embrace his militant doctrines and prepare for the coming global onslaught. China figured prominently in his world-view as a key ally with the Anglo-Saxons in counterbalancing other regional and global competitors."

[3] There have been reports that Princess Diana was Jewish, making the British royal line itself Jewish, going forward. Stranger still, she was also reportedly murdered to abort a competing royal line from Egyptian billionaire Mohamed Al-Fayed.

[4] I put the term "anti-Semite" in quotes as a misnomer. The main Semitic people are the Arabs. Opposing them is Zionism; it consists in the subjugation and extirpation of a Semitic people by European invaders. Correctly speaking, therefore, Zionism is the main force of anti-Semitism today. The proper term for an anti-Jewish attitude is "Judeophobia," while "anti-Semitism" could really only refer to both Arabs and Oriental Jews in the same breath.

Thriving on opposition, the conspiracy thus *foments Zionism and Judeophobia at the same time, through opposing factions*. This is an extremely important idea to grasp, although not a simple one; on the contrary, it works so well because it *is* a sophisticated and cunning stratagem. If we do not see through it, then we remain *Pawns in the Game*.

It has been said that an intelligent enemy is more valuable than a foolish friend. Is our adversary helping us evolve by forcing us to use our brains? Oversimplification lays one open to be entrapped. History is complex, a skein of entwined threads, a multi-player game, rather than a simple straight arrow.

A suitably murky case to be unraveled was the infamous Dreyfus affair (1894-1906), which served to foster hostility between France and Germany at the time Edward VII of England was preparing the Triple Entente to encircle the Germans in the Great War. From our viewpoint in history we easily forget that for centuries, most Jews in Western Europe were German. Most Jewish surnames still are German. Dreyfus himself was a Jew from Alsace, the German-speaking region which belongs to France (his surname means "Three-Foot" in German). "Yiddish" itself is but the German word *Jüdisch*, and it is by and large a German dialect.

A second purpose served by the Dreyfus scandal was to exacerbate both Judeophobia and passionate reactions against it. This lent fuel to Herzl's Zionist agitation, which first gained traction at the World Zionist Conference of 1896. The *clou* is that the Dreyfus affair may have been a psy-op arranged by agents of the Baron de Rothschild. Both the real spy who set up Dreyfus as the scapegoat, and the anti-Jewish journal that fomented race hysteria, were allegedly paid by Rothschild. Create the problem to sell the solution.

Once again, common sense tells us that common people everywhere have the same goal — not to fight wars, but just to have a better life for their children. It also tells us that the billionaires who run the world stick together, across ethnic lines, and do not care for any of us common people. Indeed they will sacrifice us as cannon fodder at the drop of a hat, regardless of ethnic or religious affiliation. In the 1940s, the little Jews paid with their lives so the big ones could become rulers of their colony in Palestine. Some writers, such as Henry Makow, have gone so far as to say the Jewish Illuminati banksters are not real Jews at all, but a heretical, satanist sect.

The financing of Nazism by the Anglo-Americans has been exposed by several authors (including our own Glen Yeadon in *Nazi Hydra,* Tarpley/Chaitkin in their *Unauthorized Biography* of G.H.W. Bush, and Henry Makow in *Illuminati,* vols. 1 and 2.) History contains tantalizing hints at collaboration between Zionists and Nazis, as well. In his book *The Transfer Agreement*, author Edwin Black (like Makow, himself the Jewish son of holocaust survivors), exposed the 1933 deal between Nazis and Zionists that created the basis for the state of Israel, while saving the incipient Nazi regime from being crushed by worldwide public opinion. There is also Ben Gurion's damning remark, "Were I to know that all German Jewish children could be rescued by transferring them to England and only half by transfer to Palestine, I would opt for the latter, because our concern is not only the personal interest of these children, but the historic interest of the Jewish people." Or was it rather his own interest in becoming the head of a new state, in the interests of the Anglo empire.

Carr attributes the design for Three World Wars to the unsavory 19th-century Scottish Rite Freemason, Arkansas slavocrat and sadist Gen. Albert Pike. The first war would set the Anglo-Americans against Europe's Central Powers, and thus overthrow the Czars in Russia, paving the way for Communism. "The Second World War must be fomented by taking advantage of the differences between the Fascists and the political Zionists." In each conflict, humanity is forced to choose between two materialistic, atheistic ideologies, and to descend into barbarism to destroy each other. The Third World War — the one we are in now — would be "between the political Zionists and the leaders of the Islamic World." Carr wrote in 1956, Knuth in 1944.

Looking at the turning points of the year 1917, it becomes hard at least for me to believe in sheer coincidence. The US was brought into the Great War in the spring, ensuring Germany's defeat, which would pave the way for fascism. The Bolshevik Revolution was fostered in Russia, leading to the communist takeover on November 7. On November 2, the Balfour Declaration set out the plan for Zionist colonization in Palestine, and in December, the British defeated the Turkish empire in Jerusalem. Thus in one year all the key events were arranged in the proper sequence to set the scene for the "Three World Wars" scenario. It was the culmination of steps taken in the 1890's, such as the secret agreement, the World Zionist Conference, the new US empire in the war on Spain, the Triple Entente against Germany, followed by the private takeover of the money power under the "Federal Reserve" just before the Great War.

In our time, the foundation of the garrison state of Israel (by ethnic cleansing of the native population of Palestine — itself a sort of low-intensity, ongoing genocide) has created opportunities of unlimited amplitude for psy-ops employing the Zionist card in all suits — be they Christian dispensationalist, anti-Jewish, Muslim, or anti-Muslim tendencies, etc. The occupation of Arab lands has allowed a thorough infiltration of Arab society, making it easy to recruit plenty of patsies, extremists and suicide bombers who can be used to further foment a hysteria of a "Clash of Civilizations," with provocations like 9/11, 7/7 and others too countless and frequent to mention.

I will give a small example of the Zionist card from my own experience in the "9/11 Truth" movement. Assume you and I are on the same page about The Big Lie, knowing "9/11 was an inside job" as a proven equation; then terms like WTC7 demolition, Silverstein and Comverse Infosys should be familiar variables. If the Mossad was not involved in 9/11, then the Anglos built in enough clues pointing to Jews in order to use the "anti-Semitic" card against polite inquirers. Such as the curious appearance on Sept. 10th of an article by a US military source arguing that Israel would be capable of launching an attack on the US, masked as an Arab one... one can take it either way. Major leads implicating Israel were leaked via the Zionist mouthpiece Fox News, then hushed up... What is clear is a collaboration between Christian and Jewish Zionists so intimate, so hand-in-glove that it is tendentious to single out one or the other party.

Sure enough, soon after its founding, the truth movement was badly riven by a case of the Dreyfus case. One faction feared the double whammy of an "anti-semitic *cum* conspiracy theorist" label would spell the doom of utter banishment beyond the pale, and exhorted the membership to avoid any mention of possible Mossad involvement. A few at the other extreme posited a defenseless America caught off guard by an Israeli attack — an *outside* job, almost as unlikely a tale as the government's cave-dweller conspiracy theory. And quite unnecessary when so many key posts under Bush were held by the neo-cons, many of them Israeli dual nationals. Yet today, without flying neo-con colors, the Obama regime has extended the Bush wars to Pakistan, Libya, and Syria — as if Jewish Zionism might be only the tip of the Christian Zionist iceberg.

Perhaps one can view the 9/11 evidence pointing to Israel as a way Zionist leaders can get cohesion in the Jewish rank and file behind their projects, much as the terror bombing of synagogues in Iraq by Zionist provocateurs in the 1950's led Iraqi Jews to flee to Israel, a story told in a famous book by an Iraqi Jew.

As I was writing this in 2011, conspiracy theories were buzzing that the vice charges arrest of French socialist candidate Strauss-Kahn was set up by the Thatcherite American favorite Sarkozy. In 2004, when US voters had a "choice" of two Skull & Bones brothers for president, it led to some hilarity among the dissident crowd. But would anyone be so rude as to point out that both Sarkozy and Strauss-Kahn are Zionist Jews? Not likely, unless they want to be styled "anti-Semitic." When only 1% of the French population are Jewish, what's the probability of both candidates being Jews in a random world? If such *Judeophilia* would lead to the nomination of excellent candidates, that would be another story, but both Sarkozy and Strauss-Kahn are serial adulterers, degenerate reprobates, and CIA assets. In fact, Sarkozy is the stepson of Frank G. Wisner II., who was the son of the high-level OSS and CIA official. Or take the US primaries of 2016. The Democratic choice was neo-con Israel-firster and butcher of Libya, Hillary Clinton, or "socialist" Jew Bernie Sanders, who has backed off from his earlier support for Palestine. And the Green Party candidate for President is a very fine Jewish lady named Jill Stein.

As I was updating this in 2016, President Obama nominated Jewish judge Merrick Garland to the Supreme Court. Yet three of nine SCOTUS seats are already held by Jews: Ruth Bader Ginsburg, Stephen Breyer and Elena Kagan. We've all known it's not really a democracy, it's a plutocracy, or an oligarchy, or something — almost a *Judeocracy*.

It's interesting how Jewish intellectuals carve out leading positions in all camps, left, right, anti-Muslim and what have you; Chomsky vs. Leo Strauss vs. Daniel Pipes etc. The eternal Jewish mother hedging her bets like a portfolio manager. It's what the CIA does too — co-opt everything, and go for the media like the jugular vein. How's that for a winning strategy, especially when the competition is not allowed to complain about it.

An anecdote. I was at the house of an Arab acquaintance, where she introduced me to a Jewish couple, her long-standing close friends. They were suitably radical and vocal supporters of the Palestinian cause, and the man held a post in one of the tiny leftist political splinter parties. Yet when I proposed to him that "9/11 Truth" was our ideal defensive weapon against the war on Islam, he demurred that "there is no telling where that Pied Piper would lead." OK, in other words, I thought — "What if Jews *were* to blame for 9/11? We don't want to go there!"

No matter how well-intentioned our guardians are, it is a thought-prison if we depend on them. No matter how fair-minded they may wish to be, everyone has a bias, everyone has got to look out for their own interests. You let others think and speak for you at your own risk. We don't dare even protest about not being in charge of our own country, or we're shunned as politically incorrect, nazis and untouchables.

Researcher Kevin MacDonald once estimated Jewish control of up to 67% of the media in the US, with details of corporate control to back it up. He theorizes that the Jewish people have a very competitive group strategy. Whatever the truth of it, it's obvious that the Jewish minority, about 2% of the US population by numbers, accounts for a lot more than 2% of what really counts as influence in our society.[5] Ah, the infamous "Jewish problem" — or is it a Gentile problem? Certainly people have the right to be over-achievers! And certainly Jewish people make many positive and original contributions. With their different heritage, they have a facility of viewing our society from a more objective perspective, which I have always found refreshing. Nonetheless, to my mind, too many major Jewish thinkers in modern times had awfully negative impacts: Marx, Freud, Bernays, Leo Strauss. Better a traditional than a bad original. For two cities in Japan, even Einstein's work would have been left better undone.

The tendency to overachieve might just be the core of the issue. There is a downside to overachievement; one aspect of it has been dubbed the Peter Principle, where people are promoted to a level beyond their competence. I submit that when people focus too much on achievement, the logical consequence is that mediocre but highly motivated individuals will occupy positions that would otherwise go to more gifted and suitable candidates, who do not have the support group or other tactical skills to elbow their way to the top. Look at the corrupt state all the professions are in that attract the ambitious: law, medicine, politics and the media.

Even if the influence of Jews is great in proportion to their numbers, to blame the Jews for every bad thing is a mirror image of the Chosen People myth. All peoples have made valuable contributions to human progress, even if each society exaggerates its own role and ignores others. And in some way the Hebrews were chosen to carry a message. Jesus, the Christian savior, was a Jew, although we believe his mission was to share the light with us Gentiles, so we could be chosen people too...

In the United States, due to the tragic historical burden of slavery, it is especially difficult for us to discuss ethnic differences dispassionately. The Holocaust makes this a taboo in regard to Jewishness. Yet people do differ. Of course we must be on guard against stereotypes; there is a greater variation between individuals in a group than there is between different ethnic groups; yet group differences can nonetheless be delineated.

Having lived some years in various European countries, a welcome break from America's racial tensions, I was able to notice an interesting pattern. Any virtue that a nation has in its nature is offset by a corresponding weakness.

This may indicate how difficult it is for humanity to move forward *en masse*; we seem to take a step backwards for each step forward. It also means *Vive la différence*: the human ideal we seek is shared out among all of humanity, is not the monopoly of any one group. If we are branches striving to reach the goal of human evolution in different directions, it will be reached by a meeting of minds, not by one group trying to dominate.

---

[5] According to Wikipedia, "American Jews as a group tend to be better educated and earn more than Americans as a whole. Forty-six percent (55% of Reform Jews) report family incomes of over $100,000 compared to 19% of all Americans, with the next highest group being Hindus at 43%. And while 27% of Americans have had college or postgraduate education, fifty-nine percent (66% of Reform Jews) of American Jews have, the second highest of any religious group after American Hindus."

As an example, the Germans are wonderfully conscientious and reliable. The drawback is they can be dogmatic. I happen to be more lackadaisical, jaywalking at crossings more with regard to the traffic than the color of the lights. I will never forget how I was bellowed at in Berlin at the curb, *"Ist rot!"* as if I could not *see* the light was red. The Germans themselves wryly admit, *"Die Deutschen können nur marschieren."*

I found this phenomenon of compensating strengths and weaknesses across a broad spectrum of characteristics and latitudes. Let us try and see how it might apply to the Jewish character. As we saw, it is generally accepted that the Jewish people are great achievers, and this is a strong point. The ambition to realize one's own potential. Being essentially selfish, however, the flip side of ambition is that over-achievement may not be optimal in the greater scheme of society at large. Could this be why the contributions made by the above famous thinkers were of such doubtful benefit?

One school of thought about the experience of the Jews in history — subscribed to not only by their detractors, but, I believe, by Theodor Herzl himself — holds that the Gentile body politic is irritated by something about the Jewish minority in their midst. This is given by anti-Jewish apologists as a motive for the pogroms in Poland and Russia. Yet one must wonder how much of the friction there was due to the medieval mentality of Christian Europe? Interesting, then, how this citation in David Livingstone's *Terrorism and the Illuminati*[6] contrasts with the Biblical record:

> Heccataeus of Abdera, a Greek historian of the fourth century BC, referring to the Egyptians... "The natives of the land surmised that unless they removed the foreigners [Israelites] their troubles would never be resolved. At once, therefore, the aliens were driven from the country... the greater number were driven into what is now called Judea, which is not far from Egypt and at that time was utterly uninhabited. The colony was headed by a man called Moses."

Evidently, both the Egyptians and Romans deserved to be rebelled against, as well as the Babylonians. Livingstone ascribes the rise of Illuminism to a kind of rebellion: an attempt by the Jews during their Babylonian captivity to turn the tables and regain the Promised Land by the use of magic, an art in which Solomon had excelled centuries earlier.

Heccataeus is less flattering to the Hebrews than the Bible account. He has them as banished for their trouble, rather than liberated, the Exodus being an early Diaspora. Banishment was a useful option for conflict resolution in earlier times, when the Earth was sparsely populated, and passports were not required. Today's shrunken planet no longer offers us this luxury; it is either get along with each other or kill each other.

Ironically, the anachronism of an unpopulated Palestine remained as an *idée fixe* in Zionist propaganda of the 20th century AD. Herzl's solution was for the Jews to become a majority in their own country. Yet as this was done by crushing the Palestinians into an oppressed minority, the state of Israel became a far greater irritant to world peace than the Jewish diaspora ever was. Another misplaced ambition! Ambition, the yoke that drives so many useful idiots for the powers that be.

---

[6] As well as documenting the bloodlines, *Terrorism and the Illuminati* is an attack on the British-inspired synthetic Wahhabi-Salafi sect of Islam and equally grotesque British-fostered Saudi dynasty of hordes of princelings, which is commonly styled as "feudal," as grossly unfair as that may be to the achievements of the Middle Ages!

Returning to our modern thinkers, of course, they can't predict what use will be made of their ideas. Darwin, for example, an Anglo Gentile with a radical idea, might have had no truck with Social Darwinism. The *über* classes seized on his theory as a justification for their own ideology of red in tooth and claw. We are taught that evolution is all about competition; the role of cooperation is never mentioned. Yet our bodies are stunning examples of the cooperation between individual cells! Or, as Matthias Broeckers would have it, complex life forms began as a *conspiracy* of a group of cells against the unorganized competition. Conspiracy he defines broadly as the confluence of competition and cooperation that is the great hidden power behind events.[7]

The Internet might be a huge step in human evolution towards universal cooperation, sharing and equality. Linking individuals across the globe is as revolutionary as when the first nervous system enabled rapid signaling between individual cells. Traditional mass methods of control by ideology, coercion or money would be analogous to the more primitive system of signaling by chemicals in the bloodstream, or the sap of a plant. Both systems may continue to exist side by side.

Were Promethean figures like Karl Marx or Charles Darwin part of some necessary pattern of "creative destruction"? Or is the term as self-contradictory as it sounds? Obviously mankind could not continue forever as vassals of the Church and the aristocracy. But I believe that evolution was occurring anyway in Christendom. Science was set to shake Christian faith to its timbers, without the aid of revolution. The Soviets used to claim their revolutionary ideology increased production, when in fact the growth was due not to "historical determinism," but to the application of technological developments. Revolution, especially violent revolution, is almost always bunk. "Rulership of the world is not worth one drop of innocent blood on the ground."

Here is a different theory of progress and revolution in modern history: A power élite are able to identify evolving trends and seize the popular energy they contain, turning them into revolutionary forces that can be weaponized against old power structures, in order to gain sway over empires. The revolution is hijacked before it starts.

This is exactly the kind of social engineering that goes on today, with color revolutions coming off the assembly line at a lightning tempo. The secrets of holding power were worked out millenia ago.[8] So why not in 1789? If this could happen in the sphere of the physical sciences, as when JP Morgan took control of Nikola Tesla's work, then why not in the human sciences?

The Enlightenment in France was an intellectual ferment fed by greater prosperity and wider horizons in the burgeoning French empire of the Bourbons. The Jacobin revolution turned France's own energy against itself, to crush it and its empire.

---

[7] In *Conspiracies, Conspiracy Theories and the Secrets of 9/11*.

[8] Perhaps because we live in an age of technological progress, we too often assume that people in earlier eras were primitive. Not so. Ancient languages, for example, tend to be much more complex than modern ones. The medieval church had an excellent understanding of applied human psychology and conditioning. Their "old-fashioned" doctrine of the seven deadly sins or passions is a much more accurate and useful depiction of human nature than any of Freud's confabulations, or the "Enlightenment" idea of the human mind as a "blank slate."

Few Frenchmen seem able to consider this rather obvious fact, so indoctrinated are they in the ideology of the Revolution. It led to Napoleon and the loss of Louisiana to the Anglos — a world-crushing victory for the New World Oligarchy.

The French Revolution was perhaps the most decisive psy-op ever carried out by the so-called "New World Order" plotters. One persistent theory is that it was instigated by the Illuminati, perhaps with the founder of the Rothschild dynasty as the brains behind it, as Carr believes. Another theory points to the circle of the "philosopher" Jeremy Bentham, but one finds very little written about this. It's interesting, though, that so many of the "glitterati" in the British pantheon seem to have played geopolitical roles, to have doubled as intelligence assets. Prominent examples that come to mind are Lord Byron and T. E. Lawrence, but the list is long.

In 1989, the bicentenary of the *Révolution de la Guillotinerie*, a ground-breaking volume was published based on documents in private archives. Entitled *Les Hommes de Londres*, it indicted William Pitt and the British secret service for the Reign of Terror. It does not even mention Rothschild or Bentham, or any Jewish names in the index at all. (Carr on the other hand pities Pitt as the victim of the moneylenders!)

Seeking the truth of history is no easy task. It's a great confidence game, both the making and the purveying of history. And with so many threads, there is always a great risk of confirming one's own prejudices. Through selective perception, we each impose our own pattern on the immense field of facts.

Our two distinguished authors of yesteryear each saw through an important piece of the charade in his own way, without the benefit of the Internet to do their research, but with the immediacy of living through two great world wars.

Knuth starts his historical narrative with the Napoleonic Wars and the Concert of Europe. Carr steps further back, to Cromwell's revolution in the mid-17th century. He adduces correspondence showing that Cromwell was financed by Dutch Jews, in exchange for an agreement to allow the Jews to return to England. To prepare the ground and undermine the King, "The plotters injected controversial issues into politics and religion to divide the people into two opposing camps."

Neither Knuth nor Carr mention the thesis proposed by Webster G. Tarpley: that England was taken over at the top by the Venetian empire around this time. On this view, Venice inspired the breakaway from Rome by Henry VIII in the 16th century. The Venetian agent Lord Robert Cecil engineered the 1605 Gunpowder Plot to attack English Catholics and set the stage for war with Spain, i.e., to found the British Empire. Some Venetians were Jews; in general they were agnostic or mortalists, who did not believe in an afterlife. Shakespeare (whose drama *The Merchant of Venice* casts a Jewish moneylender in the villain's role) was a Catholic patriot who opposed the Venetian conspiracy behind the throne, attacking them in his historical plays.

The 20th century was the bloodiest in history, with no parallel except perhaps the Mongol invasions in the 14th century. The Mongols played on divisions among Muslims, and between Muslims and Christians, to leverage their military prowess. Historians also admit that the Venetians put their unparalleled intelligence network (including the famous Polo family) at the service of the Mongols. (The British inherited this network when the Venetian elite transposed themselves to England). The Venetians were also a financier oligarchy who became rich and powerful by manipulating the rate of exchange between silver and gold. The parallel is uncanny with the way Knuth's financier *Empire of the City* built up Hitler and Stalin to launch a titanic battle which would "maintain the balance of power" so their one little island could hold sway over the world.

The Zionist war on Islam also dates back in history, perhaps more to medieval European intrigues than to alleged perennial conflicts between Jews and Moslems, who lived side by side in relative harmony in the Middle Ages. When the Inquisition struck Spanish Jews, most of them fled to Morocco and Turkey. Religious tolerance is a basic tenet in Islam, Buddhism and Confucianism. The Zionism of those days was in the Catholic Church, with its crusades to take Jerusalem. Like Carr's World Revolutionary Movement, the Venetians were enemies of both Christianity and Islam. Rome flirted with the strategy of using the Mongols to crush the Muslims and create an opening for renewed Christian suzerainty in Southwest Asia. But when the Mongols sacked Sidon, one of the last Christian cities in the Levant, the new Pope Alexander IV realized what savages they really were — and that if North Africa fell to the Mongols, Europe could not be defended. So the Pope threatened to excommunicate any Christian who allied with the Mongols. This last-minute solace helped the Egyptian Mameluke commander Kutuz to counterattack and rout Halagu Khan's army at the battle of Ain Jalut — Goliath's Spring — in Syria. It was the high water mark of the Mongol tide.

If the Venetians had had their way, the Mongols would have swept over all of North Africa and Europe. Muslims had saved Christendom, but this also meant the end of the Christian dream of retaking the Holy Land. The seed was sown for the modern project to install the Jews in Palestine, as a base to decimate Islam once more.

A rough historical precedent for the modern Palestine beachhead might be the Kingdom of Khazaria, which was supported by Constantinople as a Jewish bulwark against Muslim expansion, in the seventh through ninth centuries. As we know, Israel would not last long without life support from Zionism in America. When the Byzantines withdrew their support from Khazaria, it was overrun by Orthodox Christian Russians in the tenth century.

The Rus in turn were crushed by the Blue Horde of Genghis Khan's grandson Berke Khan. By a stroke of luck, a Sufi dervish converted Berke to Islam in 1248, and his fiefdom became the first Muslim Khanate. Angered by his cousin Halagu's sack of Baghdad, the crown city of Islam, Berke took up arms against him, saving the West from the same fate.[9]

Some authors believe the Illuminati, with their famous pyramid symbol, descend from ancient Egypt or Babylon (present-day Iraq), perhaps appearing to associate them in some way with today's Muslim world. However, the Babylonian source is Jewish Kabbalism, and the Egyptian link is not to the Pharoahs, but to the twelfth-century heretic Hasan al-Sabah, whose Assassins targeted Muslim monarchs rather than Christian kings.

---

[9] When I see the term "Judeo-Christian tradition" I have to wonder, is it possible to fall asleep for 1400 years? Playing a broken record, still not cognizant of the youngest and most dynamic branch of the Abrahamic tradition, Islam. Or is it not sleep but Western myopia and racism — deep-rooted forms of zionistic thinking.

Another view is that the Illuminati *per se* were fabricated as a temporary cloak for British intrigue, with no real existence before or after Adam Weishaupt. The lack of an agreed-upon tag like "the Illuminati" is one of the money monster's defenses. How can people come together to fight against something when they can't agree what to call it? Critics have tried many labels — New World Order, ruling elite, finance oligarchs, Bilderbergers, international banksters, money masters, cabal, clique, Anglo-American empire calling itself the international community, *ad infinitum*.

At any rate, the 19th-century Skull and Bones Club and Albert Pike's Scottish Rite of Freemasonry were probably simply invented outright, to be weapons in the British campaign to regain control over the American colonies. (Tarpley's latest book on Mitt Romney shows how Mormonism was one such invented weapon.) Some of the Founding Fathers themselves were traditional Masons; does that mean Freemasonry was running both sides of the Revolutionary War? Or is it simply that the format of a secret society is useful for strategic operations? The stated ideals of Freemasonry and Illuminism are close to those of the American Republic; Jefferson enthused even over the French Revolution. The ideas of the French Enlightenment were used to foment the darkest chapter in France's history, and to her eventual downfall. Were those ideas bad in themselves?

My take on this riddle is that it is a matter of sincere vs. counterfeit ideals. Again and again, sincere idealists are tricked by the boomerang. They are swept into movements that are cynically steered to achieve the opposite of what the members expect — in the end, they actually shore up the empire of the money power. To understand this entrapment we do not need to extract hints from 18th-century fragments. Just look at the CIA-sponsored "color revolutions" of Eastern Europe, which paved the way to neo-colonial kleptocracies, or the "Arab Spring" of 2011, the springboard to the invasion and destruction of Libya and Syria, the most egalitarian states in the Arab world.

Brotherhoods, secret societies, and the desire for knowledge and power have existed since the dawn of civilization. The basic psychological techniques used to exert power over others must have been learnt many thousands of years ago, when people first tamed animals. *Until more people make the effort to be more aware of this ancient technology, humanity is destined to be saddled by one or another unscrupulous power clique.* Becoming wiser ourselves, rather than arguing whether to blame the cunning Jews or Jesuits, Anglos or Freemasons, is going to be the solution.

As Christopher Clark points out in *Triumph of Consciousness*, the rich and powerful are not geniuses, but they do know the old tricks how to manipulate mankind; so we will be at their mercy until we become more aware, more conscious, than they are. We create divisions ourselves by our self-centeredness. In this world, even the great religions, monumental efforts to raise up human consciousness, deteriorate into another pretext for mutual opposition. If we get the government we deserve, it means political solutions fail without enough people of sufficient merit to support them.

With the advance of civilization, the techniques of rulership had to become more sophisticated. In the ancient age of tyrants, might made right; power was respected for itself. With the spread of religion, psychological operations and moral hypocrisy became indispensable weapons. The murders of Jesus and of Hussein, Mohamed's grandson, were facilitated by rabble-rousing ruses that foreshadowed modern methods.

It is taking thousands of years for the mentally lazy human race to stop trying to "Keep it simple, stupid" with things that are devious by nature. Great cunning is required for the few to retain their power and advantages over the many. We the people are innately far more powerful, immensely more numerous. *Their only option is to use our power against us.* It can be done by massive deceit, brainwashing, incessant distractions, and by corrupting us to scuttle our integrity for a trifling advantage of status. And this is what we will see on all sides, if we only look around.

The instrumental roles of Freud and Bernays in fostering consumer society slavery are ably depicted in the Adam Curtis BBC documentary, *The Century of Self*.[10]

What Freud did was to rebrand and sanitize the seven deadly sins as "unconscious drives," which needed to be expressed, not suppressed. Bernays then taught corporations how to use these forces to drive sales. It would hardly have been acceptable to build marketing campaigns on the overt exploitation of Greed and Gluttony, Envy, Sloth and Lust, *per se*, as long as those terms were popularly known as soul-killing evils. So Lust has been glamorized in an incessant stream of titillating images. The palliative for the pitiable results of Gluttony and Sloth seems to be electric shopping carts for the obese. Envy and Greed are now "self-realization" and "a better standard of living." No matter if the rest of the planet must be mercilessly plundered to fulfill the desires of hundreds of millions of insatiable consumers. Pride is now something to be proud of, and Wrath works just fine for the military portion of the Milinplex.

Equally fascinating is the Adam Curtis documentary *The Trap*. The trap is the thesis that we only need negative liberty, or freedom from government interference, and should be suspicious of positive liberty, which includes FDR's idea that government should try to provide freedom from want, ideas of a social contract, and all "do-gooding" generally. This thesis was propounded by Anglo-Jewish philosopher Isaiah Berlin in 1958, and it inspired decades of "reformers," who set about shredding the fabric of society the world over. Rather than freedom, it brought chaos, misery, war and inequality. It was not even original; it was a mere reduction of 19th century *laissez-faire* and social darwinist doctrine.

A tirade on the Abrahamic religions, Judaism, Christianity and Islam

What does Islam say about the Judeo-Christian tradition? I searched the Quran and found these interesting answers.

سـورة المائـدة Al-Ma'idah (The Table Spread), 5:82 (Asad)

Thou wilt surely find that, of all people, the most hostile to those who believe [in the Quran] are the Jews as well as those who are bent on ascribing divinity to aught beside God [materialists]; and thou wilt surely find that, of all people, they who say, "Behold, we are Christians," come closest to feeling affection for those who believe: this is so because there are priests and monks among them, and because these are not given to arrogance.

---

[10] The power of conditioning is such that even when people sense this in themselves and are attracted to the idea, they continue in the trained behavior patterns. Viewers of *Century of the Self* were many more times as likely to complain about the picture quality of the film — a consumer attribute — than viewers of other Adam Curtis programmes.

A riposte to that came when British intelligence invented modern Christian Zionism in the 19th century.

Concerning Jewry, if the angels fear to tread here, the Quran does not.

سورة البقـــرة, Al-Baqara, Chapter #2, Verse #96

And verily, you will find them (the Jews) the greediest of mankind for life [ambition] and (even greedier) than those who ascribe partners to Allah (and do not believe in Resurrection — Majus, pagans, idolaters). Everyone of them wishes that he could be given a life of a thousand years. [This might be a hint at the mortalist heresy. Of course, most of us would like to live as long as we can! Yet the afterlife was more important to other civilizations such as the Egyptian, Hindu and Christian medieval.] But the grant of such life will not save him even a little from (due) punishment. And Allah is All-Seer of what they do.

سورة الأعراف , Al-Araf, Chapter #7, Verse #168

And We have broken them (i.e. the Jews) up into various separate groups on the earth: some of them are righteous and some are away from that. [Viz. Carr's note about good Jews, and good and bad in every group. There are very different Jewish types or tendencies, including a good many idealists.] And We tried them with good (blessings) and evil (calamities) in order that they might turn (to Allah's Obedience). [This is the schooling we are all going through, Israel and Palestine certainly no less than the rest of us.]

It was reassuring to find the Quran seems to affirm my judgment: it is a people on the whole ambitious and worldly, yet with many good people among them (including a goodly proportion of my own authors — for example, Anna Baltzer, who wrote *Witness in Palestine*, has to be one of the nicest people in the world). *More Jews of good intentions need to let go the easy answer of accusing their critics of anti-Semitism, and engage in serious inquiry about their people's role in this world.* Is it true, for instance, as some writers have claimed, that almost all the Bolshevik leaders were Jewish? And were not the Bolsheviks responsible for killing more innocent people than any of the other mass murderers in history? These questions are amply drowned out by the drums of the holocaust industry.

It is a widespread misconception to think of Islam and Judaism as opposed, common among those who do not understand the continuity of the Judeo-Christian-Muslim legacy. Islam is a branch of the Abrahamic tradition, sharing the same early prophets as the Jewish dispensation. In Muslim mysticism, the immortal guide of the Sufis, Khidr Elias, is a Jew, and Jesus Christ "the Great Rabbi" ranks as a teacher next to Mohamed. Islam and Judaism also share similar mores regarding food and hygiene, of course.

Regarding the Judeo-Christian view, I got into a discussion recently with a Bible believer who couldn't figure out my "Free Palestine — End the Occupation" bumper sticker. According to him, "Israel" belongs to the Jews because they are God's Chosen People. Literally! But I seem to gather that Jehovah was only a tribal god? Something rather primitive, then, on a level no higher than "My Dad Can Beat Up Your Dad." The orthodox Jews were so entrenched in tribal thinking that they rejected their greatest prophet, Jesus, because he wanted to share his teaching with all the world, beyond the tribe.

This is not to say that all Jews had to become Christians and all Christians to become Muslims. There is something to be said for concentrating experience within a smaller community, as well as for dispersing and sharing it.

Still, "God's chosen people" is a tautology at best — the Jews chose "Jehovah" who then "chose" them... The anthropomorphic Chosen People concept flies squarely in the face of pure monotheism. The "Judeo-Christian tradition" pretends the Jews were the first monotheists, but are the Jews and Christians even monotheists at all? Neither a tribal god nor a trinity makes One God. At any rate, the Egyptians hit on monotheism much earlier, in the 14th century BC. (A great deal of the "Hellenistic-Hebraic" legacy of ideas was probably Egyptian. The Greeks freely admitted their debt to Egypt, as do the Chinese; but proud Europe is reluctant to accept a provenance beyond her own shores.)

Jehovism is polytheism, our god vs. your gods, and Christianity is duotheism, urging us to accept Jesus Christ as "God Jr." This supposed honor is actually a big devaluation for Jesus — he was a unique spiritual giant of the first water, whereas every briefly-reigning Roman caesar or Greek hero was styled a son of god. Only paganism, not monotheism, could set up a chosen people, or a chosen son, next to the Creator of the entire universe. (To be fair, most people then did not realize quite how big the universe might be.) Jesus' disciple Peter said, "God is no respecter of persons." That was a firm slap at the idolatrous notion of a chosen people.

Jesus asked how people could love God before they love one another. That is the rebuke to all who rob and murder in the name of religion.

When one member of the human community suffers we all suffer, and only a fool seeks happiness in causing others unhappiness. This is the error of Illuminism, Zionism, empire-building, and every form of worldly supremacism and exploitation.

A Note to a Friend in the 9/11 Truth Movement

I probably helped start the Anti-Mossad angle on 9/11 with my "Backword" to Ahmed's *War on Freedom*. My motive was I thought it was a way to help get the Israelis off the Palestinians' backs.

The problem is that being called a conspiracy theorist is bad enough without being double-labeled an Anti-Semitic conspiracy theorist — then you're really finished.

So there are no short cuts using the Jewish card — you have to deal with it comprehensively and without anything suggesting race hatred.

Even if it is true that top Zionists instigated the Holocaust, the average Jew will never believe this, especially if he is put on the defensive.

One way or the other, the little Jews were victims, and the Jews still have this victim complex, which causes them to victimize the Palestinians.

There is no way to break the vicious cycle by picking on people and making them feel like victims again.

***

But what about the Palestinians? How long do they have to keep suffering because their invaders and oppressors need time to stop feeling like victims? How long do they have to lie down and be the psychiatrist's couch for a neurotic people?

Another thought which became very timely in 2012, with the CIA-backed Foreign Salafist Army (the so-called "Free Syrian Army" or FSA) of Al-Qaeda and Wahhabite jihadis running amok, laying waste to whatever they can in Syria:

"Focusing on Israel and religious affiliation lets Saudi Arabia off the hook, yet it is as much part of the imperialist equation in the Middle East as Israel, using the oil wealth to finance the subversion of the Islamic faith worldwide, isolating the ummah in backwardness, making Islam a laughing stock, neutering opposition to Zionism, and encouraging Arab countries to be US puppets."

The think tanks of Whitehall and the Pentagon at least can't be accused of being simplistic.

It seems that a fourth world war is now shaping up, a hybrid of the Bolshevik and Zionist cold wars. On one side the US, Israel and NATO; on the other, the as-yet wobbly BRICS block (Russia, China, India, Brazil, South Africa), with the resource-rich Muslim world and Africa as the gladiators in the arena — the proxies and the battleground.

***

Herzl's Zionism is now over 100 years old. As I wrote in 2000-2001 for Media Monitors Network, Zionism, Fascism and Communism were a triplet of 20th-century sister extremist ideologies. Bolshevism endured 72 years from 1917 to 1989. Nazism held power for only about 12 years from 1933 to 1945. The Israeli occupation of Palestine almost 70 now. Is it only a question of time before Zionism falters and fails too?

In 2011, war broke out on the Gaza Strip. Amazingly, considering the narrow prison-camp existence of Gaza, Hamas managed to launch hundreds of rockets at military targets in places like Tel Aviv, and Hamas gunners scored a kill against an Israeli F-16 fighter. The Israeli military supposedly did not want this war, nor do they want a war with Iran. Instead, the mad bulldog Netanyahu is the Churchillian architect of military folly here, in the pursuit of a higher geopolitical strategy.

In other words, despite support by the global brainwashing machine, the disguise of the so-called Islamists and their media channels like Al Jazeera has grown thin with the jihadist attack on Syria. The war on Gaza is a perfect chance for them to profile as the Islamist opposition to Israel. Yet Gaza remains pinned to the floor. Even West Bank Palestine has neither army, navy nor air force. How convenient to "support" Palestine while undermining Syria and Iran.

In a game between chess masters, the complexity of gambits and intrigues grows until the patterns become too involved for one or the other player to keep track of. Something like this seems to be happening in the Middle East.

"Games occur within games... Alliances are topsy-turvy, defy logic, are unfamiliar and shifting. Theocratic regimes back secularists; tyrannies promote democracy; the US forms partnerships with Islamists; Islamists support Western military intervention."[11]

On to the game.

---

[11] NY Times book review of *This Is Not a Revolution* by Hussein Agha and Robert Malley

The Empire

of

"The City"

(World Superstate)

The Five Ideologies of Space and Power

The 130 years of power politics of the modern era

by

Edwin Charles Knuth

1946

The Empire
of "The City"

Edwin Charles Knuth

First Published by the Author,
Milwaukee, 1944, 1946

Library of Congress Catalog information
LC control no.: 46004991
Auhor: Knuth, Edwin C
Main title: The empire of "the city" (world superstate)
Published/Created: Milwaukee, 1946 [2nd edition]
Description: 111 p. 24 cm.
Subjects: World politics.
                Great Britain --Foreign relations.
                United States --Foreign relations.
LC classification: D450 .K57 1946

CONTENTS

ACKNOWLEDGMENTS

I wish to thank the following publishers for their courtesy in granting me permission to quote from these books:

America's Strategy in World Politics by Prof. Nicholas J. Spykman (Harcourt, Brace and Co., Inc.)

Background of War by the Editors of Fortune, (Alfred A. Knopf, Inc.)

Barriers Down by Kent Cooper (Farrar & Rinehart)

The Case for India by Will Durant (Simon & Schuster, Inc.)

The Day of the Saxon by Homer Lea (Harper & Brothers)

Isolation to Leadership by Prof. John H. Latane (The Odyssey Press Inc.)

The Intimate Papers of Colonel House by Prof. Chas. Seymour (Houghton Mifflin Company)

Liberty-Equality-Fraternity by Dr. Nicholas Murray Butler (Chas. Scribner's Sons)

The Life of W. E. Gladstone by John Morley (The MacMillan Co.)

Closeup of Lord Keynes by Noel F. Busch (Time, Inc., 1945)

Merchants of Death by H. C. Engelbrecht & F. C. Hanighen (Dodd, Mead & Company)

My Memories of Eighty Years by Chauncey M. Depew (Chas. Scribner's Sons)

Old Diplomacy and New by A. L. Kennedy (D. Appleton-Century Co.)

Pan-Americanism by Prof. Roland G. Usher (D. Appleton-Century Co.)

Pan-Germanism by Prof. Roland G. Usher (Houghton Mifflin Company)

Shall It Be Again? by John K. Turner (The Author)

The United States and Great Britain by Rear Admiral Chas. L. Hussey (The University of Chicago Press)

The War and Democracy by J. Dover Wilson (The MacMillan Co.)

E. C. Knuth
Member, National Society of Professional Engineers

INTRODUCTION TO THE 2ND EDITION

At the end of World War I, the author, then 27 years old, was released from the U. S. Army as Second Lieutenant of the Coast Artillery Corps. Like many other servicemen, he was filled with resentment as the deluge of utterly obvious and brazen falsehoods—by which participation in that war had been forced upon the American people—was exposed, and became more evident day by day after the war was won.

That the reasons advanced to the American people for their entry into World War I were largely fraudulent became common and accepted knowledge. More than 25 years after the war ended, the eminent American historians, Charles A. and Mary R. Beard, stated in their "Basic History" (page 442) that "the gleaming mirage that pictured the World War as purely or even mainly a war for democracy and civilization dissolved beyond recognition...." The well-known Internationalist publicist, Walter Lippmann, stated in his "U. S. Foreign Policy" (page 24) in effect that the real reasons for going to war in 1917 have never been admitted.

Many people realize that this mystifying situation—in which an alleged democratic and self-governing nation is actually controlled against the will of the people in its foreign affairs—is a clear indication that there must be a very powerful and well-financed secret organization which plans and directs American foreign affairs. For lack of a more specific identification this suspected secret organization is popularly referred to as the International Financiers.

When the propaganda mills began their characteristic grind towards war in the early 1930's, the writer began a more definite study of international power politics, and soon found it an entrancing and revealing subject. There was, however, no more free speech. The most amazingly documented aspects of a vast secret world order of International Finance could find no hearing in a situation where some Congressmen denounced overwhelming nationalist expression of views in their mail as mere organized subversion.

The shelves of our public libraries hold thousands of books pertaining to some aspect of this vast subject, most of them dry as dust to the average reader, as they remain unread by the public through the years. Most of these scholarly works are devoted to some passing phase of power politics in some part of the world of which their author has made a specialized study, yet they have invariably been forgotten as the public lost interest in that particular incident. In running through these works, some amazing nuggets of information come to light here and there. When fitted together, what gradually unfolds is the stunning history and legal structure of a sovereign world state located in the financial district of the loosely knit aggregation of boroughs and cities popularly known as the City of London. The colossal political and financial organization centered in this area, known as "The City," operates as a super-government of the world; no incident occurs in any part of the world without its participation in some form. Its pretensions are supported in the United States by the secret International Pilgrim Society, sponsor of the Cecil Rhodes "One World" ideology which was launched about 1897. The president of its American branch is Dr. Nicholas Murray Butler, also president of the allied Carnegie Endowment for International Peace. The ultimate objective of this camarilla was defined by one of its noted propagandists, the late William Allen White, thus: "It is the destiny of the pure Aryan Anglo-Saxon race to dominate the world and kill off or else reduce to a servile status all other inferior races."

After reducing the vast mass of data forming the basis of this work into a logical and readable sequence, it was finally put into print and privately published after long delay, and copyright was granted May 22, 1944. About 200 copies were sent to various members of Congress, thus largely performing the purpose of the first edition. Several members of the Senate Foreign Relations Committee accorded some attention to this.

On August 12, 1944, Senator Henrik Shipstead of Minnesota wrote, "The document containing the result of your research was so interesting that it spoiled most of my sleep that night ... I have been doing some research along the same lines and I find my time in that respect is limited. You have done a great deal of work that will save me a great deal of time." On August 21, 1944, he wrote, "People ought to be induced to read it. It is a documented piece of work and therefore should command respect and arouse interest."

This work seems to appeal most strongly to men of professional standing, and to people of the elder generations. A number of lawyers, doctors, clergymen, architects and engineers of the writer's acquaintance have expressed their great interest and commendation. Publishers approached have been reluctant to undertake it, and several stated that there would be little demand for a serious work of this kind, as the American public is not interested in that kind of reading matter. One large Eastern publisher frankly wrote that he was obliged to disregard the recommendations of his readers on advice of counsel.

Chapters I and XI, and the Conclusion, are new additions to this second edition of "The Empire of The City." Chapter XI, "A Study in Power," was published separately and copyrighted February 22, 1945.

I. THE FUNDAMENTAL BASIS OF INTERNATIONALISM

In 1912, the noted internationalist Homer Lea—in a scientific study of basic elements of world politics—forecast as imminent and inevitable a series of gigantic world conflicts, of which World War I, World War II, and a now almost certain and close at hand World War III, form a part.

Mr. Lea's great work, *The Day of the Saxon*, was first published in 1912 in very limited edition, and was republished in 1942 by Harper & Brothers. It can be said to form a major book of the Internationalist "Bible", and is one of the very few works on Internationalism that treats this usually deliberately distorted subject with scholarly candor, being particularly designed for the enlightenment of the elect. The following paragraphs are selected from Chapter II of this book:

> The character of the British Dominion is different from any of the great empires that have preceded it. It not only consists of one-fourth of the land surface, but the suzerainty of the Five Seas.... That British rule should, in various degrees of sovereignty exercise its dominion over seventeen-twentieths of the world's surface is significant of just that degree of repression towards all other nations, their rights and expansion by land or by sea.

> Peace and its duration, like war, is determined by natural laws that in their fundamental principles do not vary nor are found wanting.

> In conformity to these laws we find that the future peace of the Empire stands in decreasing ratio and must so continue until it is either destroyed or reaches a point of world dominance.

> There can be no retention of present British sovereignty without the repression of the territorial and political expansion of other nations—a condition that must culminate in war, one war if the Empire is destroyed; a series if it is victorious.

> In this epoch of war upon which the Empire is about to enter, hopes of peace are futile; constitutions and kings and gods are without avail, for these are the old, old struggles that govern the growth and dissolution of national life.

This was written before the outbreak of World War I and in light of world events since then, should be very impressive. Mr. Lea states further in Chapter 8, "For England to preserve to herself the balance of power in Europe, it is necessary to limit the political and territorial expansion of any European state."

On page 13 of the first edition of *The Empire of 'The City'*, privately published and copyrighted 1¼ years before V-E Day, the writer predicted the coming war with Russia on the basis of the well-defined and unmistakable thread of continuity and the plainly evident pattern of the machinations of the Balance of Power by the secret British "One World" order over the past century.

The grand plan of the "One World" Order decrees that it is necessary to limit the political and territorial expansion of Russia PROMPTLY AND PEREMPTORILY. Otherwise the victory over Germany will be of no avail, will in fact substitute a far more dangerous and potent challenge to British sovereignty.

[Editor's Note: Turkey has been controlled by Sabbataens since the 1500s—crypto-Muslims. It was further predicted that Turkey will resume her traditional position as the spearhead in the renewal of the timeless and savage British-Russian struggle for domination, briefly interrupted since 1912 to eliminate the newly arisen German Empire and its threat to the victor. It seems likely that the coming conflict will find Finland, Latvia, Lithuania, Slovakia, Bohemia, Poland, Romania, Hungary, Austria, Serbia, Greece, Turkey and Persia allied with the alleged forces of freedom. Geopolitics—the study of the struggle for space and power— forms a well-developed science with an extensive bibliography, which conclusively impeaches the superficial fabrication with which the American people in particular have been implanted with consummate cunning: that the great World Wars are caused by brutal attacks upon world law and order, instead of being the fully anticipated consequences of the most diabolical double dealing and planning by the secret "One World" order of "The City."]

The probability of war with Russia, now highly evident and the subject of wide comment, was variously indicated and denounced as vicious and subversive propaganda at the time the first edition of this book went into print. As is usual, the real reasons for this very probable and nearby war are easily kept submerged because of the truculence, insolence and contempt with which Russia has forestalled and checkmated the "One World" designs—with which she has had an intimate acquaintance over 130 years—fits perfectly into the sham posture of bruised democracy and violated decency.

In Chapter III of *The Prince*, his great classic on the science of power, Machiavelli warns: "... the distempers of a State being discovered while yet inchoate (in their early stages), which can only be done by a sagacious ruler, may easily be dealt with; but when, from not being observed, they are suffered to grow until they are obvious to every one, there is no longer any remedy." Is there perhaps yet time for the Congress, ruler in this sense of United States, to acquire the sagacity and the courage to deal with this menace of war with Russia? Is it in the public interest to expose the grand plan of the "One World" camarilla at a time when they are so near to finding achievement of this plan? They need to "sacrifice" perhaps only ten to twenty million more lives (in addition to the over one hundred million lives already sacrificed) in order to realize the great dream of their founder, Cecil Rhodes: a world ruled by a benevolent despotic intelligentsia, and so to create "peace for all eternity"?

The answer appears in the creed of America as defined by Thomas Jefferson: "Here we are not afraid to follow truth wherever it may lead, or to tolerate any error so long as reason is left free to combat it."

How has it been possible to erect this Internationalist structure of misrepresentation and deception in our midst and to protect it from exposure for nearly a half-century? Why have not our professors of history, our college presidents and educators, or our crusading newspapers exposed this monstrosity?

Some of the reasons are developed in the following chapters in documented detail. But there are also some evident and very practical reasons. Our newspapers are absolutely dependent on the advertising of great business interests for their existence. Perhaps the principal function of college presidents is to collect the funds upon which the existence of their institution depends, to be on the right terms with the right people.

News that definitely points to the existence of the secret world super-government of "The City" is treated with dense silence. The current activities of what has been identified as the most powerful international society on earth, the "Pilgrims," are so wrapped in silence that few Americans know even that it has been in existence since

1903. As a glaring example, let us consider the Senate hearing held on January 28, 1940. Senator Gerald Nye cross-examined Henry Morgenthau Jr. as to the contacts of his father with the peculiar activities of the mysterious and secret British statesman Viscount Reginald Esher. The surprising part is that not even one newspaper in the United States gave an inch of space to this immensely sensational exposure; while Senator Nye, like many other statesmen who have ventured too far into forbidden realms was effectively "submerged". As appears hereinafter, the late President David Jordan of Stanford University did much to expose the machinations of this International camarilla, with the that he was subjected to indignity and persecution during the World War I period; as was also the late Congressman Lindbergh of Minnesota, father of Colonel Charles Lindbergh.

As may be evident from the numerous quotations herein, many of the great teachers and professors of our universities have tried to throw some light into this situation with little success; their works have been accorded little recognition. As "controversial" matter, these works have been treated with the contempt of silence. One source estimates the average circulation of books of this kind at little over seven thousand copies.

Contrast this with the massive million-copy circulations of the highly acclaimed and widely publicized products of the proponents of Internationalism; with the complete domination of the radio by Internationalist propagandists; with billion dollar funds out of the public treasury devoted to "educating and informing" the people; with the newspapers filled with matter supplied by foreign "information" services; with opposition controlled so as to be based on such superficial and spurious reasons as to merely help hide and detract attention from the real reasons. During the Coolidge administration, the Republican Party reached such a high status as the defender of Nationalism that Mr. Coolidge has been accused in some Internationalist circles of being directly responsible for the Internationalist recession. This recession opened the way for the rebirth of Nationalism in the Totalitarian countries, among which Russia must be included. However, this Republican Nationalism has declined steadily under the encroachment of the Internationalist Money Power, so that charges of manipulation and bribery were brought after the 1940 campaign. The candidate of 1944 was the admitted pupil of a noted Internationalist and trustee of the Carnegie Endowment for International Peace. The results of the 35 years of operation of the Carnegie Endowment for International Peace speak for themselves.

A resolution by Senator Langer, Republican Senator from North Dakota, was to investigate the charge of C. Nelson Sparkes in "One Man—Wendell Willkie". The accusation was that Mr. T. J. Lamont (former president of J. P. Morgan & Co. and chairman of the executive committee of the Pilgrims) had bought the votes of delegates to the Republican National Convention of 1940 with a "roomful of money". However, this resolution was effectively submerged without any adequate public explanation.

After this brief review of recent manifestations of the parasite of foreign finance which has intertwined itself into the vitals of the capitalistic system, and which like the "Old Man of the Sea," has seated itself on the shoulders of democracy to dominate its fate; we will now turn back the pages of time 130 years to trace the development, machinations, and structure of this octopus of power in documented, step by step, historical detail as revealed by eminent scholars and writers through the years.

II. GEOPOLITICS AND THE BACKGROUND OF MODERN WARS

The events of the past ten years have brought forth a great number of books treating some aspect of Geopolitics, defined by one writer as the struggle for space and power. Among the hundreds of new works on this subject perhaps the most outstanding is *America's Strategy in World Politics*, by Nicholas J. Spykman, Sterling Professor of International Relations, Yale University, published in 1942, and sponsored by The Yale Institute of International Studies. Like most books on this subject, Prof. Spykman's excellent work is profound and comprehensive, and cannot be readily grasped by anybody not already acquainted with the outline of modern history and of modern power politics.

The modern era of world history can definitely be assumed to have had its inception with the end of the Napoleonic War. Many of the problems now affecting the nations of Europe, and the world in general, arose from the reconstruction of the map of the world as a result of that war. The virtual end of the Napoleonic War came with the crushing defeat of Napoleon at Leipzig in the gigantic "Battle of the Nations" in October, 1813, by the allied armies of Russia, Austria, Sweden and Prussia. Soon following was the abdication of Napoleon and his banishment to Elba in April, 1814.

In his treatment of *Britain and the Balance of Power* (pages 103 to 107), Prof. Spykman describes the British policies in foreign affairs, which he alleges have earned her the designation of "Perfidious Albion". He develops the British policy as a constant succession of cycles of shift partners, isolation, alliance and war; the defeat of Napoleon marked the end of one of these cycles. A tabulation of the modern wars of the world (as seen below), which assumes the Napoleonic War to be modern cyclical war No. 1, would indicate the present war as cyclical war No. 7 and very possibly as cyclical war No. 1 of a new grand cycle.

In his "Conclusion" (pages 446-472), Prof. Spykman ventures the opinion that Britain cannot permit a complete German defeat as that would leave the European continent in the grip of Russia; and that she cannot permit a full Japanese defeat as that would leave Asia in the grip of an awakened and revitalized China. He is further very doubtful of complete world hegemony by some type of British-American union, and concludes that only Japan would be able to supply the missing weight. Thus, strangely, Prof. Spykman would restore the overwhelming power that the alliance of the imperialistic expansion held in 1897-1920. Europe was in balance by the British alliance with France, Asia was in balance by the British alliance with Japan, and the world was in balance by the British alliance with the United States under the secret agreement of 1897.

One of the most forthright revelations of the secret agreement of 1897—and of the malignant disease which underlies modern civilization, which threatens to tumble the world back into chaos and barbarism—was disclosed in a speech by Chauncey M. Depew, New York Senator and high political and financial power of his day. At the Republican National Convention of 1900, in seconding the nomination of Theodore Roosevelt for the Vice-Presidency of the United States, he stated:

> What is the tendency of the future? Why this war in South Africa? Why this hammering at the gates of Peking? Why this marching of troops from Asia to Africa? Why these parades of people from other empires to other lands? It is because the surplus

productions of the civilized countries of modern times are greater than civilization can consume. It is because this overproduction goes back to stagnation and poverty. The American people now produce two thousand million dollars worth more than we can consume, and we have met the emergency; and by the providence of God, by the statesmanship of William McKinley, and by the valor of Roosevelt and his associates, we have our market in the Philippines, and we stand in the presence of eight hundred million people, with the Pacific as an American lake...

In the following tabulation, the modern cyclical wars of the British Empire in its unceasing struggle to maintain control of the dynamic and rapidly shifting balance of world power are numbered in order. The intermediate cyclical or pivotal wars are indicated by the letter O, and the wars of imperialistic expansion by the letter X:

Cyclical Wars and Imperialistic Wars	Major Powers allied with British Empire	Major British Opponents
1—Napoleonic War 1793-1815	England, Prussia, Sweden, Russia and Austria	France
2—Turkish War 1827-1829	England, France and Russia	Turkey and Egypt
3—Crimean War 1853-1856	England, France, Turkey and Sardinia	Russia
O—Civil War 1861-1865	England, France, Spain and Confederate States	Russia, (Prussia) and United States
O—Franco-Prussian 1870-1871	France, (England and Austro-Hungary)	Germany, (Russia and Italy)
4—Russian-Turkish 1877-1878	Turkey, England, (France and Austro-Hungary)	Russia (and Germany)
X—Egyptian War 1882-1885	England, France (and Austro-Hungary)	Egypt, (Turkey and Russia)

Era of imperialistic expansion under the wing of the overwhelming British-French-American-Japanese alliance of 1897-1920:

Cyclical Wars and Imperialistic Wars	Major Powers allied with British Empire	Major British Opponents
5—Spanish-American War 1898-1899	United States (and England)	Spain (and Germany)
X—Sudan War 1898-1899	England	Sudanese-Egyptian Nationalists
X—Boer War 1899-1902	England	Orange Free State and South African Rep
X—Partition of Siam 1899-1909	England and France	Siamese Nationalists

O—Russian-Japanese **1904-1905**	Japan (and England)	Russia (and Germany)
X—Morocco Conflict 1904-1906	"The Allies" (and Italy)	Germany and Austro-Hungary
X—Persian Conflict 1907-1912	England (and France)	Russia (and Germany)
O—Morocco "Affair" 1911	England and France	Germany
O—Tripoli War 1911-1912	Italian "reward" or "material quid pro quo"	Turkey
O—1st Balkan War 1912-1913	Greece, Serbia, Bulgaria and Montenegro	Turkey
O —2nd Balkan War 1913	Rumania, Greece and Serbia	Bulgaria
6—World War I 1914-1918	"The Allies" and Italy, Rumania, Greece, Serbia, Montenegro, etc. (Pop. 1,200,000,000)	Germany, Austro-Hungary, Turkey, and Bulgaria (Pop. 120,000,000)

(The era of imperialistic expansion, inaugurated by the internationalist William McKinley, Chauncey M. Depew and Theodore Roosevelt of the party of "The Full Dinner Pail" of 1896, was ended in 1920 when the people of the United States buried the interventionist candidates on the Democratic ticket of that year, James E. Cox and Franklin Delano Roosevelt, under a gigantic landslide.

The alliance with the British Empire was resumed with the election of the party of "The More Abundant Life".

No. O—South American Conflict and world-wide boycott 1934-1939	"The Allies"	Germany
7—World War II 1939-? (World War II appears to be cyclical war No. 1 of a new Grand Cycle)	"The Allies" (Pop. 1,100,000,000)	Germany, Japan, Hungary, Romania, Bulgaria, Slovakia, Finland, (Italy, France and Spain) with subject areas (Pop. 700,000,000)
New Cycle		
No. 2—Russian seizure of warm water ports	"The Allies", Turkey, etc.	Russia and new Soviet states

The term "conflict" as here used refers to diplomatic intrigue, incitation to internal disorders, and military or naval demonstrations and clashes short of formal war. Names of countries shown in parenthesis indicate allies that made no formal entry into war, due to limited length of the conflict or due to being opposed by or paired with a major opponent. The same indication has been used to indicate the present doubtful position of Italy and France.

The predicted clash with Russia, within this decade of the British allies, assisted by Turkey, seems an utterly logical conclusion. Every Russian diplomatic move and every

Russian war for the past one hundred thirty years has been a part of a campaign—which has cost many millions of lives—to reach Constantinople and the "Dardanelles." The price exacted by Russia for her entry into World War I was Constantinople—the city of the Tsar, the city of the Caesar, the Tsarigrad. World War II has a very surprising resemblance to almost every aspect of the colossal Napoleonic struggle, and the ground-work is apparently being laid to repeat the bloody 130-year grand cycle outlined here.

China, Russia, the United States and Germany are, in that order, the most populous independent nations in the world, and therefore represent the most dynamic and most dangerous competition to the British Empire. All of them have been the victims of recurrent British repression. The Russian and German cycles of repression were listed in the previous tabulation.

The Chinese cycle follows:

War and Period	British Allies	British Opponent
Opium War, 1840-1843	England and France	Chinese Dynasty
Revolution, 1857-1858	England and France	Chinese Nationalists
Storming of Peking, 1860	England and France	Chinese Dynasty
Revolution, 1860-1865	England and France	Chinese Nationalists
Yellow War, 1894-1895	Japan (and England)	Chinese Dynasty
Revolution, 1898	England-France-Japan	Chinese Nationalists
Boxer War, 1900-1901	All the Great Powers	Chinese Nationalists
Revolution, 1911	England-France-Japan	Chinese Nationalists
Revolution, 1926-1927	England, France, Japan, Portugal, Spain, Holland	Gen. Chiang Kai-shek
Manchurian Conquest, 1931	Japan	Gen. Chiang Kai-shek

In *China in Revolt*—published in London in 1927—T'ang Leang-Li writes of the events which led to the British war with the Chinese Nationalists under Chiang Kai-Shek in 1926-1927. The City of Wanhsien, population 750,000, was bombarded on Sunday evening, September 5, 1926, by a British fleet, causing civilian casualties of 2,000 and destruction of a great part of the city. This occurred despite the fact that General Yang Sen had merely detained the British steamer Wanliu to investigate a "river outrage". Negotiations had been in progress a day or two. It also happened despite the fact that bombardment of an unfortified town is forbidden by international law. The bombardment was made the subject of a message of congratulation to the naval authority by H. M. Government. T'ang Leang-Li makes further charges regarding repeated raids on the Kuo Min Tang headquarters in the British Concession at Tientsin, in November and December of the year before. These raids conducted by the British police resulted in numerous Nationalists, including several girl students, being handed over to their mortal enemies—notoriously savage in their dealings with political opponents—for court-martial. This act can only be interpreted as a desire on the part of the British authorities at Tientsin to assist in a plain and deliberate massacre; British agents in China continue to pursue the traditional policy of blackmail and bullying. The British policy of the Iron Hand, far from intimidating the Chinese people, has instead resulted in the rallying of the Chinese masses to the banner of the anti-Imperialist Chinese National Party (Page 156.)

The author describes in detail the spider-web of exploitation that International Finance has effectively woven about China, and the traditional British policy of promptly attacking and eradicating any Chinese government indicating initiative and growing strength.

Few Americans realize that as late as 1932, Japan was engaged in subduing Manchuria as a British ally, with British support and protection, against the protests of the League of Nations, the United States and China.

General Chiang Kai-shek led the Chinese Nationalist revolution of 1926-1927 against the domination of the British. Japan assumed the greater part of the fighting and the expense to overcome this "rebellion" and thus was awarded Manchuria by the British international financial oligarchy. It is of interest to note that every war listed as a "Revolution," including the "Boxer" War, was a war against foreign imperialists holding the Chinese Government in bondage, a war against the bankers of the City and against the "foreign devils."

The statesmen of the international financial oligarchy made numerous deceptive and illusory promises to many peoples and nations before and during World War I to induce them to fight and defeat their aggressors in absolute and total victory. Woodrow Wilson promised many more things, yet after this "total victory" had been won, these promises were revoked almost without exception. Mr. Wilson's promises of "New Orders" and "New Freedoms" to the subjects of the British Empire were all retracted, resulting in an immense wave of riot and revolution over a period of years following World War I. The following are some of the most outstanding of these instances of bloodshed:

Egyptian Revolution......................................1919 - 1921

Anglo-Irish War..............................Jan. 1919 - May, 1921

Ulster War.......................................July, 1920 - June, 1922

Massacre of Amritsar..................................April 13, 1921

Indian Revolution..1921 - 1922

Egyptian Revolution......................................1924 - 1925

The *Chicago Tribune* of Sunday, February 6, 1944, featured an editorial "A Dwarf Between Giants", which states that the British Foreign office generally have run America's foreign affairs for fifty years, and that for the eleven years the British have had no difficulty in guiding our policy. This truth is apparent from the following chapters that give a detailed description of the means, the men, and the methods by which this was accomplished.

[Editor's Note: The British Commander of the Massacre of Amritsar was brought back to England and hailed as a hero. The details of this needless slaughter should be studied.]

III. THE EASTERN QUESTION

The end of the Napoleonic war left the mighty Turkish Empire forming a great crescent directly across the path to India. At that time Turkey included much of what is now Yugoslavia, Greece, Romania, Bulgaria, and northern Africa up to Tunis. It was also a potent threat to further British expansion in the Mohammedan East. An uprising in the Greek provinces of Turkey provided a suitable cause for war. Russia joined the British-French alliance as the protector of her brethren of the Greek Catholic Church and to promotion her aspiration to gain access to open water through the Porte. A British-French-Russian fleet destroyed an allied Turkish-Egyptian fleet on Oct. 20, 1827. The British and French then withdrew, leaving Russia to fight Turkey alone. Russia defeated the Turks and the war ended on September 24, 1829.

The British and French would not allow Russia to enjoy the fruits of victory; she was not permitted to open the Porte or gain free access to open water. For over one hundred years, to this day, Russia's efforts to gain unrestricted access to a warm water port through the Porte, the Baltic, the Persian Gulf or the Yellow Sea have been frustrated by the "policy of encirclement." This subject will come up for troublesome discussion in the near future.

After having been reduced to utter bankruptcy, inflation and despair by the frightful bloodletting of the gigantic Napoleonic World War, the new French Government was readily subsidized by the International Bankers in an alliance which made France the perennial junior partner in their world imperialism for over one hundred years until the recent collapse of France. France has been the ideal partner for she has always conceded to the Lion, "the Lion's share"—a share which has always been about 75% or more, even in the case of World War I.

Several million Greek Orthodox Christians still remained under Turkish rule after Russia achieved Greek independence in 1829. These people were subjected to the most inhumane and monstrous cruelties by Mohammedan persecution, a condition that continued over a long span of years until modern times, despite repeated promises of reform by the Turkish Government. As the Czar considered himself the protector of these Greek Orthodox Christians, this provided a constant cause of friction and grievance. Together with the British and Turkish obstruction to the Russian pressure for free passage through the Porte, this situation—known as "The Eastern Question"—overshadowed the power politics of Europe for almost three quarters of a century and formed the basis for a succession of bloody conflicts.

The Standard History, 1899, quotes:

> The ascendancy of Russia was accompanied by the rise of a wholly new policy in Europe with regard to the Eastern Question. The old feeling that the Turk was the common enemy of Christendom, that every victory over the Crescent, no matter by what power it was gained was a subject for general triumph, completely disappeared. On the contrary, the Turkish power was to be maintained, because Russia was dreaded.

Britain resurrected the principle laid down by William Pitt who had argued that

> the true principle by which the foreign policy of England should be directed, was the fundamental principle of preserving the balance of power in Europe; and that the true

doctrine of the balance of power required that the Russian Empire should not, if possible, be allowed to increase, nor that of Turkey to diminish.

Twenty-four years after Russia had helped Britain overcome the menace of the Mussulman to her eastern possessions, the first war broke in the "Eastern Question"—the great Crimean War, in which Britain, France and Turkey (later joined by Sardinia, predecessor of modern Italy) defeated Russia in 1853-1856 at a cost of one million lives. The House of Savoy, rulers of Sardinia, entered this war in a political deal which placed it on the throne of a newly united Italy in 1861, through British victory.

The years of 1869-70 found Britain and its balance of power in an exceedingly precarious position. Due to Britain's interference in the American Civil War, an angry and resentful America, now possessing the world's greatest army and a powerful navy of the new and terrible ironclads, demanded redress for heavy damages due to British lend-lease to the Confederacy. Russia fully signified her intention to fight to avenge her recent loss (the war of 1853-1856) by sending two fleets to the United States when war seemed most imminent between the United States and Britain, during the Civil War. In a further incident of strange significance, the Queen of Spain was dethroned in a revolution.

This auspicious moment was seized by Prussia, largest of the many small German-speaking states of central Europe, to abandon her role in the local politics of Europe and to enter on the stage of world power politics. Her ambitious prime minister, Count von Bismarck, had already unified the German states into a loose confederation, and now attempted to place a Prussian princeling on the vacant throne of Spain. This was a step towards a natural alliance, for Spain was and still is the implacable and unforgiving foe of Britain, the nation that seized its colonies and reduced it to a state of poverty and decay.

The move of Bismarck to place a German ruler on the throne of Spain was summarily challenged by France. The name of the German candidate, Prince Leopold of Hohenzollern-Sigmaringen, was withdrawn within about ten days, by July 12, 1870. In accordance with the established tradition of the British-French financial oligarchy never to accept anything short of unconditional surrender, on July 14, 1870, the French government further demanded an abject personal apology from King William I of Prussia.

When this personal apology was refused, France declared war the following day. Britain, as usual, made no immediate move; six months and twelve days later, on January 27, 1871, the defeat of France was utter and complete. Nearly all the German States promptly joined in the war, and by the end of July, the highly skilled German military chief, General von Moltke, had 700,000 men along the French frontier. Emperor Napoleon III took over the chief command of the French armies. Napoleon III was captured by the Germans together with 120,000 men at the Battle of Sedan, on September 2, 1870. On January 19, 1871, King William I of Prussia was formally proclaimed Emperor of the new German Empire, a union of four kingdoms and twenty-one other principalities of central Europe. Although the war had been very short, nearly 500,000 men perished.[1]

---

[1] A message was transmitted for the French Emperor on July 5, 1870, by Baron Rothschild of Paris to Baron Lionel Nathan Rothschild of London. The message was deciphered by

This war occurred in the adult life of thousands of American citizens now living, and in that same span from 1871 to today perhaps 25,000,000 to 30,000,000 human beings have lost their lives in the struggle of the "Balance of Power." This is a "Big-League" game, and we are now the principal participants.

The crash of the European Balance of Power was promptly exploited to its utmost by the nations of the continent. The head of the House of Savoy revoked the agreement with the British-French oligarchy by which he had been made King of Italy and sent an army

---

Nathaniel Maier Rothschild, still head of the House of Rothschild at the beginning of World War I, and by him delivered to Mr. Gladstone early on the morning of July 6th. The message was to inform Mr. G. that the council of ministers at Madrid had decided to propose Prince Leopold of Hohenzollern for the Spanish throne, that his candidature would be intolerable to France, that the Emperor hoped Mr. Gladstone would endeavor to secure its withdrawal.

Mr. Gladstone stated his reluctance to interfere with the liberty of the Spanish people to choose their own sovereign. He was nevertheless later confronted with a dispatch to the King of Prussia drafted by Lord Granville and asked to sign the same. Again Mr. Gladstone was reluctant, but after several days of hesitation, he added to Lord Granville's draft an appeal to the magnanimity of the King, begged him to consider the danger to the peace of Europe, and enjoined him further to say nothing to give ground for the supposition that England had any business to discuss the abstract right of Spain to choose her own sovereign. (Morley's Life of G., Book VI, Ch. IV.)

Gladstone's appeal was supported by an energetic representation to Berlin by Austria, seat of the third Rothschild dynasty, and the King of Prussia immediately ordered the candidacy of Prince Leopold withdrawn. Having inveigled Mr. Gladstone into a definite position, the tone of France suddenly became harsh and menacing. Evidently mistaking the quick compliance of King William I as a sign of weakness and fear of an apparently united Austrian, British and French coalition, they demanded two days later, on July 14th, that the Prussian King make a personal pledge that he would never again sanction any similar political move. This was an ultimatum of unparalleled effrontery demanding in effect that Prussia in utter humiliation acknowledge herself a vassal of France, with no further voice in the council of Nations. The King politely declined the French demand and France declared war the next day. Each and every war of modern times has been preceded by an interchange in similar form of arrogance and contempt by the statesmen allied with International Finance, with a disdainful refusal of any basis of settlement making any reasonable concession.

Gladstone was horrified; and this great opponent of Toryism and its wars stated that the diplomacy on the side of the Government of France anterior to the war made up a chapter which for fault and folly taken altogether is almost without a parallel in the history of nations. With one stroke, France united the quarreling and jealous small German kingdoms and principalities of central Europe into a great empire and threw itself under the grinding wheels of Bismarck, to be utterly demolished in six months time. The French calculations proved entirely wrong. The illusion of International Finance that Russia had been immobilized for 100 years by the Crimean War of only 14 years before quickly vanished, with a vindictive Russia holding Austria at bay and repudiating her terms of surrender in that war. The German victory was too sudden to permit the financiers of the City and the Conservatives to unseat the anti-imperialistic Liberal, Gladstone; and to intervene.

to seize the Pontifical States of Italy, which were under the temporal rule of the Pope as their absolute sovereign. The troops of the Pope surrendered on September 20, 1870, and the capital of Italy was moved from Florence to Rome on July 8, 1871.

Russia at the outbreak of this war denounced the treaty of 1856 and rebuilt her Black Sea fleet and fortifications, and prepared to resume her offensive in the "Eastern Question," thus undoing everything for which a million men had died a brief 15 years before. She had openly supported Prussia and any move on the part of England would have promptly brought her into the Franco-Prussian war, and she now was free to act. Her first move was a drive into Turkestan up to the borders of Persia, Afghanistan and India. In this campaign she defeated the Khan of Khiva in the spring of 1873, the Turkomans in the fall of 1873, and the Khan of Khokand in the summer of 1875.

In the meantime Russian political penetration roused the peasants of the Turkish provinces of Herzegovina and Bosnia into rebellion in July, 1875, and this was followed by declarations of war by other Turkish political subdivisions; Serbia and Montenegro in 1876, and Bulgaria and Romania in 1877. The stage was then set for Russia's answer to the Eastern Question and her revenge for the horrors perpetrated on her religious compatriots; the war that followed was fought with bestial fury, with no quarter given or asked. The Turks fought with frenzied determination and losses were immense on both sides. The odds were too great. Nine months after declaration of war, the Russian army was encamped in the suburbs of Constantinople, with the Turkish army totally dispersed. The Russians had been well prepared, for two immense armies totaling 500,000 men had moved over the border into Turkey within a few hours after the declaration of war.

The conduct throughout this war was exceedingly brutal. Turkish prisoners were kept herded out in the open in bitter winter weather without food or shelter for many days, to die by the thousands. The American military observer, Lieut. F. V. Greene, relates in "*Army Life in Russia,*" (published in 1881) that in passing one of the burial trenches filled with the bodies of naked Turkish dead, he saw among the corpses a living man; his head and one arm only visible, speechlessly beckoning for aid. Greene called attention to this man but nothing was done for him. Nevertheless, when the Russians reached the suburbs of Constantinople, they did not enter the city to loot and destroy. On the contrary, the Grand Duke Nikolaus made a formal call on the Sultan to pay his respects, duly returned by the Sultan.

A treaty of peace was made at San Stefano, near Constantinople, on March 3, 1878, between Russia and Turkey; which was promptly challenged by Disraeli. Britain had been unable to come to Turkey's assistance, but had charged Russia with deliberate violation of the Treaty of Paris in attacking the integrity of the Ottoman Empire. To save face, she declared she would remain neutral as long as British interests were not attacked, and these were defined as follows: First, the navigation of the Suez Canal must not be blockaded or interfered with. Second, Egypt must not be attacked or occupied. Third, Constantinople must not pass into any other hands than those of its present possessors. Fourth, the existing arrangements concerning the navigation of the Bosphorus and the Dardanelles must not be changed.

Unable to oppose Russia by force, Britain appealed the Treaty of San Stefano to the Concert of Europe, an informal organization of the nations of Europe which had attempted to install a system of law and order into the affairs of the world since the

Napoleonic wars. Russia obediently waited on the outskirts of Constantinople for six months after the close of the war; her soldiers eager to go home after their great victory, ill-housed and exposed to the weather and ravaged by disease, until the European Concert had concluded the Treaty of Berlin on July 13, 1878. That part of the Eastern Question pertaining to the Turkish atrocities was now fully settled with general freedom for the Balkan nations, and Russia had demolished the Porte. On the other side of the Porte, however, stood the British fleet. That part of the Eastern Question has never been settled, for the new alignments of the Balance of Power left Russia helpless in Europe thereafter. With their Turkish ally of no further use, the British banking oligarchy subsidized the government of Turkey's vassal state Egypt the next year with a largely fictitious loan. The Egyptians rose against this seizure under the leadership of their War Minister Arabi Pasha with the battle cry of "Egypt for the Egyptians". While the French and British fleets demolished the Egyptian fleet in July 1882 and defeated Arabi's army shortly afterwards, the revolution continued for many years. In 1885, the renowned "trouble shooter" of the British Empire, Gen. Chas. G. Gordon lost his life in the Egyptian war. Final victory was not achieved by the British until 1898, when Lord Kitchener defeated the Mahdi. General Gordon—also known as Gordon Pasha and Chinese Gordon—thus played a large role in the British and French subjugation of China.

Turkey, once the world's greatest empire, and still the nominal leader of the vast Mohammedan world, has had a number of years of fair prosperity and modernization and has profited much from the present war. The Mohammedans, largely under British and French rule, have a great store of grievances against this rule, real and fancied. With the relatively small Christian white population of the world engaged in annihilating themselves in a shambles of intolerance caused by illusion and deceit; a world-wide uprising of the Mussulman is not so far-fetched.

IV. THE CONCERT OF EUROPE

The leading powers of Europe had adopted a custom of holding a conference whenever any particularly perplexing problem arose to threaten the peace. The successive treaties and agreements adopted at these conventions in time covered a large part of the customs and interaction between these nations. This concert of the nations in time assumed an official status. The effect of this was to create a type of League of Nations; which, while not in itself an entity, nevertheless was ruled by the will of the majority.

Among the earlier meetings of the Powers were the Congress of Vienna in 1814-1815, of Aix-la-Chapelle in 1818, Carlsbad in 1819, Verona in 1822, and London in 1830. The Concert of Europe attempted again and again to bring about a settlement in the Eastern Question. Only British consent kept the Congress from quickly disposing of that part of the Eastern Question affecting the Mohammedan persecution of the millions of Christians in the Turkish conquered Balkan nations, by united action of all the nations of continental Europe. These small nations had been conquered by the Turks after the Christian world had collapsed due to economic causes and a frantic new deal type of spending, which had eventually exhausted the inexhaustible treasury of Rome, that great empire which included nearly all of Europe, present-day Turkey, and other parts of Asia and Africa.

Civilization has risen to great peaks and fallen to deep valleys again and again throughout the centuries, and Rome marked the last great peak of civilization. Let us note that Rome built 50,000 miles of hard-surfaced cement roads in its day. For one thousand years after the fall of Rome, not one mile of cement road was built in Europe. Even the secret of making cement was only rediscovered in recent years. With its capital spent, all Europe plunged into chaos, with its immense natural wealth of little avail.

That inexorable self-interest which will sacrifice everything and anything to the future expansion and well-being of the British Empire was clearly and shamelessly exposed in every discussion of the Eastern Question during the years. The traditional British explanation of their war aims originated in her war with France for hegemony of the seas of the world. The explanation was that it was not their intent to fight the French people— only to rid Europe of the Scourge of Napoleon, bring peace to Europe and preserve the rights of nations. This has since been repeated in war after war with only a slight transposition of names, yet was not used in this instance. Every aspect of human decency, human compassion, the freedom of men and the rights of small nations, left British statesmen cold, yet were championed entirely by Russia. Ghoulish atrocities committed under that command of the Koran: "O true believers, wage war against such of the infidels as are near you," were loftily ignored in the expediency of the empire; nothing was to be permitted to upset the then secure Balance of Power.

In treating the Eastern Question in his "Army Life in Russia," Lieut. F. V. Greene, the former military attaché to the U. S. Legation at St. Petersburg wrote:

> Deprived of her colonies and her commerce, England would at once sink to the level of the smaller states of Europe, following in the wake of Holland and Venice and Spain, who in their days have been great and powerful, but who have declined with the loss of their foreign possessions and the commerce which they sustained. ... No single event could strike so serious a blow as the loss of India. Of all the great possessions—it is

hardly a colony—it is the most alien to the British race, and it is held as a mere money-making investment. Its people are ground with extortionate taxation, are allowed no voice in their own affairs, are treated with studied scorn. ... It is held as a market in which to buy cheap and sell dear, and as a place in which younger sons and needy relations can amass fortunes to be subsequently enjoyed in England. Its loss would result in a financial crisis which would shake the whole fabric of England's commercial prosperity, and deal a blow at her political prestige from which she could hardly recover.

Lieut. Greene stated further in this book:

I have also attempted to give prominence to the Russian views of the question—which, in the main, I believe to be the correct ones—because Americans are in the habit of hearing only the other side. Our language being the same as that of England, and the opinions of the Continent being transmitted to us principally through the English press, we receive constantly the most prejudiced, unfair, and at times false statements about Eastern affairs.

Of the diplomatic discussions over the Turkish revolutions which immediately preceded Russian intervention he wrote:

Austria, Germany, France and Italy all in turn pressed England to accept the memorandum, or to suggest any modifications she might desire in its language. She declined to do either. They then asked Lord Derby if he had any proposition of his own to make, and he replied none. 'Her Majesty's Government deprecated the diplomatic action of the other Powers in the affairs of the Ottoman Empire.' Russia then asked what the drift of England's policy was; what were her ideas in the matter? To which Lord Derby replied, that he thought nothing remained but to let the struggle continue until success should declare itself on one side or the other. In other words, in British phrase, form a ring and let 'em fight it out with the usual result of indiscriminate slaughter and pillage ...

The political aims of nations change little through the years; one hundred years in the life of a nation are perhaps as ten in the life of the individual. In the case of Britain, it would appear that the leopard did not change his spots. Take the fact that Sir Edward Grey used almost exactly the same tactics as the Lord Derby in evading the urgent representations of Germany in her effort to escape World War I in 1914. This was recorded by J. Ramsay Mac-Donald—later Prime Minister of Britain—in his article, "Why We Are At War. A Reply to Sir Edward Grey," in which he accused Sir Edward Grey of the war guilt. It is utterly impossible to reconcile these lofty and disdainful expressions of Lord Derby with the crushing debacle that followed once Russia removed Turkey from the British Balance of Power with one ferocious lunge, thus disproving the view of many Englishmen that the march of Russian conquest had been set back one hundred years by the Crimean War of only 21 years before.

Surprised and frightened Britain now turned to the Concert of Europe, which she had heretofore flouted, for assistance. The British-French financial oligarchy had been grooming Austria for some years as a British ally in the growing German and Russian menace through their related banking house at Vienna. To influence the Congress of Berlin in its consideration of the Treaty of Stefano, it was threatened to have Austria attack Russia with British financial support. In addition, British reserves were called out. War-weary Russia was obliged to accept new terms and the Treaty of Berlin was signed on July 13, 1878. It deprived Russia of any territorial gain, but allowed her an indemnity for part of her war cost. In general, the freedom of the Balkan nations was admitted with various modifications to remove their governments from any Russian influence. Armenia was left under Turkish rule, to furnish another Eastern Question in very recent years. Herzegovina and Bosnia, whose rebellion in July 1875 had started this era of bloody slaughter, were given to Austria for her support of Britain over their furious protests. It was rebellion in these provinces of Austria which lit the fuse of World War I, 36 years after they had become Austrian provinces. Britain seized Cyprus in order to create a base to halt any further designs by Russia on the Porte. All the nations of Europe now considered the Eastern Question fully settled and Russia also realized the futility of any further efforts in the face of the new powers. Europe had assumed its modern complexion, with the new "Great Powers" of Germany, Italy and Austria-Hungary in full strength. The successful settlement of the Eastern Question had raised the Concert of Europe to the status of the de facto government of the world. The British Balance of Power was in abeyance, and there was an era of stability. Germany in particular engaged in no major conflict for 43 years.

V. THE EUROPEAN CONCERT ENDS IN THE EAST

Immediately after the Russo-Turkish war, the British-French oligarchy was engaged for some years in the conquest of the former Turkish vassal state Egypt and the Egyptian Sudan. Their world-wide program of aggression and expansion was badly curtailed by the restrictions imposed by the Congress of Europe, which had extended its sphere of influence to cover the entire world. There was continual pressure, sometimes referred to as piracy, on the part of the great European members of the Concert for equivalent compensation of every other nation for each British-French penetration and expansion. The growing fleet of a powerful Germany was a particularly insistent persuader and irritant in this attitude.

This irksome situation of general interference in the affairs of the British-French financial house was aggravated by the threat of revolution in many of its colonies. The most dangerous of these threatened revolutions was China, circa 1894. China had been subjected to British-French commercial and political control in the Opium War of 1840 (see note). Since that time there had been a succession of uprisings of the Chinese Nationalists to throw off this yoke. The British and French were obliged to fight this Chinese aggression from 1840 to 1843, from 1857 to 1858, from 1860 to 1865, in 1894, in 1898, in 1900, in 1911 and in 1927. In addition, there were nearly endless minor aggressions in one part of China or another. For this aggression, China had indemnities assessed against her which ranged from about $28,750,000 in 1843 to $750,000,000 in 1900. The government of China in 1894 was in the hands of a British mercenary, Li Hung-Chang, a former lieutenant of the noted British "trouble-shooter" Chinese Gordon, who ruled as Viceroy.[2]

This brewing and most certain revolution was known to be well-organized. Along with the growing pressure of the European Concert for a more equitable participation and distribution of the raw materials and resources of the world, the international oligarchy faced a rapidly growing menace abroad at a time the Gladstone Liberals were still loud, vocal and unmuzzled. While Mr. Gladstone had been openly charged with treason for his opposition to British imperialistic aggression; the benign character of that dual and double-headed Dr. Jekyll and Mr. Hyde structure of government, known to Americans simply as the British Government, was still at one of its peaks of strength. Thus the financial oligarchy found itself in a very weak and vulnerable position in dealing with the imminent Chinese uprising.

Of this concealed dual nature of the British Government, George Burton Adams (late Professor of History, Emeritus, Yale University) authoritatively develops in his *"Constitutional History of England"* that the members of the British Cabinet are strangely impotent. They are not permitted to make any written notations of proceedings of the Cabinet. They have no access to records of proceedings, if any, made by the Prime Minister. They are not permitted to make reference afterwards to anything that had transpired at a meeting of the Cabinet (page 493). Adams further develops the utter lack

---

[2] Of the Opium War in 1840, Mr. William E. Gladstone said: "I am not competent to judge how long this war may last. ... but that I can say, that a war more unjust in its origin, a war more calculated in its progress to cover this country with disgrace, I do not know and I have not read of."

of power of the House of Commons and of the House of Lords (pages 472-474). "The House of Commons no longer controls the Executive; on the contrary the Executive controls the House of Commons." (Page 495.) There is a distinction between the Government of Great Britain, which is largely confined to the internal government of the British Isles, and the British Government, which controls the British Empire.

Referring to "Great Britain, Banking In" in the Encyclopedia Americana, it appears that the Bank of England is not subject to control by any governmental agency of Great Britain, and that it is above all government, despite the fact that it is privately owned and its directors are nominated by its proprietors. In the Encyclopedia Britannica of 1891 it is termed "a great Engine of Government." It is obvious that this privately owned foreign institution is now in grave financial difficulties with its loans, bonds and mortgages disavowed all over the world, and that it is being bolstered by huge funds siphoned into it from the United States treasury.[3]

[Editor's Note: The Bank of England was nationalized in about 1946. However this did not change the ownership of assets deposited in the bank such as the "'consorts" owned by the Rothschilds. These bear interest at 12%, are transferred by inheritance only and are not redeemable nor subject to tax. These are the profits from the time of the Battle of Waterloo. The interest gleaned from the consorts since 1808 is probably near the sum of 4 quadrillion dollars. The Inner City of London is allodial or freehold title land not subject to the King.]

The startling aspect of the dual nature of the British Government has the support of many eminent authorities on the subject, despite the fact that millions of American school textbooks, works of popular reference, and the works of thousands of pseudo history experts, have woven a fabric of deceit and created popular acceptance of an illusion and a fallacy by the cumulative live force of constant repetition.

The impeachment of this dual structure of government by Prof. Adams is fully supported by the authoritative *Laws of England* of the Lord of Halsbury, a massive work of many huge volumes. It is also supported by the specific statements and writings of

---

[3] The 1943 edition of the Encyclopedia Americana (Vol. 13) makes this stunningly significant statement of the Bank of England, that full partner of the American Administration in the conduct of the financial affairs of all the world: "... Its weakness is the weakness inherent in a system which has developed with the smallest amount of legislative control ... its capital is held privately, and its management is not in any way directly or indirectly controlled by the state. On the other hand, during its whole history, it has been more or less under the protection of the state; its development has been marked by successive loans of its capital to the state in return for the confirmation or extension of its privileges, and it still continues to exercise powers and owe responsibilities delegated by the state . The Bank of England is controlled by a governor, deputy-governor and a court of 24 directors who are elected by the proprietors on the nomination of the directors ..." (This is a description of a privately owned structure of government, sovereign in its own right, and over and above the laws of England. A status admittedly attained by bribing dishonest officials of the Government of the British Isles through the years to gradually extinguish the freedom and rights of the people.)

The Bank of England is a secret holding company of colossal size. The true nature of this strange bank is indicated by a reference in "England's Money Lords Tory M. P.", by Simon Haxey, to Lancashire Steel Corporation, subsidiary of the Bank of England (page 158).

David Starr Jordan (late president of Stanford University), Gladstone, David Lloyd George, J. Ramsay MacDonald, Vincent C. Vickers (director of the Bank of England and of Vickers-Armstrong armaments works), Harold J. Laski and many others. *Better Times* by Lloyd George in 1910 is particularly revealing.[4]

The manipulations of the financial oligarchy at the Berlin Convention to modify the Treaty of San Stefano enraged many of the people of Europe and there followed some serious racial riots in Germany and Russia. The coming war in China against the financial oligarchy would very likely have been quickly followed by an uprising in India, with the whole British Empire subject to a searching investigation of the entire Concert

---

[4] The wide latitude of action of the agents and servants of the CROWN and their remarkable immunity from the interference of English Courts and of English law appears in the "Laws of England" of Lord Halsbury as apparent from the following selected passages:

Vol. 6, page 388, par. 582— ... Nor can the Crown, by proclamation or otherwise, make or unmake any law on its own authority apart from Parliament, except in colonies to which representative institutions have not been granted. (This excepts only England, Canada, Australia, Union of South Africa and New Zealand, who between them have only 13% — almost the total white population of 68,000,000 of the Empire — of the people of the British Empire, from the utterly absolute and autocratic rule of the Crown, THE Bank and THE City.)

Vol. 23, page 307, par. 641 — If under a treaty with a foreign state, a government has received funds for the benefit of a private person or class of persons, although a moral obligation may thereby be imposed upon the government to pay the funds so received tosuch persons, no action or petition of right, will be at their suit to recover the fund, and the intended ultimate beneficiaries cannot compel the government to carry out the obligation.

Par. 642 — An executive or administrative act of a subject, though in the first instance done without the authority of his Sovereign, will have all the effect of an Act of State if subsequently ratified. (This provides the facilities to make the law afterwards to fit the case, as developed by Prof. Edwin J. Clapp in "Economic Aspects of the War" published 1915 as having been the procedure in the matter of the American ship Wilhelmina.)

Par. 643 — The Sovereign can do no wrong, and no legal proceedings can be brought against him...

Par. 648 — As regards Ireland, all of the official acts of the Lord Lieutenant are Acts of State apparently even if ultra vires (transcending authority conferred by law).

Par. 650 — The official acts of every state or potentate whose independence has been recognized by the Crown, and of their authorized agents, are Acts of State. No action can be brought in respect of such acts; even where the agent is a British subject, and where, in carrying out the Act of State, he is committing an offense against English law...

This gives a fair outline of the adroit and dexterous machinery of government which is able to adjust itself to any situation and clothe it with a veil of justice and right, and which provides the tool to make the 435,000,000 colored people of the British Empire its utterly voiceless subjects; and which in addition has had virtually complete control of the government and commerce of China for over one hundred years, and of other apparently independent countries. It can reasonably be stated that over half of all the people of the world have been its subjects up to recent times. Of this government the late President Jordan of Stanford University said: "Everything runs as though newly oiled, and the British public hears nothing of it."

of Europe, in which the British would have had only the very weak French support. However, the great depression of the '90's provided a solution, with the whole world in the grip of over-production and lack of markets.

It appears that about 1895 the first of the series of secret treaties between Japan and Britain, which made Japan virtually a British robot, was made. The British financial oligarchy practically took over the Japanese banking system to finance her wars and the immense industrial expansion that eventually swamped the world with goods "made in Japan". Of this deal, the former Kaiser Wilhelm II wrote in his *Memoirs* published in 1921: "Some day when Hong Kong has gone the same way, England will repent of her act. ... When once Japan has made a reality out of her watchword 'Asia for the Asiatics' and brought China and India under her sway, England will cast her eyes about in vain search of Germany and the German fleet."

France had now recovered from the beating of 1871, and the oligarchy was ready to lay the groundwork for a new world-wide balance of power, to supersede the noxious supervision of the Concert of Europe. By the treaties that followed on January 30, 1902, and in 1905, Japan became as close and subservient an ally of Britain as was France. This alliance continued for about 35 years until it was ended by the assassination of the Japanese statesmen associated with the international financial oligarchy.

The thought that this Frankenstein of the financial oligarchy would eventually turn against its creators was expressed by Prof. Usher in his *Pan-Americanism* published in 1915, in these words:

> Nor should it be forgotten that the financial indebtedness of Japan, which taxes the capacity of that country to meet the interest and principal payments, is all owed in Europe and America. So far as any tangible evidence of that capital is in existence in the world, it is in Japan. ... The Japanese have only to repudiate their entire indebtedness to free the nation from a staggering load and put it at once in the possession of its whole economic development at the price of what they have already paid. The control of the Pacific, the annexation of the Spice Islands and the Philippines, the expulsion of foreigners, the assurance for all time of financial independence—these are indeed things to conjure with. And we who can clearly see so much at so great a distance with so little aid, may well pause to wonder how much more the Japanese themselves can see, and how long caution and prudence will counsel them to wait before attempting the attainment of such desirable ends.

The oligarchy sent its Chinese henchman, Li Hung-Chang, on a tour of the European capitals in 1896. The purpose for this tour was to negotiate a Chinese concession to each of the Great Powers to allay their rising resentment, and to meet the coming Chinese Nationalist revolt. Each concession carried with it the requirement to help keep order in China. In this deal Russia was leased Port Arthur by the famous Li Hung-Chang-Lobanov Treaty of May, 1896, and subsequent agreements of September 8, 1896 and March 27, 1898 . Germany was leased Kaiochow on March 5, 1898. Italy and Austria-Hungary were also given certain rights. The imminent Chinese revolt against the British yoke was represented to the people of the world as an indication of the extreme inner weakness of the Chinese dynasty and as an indication that China was on the point of falling apart in national disintegration, and that it was at the stage where the only solution was a division between the Great Powers.

That the weakness of the Chinese dynasty was not as great as represented may be apparent from the fact that the Emperor Kwan-Hsu ventured to dismiss the British hireling Li Hung-Chang with the support of the Nationalists in the summer of 1898. As a result, the Emperor was deposed by the British, and Li Hung-Chang restored to influence under the nominal regency of the Empress Dowager. There are few instances in all history where there was more dissembling, falsification and feinting on the part of the Powers to keep the facts from the world as they were all implicated. The American political machine of 1896 was faced with the difficult task of pulling the United States out of the great depression of the '90s and to fulfill their promise of "The Full Dinner Pail." The task was difficult, for in the words of Chauncey Depew, great financial and political power of that day, we were producing two thousand million dollars worth more goods than we could consume, and this overproduction was going back to stagnation and poverty. In this critical period a deal was struck by which the American Wall Street became a branch office of the Bank of England.[5] (See footnote.)

The United States started its war with Spain ostensibly to free Cuba from Spanish oppression. Spain had fully accepted an American ultimatum on April 10, 1898, but this fact was ignored by President McKinley in asking for a declaration of war on the following day. On April 25, 1898, war was declared as existing since April 21st. The fleet of Admiral Dewey had been prepared for battle at Hong Kong, and after receiving word of the declaration of war on April 27th, sped to Manila and attacked and sank the Spanish fleet there on the morning of May 1, 1898. The American people were electrified by this unexpected and dazzling victory, and the resulting jubilation served to bury some questionable aspects.

Within the next few days the warships of various other Powers began to arrive at Manila, and there assembled a German fleet under Vice-Admiral von Diederichs and a British fleet under senior Captain Chichester. Admiral von Diederichs questioned the American action, which was his prerogative according to the then still tacitly accepted International agreements or International Law as promulgated by the Concert of Europe. It was the established right of every Great Power to be explicitly informed of any contemplated political change in any part of the earth, and to be given ample time to enter its objections and counter-proposals in every disagreement between any other nations, before any nation made an aggressive move.

The German fleet included some large and powerful armored ships and was superior to that of Admiral Dewey. Furthermore, the German Navy of this period was larger than that of America, as were also the navies of France and Russia. Despite this, Admiral Dewey assumed a highly bellicose attitude and in one exchange is said to have stated to Lieutenant von Hintze (later a foreign minister of Germany): "... and say to Admiral von Diederichs that if he wants a fight he can have it now." The reply of the British commander Chichester is said to have been equally to the point: "There are only two

---

[5] Prof. Usher stated in "Pan-Germanism" of 1913, Chapter X, pages 139 and 140; that an understanding was reached, probably before the summer of 1897, that in case of war the United States would promptly declare in favor of England and France and would do her utmost to assist them; and that there seems to be no doubt whatever that no papers of any sort were signed. He quotes further: "The alliance, for it was nothing less, was based upon infinitely firmer ground than written words and sheets of parchment ..."

persons who know what my instructions are. One of those persons is myself, and the other is Admiral Dewey."

Various writers and historians differ as to the precise words used by Admiral Dewey. They were "off the record" but there is no question that Admiral Dewey used the fact he was addressing Admiral von Diederichs through a third person to use terms that had heretofore been considered inadmissible in the communication between representatives of nations. The dispute at Manila raged for three months. On August 13, 1898, the day after the war had ended and before word reached Manila, Captain Chichester is recorded to have placed his ships between the German and American fleets. The Germans then withdrew from Manila fully aware that the established law and order of the Concert of Europe had been superseded by "The New Order of Freedom" of a now fully revealed British-French-American-Japanese alliance, and that their commerce and trade in the Pacific was on the wane.

Nicholas Murray Butler stated in an address delivered Sept. 1, 1940, at the Parrish Memorial Art Museum, Southampton, Long Island:

> Consider for a moment the progress which was making from 1898 to 1920 in the building of a system of world organization and international cooperation that should control and guide the new economic forces which the Industrial Revolution had set at work. The purpose, of course, was to increase prosperity for all peoples, great and small, and to protect the foundations of international peace through international cooperation. ... Immediately, the progressive and liberal forces of the world rallied to respond to that appeal. ... It was the influence of the American delegation which gave to the first Hague Conference of 1899 the measure of success it attained. ...
>
> The Spanish-American War in 1898 was absolutely unnecessary, and if it had not been insisted upon by the belligerent press, aided by numerous influential leaders of opinion, including Theodore Roosevelt, Cuba would have become free without any armed hostilities whatsoever. The cost to the people of the United States of that unnecessary war is quite appalling, since highly organized and efficient lobbies have provided for a system of pensions to persons whose relation to the war was only nominal, which have already amounted to tens of millions of dollars and will continue yet for a long generation. Isolation is the last thing of which the American government and the American people can be accused. ...
>
> It is therefore obvious and of record that the American people were betrayed by the failure of those who were chosen to public office in 1920.

(It is interesting to recollect that the Spanish-American War, whose eventual cost is here admitted as appalling, lasted a little over 3½ months.) The condemnation of the Spanish American War and of the part played in its making by Theodore Roosevelt and others by Dr. Nicholas Murray Butler is a typical example of an imperialist deprecating imperialism, of the pot calling the kettle black. There are few wars that have not been later deplored as having been utterly futile and unnecessary by someone of eminent standing whose connection with the International Imperialists was as positive as is that of Dr. Butler, the eminent chief of the Pilgrim's secret society of International finance. It all seems part of the general scheme to create confusion and contradiction in the minds of the people and so avoid disclosure of the highly disciplined organization of the international financial oligarchy and its planned objective: eventual world domination.

In *My Memories of Eighty Years*, published 1924, Chauncey M. Depew records on page 270 a conversation in which Lord Rothschild offered Puerto Rico and the Philippine Islands to the United States and stated the willingness of the Spanish Government to give independence to Cuba and to comply with every demand the United States can make. Regretfully he records further: "The proposition unfortunately came too late, and Mr. McKinley could not stop the war. It was well known in Washington that he was exceedingly averse to hostilities and believed the difficulties could be satisfactorily settled by diplomacy, but the people were aroused to such an extent that they were determined not only to free Cuba but to punish those who were oppressing the Cubans."

The facts are that McKinley suppressed Spain's formal acceptance of American demands and asked for war the day after receiving that acceptance, and that it took every resource of high finance and its controlled jingo press to rush America into war before any resistance could be organized to oppose the war-makers. Mr. Depew guilelessly admits his significant conversation with Lord Nathan Rothschild over 25 years later when it apparently no longer has any current interest. This renowned after-dinner story teller and revered Pilgrim founder goes on to repeat the fable of why our war with Spain which is now accepted American "History." Of how "History" is made, John K. Turner states in *Shall It Be Again*, published 1922:

> Remember that for more than four years one side was permitted to speak and the other forced to remain silent. 'The perspective that only time can give,' some say, 'is necessary before the true history of our war can be written, and before proper criticism can be made.' But the end of the fighting saw a vast and complicated machine feverishly at work to crystallize into 'history' the story of the war as it was told to us as propaganda in the heat thereof ...

Mr. Turner refers to the activities of another great Pilgrim at the conclusion of World War I on page 367:

> Our illegal war in Russia was pleasing not only to Paris and London bankers, but to New York bankers as well. ... Mr. Lamont, a partner of Morgan was permitted to send an advance copy of the peace conditions to his Wall Street associates. While acting for the American people at Paris, Lamont participated in the organization of the China Consortium and the International Convention of Bankers on Mexico. So, along with the peace arrangements we find the beginnings of the 'definite plan of international cooperation in the financing of foreign enterprises,' advanced by Pres. Farrell of the U. S. Steel Corporation, a year before!

[Editor's Note: It seems indisputable that this plan has been operating since 1897.]

VI. THE NEW ORDER OF FREEDOM

British approval of America's entry into the new world Balance of Power was open and widespread. The Right Hon. Joseph Chamberlain, Secretary of State for the British Colonies, made this comment on the secret pact between Britain and America: "We now see our cousins across the water entering the lists and sharing in a task which might have proved too heavy for us alone." The London Saturday Review quoted: "The American Commissioners at Paris are making this bargain, whether they realize it or not, under the protecting naval strength of England, and we shall expect a material quid pro quo for this assistance ... we expect her assistance on the day, which is quickly approaching, when the future of China comes up for settlement ..." The pact between the British and American internationalists was made in the utmost secrecy, but many of the leading statesmen and educators of that day sensed what was going on, and many of the great speeches and articles in opposition to this fantastic conspiracy were included in *Republic or Empire?* by William Jennings Bryan, published in 1899. Among these is a speech delivered at the University of Michigan on February 22, 1899, by former Congressman Charles A. Towne. He said:

> ... upon the decision by the American people of problems now imminent depends the future weal or woe of our country, and hence that of the human race for ages to come ... by a considerable portion of the public press the language of distrust of present tendencies is ridiculed as a form of hysteria or denounced as an attack on the Government, and that a man who ventures to raise a cry of warning is either charitably characterized as a fit candidate for a lunatic asylum or violently assailed as an enemy of his country ... It is to mix up in alien quarrels, which we have deprecated always and with special emphasis of late, at precisely the time when by all indications they are about to fulminate in the most colossal and destructive war of modern times.

It appears from the words of Mr. Towne that the treatment of "isolationists" has not changed in the 44 years that have passed; nor has British censorship and control over American sources of foreign news changed in the 65 years since Lieut. F. V. Greene commented on that control in his "Army Life in Russia," of 1878.[6]

---

[6] In "Barriers Down" published in 1942, Kent Cooper, General Manager of the Associated Press, discloses a 20 year battle fought since the end of World War I for the right to give the American people the truth about the news of Europe and the world. He gives it as his opinion that the control of "the greatest and the most powerful International monopoly of the 19th Century" in developing international attitudes and prejudices has been an undisclosed cause of wars for the past 100 years (page 7). The mischief planted during the fifteen years following World War I had become too great for the new relationship of the Associated Press to overcome (page 264).

He develops that the determination of France and England to keep Germany encircled by small allied nations, was supported by Reuters and Havas with their own "cordon sanitaire." (Page 106) Havas, the allied French agency, is a subsidiary of the French Government; and an impressive array of practical and historical fact would indicate that most French governments of the past 100 years have been subsidiaries of the French House of Rothschild in practice if not in theory.

Mr. Cooper states that the account is that international bankers under the lead of the House of Rothschild had acquired an interest in the three leading European agencies (Reuter, Wolff

Immediately after the nations of the world had been lined up in the "New Order," the long-awaited rebellion of the Chinese Nationalists broke out. The British organization to meet this menace functioned well and the cream of the British, French, Russian, German, Japanese, American, Italian and Austro-Hungarian armies soon gave the Chinese a severe beating for their aspirations of National freedom in what was known as the "Boxer War" of 1900. China was assessed an indemnity of $750,000,000 for her brutal aggression, later reduced due to American intercession and renunciation of her share. To impress upon the Chinese the utter dissolution of their national entity, the soldiers of all nations were marched through their "Forbidden City," thus desecrating their holy of holies.

With the other Great Powers of Europe locked up in the "policy of encirclement" on the continent of Europe by the overwhelming sea-power and imposing military and commercial over-balance of the new British Balance of Power, there was inaugurated an era of almost unrestricted territorial acquisition and plunder. The first was the attack and seizure of the Orange Free State and the Transvaal Republic in the Boer War of 1899-1902, in the face of feeble and futile German protest. A mobilized British force of 448,435 eventually defeated 60,000 to 65,000 Boer soldiers.

The next move was to restore the status quo of China as the sole province of international finance and—with a nucleus of an overseas army released by the victory over the Boers—to hold in check the reactions of the other European powers. The eviction of Russia from her warm port on the open Yellow Sea was inaugurated by the treaty of January 30, 1902 with Japan. The Japanese war machine was rapidly built up with British financing and in July of 1903 a demand was made on Russia to abandon her position on the Kwantung Peninsula. Russia had spent $300,000,000 in improvements since she had leased Port Arthur from Li Hung-Chang six years before, and the Japanese challenge aroused a large measure of scorn in Russia, tempered only by the knowledge that this was a British challenge.[7]

---

and Havas). (Page 21) Reuters, whose headquarters were in Old Jewry, or the Bank of England, in the City, was the chief of the three. It was the staggering presumption of this firm that the news of the world was its own private property, to be withheld, to be discolored to its own purposes, or to be sold to whom and where they directed. Rengo of Japan was obliged to pay a territorial "Franchise" fee, plus a service fee for news furnished. When Rengo attempted to buy news from the Associated Press; Reuters assessed a "service" fee on the Associated Press for the "right" to sell news to Rengo.

[7] When John Hay, in a characteristic assumption of sanctimonious hypocrisy, remonstrated with the Russian Minister at Washington in May, 1903, stating that the inevitable result of the policy of aggression being pursued by Russia would be the dismemberment of China, Count Cassini shouted: "This is already done. China is dismembered and we are entitled to our share."

Norman Dwight Harris in "Europe and the East," published 1926, significantly states of British and Japanese cooperation in the affairs of Korea after the Sino-Japanese or Yellow War of 1895, that the Korean finances were re-established through Sir McLeavy Brown, a gifted British financial expert.

Already in 1900, with the Chinese revolution just in satisfactory solution by joint action of the Great Powers; the notorious international promoter of armaments, Basil Zaharoff, went to Japan to make a deal by which Rothschild controlled Vickers acquired armament and

There followed several months of inconclusive diplomatic interchange. Then, on the night of February 8, 1904, a Japanese torpedo flotilla sped into the harbor of Port Arthur. With the Russian warships brightly illuminated and off guard and a large part of the crews on shore, terrific damage was inflicted, including the sinking two battleships and a large cruiser. Many will recall the immense jubilation of the controlled American jingo press at this brilliant Japanese feat, and many of those of middle-age should still have a vivid recollection of the overwhelming wave of pro-Japanese sentiment that swept this country.

The Japanese then transported nearly half a million men over one thousand miles of open water and fought the two most massive engagements of modern times within eight months of the outbreak of the war: the battles of Liao-Yang and Mukden; the latter involving about 750,000 men and casualties of 130,000 men in less than a week. The Russians outnumbered the Japanese, but were utterly crushed in a campaign of marvelous military efficiency under the command of Field Marshal Oyama. The Japanese ally had justified himself, and a new treaty was immediately formed in August 1905. It was signed concurrently with the signing of the Treaty of Peace between Japan and Russia, which bound Britain and Japan to immediately come to the assistance of each other even if only one power was to attack. Undoubtedly, this treaty secretly included the removal of Germany from Kiaochow in the upcoming and preplanned World War I, as well as the awarding to Japan of the islands of the German Marianas, Caroline and Marshall groups. These islands stretched out about 5,000 miles east and west and 3,000 miles north and south across our path to the Philippines; bracketing and nullifying our position in the Philippines, projecting Japan's influence 5,000 miles closer to America's shores, and transforming the Pacific Ocean into a Japanese lake. The existence of this secret deal giving Japan these islands did not become known to America until Wilson sat down at the Peace Table at the end of World War I. His objections to the various secret treaties that then came to light caused most of the secret deals to be revoked by the British; however, this deal was not revoked.

The affairs of the Far East were now stabilized; in the opinion of some Englishmen, for one hundred years to come; and all eyes turned to the new district of dissension in Africa. On April 8, 1904, a secret treaty was signed between Britain and France stabilizing the relative positions of these nations in Africa; in plainer words, dividing Africa between them. Trouble immediately erupted in nearby Morocco, an independent empire, then occupied by the French in accord with the treaty with Britain. Germany promptly protested the French action as a breach of the Madrid Convention of 1880 (signed by 15 nations), which had defined the precise status of Morocco. To offset and meet the breach of this Convention, Germany herself occupied the port of Casablanca.[8]

---

munitions plants in Japan. Zaharoff's prescient foresight of war profits ahead marked his career. Lord Beaverbrook said of him: "The destinies of nations were his sport; the movement of armies and the affairs of government his special delight. In the wake of war this mysterious figure moved over tortured Europe."

[8] From *A Short History of English Liberalism* by W. Lyon Blease (published 1913 in England), Chapter XI regarding Liberalism Since 1906: "In 1904 Lord Lansdowne made an agreement with France by which the two contracting Powers settled all their outstanding disputes. This was intended by its author to be only the first of a series of international

In order to arrive at an amicable settlement, a conference of the Powers was called at Algeciras, which lasted from January 16th to March 31st, 1906. The British-French oligarchy passed the initiative at Algeciras to President Theodore Roosevelt, who through Ambassador White informed Germany in harsh and unequivocal terms to get out of Casablanca, that America would not tolerate any German port on the Atlantic. Thus the pact of the Pacific was extended to the Atlantic, our partnership in the British Balance of Power asserted in no uncertain terms. America forced virtually complete recognition of French pretentions and of the division of Africa between Britain and France. The financial oligarchy purchased Italy's vote at this conference against her German ally, by awarding Tripoli, then a Turkish province, to Italy; and promising British aid in its capture. It is an interesting coincidence that Theodore Roosevelt proposed the nomination

---

agreements. It was converted by Sir Edward Grey into a weapon of offence against Germany, the country upon which ... the animosity of modern Toryism had definitely settled. The fortunes of Great Britain were bound up with those of France. The theory of the Balance of Power was revived, every diplomatic conference was made a conflict between France and Great Britain on the one side and Germany on the other, and in 1911 the lives and the wealth of the British people were endangered, not to maintain any moral principle or any British interest, but to promote the material interests of French financiers in Morocco. (Page 364.)

"When Germany proposed at a Hague Conference, that international agreement should abolish the system of destroying private property at sea, Great Britain refused even to discuss the point ... The right to destroy her commerce was our most powerful weapon against her, and as our peace policy was determined by our war policy, we preserved this relic of barbarism. The inevitable consequence of our diplomacy was to give German Jingoism an irresistible argument for the increase of the German Fleet. The increase in the German Fleet was described in threatening language by Mr. Churchill, and was matched by an increase in our own ... There may have been information in the possession of the Foreign Office which justified this persistent hostility towards Germany. That country may have been animated by some desire to destroy our commerce, or to appropriate our Colonies. So far as we are allowed by our governors to learn any facts at all, there is no more than a shadow of a foundation for such an assumption. Up to the end of 1912 we were bound straight for a conflict, of which not one Englishman in ten thousand knew anything definite, and not one in a thousand knew anything at all. (Page 365.) (Note that this was written before World War I.)

"It is not the business of Great Britain to dictate to established Governments, or to go to war with them for the better regulation of their internal affairs. Nor is it the business of a British Government to refuse to make agreements with any foreign Government for the management of matters in which they are jointly concerned. But it is the duty of a British Government not to corrupt its own people by involving itself intimately with a Government whose methods are not only different but are utterly alien from its own. An alliance with France is bad only in so far as it is turned into a combination against Germany. An alliance with Russia is in itself unnatural and horrible." (Page 367.)

These words written in 1913 by a Liberal Britisher about Britain apply with surprising exactness to the extent of the understanding and knowledge of the average American citizen as to why the United States is at war 30 years later.

(*) Bertrand Russell in "Justice in War-Time" (p. 168), published by The Open Court Pub. Co. in 1917.

of John Hays Hammond for vice-president of the United States on the Republican ticket of 1908. Mr. Hammond was one of the four men sentenced to death in 1896 as a result of the Jameson Raid in South Africa, an effort to seize territory for the British Empire. Cecil Rhodes paid an indemnity of $250,000 to free Hammond and his brother, Col. Francis Rhodes.

With the African difficulties settled (perhaps for one hundred years) the scene flashed to the "Middle-East." Russia, balked in her efforts to attain a foothold on open water in the Near-East and in the Far-East, was now attempting to penetrate to the Persian Gulf. She had gradually occupied the northern half of Persia, while Britain had occupied most of the southern half to resist her, with a small neutral zone in between. In order to meet the Russian menace, the British-French oligarchy decided to subsidize a certain section of the Russian Government, and a loan was arranged in April, 1906, of which a British writer (*) said: "The part played by the Foreign Office in advising the City is not easy to ascertain, but no one can doubt that our financial magnates were perfectly conscious of co-operating with the Foreign Office when they undertook to lend money to the Russian Government." The purpose of the loan was to strengthen the hand of those elements in the Russian Government favorable to International Finance, and to halt a growing tendency to an understanding with Germany.

The same British writer goes on to say: "... incidentally, we could not but help the Russian Government in suppressing the Duma, in reconquering Poland, and in depriving the Finns of the liberties which the Tsar had sworn to defend ..." As a result of the British subsidy, the first Duma, whose probable pro-German leanings were greatly feared, lasted only ten weeks from May 9 to June 22, 1906. Although the Russian Emperor apparently was not in accord with this suppression of Russian liberty, its consequences eventually cost his life. The Anglo-Russian Agreement of August 31, 1907, made on the basis of the loans of the British and French bankers, did nothing to end Russian pressure.

In November 1910, Russia and Germany concluded the Potsdam Agreement, giving Russia a free hand in Persia. The same British writer states of this: "From this time on, we became completely subservient to Russia in Persia, since we lived in terror of a rapprochement between the Tsar and the Kaiser." As usual, the public was totally unaware of the wider scope of the power politics involved and accepted the stock tale of Persia being taken over by the two adjacent powers due to discord in Persia itself.

The British took a peculiarly artful advantage of the public ignorance in America in this instance by having the new British-controlled government of Persia (the Shah and his government had fled to Russia) appeal for American Government assistance in regenerating Persian finances, and so help restore the country's order and independence. The success of this superficially plausible and highly commendable undertaking would of course have meant complete and final defeat of the last Russian hope for access to open water, the dream of centuries. Russian antagonism to this splendid and humane objective was then thoroughly capitalized and exploited with the aid of alleged American financial experts, causing wide-spread indignation in America. The British-French loans to Russia had at this time reached vast proportions, as indicated by subject matter from the "Pan-Germanism" of Prof. Usher quoted heretofore. This, together with the storm of American hostility, raised the weight of the Russians allied with the International Financiers so as to cause Russia to recede from her stand; giving British diplomacy another mighty victory in the policy of encirclement.

The foundation for The Great War, which had been started on May 1, 1898, was now nearly ready. Germany had made many other frantic efforts [9] to evade the iron circle slowly closing about her national existence. The most outstanding was her effort to overcome a large part of British supremacy on sea by bypassing the Suez Canal with a railroad in Turkey to the Persian Gulf, the so-called Berlin to Baghdad Railroad. Although they obtained permission from Turkey to build this line in the fall of 1899, shortly after the nullification of the Concert of Europe by the new British Balance of Power, she had been halted again and again by threat of war, and by the outbreak of war in 1914 still had not finished it.

The Berlin to Baghdad Railroad in general involved only an extension of about nine hundred miles to existing railroads, it was located entirely in Turkey and was being built with the full consent of that country. In the fifteen years from 1899 to 1914, the Balkans were called the sore spot of Europe, simply because of the jockeying with this railroad. The notorious agent provocateur of war, Sir Basil Zaharoff, was an active figure in the secret diplomacy of Europe in this period. One writer has said of this Greek-French super-salesman of the armament plants of International Finance, and British nobleman: "His monument is the graves of millions; his epitaph, their dying groans."[10]

---

[9] The part Britain played in the 1907-1912 conflict with Russia, which followed their agreement of August 31, 1907, to divide Persia between themselves added much to the misery and poverty of the Persian people. Mr. Arthur Bullard stated in an article that appeared in the Century Magazine for December, 1915, on "The British Foreign Policy and Sir Edward Grey": "From a humanitarian point of view the British record in Persia is the blackest in recent history. It is on a par with their Chinese opium war and their ultimatum to Portugal in 1790."

[10] Among the shadowy and mysterious figures that silently flitted about the stage of European power politics during the period of incubation (1895 to 1914) of the Great War, figures that all were imbued with that intense "passion for anonymity" generally associated with the great British-French banking dynasty, was Viscount Reginald Esher. Viscount Esher was born in 1852, the son of a noted jurist and interpreter of English law, and died in 1930. Despite the fact that he was for forty years one of the most powerful statesmen in all the world, his actual position was very obscure; his name was utterly unknown and has remained unknown to the American public. In a hearing before the Committee on Foreign Relations of the United States Senate on January 28, 1940, it was developed that his whole position was derived from the fact that he was the most secret confidant and counselor of the "monarchy." It is quite apparent that by the term "monarchy" there is here meant the "King-in-Council" or Crown; or in other words the City and International Finance.

Harold J. Laski said of this man in the New Republic that he was "for a generation the unnamed member of Cabinet after Cabinet, indispensable to them all and not responsible to any." There was made a plausible arrangement to give a public aspect to his position of most secret confidant of the "monarchy" by his editing and arrangement of the letters and papers of Queen Victoria. His journals were published in limited edition under the title "The Captains and the Kings Depart." On August 3, 1917, he recorded: "No American is likely to be killed before November. This is unfortunate, as Wilson may require to be steadied before then and only the death of young Americans can ensure him stability."

The principal reason for the frenzied secret diplomacy and bloodshed to halt this railroad was that it would have been a shortcut from Berlin to the East and India, completely bypassing the Suez "tollgate" of the British-French financial oligarchy. It also would have had a considerable advantage over the route from London to India via the Suez Canal. Lord Cranbourne, Under-Secretary for Foreign Affairs, in January, 1902, stated that the maintenance of the status quo in the Persian Gulf was incompatible with the occupation by any Power of a port on those waters. British interests based their opposition on the fact that this railway would destroy the trade that English capital and English merchants had painfully built up along the Suez Route. An important aspect of this trade was the sale of coal to the ships of other nations at prices set by that English capital. In order to provide a coaling station for her ships on the route to her own inner Africa colonies, Germany authorized a German syndicate to purchase dock facilities at Agadir, an utterly unimportant town on the southern end of the Moroccan Coast, with no railroad connection, cut off by mountains running out into the desert. This was not a political penetration as the town itself is cut off from the entire world. Nevertheless, interference was set up; and when the German gunboat Panther was sent to investigate, it was forced out of the harbor by British and French cruisers standing by, guns ready, in one of the most humiliating episodes of modern history. This incident in July, 1911, received wide attention as the "Morocco Affair" and was one of the last preludes to The Great War.

The outbreak of the Great War was fully expected by every government in the world; it took not one of them by surprise. The illusion which was artfully fostered in all the world that Britain was the victim of her treaty to defend Belgium neutrality, and of a wholly unexpected and brutal attack on Belgium, is evident from a sentence in a letter written to President Wilson by Colonel E. M. House, dated at London, May 29, 1914, in which he stated: "Whenever England consents, France and Russia will close in on Germany and Austria." The greater part of British sea-power from all over the world had been gathered in Home waters on that day; although Archduke Franz Ferdinand, active ruler of Austria-Hungary and leader of the foes of International Finance, was not assassinated until June 28, 1914, and war was not to start until August 1, 1914. Sir Arthur Nicolson was for many years one of the foremost diplomats of the world. He retired in June, 1916, from the British Foreign Office. He can well be credited with a great part of the success of British diplomacy in restraining and confining the explosive economic pressure of the rapidly multiplying sixty millions of Germany squeezed in an area about four-fifths the size of the State of Texas; a pressure which erupted into World War I. Sir Arthur served for nearly a half-century in the Foreign Office and in nearly every important legation in Europe, the Near-East, the Middle-East and the Far-East.

The Algeciras conference held in January 1906 was to consider the German protest against the Cambon-Lansdowne Agreement of April 8, 1904; as it had divided Africa and other parts of the world between Britain and France in utter disregard of existing agreements. While every other Great Power was represented by two delegates, Sir Arthur alone represented Great Britain; he completely dominated the Conference. The Jewish Sir Donald Mackenzie Wallace was present only as an observer for British financial interests. Due to the Intervention of Theodore Roosevelt, this partition of Africa was approved by the Conference. It ended in a complete diplomatic fiasco for the Germans, with even the delegation of their Italian ally against them due to previous secret concessions in Africa, which they had received from British Finance.

The tortuous currents and counter-currents of international machinations and intrigue over this period of nearly fifty years are described in intimate personal detail in *Portrait of a Diplomatist* by Harold Nicolson, a son of Sir Arthur, published in 1930. Mr. Nicolson states (Ch. XIV—The Outbreak of War—p. 298-299) in effect that the events of the several days immediately preceding the outbreak of World War I were merely of dramatic interest with no practical significance. He adds that the war was the result of cumulative international stupidity since 1878. He further records (page 314) that his father wrote an article during that war expressing his indignation regarding the conclusion that Germany had started or was responsible for the war. The article was refused publication. In that article, Sir Arthur Nicolson urgently warned that terms of oppression or humiliation of the defeated would make durable or lasting peace impossible.

The following memorandum of a conference with President Wilson on December 10, 1918, was made by Dr. Isaiah Bowman, one of the American economic experts at the Peace Conference:

> ... the President remarked that we would be the only disinterested people at the Peace Conference, and that the men whom we were about to deal with did not represent their own people. ... The President pointed out that this was the first conference in which decisions depended upon the opinion of mankind, not upon the previous determination and diplomatic schemes of the assembled representatives. With great earnestness he re-emphasized the point that unless the Conference was prepared to follow the opinions of mankind and to express the will of the people rather than that of their leaders at the Conference, we should soon be involved in another break-up of the world, and when such break-up came it would not be a war but a cataclysm. (Vol. 4, p. 280, Intimate Papers of Col. House.)

Not only did those that "did not represent their own people" flout and nullify the views of President Wilson, but they also callously ignored the warning of their own foremost diplomat, Sir Arthur Nicolson, for many years the feared and formidable opponent of Germany in almost every major diplomatic clash, and the invariable victor due to the invisible support of International Finance. Philip Snowden, later a member of a Liberal British Cabinet, said of the peace treaty:

> The Treaty should satisfy brigands, imperialists, and militarists. It is a death-blow to the hopes of those who expected the end of the war to bring peace. It is not a peace treaty, but a declaration of another war. It is the betrayal of democracy and of the fallen in the war. The Treaty exposes the true aims of the Allies.

VII. THE NEW ORDER ENDS IN THE EAST

The common people of the world were kept in utter darkness as to the nature of the moves made in the great game of international power politics through the years, and the fact that it was a foregone conclusion that these moves would inevitably lead to gigantic slaughter. Therefore, the outbreak of the Great War was to them a complete surprise, as it was also to the greater part of the representatives of the people in the government of the United States and in the government of the British Isles. The reasons given to the public for the war were purely superficial and fraudulent. Belgium was a full British ally before she was invaded. The treaty as to Belgian neutrality, which was alleged to have formed the basis for British intervention, was non-existent.

Specifically, the British foreign office pointed to a treaty signed April 19, 1839, as providing a basis for mandatory British intervention. It would take a considerable stretch of the imagination to read into the broad general terms of this treaty any such mandate. The British had in the meantime grossly violated far more definite terms of more recent treaties again and again, as witness the complete disregard of the 1880 Convention of Madrid signed by 15 nations, in their agreement with France that occurred on April 8, 1904, dividing all of Africa between the two nations. It is very interesting to note the artless way in which the British Foreign Office stated that its foreign policy of 1914 was still unchanged from 1839, in view of the rivers of blood shed in that foreign policy during those 75 years.

The chicanery and deceit of international power politics was never better exposed than at the so-called "Peace Table" after the Great War. Herbert Hoover, who was a member of the American commission at Paris, tells of this in his article of November 8, 1941, in *The Saturday Evening Post*, entitled "You May Be Sure I Shall Fight Shy." Mr. Wilson was stunned to find we had been fighting for the success of secret agreements of which the United States had no knowledge. Some of these agreements were actually designed to check further political and commercial expansion of this country; such as awarding the vast island chains in the Pacific to the Japanese so as to cut us off from India, China and the Philippines. Italy had been promised a definitely described colonial area in another secret agreement for deserting her German and Austro-Hungarian allies; then later was blackjacked into the war with the threat to make peace and let her betrayed allies deal with her alone.[11]

---

[11] *The Intimate Papers of Col. House*, (arranged by Chas. Seymour, Provost and Sterling Professor of History, Yale University, and published in 1926 in four volumes) develop that a secret treaty covering Italy's reward for entering into World War I on the Allied side was formally signed in London on April 26, 1915. It was followed by Italy's declaration of war on Austria: May 23, 1915; and on Germany: August 27, 1916.

From Mr. House's notes it would appear that this secret treaty, as well as one of March, 1915—promising Constantinople to Russia—was discussed at an intimate dinner meeting at the White House on April 30, 1917. Only Mr. House, Mr. A. J. Balfour and Mr. Wilson attended. It seems that Mr. Balfour did not later furnish Mr. Wilson any particulars or details of the secret treaties as he had promised, so that Mr. Wilson testified before the Senate Foreign Relations Committee on August 19, 1919, that he had no knowledge of the existence of these secret treaties as a whole. (Appendix, Vol. 3, p. 61.)

This secret deal was retracted and Italy was given little for her 2,197,000 war casualties. The British Government seized for itself nearly all of the captured areas, taking 1,415,929 square miles and allowing France a mere 360,000 square miles for her immense casualties of 6,160,800 men.[12] Italy was bankrupted and wept by revolution as a result; out of this chaos emerged the inevitable dictator: Benito Mussolini. Thus, was a powerful and faithful ally (and let those inclined to scoff contemplate the 680,000 Italian dead given to the British cause) transformed into a bitter enemy.

In this atmosphere of corruption Mr. Wilson launched his proposed League of Nations as a successor to the former Concert of Europe in creating law and order among the nations of the world. In its original form it reflected Wilson's idealism; but in its final form, it was simply a fraudulent instrument to give a legal aspect to the control of the affairs of the world by International Finance.

In his *Memoirs of the Peace Conference*, David Lloyd George stated that the prospect of a mandate for Armenia and Constantinople appealed to Wilson's idealism and he therefore made a proposal on May 14, 1919, to the Council of Four which was accepted by President Wilson "on behalf of the United States of America and subject to the consent of the Senate thereof." Had the Senate succumbed to this crafty stratagem, it

---

In the appendix on page 62 of vol. 3, occurs this statement: "There are those who believe the President laid too little stress upon the treaties and that he should have had some understanding with the Allies regarding them before he committed the United States to war." Vol. 3, page 322, records a meeting with the President, and states: "The President was especially disturbed by the Treaty of London and the arrangements made for the partition of the Turkish Empire. Mr. Wilson was aware of the extent to which Britain and France were committed to Italy by the Treaty of London ..." Strangely, this meeting occurred January 4, 1918; and in other parts of his notes he attempts to explain Mr. Wilson's forgetfulness in the matter of this treaty when he testified August 19, 1919, he knew nothing of these treaties as a whole.

On page 50 of Vol. 3, is recorded a copy of a letter dated Jan. 30, 1918, from Mr. A. J. Balfour to President Wilson, in which Mr. Balfour admits the secret treaties had been made by Britain under the stress of the necessity of getting Italy into the war, and expresses his doubt as to whether performance of Britain of her promises to Italy would be for the best interests of Italy. Thus the way was paved for the expulsion of Italy from the Peace Conference and the change from "The Big Four" to the big three, and eventually to "The Big One:" Mr. David Lloyd-George.

Mr. House's record of a meeting with Walter Page, American Ambassador to Great Britain, on September 25, 1916, appears on page 319, Vol. 2, in part as follows:

"He said the British resent our trying to bring about peace ... I did not think this was as ignoble an effort as it seemed to Page. He declares none of us understand the situation or the high purposes of the British in this war. I replied that we resented some of the cant and hypocrisy indulged in by the British; for instance, as to Belgium. Page admitted that the British would have been found fighting with France even if France had violated Belgium in order to reach German territory more effectively..."

From Vol. 3, page 41: "... neither the President nor House felt that it was possible to endanger unity with the Allies by raising a protest against the secret treaties."

[12] Enc. Brit

would have placed the United States at the focal point of infection of the wars of Europe, at the tangled crossroads of the centuries-old Russian surge towards open water and the German surge towards Baghdad, the Persian Gulf, the Orient and Africa. It would have simplified immensely the British problem of the Balance of Power, and made of the United States the immediate opponent of every European aggressor, and relieved the British Empire of this crushing load. Italy's dissatisfaction with the Peace Treaty, the seething ambitions of all the newly created buffer states to profit at the expense of each other, the war between Poland and Russia, the war between Greece and Turkey, the clash between Bolshevism and Fascism in the long and bloody Spanish War, and many more of the endless intrigues and hostilities that followed the Great War in the human cesspool of Europe, would have involved the armed intervention of the United States at the expense of the American taxpayer. This situation was sensed by American statesmen and the American public. The proponents of this League of Nations and of the internationalist group on the 1920 Democratic ticket—Mr. Cox and Franklin Delano Roosevelt—were buried in a landslide so deep it seemed that the Internationalist control of America should have been buried forever. As a matter of fact a great number of people neither remember the names of the candidates on this Democratic ticket of 1920, nor the fact that Mr. Roosevelt made over 1,000 speeches in favor of continued internationalist intervention in the campaign.

The election of 1920 removed America from the British Balance of Power, as the succeeding Republican administrations were true to their trust and mandate, and this country did not re-enter a British alliance until 1933. With the American withdrawal, history was repeating itself. Britain was in the same situation that she had been in after France was demolished in the Franco-Prussian war of 1871. At that time, she had come under the wing of the Concert of Europe for a number of years until France could recover and Japan and America could be groomed as running mates; she now used the League of Nations for a number of years, until the newly formed buffer states reached a level of greater maturity under governments favored and supported by International Finance.

Poland grew to the status of a major ally, and in the formidable British-French-Polish bloc there were in addition Czecho-Slovakia, Yugoslavia, Greece, Belgium and Holland. Other countries, particularly Romania, were for some years the battleground of opposing factions in the pressure to join this alliance. When Hitler and Franklin D. Roosevelt came to power within a few hours of each other in 1933, the battle to submerge Germany again was under way. One of the early American contributions was the "Most Favored Nation" treaty, open to any and all nations in the world, except Germany, which at the time was one of our best customers.

The peculiar ability of the arms and munitions makers to foresee war and to be prepared and ready to make profits is illustrated by an observation of H. C. Engelbrecht, Ph. D. and F. C. Hanighen in their "Merchants of Death" published in 1934:

> Fifteen years have elapsed since the 'war to end all wars.' Yet the arms industry has moved forward with growing momentum as if the pacific resolutions of the various peoples and governments had never existed. All these technical improvements, all the international mergers, the co-operation between governments and the industry bear an uncomfortable resemblance to the situation during the epoch preceding 1914. Is this present situation necessarily a preparation for another world struggle and what, if any, are the solutions to these problems?

Strangely significant, the great British industrial firm of Vickers, Ltd., in a major program of expansion with Rothschild financing, had entered the armaments and munitions field in the explosive year of 1897, at the very outset of the era of imperialistic expansion that brought on the Great War.

The eventual curious conjunction of apparently unrelated and widely separated acts in the world of politics and war seems to be well described in words Abraham Lincoln used to comment on a political conspiracy of his time:

> When we see a lot of framed timbers, different portions of which we know have been gotten out at different times and places, and by different workmen ... and when we see those timbers jointed together, and see they exactly make the frame of a house or a mill. ... in such a case we find it impossible not to believe that. ... all understood one another from the beginning, and all worked upon a common plan, drawn up before the first blow was struck.

The Chinese Nationalists staged another of their periodical revolts against the British-French oligarchy and its Japanese ally in 1926. As usual, a number of Americans were killed in the general uprising against the foreign usurpers. A large force of Marines was sent to China under General SmedleyButler to protect American interests. The British invited Admiral Clarence S. Williams, the commander of the Asiatic fleet to join them in shelling Nanking, the capital of the leader of the rebellion, General Chiang Kai-shek.[13]

President Coolidge declined to permit the American fleet to join in this venture, thus causing the whole world to sit up and take notice that America was no longer a robot of the International clique; this decision caused one of the greatest upsets in the history of international power politics. Sumner Welles, a minor career diplomat during the Coolidge administration, attracted wide attention to himself by resigning in protest to the Coolidge foreign policy. Americans generally failed to grasp the significance of the outburst of hostility, insult and indignity to which American tourists were subjected in France and England directly after this incident.

Japanese writers had been bitterly indignant at a situation in which Japan had to fetch and carry at the bidding of the British-French financial oligarchy, had then invariably been obliged to turn over to them the fruits of victory, and finally to pay the oligarchy huge interest charges on the money to fight its wars. This open break in British-American relations placed the oligarchy completely at the mercy of the rebellious Japanese factions. Without American participation, this situation in China lacked the essential flavor of democracy and left the oligarchy without sufficient forces to meet the rebellion, opening them wide to the attack of their many internal British and French enemies.

The forces they had marshaled to again bring decency and democracy to China presented a somewhat dismal and moth-eaten aspect in comparison to the forces they had marshaled to subdue the Nationalist uprising of 1900. That time they had the assistance of the elite crack troops of America, Germany, Russia, Austria-Hungary, Italy, France and Japan to help them subdue the brutal aggression of the Chinese. This time they made a shabby pretense of this being a humane and unselfish effort to restore order in China as they gathered together troops from lands still under their pay. They could only induce

---

[13] See "Old Gimlet Eye" (Smedley Butler) by Lowell Thomas, (p. 288) chapter on "Treading Softly in China."

Portugal, Spain, Holland, France and Japan to answer their plea for help. They were obliged to sublet practically the entire job to Japan, and it was performed with the usual Japanese snap and vigor. The consideration for the contract was an agreement giving Japan a rider participation in the commercial and political control of China, and conceding to Japan the occupation of Manchuria.[14]

In order to minimize and discount their deal with Japan, enforced on them under the stress of circumstances, the financial oligarchy now subsidized its recent foe, General Chiang Kai-shek. They financed the Chinese aggression against Japanese occupation and infiltration, and thereby thoroughly enraged the Japanese who felt that they had made an honorable deal and that they were now being double-crossed. International Finance had taken over the Japanese banking system under the treaty of 1902, and the great Japanese commercial expansion that then followed and which had flooded the world with Japanese goods, had been promoted by British capital. The wheels of the great Japanese industrial machine slowed down with those of all the world, leaving the Japanese with a huge interest load and rapidly falling revenue. This aggravated the very conditions which had been emphasized by Prof. Usher as a very probable cause for a Japanese war in his "Pan-Americanism" of 1915 in that excerpt quoted heretofore.

In this critical period the International clique was restored to power in the United States by the election of 1932. In giving the British unqualified support, the American Administration chose to ignore a few important facts. The position of the British interests in China had been dependent to a great extent upon Japanese support since the year 1895. The Japanese could have made common cause with the Chinese Nationalists or with Russia at various inopportune times, with a certain major disaster to the British Empire. This was mainly a quarrel between Japan and the British interests as to Japan's share of the profits of the exploitation of China.

There was here a very close repetition of the plausible deal made in the case of Persia in 1911, when the British had ejected the Shah and set up a subsidized government of their own, then appealed to the American International clique to aid them in restoring control to the Persian Government, thus to balk the vital Russian surge to the sea by a simple strategy. In this instance, the secret control of China had been in British hands since 1841, so they utilized a revolutionist against their own secret government and made him the nominal front man, then appealed to the American International clique to aid

---

[14] From *"Background of War,"* published 1937 by Editors of Fortune:

"When the Lytton Committee made its report indicting Japan, and when China thereupon fought for the impositions of sanctions under Article XVI of the League, the British Foreign Secretary opposed the demand so eloquently and so effectively that the Japanese delegate, Mr. Matsuoka, told the American correspondents that Sir John Simon had said in half an hour what he had been trying to tell the Assembly for weeks. From beginning to end of the Manchurian incident Great Britain resisted every effort to impose upon the aggressor country the penalties expressly provided by the League Covenant ... the liberal British review, The New Statesman and Nation, charged ruling-class perfidy. Behind Sir John Simon's pro-Japanese policy during the Manchurian dispute there lay the hope in the minds of businessmen, who were very adequately represented in the House of Commons, that Japan would fight Russia and repay our friendly encouragement in her piracy in China by a reasonable attitude when it came to dividing the spoils." (page 8-9.)

them in restoring the government of China to its rightful head; thus balking the deal they had made with Japan by a simple strategy.

That the British did not correctly evaluate their Japanese ally at the beginning of their relations would appear from the ideology of Cecil Rhodes, cited hereinafter; which was written at about the stage of the first alliance with Japan, and which embraces in the dawning British world state "the seaboard of China and Japan."

Chiang Kai-shek was forced to choose between two evils in going along with the British oligarchy after his defeat in 1927. It is very obvious, however, that he still has his Nationalistic aspirations, and that his open efforts to gain support in the United States for his dream of Chinese independence has caused a discordant note in his relations with the British. British dictatorship over American lend-lease has given him a very shabby deal. This latter fact was graphically treated in a recent book, *Between Tears and Laughter* by the Chinese writer Lin Yutang.

VIII. THE LIBERALS VERSUS THE CONSERVATIVES AND WAR

The ebb and flow of British Imperialism and the predominance of the benign or the evil character of the Dr. Jekyll and Mr. Hyde British Government is definitely linked with the two major political parties of Britain as is readily apparent from the following tabulation of successive British Governments within present-day personal recollection:

Period	Prime Minister	Party
1868	Benjamin Disraeli	Conservative (Tory)
1868-1874	William E. Gladstone	Liberal
1874-1880	Benjamin Disraeli	Conservative
1880-1885	William E. Gladstone	Liberal
1885-1886	Lord Salisbury	Conservative
1886	William E. Gladstone	Liberal
1886-1892	Lord Salisbury	Conservative
1892-1894	William E. Gladstone	Liberal
1894-1895	Earl of Rosebery	Pseudo-Liberal
1895-1906	Lord Salisbury et al	Conservative
1906-1916	A period of confusion	Unionists (incl. Conservatives)
1916-1922	D. Lloyd George	Coalition (Conservative majority)
1922-1923	A. Bonar Law	Conservative
1923-1924	Ramsay MacDonald	Liberal-Labor
1924-1929	Stanley Baldwin	Conservative
1929-1935	Ramsay MacDonald	Liberal-Labor
1935-1937	Stanley Baldwin	Conservative
1937-1940	Neville Chamberlain	Conservative
1940-	Winston Churchill	Conservative

For the purpose of ready identification, the Conservative Party can be represented with the barbed tail, horns and cloven hoof of International Finance, intrigue and war. The Liberals can be conceived to bear that torch of freedom and liberty usually associated in the public mind with England itself as compared to the other countries of Europe. That this aspect is substantially true becomes readily apparent in noting the trend of events under Liberal leadership and under Conservative leadership. Not only did the

Conservative Benjamin Disraeli disestablish the Concert of Europe, but he deliberately led all Europe to the brink of war in the eastern question, after he had incited the ferocious Russo-Turk war of 1878.

When his ally Turkey was defeated and of no further use, Disraeli promptly inaugurated the subjugation and plunder of Egypt, vassal state of Turkey. The penetration was by the usual formula of partly fictitious loans to a dishonest government and the building up of a heavy interest burden on the people. The subsidized Egyptian government was too weak in the face of the Nationalist revolution against this depredation of the public treasury. The British-French oligarchy was then "obliged" to enter the civil war to protect their loans, thus inaugurating the long Egyptian War which was not settled for twenty years.

This brewing war upset the Disraeli government; his Liberal successor, William E. Gladstone—greatest of all British statesmen—proceeded to withdraw from the Egyptian war. He commissioned the renowned agent of Imperialism, Gen. Chas. G. Gordon, to arrange for evacuation of British forces and British interests from the Egyptian Sudan. However, Gen. Gordon proceeded to act in complete contradiction to the prime minister's orders and in obvious accord with that ingenious dictum of Imperialism cited heretofore from the *Laws of England*: "An executive or administrative act of a subject, though in the first instance done without authority of his Sovereign, will have all the effect of an Act of State if subsequently ratified." Thus had General Gordon met with success in his illegal venture, that success in itself would have upset the government opposed to it, and rose to power a government prepared to ratify it. Unfortunately, for General Gordon, he had climbed out far on a limb; and the Liberal Government, accustomed to this sort of trickery, simply left him in the lurch, with the result that he was killed in his venture; having vainly waited for months at Khartoum for succor.

In 75 years, from 1868 to 1943, there have been only two true Liberals to attain leadership of the British Government: William E. Gladstone and J. Ramsay MacDonald. During the period of 1906-1916, indicated in the foregoing tabulation as a period of ostensible confusion in national politics, the foreign power: politics of Empire were not at all in a state of confusion. In its dexterous and chameleon-like ability to change its nature untrammeled and unhindered by the limitations of any Constitution, the foreign policy of Britain was centered not in any government. It was, however, centered in the hands of only one man: Viscount Edward Grey. He became Secretary of State for Foreign Affairs in December, 1905, and retained that office for an incredible ten years until December, 1916, in a virtual dictatorship. The views of Mr. William E. Gladstone, four times Prime Minister of Britain on a Liberal platform up to 1894, are very significant as he was the last Liberal Prime Minister before the Imperialist rampage that started in 1897 and continued up to World War I in 1914. The following quotations and notes are all from *The Life of William Ewart Gladstone*, by John Morley, published in 1903:

> When England rejected the Berlin memorandum of May 13, 1876, in the Eastern Question which had been adopted by Russia, Austria, Germany, France and Italy — Gladstone said of Disraeli: 'His government is supposed now to stand mainly upon its recent foreign policy: the most selfish and least worthy I have ever known ... (Book VII, Ch. IV)

A letter to the Duke of Argyll:

> ... Dizzy's speech (so I call him with all due respect to the peerage), gave me a new light on his views. He is not quite such a Turk as I had thought. What he hates is Christian liberty and reconstruction. He supports old Turkey thinking that if vital improvements can be averted, it must break down; and his fleet is at Besika Bay, I feel pretty sure, to be ready to lay hold of Egypt as his share. So he may end as the Duke of Memphis yet.

Another letter to the same: "I have a strong suspicion that Dizzy's crypto-Judaism has had to do with his policy. The Jews of the east bitterly hate the Christians."

Morley's note: "Mr. G, however, found comfort in the thought that by the agitation two points had been gained: the re-establishment of the European Concert in the conference of Dec., 1876, and extrication from a disgraceful position of virtual complicity with Turkey."[15]

While Mr. Gladstone was definitely opposed to rapacious Imperialistic aggression and expansion, he was nevertheless an Imperialist. However, his imperialism was aimed at reconstructing and integrating and strengthening the existing empire, and he spent an immense amount of effort in attempting to arrive at a settlement in the dissatisfaction of the Irish. Had his lead been followed and had he been given full support, it is a reasonable assumption that Ireland would still be a full and loyal member of the British Commonwealth of Nations. He admitted that at one point in his career he had held with those favoring disintegration of the Empire. In 1872 he stated that opinion in the country was at last rising against disintegration. "In my judgment," he said, "no minister in this country will do his duty who neglects any opportunity of reconstructing as much as possible our colonial empire ..." (Book VI, Chapter VIII.)

The Liberal government of Gladstone was followed by twenty years of unbridled imperialistic aggression and expansion under unbroken Conservative control, ending in the gigantic slaughter of World War I with its total casualties of 37,494,186 and its 8,538,315 dead. These years of incubation for World War I (1897-1914) included the imperialistic aggression and seizure of the South African republics, the imperialistic "Boxer" war, the imperialistic Russo-Japanese War, the division of Africa to compensate France for British seizure of South Africa and Egypt, the Russo-British Persian imperialistic division, and the Balkan Wars in the interest of British Imperialism. The mantle of dictator of the foreign policy of the Conservatives and of the British-French

---

[15] Although Mr. Disraeli had been baptized in the Church of England, he amazed and shocked one of his friends after coming out of a sitting in which he had defended the Church, by murmuring: "It is curious, Walpole, that you and I have just been voting for a defunct mythology ..." His friend was further taken aback when Dizzy declared that there is no English nobility: "We owe the English peerage to three sources: the spoliation of the Church; the open and flagrant sale of its honours by the early Stuarts; and the borough-mongering of our own times. When Henry IV called his first Parliament, there were only twenty-nine temporal peers to be found. Of those twenty-nine only five remain." Then he explained that the only pedigree of long civilization was that of the House of Israel and that his family was far older than theirs. (*Disraeli* by Andre Maurois, Ch. IV, D. Appleton & Co. 1929).

Disraeli found pleasure in repeating a maxim of Cardinal de Retz: "Everything in the world has its decisive moment; the crowning achievement of a good conduct of life is to know and pick out that moment."

financial oligarchy, dropped by Sir Edward Grey in 1916, was assumed in large measure by Winston Churchill, whose start in high Conservative office occurred in 1903 in the reactionary Lord Salisbury government. In 1910, during the "Unionist-Conservative" period of 1906-1916, he rose to the office of Home Secretary, authoritatively stated to be the most powerful office in the British Empire, exercising the power of life and death in criminal cases; which under much vaunted English law are not subject to appeal, giving the powers-that-be a leverage against persons convicted of a political crime deemed possible by the uninformed only in the "Dictator" countries.[16]

He conducted certain secret negotiations usually associated with the Foreign Office, together with Lord Haldane, with Germany and Austria-Hungary in October, 1911, after he had just been made First Lord of the Admiralty. He arrived at certain very important decisions as to conduct of the Dardanelles campaign, and admitted full personal responsibility; having apparently conducted this campaign without approval or disapproval of his government. The Dardanelles debacle enforced a temporary interval in his positions of arbitrary power, but in June, 1919, he was made Minister for War and Air. In this position he engaged in the persecution of the Irish. This act was made the subject of investigation by an American commission, which in its report charged that this persecution and suppression subjected the Irish to indescribable brutalities and torture, and they had been illegally deprived of their civil rights. This report was a big factor in obtaining freedom for Ireland and restoring a Liberal Government to Britain after a lapse of 29 years, in the person of Ramsay MacDonald. In 1935 the Conservatives were back in power and with them the period of incubation for the next world war was under way.

Few Americans comprehend the immensity of the British Empire. Its land area just before this war was nearly 17,000,000 square miles—not including the semi-colonial area of China—an area nearly six times greater than is the area of the United States. To the 1,415,929 square miles taken by Britain from Germany at the conclusion of World

---

[16] From *Laws of England* Vol. 6; page 348, art. 499: To levy war against the King in his realm is treason, and this provision has been held to extend to cases of riot for various purposes. Thus a riot for the purpose of pulling down brothels or breaking open prisons has been held to be treason. And where riots took place in support of a prisoner undergoing trial, and dissenting meeting-houses were pulled down, and other acts of violence committed, it was held to be treason. So also a riot in order to attain an object of a general or public nature, such as repeal of a law, through intimidation and violence, has been held to be treason ... Note (m): Insurrections by force and violence to raise the price of wages, ... or to redress grievances real or pretended, have all been held levying war."

Page 352, art. 508: The punishment for a person convicted of treason is hanging. But the Sovereign may by warrant..., direct that, in place of hanging, the head of the convicted person shall be severed from his body whilst alive, and may also direct and order how the head and body are to be disposed of.

Except for the privilege of this singular choice in the manner of dispatching one convicted, the Sovereign appears to be fully as impotent as described in the words of Andrew Carnegie "in theory still a real monarch, although in reality only a convenient puppet, to be used by the cabinet (the City) at pleasure to suit their own ends;" not able even to exercise the power of pardon that is a prerogative of a governor of an American state and of the President of the United States.

War I, there was added by purely Imperialistic aggression another incredible 1,145,764 square miles in the period from 1925 to 1938. During these years Americans generally were under the impression that everything was peaceful and quiet except for the belligerent and snarling dictators of Europe and the purges of Russia. Not only did Britain greedily seize 75% of the German colonies in utter disregard of the needs of her own allies and despite her already vast hegemony over a great part of the earth, but she was not prepared to stop there. The program of expansion was pressed year after year to the certain end that the over-populated areas of the world, deprived of any reasonable outlet for their products, would sooner or later rise in fury in a new and greater war. In 1939, the Germans seized about 100,000 square miles of Poland, but the British in that year seized 218,259 square miles in other parts of the earth. Dividing the land ruled by the British Empire at this stage by the 49,000,000 population of the British Isles would give each British a theoretical national interest in 120 times more land than each German had. Just before the war with Poland, Germany—greatest all-white nation on earth—had 104,133,000 people,[17] crowded into an area of less than 300,000 square miles. The entire British Empire had about 68,000,000 white people, ruling nearly 17,000,000 square miles of the earth's surface. We are now the victims of a grotesque and fanciful contention that the freedom and liberty of the United States is inextricably intertwined with the continued domination of these few British over nearly one-third of the earth's surface; that our own safety is dependent on the protection extended over us by the illusive power of the great British Commonwealth of Nations; that our own mighty and compact and unified country with 135,000,000 people living in early the finest and most productive 3,022,387 square miles on earth, cannot continue to exist and to protect itself without the sheltering "umbrella" of the 68,000,00 white people of the British Empire scattered all over the face of the globe, their strength dispersed in the task of keeping the 435,000,000 colored subjects of "the Crown" under control.

As Winston Churchill ingenuously assured the American people: "Give us the tools and we will do the job (for you!)." That was in 1940, and the inspired press in that year was filled with the erudite discussions of pseudo military experts as to a forthcoming British invasion of Europe in 1941. The ways and words of International Finance are indeed wonderful.

The method and manner of British territorial growth and of British rule of their colored subjects is apparent from matter printed in the Congressional Record of March 4, 1941. From the New Leader, an organ of the Independent British Labor Party, the following is quoted: "...only a little more than a year ago the British Government annexed, by order in council, 100,000 square miles to the British Empire. This was done in February, 1937, in south Arabia. It was done in defiance of treaties of long standing. It was done contrary to pledges solemnly given in the House of Commons."

There was further given from *The World Review*—a British publication—an explanation by St. John Philby that the desire to acquire new oil fields led the British to commit this type of aggression, and he described the technique by which the job was done. He said: "That aerial bombing is freely used by the Aden administration is not denied by the Government. It is actually defended by those responsible for it, as a rapid and humane method of keeping peace in the outposts of the Empire." He developed

---

[17] 1939 population as per *Whitaker's British Almanac*, 1941— Eliminated from later issues.

further that the same method of keeping peace has been used by the Royal Air Force on many occasions along the northern border of India.

It is interesting to note that these methods of "pacification" were in use at least two years by the British before the Germans used them to "pacify" Poland and London.

Of the situation in India after the last war, Will Durant, in *The Case for India* published in 1930, states: "It was Woodrow Wilson who started the Indian Revolution. Did he know what he was doing when he scattered over every land his ringing phrases about democracy, self-government, and the rights of small nations? In every country—in Egypt and Near East, in China and India—there were ears waiting for those words as the signal to revolt. ... Were not the allies winning, and destroying the last autocracy in Europe? Was not the whole world now safe for democracy?" He further discussed the brutal massacre of Amritsar on April 13, 1921, which touched off the Revolution of 1921, in which Brigadier General Dyer ordered his men to fire into a crowd of 10,000 Hindus "until all the ammunition the soldiers had with them was exhausted." General Dyer personally directed the firing towards the exits where the crowd was most dense: "...the targets; he declared were 'good." (p. 134). The massacre lasted over ten minutes. When it was over 1,500 Hindus were left on the ground, 400 of them dead. Dyer forbade his soldiers to give any aid to the injured, and he ordered all Hindus off the streets for twenty-four hours, prevented relatives or friends from bringing even a cup of water to the wounded who were piled up on the field. It developed that these 10,000 people had entered an enclosure known as Jalianwala Bagh to celebrate a religious festival and the General had shot them all in the erroneous view this was a political meeting. This did not faze General Dyer; in the succeeding revolution, the sadistic tortures inflicted upon hundreds of innocent victims exceeded those of medieval times (see page 135 of the above).

Is there anything significant in the fact that these Indian outrages were perpetrated under the direct jurisdiction of Minister of War and Air, Winston Churchill? That the news of this reign of terror was kept from Parliament for six months? That General Dyer was presented with a cash award of $150,000 for his prompt and effective action despite wide-spread indignation in England? Among the principles laid down by Woodrow Wilson, for which the United States was alleged to be fighting in World War I, were the self-determination of suppressed minorities, the freedom of the seas, and open covenants openly arrived at. These were precisely the principles which International Finance was fighting against; but, if Woodrow Wilson presumed to enter the war on their side in the mistaken idea he was fighting for these things, they had no objection until the war was won. Then these principles were roughly over-ridden and cast aside by the leading allied statesmen in terms of open ridicule and contempt. Clemenceau called the Wilson "ideals" a joke on all humanity.

Again we are fighting the war of the Conservatives and of International Finance and of the City in the deluded pursuit of the very same idealistic objectives, resurrected and renovated and sweetened with the "Four Freedoms" and the "Charter of the Atlantic." Will these idealistic objectives be achieved with the winning of the war this time? Has the leopard changed his spots? In the words of one American (who has himself failed to do so): "Let's look at the record." Winston Churchill has been in many important respects the principal agent of Conservatism and of International Finance for nearly thirty years. He differs from his American collaborators in one distinct and definite respect—he does not sail under false colors. He has stated his position in clear and unequivocal words. He has stated that the "Four Freedoms" and "The Charter of the Atlantic" do not apply to "Those owing allegiance to the British Empire." He has further stated that the British Empire has been built by the sword and will be maintained by the sword.

The principles and purposes of the British Empire, the reasons for which it was conceived and for which were expended vast rivers of sweat and blood and tears in that process of building it by the sword, were laid down in these words by Benjamin Disraeli: "Gain and hold territories that possess the largest supplies of the basic raw materials. Establish naval bases around the world to control the sea and commerce lanes. Blockade and starve into submission any nation or group of nations that opposes this empire control program."

Winston Churchill, Conservative heir to the principles and methods of that greatest of empire builders and greatest of Conservatives, Benjamin Disraeli, stoutly affirms those principles and those methods of his illustrious predecessor. Mr. Gladstone stated: "... I was tenaciously opposed by the governor and the deputy-governor of the Bank, who had seats in parliament, and I had the City for an antagonist on almost every occasion," (Mr. Gladstone and the Bank — Appendix Book 1 — Morley). That City, THE City, Citadel of International Finance, controls not only about half of the basic raw materials of all the earth directly, but also has an immense indirect influence over most of the rest of the basic raw materials of the world through its subservient financial interests. Among the principal provisions outlined in the Atlantic Charter is that of access for all nations to essential raw materials and world trade for their economic prosperity, coupled with "Genuine Freedom of the Seas". The mines, the railroads, the utilities, the plantations, and the raw materials of South America, China, India, Africa—in fact practically of all the world—are controlled by the City. Who will determine what a fair price is at which the nations of the world are to have access to these sources of raw materials, ownership of which is in the hands of International Finance. That price was a big part of the argument which brought on World War I and World War II. David Lloyd George stated in a speech at Plymouth on January 8, 1910:

> We do most of the business of the world. We carry more international trade — probably ten times more — than Germany. Germany carries her own trade largely. The international trade is ours. Well, we do not do it for nothing. As a matter of fact, our shipping brings us over a hundred millions (pounds) a year, mostly paid by that wretched foreigner. I'm taxing the foreigner for all I know. ... You've heard a good deal of talk here, probably, about the exportation of capital abroad. There is no way in which we make the foreigner pay more. We get the foreigner in four ways by that. The first way we leave to Lord Rothschild. (Better Times, published 1910).

It should be clear that this immense predominance in the business of the world and of the seas was not just due to a little British luck; that the control of the port facilities of the world, the British Navigation Acts, and other methods of restriction of the commerce of nations, backed by a fleet able to make them stick, was a potent factor. This predominance over the trade of the world is the life and the reason for the British Empire and Mr. Churchill is on record that there will be no change "incompatible with the status quo" of the British Empire.

In 1898, General J. B. Weaver stated in a speech:

> The thing calculated to wound our pride in connection with the two speeches (by President McKinley and by the Right Hon. Joseph Chamberlain), is the fact that the Right Hon. Englishman spoke first and blazed the way in these recent discoveries concerning the ways of Providence with imperialism. Note the similarity of thought. It is marked and striking. It would seem there is an entente cordiale existing between the two governments which the people know nothing about.

It is quite evident there is again an *entente cordiale* existing between the two governments which the people know nothing about; an agreement in violation of any principle of open covenants openly arrived at; an agreement without sanction of the people of the United States or of their representatives in Congress. This would appear in part from a speech at Indianapolis by Secretary of the Navy, Frank Knox, on October 1, 1941. He stated that the "great peace-minded, justice-loving" powers—the United States and Great Britain—which are "lacking in any desire for personal aggrandizement" must join forces for at least 100 years to produce "by force if need be" an effective system of international law. He went on to say that the British and American navies "ARE sweeping the German pirates from the North Atlantic" and "eventually we shall lock Nazi Germany up in an iron ring, and within that ring of sea-power she shall perish." Here is a fairly good outline of a small part of that unquestionable secret agreement which accords with the course of events in the two years since that speech was made. Here is an open admission that we were already engaged in active combat over two months before the great surprise at Pearl Harbor. The previous flat statement of the Administration that it would not permit the British Empire to be defeated, that it was prepared to fight for the preservation of that Empire, added to events that have since occurred, indicate that this secret agreement is one making us a junior partner in the British Empire, the role lost by France.

The British Empire, whose ships have heretofore carried nearly 90% of American foreign trade through the years,[18] as well as that of other countries, could not exist if any other powerful nation was permitted "Genuine Freedom of the Seas" or unrestricted access to the world's sources of raw materials, except in the limited nature of a junior partner prepared to pay for partial participation in rivers of sweat and blood and tears. The only reservation originally made by the Allies in accepting Mr. Wilson's Fourteen Points, was complete liberty as to interpretation of the phrase "freedom of navigation upon the seas."

---

[18] See World Almanac — various years

IX. THE MONEY POWER IN POWER POLITICS

As developed herein from many aspects and from many authoritative sources, the functions of the British Parliament are restricted largely to the local and domestic affairs of Great Britain itself. The parliaments of the four dominions of Canada, Australia, New Zealand and Union of South Africa are likewise confined to similar functions in their own countries. Thus, the 68,000,000 white people of the British Empire have forms of government which allow a nearly democratic form of administration of their own internal affairs, and this provides the stage-setting of Democracy behind which operates the secret "Sixth Great Power of Europe." The other 435,000,000 people of the Empire are subject to that provision of the Laws of England which decrees: "...Nor can "the Crown" by proclamation or otherwise, make or unmake any law on its own authority apart from Parliament, except in colonies to which representative institutions have not been granted." (See the *Laws of England* by the Earl of Halsbury, Vol. 6, page 388, art. 582).[19]

The colored people of the British Empire, comprising 87% of the total population, are the voiceless subjects of the international financial oligarchy of "The City" in what is perhaps the most arbitrary and absolute form of government in the world. This international financial oligarchy uses the allegoric "Crown" as its symbol of power and has its headquarters in the ancient City of London, an area of 677 acres; which strangely in all the vast expanse of the 443,455 acres of Metropolitan London alone is not under the jurisdiction of the Metropolitan Police, but has its own private force of about 2,000 men, while its night population is under 9,000.

This tiny area of a little over one square mile has in it the giant Bank of England, a privately owned institution; which as is further elaborated hereinafter is not subject to regulation by the British Parliament, and is in effect a sovereign world power. Within the City are located also the Stock Exchange and many institutions of worldwide scope. The City carries on its business of local government with a fanciful display of pompous medieval ceremony and with its officers attired in grotesque ancient costumes. Its voting power is vested in secret guilds with names of long extinct crafts such as the Mercers, Grocers, Fishmongers, Skinners, Vintners, etc. All this trivial pomp and absurdity and horse-play seems to serve very well to blind the eyes of the public to the big things going on behind the scenes; for the late Vincent Cartwright Vickers, once Deputy-Lieutenant of this City, a director of the great British armament firm of Vickers, Ltd., and a director of the Bank of England from 1910 to 1919, in his *"Economic Tribulation,"* published 1940, lays the wars of the world on the door-step of the City.

That the British people and the British Parliament have little to say in the foreign affairs of the British Empire, and that the people of the British Empire must fight when International Finance and the City blow the trumpet, appears from the paean of praise of

---

[19] From *Laws of England* Vol. 6, page 423, art. 651: In Crown colonies, namely, Colonies to which representative, or representative and responsible government, has not been granted, the right of legislation enjoyed by "the Crown" is usually exercised either through a governor, commissioner assisted by legislative and executive councils nominated by the Crown or by the governor or commissioner, "the Crown" retaining the right of veto, and, in most crises, of legislating by Order in Council.

America by Andrew Carnegie, *Triumphant Democracy*, published in 1886 by that American super-industrialist and British newspaper publisher, in the following words:

> My American readers may not be aware of the fact that, while in Britain an act of Parliament is necessary before works for a supply of water or a mile of railway can be constructed, six or seven men can plunge the nation into war, or, what is perhaps equally disastrous, commit it to entangling alliances without consulting Parliament at all. This is the most pernicious, palpable effect flowing from the monarchial theory, for these men do this in "the king's Name," who is in theory still a real monarch, although in reality only a convenient puppet, to be used by the cabinet at pleasure to suit their own ends. (Ch. XVI)[20]

In his damnation of Sir Edward Grey for the guilt for the Great War, entitled "Why We Are At War. A Reply To Sir Edward Grey," J. Ramsay MacDonald, later Prime-Minister of Britain and foe of International Finance, wrote in part: "It is a diplomatist's war, made by about a half dozen men."

There are on authentic record many instances where the City has acted not only without the consent of Parliament, but has acted in defiance of the wishes of Parliament and even in violation of its own solemn promises to the contrary of its action. From the *Laws of England* of the Earl of Halsbury it appears that the City, exercising its power as the "King-in-Council" or "Crown" has control over both the legislative and executive functions of the Empire, and as Britain has no written Constitution there is no court with any power to temper the actions of the "Crown."[21]

---

[20] From *Laws of England*, Vol. 6, page 427, Sec. 8, art. 658:

"By the law of the English Constitution (nonexistent) the Crown acts as the delegate or representative of the nation in the conduct of foreign affairs, and what is done in such matters by the royal authority is the act of the whole nation, and binding, in general, upon the latter without further sanction ... The Crown, therefore, enjoys the sole right of appointing ambassadors, diplomatic agents, consuls and other officers, through whom intercourse with foreign nations is conducted, and of receiving those of foreign States, of making treaties, declaring peace and war, and generally conducting all foreign relations. Such matters are entrusted in general to the absolute discretion of the Sovereign, acting through the recognized constitutional channels upon, the advice of the Cabinet or the Secretary of State for Foreign Affairs, unfettered by any direct supervision, parliamentary or otherwise."

Nicholas Murray Butler explained the nonexistence of a written British Constitution in a speech to the Pilgrims at New York on January 22, 1936, in these words:

"Inasmuch as the Constitution of Great Britain is not fixed and definite, but is a matter of tradition and of habit, its interpretation is not by judicial voice but by legislative act. When, as in the Parliament Act of 1911 or as in the Statute of Westminster of 1931, a grave step is taken in changing the organization of the British Government, what they are really doing is amending their constitution thereby. That is why they do not have judicial interpretation of their Constitution, because not being written, not being definite, it can and must be dealt with as habit and necessity may require..."

[21] The "Laws of England," a massive work of over 30 huge volumes, by the Earl of Halsbury—recurrent Lord High Chancellor of Great Britain between the years 1885 and 1905—published in 1909, states in Vol. 21, page 618, note k: "There is no rule of law which

Edwin J. Clapp, Professor of Economics at New York University, in his *Economic Aspects Of The War* published in 1915, brought attention to the utterly boundless authority assumed by the "Crown" in its commands to the nation of the world through its "Order-in-Council." Without restraint or reference to existing usage or so-called International law, the council can simply make new International Law to fit any situation, as required.

The Balance of Power is a creation of this financial oligarchy and its purposes are as follows:

To divide the nations of Europe into two antagonistic camps of near equal military weight, so as to retain for Britain itself the power to sway a decision either way.

To make the leading and potentially most dangerous military power the particular prey of British suppression and to have the second strong power on the other side.

To subsidize the "Most Favored Nations" with financial investments; to permit them to acquire political advantages under the beneficent protection of the Sea-Power at the expense of the nations being suppressed.

To subject the continent of Europe to the "Policy of Encirclement" so as to keep the nations of the continent in poverty and ineffectiveness, and thereby prevent the growth of sufficient commercial expansion and wealth to create a rival sea-power.

To retain that complete control and hegemony over all the seas of the world, which was acquired by defeating the allied fleets of its only real rivals, France and Spain, in 1805; and which is artfully and subtly called "The Freedom of the Seas."

To shift this Balance of Power as required so as to be able to strike down friend or foe in the rapidly shifting scene of world power politics, in that inexorable ideology that demands that everything and anything must be sacrificed where the future welfare and expansion to the eventual destiny of the Empire are affected; that eventual destiny

---

compels a Ministry which has lost the confidence of the House of Commons to resign office...

In Vol. 6, page 388, art. 582: The Crown is therefore a necessary party to legislation, and neither House of Parliament, whether acting alone or in conjunction with the other House, has a power of legislation without the Crown... The Sovereign is regarded in law as being incapable of thinking wrong, or meaning to do an improper act. Apart from legislative authority, which is vested in Parliament subject to certain concurrent rights of the Crown, the law of the constitution clothes the person of the Sovereign with supreme Sovereignty and pre-eminence."

It is clear from the above that the representatives of the people in the House of Commons, and the House of Lords, are utterly lacking any legislative initiative and that their function in such matters subject to certain concurrent rights of the Crown is largely one of silent submission, and this is in accord with the conclusions of Prof. George Burton Adams. It clearly appears that while the Sovereign and the mythical Crown are not one, the virtues and authorities ostensibly vested in the person of the Sovereign pertain with full weight as to the Crown; and an act of the Crown is not subject to question in the Parliament, as the "King Can Do No Wrong." This provides the ideal machinery of government for the absolute rule of the Crown, and the world dictatorship of International Finance of The City. The nature of this strange structure of government is further evident in this passage from the Encyclopedia Americana—Vol. 13 (Great Britain—English Judaism): "... the Crown, as chief partner in the Jewish money lending business...to secure its shares of the gains..."

outlined by its proponents as the eventual control of All the lands, and All the peoples, of All the world.

The ideology of the British Empire has been outlined in the past by various British statesmen and specifically by Mr. Disraeli (Lord Beaconsfield). The modern version which has been broadened to include the United States as a principal in the British Empire was outlined by Cecil Rhodes about 1895 as follows: "Establish a secret society in order to have the whole continent of South America, the Holy Land, the Valley of the Euphrates, the islands of Cyprus and Candia, the islands of the Pacific not heretofore possessed by Great Britain, the Malay Archipelago, the seaboard of China and Japan and, finally, the United States. In the end Great Britain is to establish a power so overwhelming that wars must cease and the Millennium be realized."

The secret societies of the above plan apparently came to life (immediately after the death of Mr. Rhodes) in the Pilgrims of Great Britain, often used by British statesmen in recent years as a public sounding board; and the Pilgrims of the United States–founded in New York City on January 13, 1903, and listed in directories of secret societies with no indication of purpose. Mr. Rhodes left a fortune of about $150,000,000 to the Rhodes Foundation, apparently largely directed towards the eventual intent of his ideology. One admitted purpose was "in creating in American students an attachment to the country from which they originally sprang ..."[22] It appears that organizations such as "Union Now," subversive to the liberty and the Constitution of the United States of America, have a large sprinkling of Rhodes scholars among their staff.

For some years there has evidently been a gradually increasing tempo in the number and degree of the attacks on the Constitution of the United States under guise of an inevitable drift towards union with the British Empire. On August 20, 1941, Mr. Winston Churchill concluded this project had reached such momentum that he could afford to extend to it his blessing in these well-chosen words:

> These two great organizations of the English-speaking democracies, the British Empire and the United States, will have to be somewhat mixed up together in some of their affairs for mutual and general advantage. For my part, looking out to the future, I do not view the process with any misgivings. I could not stop it if I wished. No one could stop it. Like the Mississippi it just keeps rolling along. Let it roll. Let it roll on in full flood, inexorable, irresistible, benignant, to broader lands and better days.

The guileless implication of something spontaneous, magnificent and overwhelming in this movement can be caustically exposed by referring to an autographed copy of *Pilgrim Partners* by Sir Harry Brittain, published in very limited edition in 1942. The sub-title of the book is "Forty Years of British-American Fellowship" and one critic stated in a review of the same: "The Pilgrims, founded in 1902, with one section in England, and one in America, was described some time ago by a leading New York paper as 'probably the most distinguished international organization in the world.' Each incoming American or British Ambassador receives his initial welcome from The Pilgrims, and gives his first address to the peoples of Britain or America respectively from a Pilgrim's gathering."

---

[22] Enc. Brit. "Cecil Rhodes."

On page 113, Sir Harry records (and the capitals are his):

AT LENGTH, IN APRIL, 1917, DAWNED A WONDROUS DAY in Anglo-American
history—the U.S.A. had joined the Allies. The Pilgrims' dream of fifteen years at length
had come to pass... (page 115). A few days later a solemn service was held at St. Paul's
Cathedral to mark the entry of the United States into the war, and the members of The
Pilgrim's Club were allotted a place of honor under the dome, behind the King and
Queen...

The Pilgrims were founded in London on July 24, 1902, four months after the death of
Cecil Rhodes who had outlined an ideology of a secret society to work towards eventual
British rule of all the world, and who had made particular provisions in his will designed
to bring the United States among the countries "possessed by Great Britain." The first
officers were Field-Marshal Lord Roberts—President; General Lord Grenfell, Chauncey
Depew, and Captain Hedworth Lambton—Vice-Presidents; and Sir Harry Brittain as
secretary. The representative committee elected included Mr. Don M. Dickinson of
Detroit, Colonel Herrick of Cleveland and Charles T. Yerkes. The present American
officers are listed as Dr. Nicholas Murray Butler, President; Major Elihu Church,
Secretary; and Mr. Thomas W. Lamont, Chairman of the Executive Committee. Sir Harry
records that he was requested to come to New York in 1915 by the Chairman of the
American Pilgrims "in order to give him a hand" in welcoming Lord Reading (Rufus
Isaacs). The dinner in honor of Lord Reading took place at Sherry's on October 1st, and
was attended by 400 representative men prominent in the banking, commercial and
political life of the United States. In Sir Harry's words "dear old Joseph Choate" (former
ambassador to Great Britain) presided. The magic number of 400, once the symbol of
reigning wealth and privilege, appears here in a new role. Men of millions here sway the
destiny, the life or death of their fellow citizens, with an organization which is subversive
to the spirit and the letter of the Constitution of the United States, an organization of
which not one in one thousand of their fellow citizens has ever heard. The purpose of
these men is completely interwoven with the dependence of their own invariably great
fortunes on the operations of "The City," citadel of International Finance. Not only do
these men collectively exert a planned influence of immense weight in utter secrecy, but
they operate with the support of the immense funds provided by Cecil Rhodes and
Andrew Carnegie.

The late Robert M. La Follette, Sr., in the course of a speech in the United States
Senate in March, 1908, asserted that fewer than one hundred men control the great
business interests of the country. His statement brought forth a nation-wide storm of
denunciation and ridicule, and even today any similar statement is invariably derided as
sensationalism and as "crackpot." Nevertheless, Senator La Follette conclusively
demonstrated a few days later from the Directory of Directors that through interlocking
directorates actually less than one dozen men controlled the business of the country, that
in the last analysis the houses of Rockefeller and Morgan were the real business kings of
America. On December 13, 1911, Mr. George M. Reynolds of the Continental and
Commercial Bank of Chicago stated to an exclusive company of bankers: "I believe the
money power now lies in the hands of a dozen men. I plead guilty to being one, in the
last analysis, of those men."

That the Rockefeller-Morgan-Aldrich machine, which was largely in control of
business and politics then, is still a potent factor over a generation later, should be

evident from the manipulations in the presidential election of 1940, charged to Thomas W. Lamont, president of J. P. Morgan & Co., and others, which has been made the subject of a Senate investigation.

Simon Haxey—in *England's Money Lords Tory M. P.*, published 1939—demonstrates in extensive tabulations that the peculiar inter-relationship and organization of the Money-Power in Britain places its control in a very few hands. He quotes Mr. Hobson, who said:

> Those who have felt surprise at the total disregard or open contempt displayed by the aristocracy and plutocracy of this land for infringements of the liberties of the subject land for abrogation of constitutional rights and usages have not taken sufficiently into account the steady influx of this poison of irresponsible autocracy from our 'unfree, intolerant, aggressive' Empire. (page 114.)

> What part do the Colonial peoples play in the battle for democracy, when they themselves have no democratic rights and the British governing class refuses to grant such rights? The pretended defense of democracy by the British Conservative Party can only be regarded by the Colonial peoples as a monstrous piece of hypocrisy. If Britain under a Conservative Government gets into difficulties, we can be quite sure that the Colonial peoples will refuse to help us, and wherever they feel strong enough, will seize power from the British governing class. The whole Empire is becoming tremendously unstable, and any great shock is certain to put an end to a situation where the business men of one small island rule over a great part of the world. (Page 115.)

The late Vincent Cartwright Vickers stated:

> ...financiers in reality took upon themselves, perhaps not the responsibility, but certainly the power, of controlling the markets of the world and therefore the numerous relationships between one nation and another, involving international friendships or mistrusts...Loans to foreign countries are organized and arranged by the City of London with no thought whatsoever of the nation's welfare but solely in order to increase indebtedness, upon which the City thrives and grows rich...This national and mainly international dictatorship of money, which plays off one country against another and which, through ownership of a large portion of the Press, converts the advertisement of its own private opinion into a semblance of general public opinion, cannot for much longer be permitted to render Democratic Government a mere nickname. Today, we see through a glass darkly; for there is so much which 'it would not be in the public interest to divulge'...

The bulwark of the British financial oligarchy lies in its ageless and self-perpetuating nature, its long-range planning and prescience, its facility to outwait and break the patience of its opponents. The transient and temporal statesmen of Europe and particularly of Britain itself, who have attempted to curb this monstrosity, have all been defeated by their limited tenure of confidence. Obliged to show action and results in a too short span of years, they have been outwitted and outwaited, deluged with irritants and difficulties; eventually obliged to temporize and retreat. There are few who have opposed them in Britain and America, without coming to a disgraceful end; but many, who served them well, have also profited well.

While the City, through its ruling power of the "Crown" and its all-powerful Bank of England, holds the purse-strings of the British Empire; the Parliament still holds the taxing power within the British Isles, and the disposition of the citizens of Great Britain.

This accounts for the incredible delay of the British Empire in getting started in its wars. There has not been the slightest indication that the situation at the beginning of this war—which did not permit the Empire to draft a citizen for service outside of his homeland—has ever been changed. This same situation existed in the case of the citizens of Canada, Australia, and the Union of South Africa; with only New Zealanders subject to draft in the services of the British financial oligarchy.

Gladstone expressed his ire at the usurpation of the functions of government by the Bank and the City, and both J. Ramsay MacDonald and David Lloyd George opposed International Finance. David Lloyd George covered this situation with the greatest sarcasm in his *Better Times* published in 1910. *Better Times* presented eighteen of his speeches that were delivered between 1903 and 1910. From "The Peers and Public Opinion" (delivered on December 17, 1909, at Walworth) there is this gem: "Who clamored for these Dreadnoughts? I remember a great meeting in the City presided over by Lord Rothschild, in which he demanded that there should be laid down eight Dreadnoughts. Well, we have ordered four, and he won't pay." He had stated previously at Limehouse in regard to this demand for more Dreadnoughts by the City: "That meeting ended up with a resolution promising that those who passed that resolution would give financial support to the Government ..."

David Lloyd George had been a red-hot radical, but made a complete about-face when he seized upon the Agadir crisis—which clearly foreshadowed the coming war in Europe—to spread out his wares before the bankers of the City in his speech of July 21, 1911, at the Mansion House in the City (and it was a deal). His career as a Liberal was doomed to an abrupt conclusion shortly in any event due to a dubious financial investment which he had entered together with his friend Sir Basil Zaharoff on the advice of the great Conservative Sir Rufus Isaacs, later war ambassador to the United States as Lord Reading; which caused an extensive scandal.

Eleutherios Venizelos, war-time premier of Greece, Georges Clemenceau and David Lloyd George were all known as the intimates and contact men of Sir Basil Zaharoff. All went into eclipse in the Liberal uprising following the war (Enc. Brit.—Zaharoff). David Lloyd George was obliged to resign in 1922 under a barrage of the British Liberal press demanding that Zaharoff be ousted from Downing Street.

In *Zaharoff, High Priest of War*, published 1934, Guiles Davenport uses the term 'système' to designate the rule of the City, and indicates that following World War I it had reached a new peak in its plan of world domination, able to remodel Europe almost at will, omnipresent and omnipotent in world politics. (Page 276.)

X. THE SECRET SIXTH GREAT POWER

In *Germany and England* by J. A. Cramb, M.A.—late Professor of Modern History, Queen's College, London—published in 1914, is quoted:

> Napoleon in 1809 attempted to wrench a planet from the hideous tentacles of this octopus, this British dominion strangling a world...And what was the stake for which England fought in all her battles against Bonaparte? The stake was world-empire; and Napoleon knew it well...In the nineteenth century there was a long series of wars in all parts of the world—in the Crimea, in India and Afghanistan, in China, in New Zealand, in Egypt in Western and in. Southern Africa; so that it might be said without exaggeration that through all these years scarcely a sun set which did not look upon some Englishman's face dead in battle—dead for England!

The British had succeeded in destroying the preponderant French military might on the continent after 20 years of almost continuous turmoil and slaughter, in which almost every nation on the continent had been embroiled at one time or another. British soldiers took little part in the fighting on the continent, even in the battles near the Channel commanded by the Duke of Wellington; for they were spread out all over the world engaged in seizing and occupying French and other colonial lands, and in fighting the United States in the war of 1812-1815. While the "Battle of the Nations" at Leipzig, in which British forces took no part, marked the end of Napoleon's control over the European continent, he later escaped from Elba in the historic "100 days," and hurriedly organized a new army. He was overwhelmed in a four day battle on June 15th to 18th, 1815, in Belgium by an opposing force of 124,074 Prussians, 60,467 Hanoverians and other Germans, 29,214 Belgians and Dutch, and 31,253 British, who were largely raw recruits despite the fact that a 20 year British war was just being concluded. The Battle of Waterloo is generally accepted as perhaps the greatest and most glorious British victory of all time; but much British money and few British soldiers won the 20 year war with France into which Napoleon did not enter as dictator until Dec. 13, 1799. The 31,253 largely inexperienced British soldiers did not single-handedly defeat the 124,588 hardened veterans of Napoleon near the village of Waterloo on June 18, 1815, and thus gain for Britain almost the sole glory for the defeat of Napoleon, while General Bluecher, the German victor at the gigantic slaughter at Leipzig, stood by in the role of spectator.

The House of Rothschild's headquarters were in Frankfurt, Germany. Through its loans to the numerous small nations of continental Europe at extremely high interest rates—and in some instances of additional premiums—it had built up what was widely considered the world's greatest fortune, capitalized by general public custom as "The Fortune" previous to the war between England and France. Apparently foreseeing the trend of events, one of the sons of the founder was sent to England to open up a branch the year before Napoleon was elected one of the three consuls of France in 1799.

The financing of the war in France and the transmission of the funds to the troops on the continent was soon in the hands of this firm. As this was a highly dangerous operation due to the presence of fast privateers, a high premium was paid for this service. The transfer was said to have been accomplished in part by signaling the French coast by semaphore or heliograph, or by ordering payment in writing in the modern manner from the continental branches of these bankers. The result of this was that the money paid by Britain stayed in Britain, while the funds on the continent were paid out, thus bodily transferring this continental banking house to Britain, with all its assets greatly enhanced by the transfer and removed into a haven safe from the grasp of greedy European statesmen and dictators.

When the conflict with France ended, the House of Rothschild was in control of British finance and was the official banker of the British Government. This odd financial octopus was acknowledged to be in some respects the greatest power on earth and was designated by some writers as the "Sixth Great Power of Europe." Although the treaties of Europe and of the world were made under its dictation for 100 years, it never signed a treaty and it never was bound by a treaty. Its position was aptly described in the position of one of its agents and henchmen, Viscount Reginald Esher, as "indispensable to them all, not responsible to any." Despite the intense "passion for anonymity" of the Rothschilds, which has veiled their affairs in secrecy through the years; there are still a number of incidents of momentous international purport, some of them cited herein, in which their connection appears in an aspect denoting remarkable prerogative and ascendancy for what is only a private banking house.

While the gigantic fortune of Maier Amschel Bauer, who had lived once in a house bearing a red shield in Frankfort, Germany, had been a potent factor in the politics of Europe before the year 1800, the 1943 Encyclopedia Americana states under the subject heading "Rothschild:" "The political events of 1813 raised the House of Rothschild to the important position it has SINCE occupied in the commercial and financial world." And further: "... much intermarriage among cousins indicates the family is destined long to retain control of European finance."

It was Nathan, founder of the British house which plays so important a role in the affairs of the City and consequently in the affairs of all the world, who is credited with advancing this House to that commanding eminence of which Professor Usher stated in his *Pan-Germanism* of 1913: "Russia, Turkey, Egypt, India, China, Japan and South America are probably owned, so far as any nation can be owned in London or Paris. Payment of interest on these vast sums is secured by the pledging of the public revenues of these countries, and, in the case of the weaker nations, by the actual delivery of the perception into the hands of the agents of the English and French bankers. In addition, a very large share, if not the major part, of the stocks and industrial securities of the world are owned by those two nations and the policies of many of the world's enterprises dictated by their financial heads. The world itself, in fact, pays them tribute; it actually rises in the morning to earn its living by utilizing their capital, and occupies its days in making the money to pay them interest, which is to make them still wealthier." (Page 83.)

In a carefully developed plan to attain financial control of all Europe, Maier Amschel established his five sons in the leading five financial centers of Europe: Nathan in London, Solomon in Vienna, Jacob in Paris, Karl in Naples, while the eldest (Anselm Maier) remained in the German headquarters. Nathan had arrived in England at a very auspicious moment in 1798, and he soon formed the depository for the vast fortune on the continent and its refuge from taxation. The bloody struggle between France and England for world supremacy in what was actually modern World War I, reduced all Europe into a vast sink of despair and bankruptcy, yet elevated the House of Rothschild to financial and political domination of all Europe and much of the rest of the world.

The Naples house ended about 1855 with the death of Karl; whose son, Maier Karl, moved to Frankfort to assume the German house of his childless uncle Anselm Maier, then 82 years old. After the death of Baron Maier Karl and his brother Wilhelm Karl, it was decided to abandon the sterile German headquarters; the cradle of the House of Rothschild. It is interesting to recollect the Disraeli observation that no country can be prosperous that does not offer prosperity to the Jews. Since 1895, the operations of the House of Rothschild and of the City have been very unfavorable to Germany throughout the world. The Vienna House ended with the Nazi occupation of Austria, and the Paris House moved to New York in 1940.

Maier Amschel laid down the maxims on his deathbed that all members of the family were always to act as one, that they choose wives out of their own family, and that they must remain true to their orthodox religion. In accordance, his son Jacob (Baron James de Rothschild of Paris) married the daughter of another son, Baron Solomon of Vienna.

Nathan of London died in Frankfort in 1836 and was succeeded by his son Lionel, who married the daughter of Karl of Naples, his first cousin. Baron Lionel Rothschild died in 1879 and was succeeded by his son Nathan, who married his cousin Emma of Frankfort, and became the first Lord Rothschild in 1885. Nathan and his brothers, Leopold and Alfred, died during World War I; and the present head of the House of Rothschild is Lord Lionel Nathan de Rothschild, born 1882. The former head of the French House, Baron Edouard de Rothschild, born 1868, has been a resident of New York City since 1940.

The Annual Encyclopedia of 1868 records that Jacob had been established in Paris in 1812 with a capital of $200,000 by Maier Amschel, and that at the time of his death in 1868, (56 years later) his fortune was estimated at over $300,000,000, and his yearly income at about $40,000,000. In comparison it may be significant to note that there was at this time no fortune in all America that equaled only one year's income of Jacob (Baron James de Rothschild). The fortune of the Rothschild family in 1913 was estimated at over two billion dollars.[23]

The biographers of the House of Rothschild record that men of influence and statesmen in almost every country of the world were in their pay. Some statesmen had the privilege of writing checks on the Rothschild bank at their own estimate of the value of their services. Disraeli was a very close friend of Lord Rothschild; and the extravagant Edward VII, acting King of England long before his mother died, was deep in their confidence. A large part of the profligate nobility of all Europe was deeply indebted to them.

Gradually through the years, the House of Rothschild has withdrawn from the public consciousness and gaze in the practice of a peculiar "passion for anonymity" to the extent that a large part of the American public knows little of them. They are generally considered in a class of myth or legend. It should be quite obvious that the gigantic fortune of this family is still a very formidable factor in the affairs of the world. The fact that the international loans to the nations of the world by Rothschild are still a live factor would appear from the many sharp barbs thrust at the omnipotent Lord Rothschild in the *Better Times* of David Lloyd George, and his further sardonic observation that Britain made money on World War I. It is reasonable to suppose that the immensity of the Rothschild fortune has taken it more or less out of the scope of the present heads of the

---

[23] *The Romance of the Rothschilds*, Ignatius Balla, 1913.

House of Rothschild and that it is merged in the general conduct of the financial, commercial and political control of the world by the City.

Today's financial system is not adapted to progress

It paralyzes the whole economic system

As recorded by their biographers, one of the most effective devices employed by the House of Rothschild through the years to destroy their competitors and to discipline recalcitrant statesmen has been that of artificially creating an over-extended inflation by extended speculation, and then to cash in and let others hold the bag. They worked this trick at intervals through the years. The Bank of England is in effect a sovereign world power, for this privately owned institution is not subject to regulation or control in the slightest degree by the British Parliament. A succinct outline of this situation appears in the *Encyclopedia Americana* under "Great Britain—Banking In." This privately owned and controlled institution functions as the great balance wheel of the credit of the world, able to expand or contract credit at will; and is subject only to the orders of the City, the City dominated by the fortune of the House of Rothschild and the policies of the House of Rothschild.

The fact that British capital played an important role in the great crash of the American market in 1929 seems beyond question. That the overextended inflation that brought on the crash could have been controlled and halted dead at any point in its rise by the great balance wheel of the world's credit seems beyond question. That the immense crash and loss in American securities served not only to damage and cripple Britain's then greatest competitor, but also to discipline a recalcitrant and unfriendly administration seems beyond question. That $1,233,844,000 of foreign gold[24] was moved out of the country in the election year of 1932 to bring further discredit to that unfriendly administration and to influence the election seems beyond question. That $1,139,672,000 in foreign gold was moved into the country in 1935 to influence an election and to recreate "confidence" and to prepare the American investor for a further milking in 1937 seems beyond question. The fact that the House of Rothschild made its money in the great crashes of history and the great wars of history, the very periods when others lost their money, IS beyond question.

---

[24] World Almanac

XI. A STUDY IN POWER

The giant oriental dynasty of the House of Sassoon, opium traders from Baghdad, became affiliated by intermarriages with both the French and English branches of the European colossus of international finance—the House of Rothschild; the first of which occurred in 1881. The House of Sassoon is now headed by Sir Victor Sassoon, a frequent visitor to the United States, who in recent years has urged "Union Now" in a newspaper interview in this country.

The history of this family is traced by Dr. Cecil Roth in *The Sassoon Dynasty*, published in London, in 1941. Already well-established financially, in 1832 this family broadened its sphere from Baghdad to Bombay; thereafter to China, Japan and the entire orient. It recently had wide control over the financial affairs of the orient through David Sassoon & Co., Ltd., of China; the Imperial Bank of Persia; E. D. Sassoon & Co, Ltd., of India; E. D. Sassoon Banking Co. of China and London; Arnhold & Co., Ltd., of Shanghai, Hankow, Tientsin, Peking, Hong Kong, Canton, Mukden, London, New York, and other places; the Bank of China; the Eastern Bank; the British Burma Petroleum Co., and other firms. Captain Derek Barrington Fitzgerald, a Sassoon grandson, is recorded (page 222 of the above) as a considerable figure in "the City," financial capital of the world.

Li Hung-Chang, viceroy of China until his death in November 1901, and agent of international finance, was reputed to be the richest man in China in his time; and was considered owner of many great enterprises financed by foreign capital through the Sassoon owned Bank of China and Japan. This bank was organized in 1894, the year Japan attacked China in the Yellow War, to function in the new political and financial alliance between the British Empire and Japan, which was inaugurated with this war. It was wound up in 1902, immediately after the death of Li Hung-Chang, and its interests were largely taken over by David Sassoon & Co.; which was reorganized into a limited company for this purpose in 1901. With the "système" at an all-time high in its political power in 1920, Sir Philip Sassoon, Chairman of David Sassoon & Co., Ltd., was appointed Parliamentary Private Secretary to the Prime Minister, David Lloyd George. Sir Philip, whose mother was Aline de Rothschild, went out of office with David Lloyd George in the political uprising against the influence of Basil Zaharoff and international finance in Downing Street; he died in 1939.

Dr. Roth states (page 236) that "Lord Esher, sitting at the hub of the inner circle of English politics, wrote to him (Sir Philip) confidentially..." Dr. Roth also records a luncheon conversation at Reuben Sassoon's home during which they discussed the composition of a Cabinet which Edward VII would find most nearly ideal. It was suggested that "Lord Esher, of course the power behind the scenes, would be the obvious Prime Minister." It is clearly indicated that the hub of British power politics was not considered to be in Downing Street, but that the Prime Minister was subject to the orders of "the power behind the scenes."

T. V. Soong, the present foreign minister of China, is also head of the Sassoon controlled Bank of China, which Mr. Elmer T. Clark describes in *The Chiangs of China*, published in 1943, (page 71) as "ruling one of the world's great financial organizations." Mr. Soong is the son of a Chinese business man who was educated as a Methodist missionary in the United States, and was there baptized Charles Jones Soon. After returning to China in 1886, Mr. Soon changed his name to Soong. He wrote that his salary of $15.00 per month as a missionary was inadequate, and he therefore made more profitable connection as a political agent of the Bank of China and Japan. His son, T. V. Soong, was educated at Harvard and was then given post-graduate training in an international banking house in New York. He was transferred to a Sassoon subsidiary in China about 1920.

Impressive historical record and authentic documentation reveal that the American kings of finance of the Rockefeller-Morgan machine entered into a secret agreement with the British-French-Dutch-Oriental combine in the early part of 1897 by which they regulated and allocated the business of the world among themselves much like the racketeers of recent years have split up the illicit liquor concessions in our big cities.

Their agreement was particularly designed to destroy the foreign commerce of Germany and of some other unfavored nations. Its operation necessarily demanded a concurrent secret military alliance, and this numbered among its ardent sponsors Theodore Roosevelt, then assistant secretary of the navy; Senator Henry Cabot Lodge; Senator Nelson W. Aldrich, widely reputed Rockefeller-Morgan associate; Chauncey M. Depew, known in some foreign countries as America's leading citizen; Rear Admiral Alfred T. Mahan, writer on power politics upon whom many foreign distinctions had been showered; and somewhat reluctantly, President William McKinley.

Japan was a member of this secret alliance through the House of Mitsiu, Rothschild-Vickers ally. There was a gradually rising dissatisfaction in Japan through the years with her split of the international take. In the early 1930's a rebellious military faction assassinated some of the officials and political associates of the House of Mitsiu, and thereby crashed a wide gap into the solid front of irresistible might with which the alleged justice-minded peace-loving powers had kept the brutal forces of aggression suppressed for over 35 years.

By its secret alliance, the United States was committed as a British-Japanese ally to the following wars and conflicts: the Boxer War of 1900 in which foreign investments had to be protected against one of the periodical uprisings of the Chinese Nationalists; the Russo-Japanese War of 1904, settled by President Theodore Roosevelt for his ally in a master-stroke of diplomacy; the Morocco Conflict of 1906 at Algeciras in which Theodore Roosevelt threw the full weight of American might into the scale to give Africa to his allies; World War I, where the language used by Theodore Roosevelt in denouncing the vacillation and delay of President Wilson exceeded the limits of ordinary decency. Theodore Roosevelt was widely renowned in foreign lands as one of the foremost exponents of Machiavellian government of modern times. Few works on international politics through the years fail to accord considerable space to his many sly presumptions of power. The death of Dr. Sun Yat-sen on March 12, 1925, left the foreign bankers without a moderating influence in Nationalistic circles, and the perennial war of the Nationalists with the bankers was promptly resumed in 1926. Their new leader, General Chiang Kai-shek, accompanied by the Soviet Russian General Michael Borodin, moved on Shanghai to loot the vaults of the foreign bankers. (*The Chiangs of China*, page 68.)

Then, in what was perhaps the most sensational upset in the history of international power politics, an incident widely condemned by internationalist writers as the direct cause of World War II, President Calvin Coolidge declined to honor the secret commitments of the United States and refused to permit American ships and troops to engage in active hostilities against the Chinese Nationalists.

In this extremity, the bankers sent Mr. T. V. Soong to negotiate with Chiang Kai-shek. He offered Chiang $3,000,000 in cash, his own pretty sister May-ling as a wife (Chiang already had a wife and family), and the presidency of China as eventual successor to Mr. Soong's deceased brother-in-law Dr. Sun Yat-sen. Chiang accepted the offer and ordered his Russian allies to get out of China; the wedding took place in December, 1927.

In 1940, Mr. T. V. Soong offered to hold off a Japanese attack on the United States until this country could prepare itself to meet the attack when it came, for the sum of $100,000,000, which in effect was to be a flat gift to China. Mr. Ernest O. Hauser records in an article (*Life*, 1941) that the President called in his financial manager, Jesse Jones; it was decided that "The merchandise was fantastically cheap at that price" and this "bill of goods" was therefore "bought." It would seem that Mr. T. V. Soong, as head of the Bank of China, was selling a "bill of goods" for his principals of the House of Sassoon, which has a striking resemblance to the "bill of goods" sold by Mr. Winston Churchill when he offered: "Give us the tools and we will do the job."

In the early 1900's, the House of Sassoon was at the peak of its power, and its members, who had all gradually drifted to London from the orient, entertained in lavish magnificence. Dr. Roth records that King Edward VII was a constant house guest and companion of its members, and that among other greats and future greats partaking of their intimate hospitality were A. J. Balfour, H. G. Wells and the rising Winston Churchill.

Mr. H. G. Wells has been engaged through the years in distorting and falsifying international history in the service of the secret empire of finance. His *What is Coming? A European Forecast*, published in 1916, was written to impel American entry into World War I. Its subject matter has been largely used to bring about American entry into World War II, with only minor transposition of names, as may be apparent from a few sentences, as follows:

> ... The Hohenzollern Imperialism towers like the black threat of a new Caesarism over all the world [p. 208]. If by dying I could end the Hohenzollern Empire tomorrow I would gladly do it [p. 214] ... The American tradition is based upon the casting off of a Germanic monarchy, it is its cardinal idea. These sturdy Republicans did not fling out the Hannoverians and their Hessian troops to prepare a path of glory for Potsdam [p. 222]... For fifty years Germany has been unifying the minds of her people against the world. She has obsessed them with an evil ideal... [p. 223]. This catastrophic war and its preparation have been their chief business for half a century... [p. 270]. We fight dynastic ambition, national vanity, greed, and the fruits of fifty years of basely conceived and efficiently conducted education, [p. 272] ...If Germany remains Hohenzollern after the war, to do their utmost to ring her in with commercial alliances, tariffs, navigation and exclusion laws that will keep her poor and powerless and out of mischief so long as her vice remains in her [p. 273].

Charles A. and Mary R. Beard in their recent *"Basic History"* state (p. 442): "On the basis of clear documentary evidence scholars dissected the myth, propagated by those

Powers, that Germany was wholly responsible for inaugurating the war ... The gleaming mirage that pictured the World War as purely or even mainly a war for democracy and civilization dissolved beyond recognition ..." The Beards recorded history, while Mr. Wells was merely selling a "bill of goods." Over 400 years ago, the Florentine statesman Niccolo Machiavelli engaged in a profound study of methods used by various rules to attain power. He lived in an age when nations were small, in some cases only walled cities, when events were moving fast and when many men were struggling for power. Due to his own confidential government position, he was able to closely observe events both in other lands and in his own; he was able to evaluate the methods of those who succeeded as well as observe the mistakes of those who failed. In *The Prince* he reduces his conclusions to definite rules or doctrines. His conclusions, in general, appear to find support in the *De Monarchia* of Dante written two hundred years before *The Prince*.

The findings of Machiavelli and other students of power decree that to obtain power it is essential to ignore the moral laws of man and of God; that promises must be made only with the intention to deceive and mislead others to sacrifice their own interests; that the most brutal atrocity must be committed as a matter of mere convenience; that friends or allies must be betrayed as matter of course as soon as they have served their purpose. But, it is also decreed that these atrocities must be kept hidden from the common people except only where they are of use to strike terror to the hearts of opponents; that there must be kept up a spurious aspect of benevolence and benefit for the greater number of the people, and even an aspect of humility to gain as much help as possible.

It is held that the vast mass of the people are oblivious and gullible, and therefore will believe a lie which is repeated again and again, regardless of how obvious may be the fundamental facts to the contrary. But, Chapter VI of *The Prince* also decrees: "... matters should be so ordered that when men no longer believe of their own accord, they may be compelled to believe by force."

Mr. Wells illustrated a practical application of the doctrines of power in his book of 1916, mentioned previously, in declaring that it was the resolve of sensible and influential Englishmen to beat Germany thoroughly and finally, and, if Germany remains Hohenzollern after the war, to do their utmost to ring her in with commercial alliances, tariffs, navigation and exclusion laws that would keep her poor and powerless and out of mischief so long as vice remained in her.

Thus, Mr. Wells first hypocritically divulged part of the exact technique which had been in use for fifty years to exclude Germany and other unfavored nations from the colossal commercial dominions and monopolies of the private empires of the dynasties of finance, and then cunningly distorted the reality of the past and the present as a proposed future punishment.

This is an application of the doctrine of power which holds that high-minded words can be used by the powerful, the demagogue and the hypocrite (or the merely self-deluded), to arouse passion, prejudice and sentimentality for the wrong reasons in favor of disguised real aims; thus to deceive the people and lead them by easy stages to sacrifice their own interests in the service of power.

It is obvious that in the early stages of the usurpation of power in any land of even partial democracy, opposition is certain to arise, and that an attempt to suppress this disagreement by arbitrary means would quickly inflame and solidify its opponents into an overwhelming attack. Machiavelli considered this aspect and indicated the correct method to neutralize this danger in stating: "Many consider, that a wise prince, when he has the opportunity, ought with craft to foster some animosity against himself, so that, having crushed it, his renown may rise higher."

This indicates the technique of modern Machiavellians in having their own stalking horses grasp the leadership of their opponents, and then as their own veiled and hidden action is gradually unfolded, have their Pied Pipers oppose them on spurious and superficial reasons in such a way as to obscure and conceal as far as possible the real reasons and objectives, thereby confusing and confounding the real opponents and leading them into a swamp of futility.

Since the Rothschild dynasty attained control of British finance 130 years ago, every major war has been fought to utter collapse of British opponents and unconditional surrender, and has left international finance omnipotent and unrestrained in organizing a new power-block to enforce the peace and to exploit the victory. Each of these successive power-blocks failed within a brief length of time due to the desertion of an ally infuriated by the British bankers' boundless greed. Each time this has led to a new war, and these wars have been of progressively greater scope and fury.

Only France has been a constant ally for over a century, and the reason seems quite evident as the House of Rothschild has controlled both Britain and France during this period. In *Inside Europe*, published in 1936, John Gunther develops (Ch. IX) that any French prime minister, at the end of 1935, was a creature of the financial oligarchy. That this financial oligarchy was dominated by twelve regents, of whom six were bankers, who were "hereditary regents" in the absolute sense of the term, and were headed by Baron Edouard de Rothschild.

War, according to Machiavelli, must be applied at almost regular intervals to maintain power. It is held that it is not an unforeseeable accident and that it is not a passing madness, but that it is a normal and indispensable tool of power. It must be applied promptly and ruthlessly to be effective in its function of maintaining and extending power.

The infinite danger of the present position of the United States in its relations with the all-pervading power and presumption of the allied dynasties and empires of finance, appears from the dogmatic assertion of David Lloyd George in his *Better Times*: "The international trade of the world is ours." The Machiavellian methods used in acquiring this power are admitted by Mr. Winston Churchill in his statement that the British Empire was built by the sword and will be maintained by the sword.

Machiavelli very urgently warned against any alliance with a more powerful friend, and counseled that in cases where this was unavoidable, the stronger friend must be regarded as a certain potential enemy who must be undermined and destroyed as soon as circumstances permit with the aid of the common enemy and of weaker friends.

The Machiavellian nature of the British Government appears from a consideration of British policy by Rear Admiral Charles L. Hussey in *The United States and Great Britain*, published in 1932 for The Chicago Council on Foreign Relations by The University of Chicago Press, as follows (p. 171):

The British have no written policy, nor even a written constitution...To undertake to outline British policy; an American must be both capable and daring. It seems the part of wisdom to turn to the British themselves for this. The editor of a British colonial weekly tersely stated it as follows: 'Britain is the workshop of the world. It lives by foreign trade, therefore, to secure and hold markets it must invest money abroad, acquire colonies and control the seas...The world must be made safe, not for democracy—for that is only a word—but for trade and commerce. ...That is the national policy of the British people, of both Liberals and Conservatives. It forms the background of all British thinking. It is not openly stated, as there is a trace of Oriental secrecy and reticence in England. It is not considered good form to shout one's beliefs from the house-tops.

XII. THE PROBLEMS OF THE PEACE

The Rhodesian ideology was outlined in a letter written by Cecil Rhodes in the autumn of 1890. It was made public by W. T. Stead in the Review of Reviews of May, 1902, immediately after the death of Rhodes. One part of it states:

> What an awful thought it is that if we had not lost America, or if even now we could arrange with the present members of the United States Assembly and our House of Commons, the Peace of the world is secure for all eternity. We could well hold your federal parliament five years at Washington and five years at London. The only thing possible to carry this idea out is a secret one (society) gradually absorbing the wealth of the world to be devoted to such an object. ...I note with satisfaction that the committee appointed to inquire into the McKinley Tariff report that in certain articles our trade has fallen off 50 per cent, and yet the fools do not see that if they do not look out they will have England shut out and isolated with ninety millions to feed and capable internally of supporting about six millions. If they had statesmen they would at the present moment be commercially at war with the United States, and they would have boycotted the raw products of the United States until she came to her senses ...

Mr. Stead further records in this same article that Mr. Rhodes worked with the support and backing of the Rothschilds in his mammoth undertakings and speculations in Africa.

When Mr. Rhodes considered the problem of "ninety millions to feed" he was looking a long way into the future, for the Great Britain of 1890 had a population of only 37,000,000 including Ireland. Like Mr. Depew, he felt the need of doing something drastic about foreign markets and demanded an immediate boycott of the very nation with which he also wanted union in order to force down its tariffs, so British goods could undersell American goods in the American market. The vicious circle started by this foreign interference would as its next step have forced the reduction of American wages to the much lower British level to regain the market, and so on *ad infinitum*.

When we entered the alliance of 1897 with the British Empire in order to create an overwhelming British control of the Balance of Power, and agreed to assist the British Empire in the permanent encirclement and repression of Germany, Russia and China (with the latter requiring immediate, urgent and active attention), we adopted one of the two opposing theories of geopolitical thought referred to by Prof. Spykman in *America's Strategy in World Politics*. The controlling factor towards this alliance was a wide acceptance of the Rhodesian ideology that with such an alliance, "the peace of the world is secure for all eternity." This fallacy has persisted practically up to the present in an utterly fatuous belief in the eternal omnipotence of British "sea-power."

The foreign trade statistics of the United States in the years since 1897 demonstrate very conclusively that the statement of Lord Salisbury in 1898: "The appearance of the American Republic among the factors, at all events, of Asiatic, and possibly of European diplomacy, is a grave and serious event, which may not conduce to the interests of peace, though I think, in any event, it is likely to conduce to the interests of Great Britain;" was far more to the point than was the fatuous eloquence of Chauncey M. Depew proclaiming in 1900 that "by the statesmanship of William McKinley...we have our market in the Philippines, and we stand in the presence of eight hundred millions of people, with the Pacific as an American lake."

That the Pacific simply became much more of a British lake than it had been is very apparent by combining the totals of the foreign trade of the United States with those lands in the British colonial orbit whose exchange largely balances United Kingdom purchases, with the figures of the United Kingdom; in other words, adding together the foreign trade of China, India, Malaya, the Philippine Islands, and the United Kingdom. We then compare the years 1897 when we joined the "Policy of encirclement" and the year 1927 when Mr. Coolidge definitely withdrew our support of the British alliance, at the time when it had become involved in the war with the Nationalists under Chiang Kai-shek.

Foreign Trade of the United States in Millions of Dollars (World Almanac):

Area or Country		*1897*	*1927*	*Increase*
The Orbit of British Finance (United Kingdom, China, India, Malaya, Philippine Islands)	Sales to	$555	$1071	93%
	Purchases	$176	$1035	488%
Germany (relatively smaller and poorer in 1927)	Sales to	$153	$482	215%
	Purchases	$70	$201	187%
Grand Total of U.S. Foreign Trade with all Nations	Sales to	$1061	$4865	363%
	Purchases	$764	$4185	448%

In 1927, a weak and impoverished Germany still accounted for 41% of the narrowing favorable margin still remaining to the United States in its sales to all the nations of the world over its purchases. On the other hand the highly favorable margin of sales over purchases in our trade with the British orbit which existed in 1897 had almost disappeared in 1927. The year 1927 was in most respects the best year of the post-war era of prosperity preceding the great depression. Our sales to a defeated and smaller Germany in 1927 were over three times greater than they had been in 1897, while our sales to the British orbit, which had profited immensely from the imperialistic expansion of 1897-1920 and from further war and post-war expansion, did not even double; it actually contracted due to the much greater volume of post-war business activity and lesser purchasing power of money. However, we did very well by our British ally, for we bought six times more goods from the British orbit in 1927 than we did in 1897.

Our trade with Germany was about as important as our trade with all of Latin America. Germany was a heavy buyer of American raw materials and an American competitor in selling manufactured goods in Latin America. The Latin American countries, particularly South America, were the United States' competitors in selling raw materials to Germany, and were buyers of American manufactured goods. We competed with Germany in the Latin American market throughout modern times, and held our own very well. The deadly menace of this competition to our continued national existence was not evident until it was given a promotional build-up for the world-wide boycott of German made goods inaugurated by the International Conference called at Amsterdam in the early part of 1933 in retribution for German misdeeds. The United States promptly joined in this boycott with its "Most Favored Nations" treaties to which every country in the world, except Germany, was eligible. This was not a step short of war; it was war, and it was sure to lead to eventual bloodshed. Had a boycott of this type been enforced against a relatively small and weak country like Cuba or Venezuela, it would have ended in open fighting. When German toys, dolls, cutlery, wines and other goods disappeared from the counters of American merchants (to be replaced by goods marked "Made in Japan"), the German market for American wheat, meat and cotton disappeared also, and there was invented the remedy of plowing under surplus crops and of killing off surplus little pigs.

When the American financial-political machine of 1897 decided that a very drastic expedient was necessary to forcibly acquire foreign markets to absorb the two thousand million of production in excess over what we could consume. The population of the United States was about 76,000,000, and averaged about 25 per square mile of what is nearly the finest and most productive land on earth. When the American machine of 1933 decided upon a similar expedient for similar reasons, their principal opponent was a nation that—according to recent statistics—has a population averaging 352 per square mile of land that contains almost as much mountainous and unproductive area in proportion as the United States. In attempting to evaluate the explosive and dynamic opposing forces in this situation, forces that threaten to destroy this civilization, Prof. Usher in his *Pan-Germanism* of 1913 states (page 247): "England, France, Russia, and the United States already possess the choice places in the world; their position is already everything they could reasonably hope to have it; and they scarcely deserve to be praised for unselfishness when they insist upon preserving a situation which is so very much to their advantage ... Nor is it proved that they have obtained it by the observance of the ethical precepts which they would now be glad to apply to Germany ..." As to Germany's position he states (page 233): "If Germany is wrong, others too have been wrong; indeed, if her conduct is unjustifiable, no country in the world can establish its moral and ethical right to existence." It is noteworthy that since this was written in 1913, England and France improved their already dominant position immensely, largely at the expense of Germany; thus to aggravate the problem.

If an America with only 25 people per square mile and almost unlimited access to the good things of this earth was headed back into stagnation and poverty unless it could sell $2,000,000,000 more than it could consume, and a Britain in control of one-third of the markets and the raw materials of all the earth had such great need of the American markets and workmen that the great high priest of "Union Now" would advocate commercial warfare against the United States (in 1890) in order to force their surrender to Britain, where will all this end? Britain's present scramble to forestall us in the markets of the world should be a fair indication of trouble ahead, not only in our foreign affairs but also at home when the American workman can no longer be kept employed by giving our surplus production away and charging it to the American taxpayer. In following one of the two opposing theories of geopolitical thought and in the alleged purpose of retaining for the United States its foreign markets, more money has already been spent than the gross total of our sales to all the world in all the years of our existence. This expenditure makes a mockery of what profit or capital may have been derived from this source, and makes a mockery of all proved economic thought. The fundamental facts are that nations do not trade with one another because they are political allies or political opponents. Foreign nations buy from the United States because they need what she has to sell and because they want to sell their own products in return.

The actual position of the United States in the power politics of the world was well outlined by Prof. Usher in *Pan-Germanism*, Chapter X, pages 141 to 143:

> The possibility of invasion (of the United States) is made of no consequence by the simple fact that no foreign nation possesses any inducement for attempting so eminently hazardous an enterprise. The United States possesses literally nothing which any foreign nation wants that force would be necessary to obtain, while, by making war upon the United States, she would certainly expose herself to annihilation at the hands of her enemies in Europe, who have patiently waited for decades in the hope that some one of them would commit so capital a blunder ... the complexity of the problems of no one group of states, whether in Europe, in the Middle East, or in the Far East, could possibly allow the United States to play a prominent part. In each, the natural antipathies counteract each other. Only the fact that every nation is anxious to maintain or win power or wealth in Europe and Africa and Asia makes the United States of value to any of them. Indeed, it is only as European questions become themselves factors in the larger problem of India, Morocco, and the Mediterranean that they concern the United States at all. As soon as European politics became world politics and Asiatic and African problems became European; the United States began to be a factor in their solution. She has, to be sure, no vital stake in any one of these fields ...

There have probably been over 100,000,000 casualties and over 25,000,000 dead in the wars of the European Balance of Power in the modern era. As the greatest interval between major wars in this 130 year period has never been over 24 years—and the minimum interval only 12 years—every generation (usually assumed to be about 33 years) has had one or two major wars; this recurring slaughter has been the subject of much inconclusive and perplexed discussion.[25]

A monstrous structure of bigotry and intolerance has been artificially devised throughout the Christian world which dogmatically rejects any recognition of the fundamental disease underlying the recurring symptoms of war. Most of the political leaders of the United States have not been acquainted with the most elementary fundamentals of the two opposing theories of geopolitical thought, and in making these two opposing theories merely two sides of a debate have given vent to surprisingly simple-minded statements.

Many of the problems of the peace being discussed now still bear a striking resemblance to those that confronted the world following the gigantic slaughter of the Napoleonic War; the end of that war found the people of Europe stunned with horror, imploring their statesmen and rulers to find some solution of this recurring slaughter of innocent human beings. This is apparent in the following quotes from *The War and Democracy* by J. Dover Wilson, published in London in 1918:

> The Congress of the Powers which met at Vienna in 1814 to resettle the map of Europe, after the upheavals and wars of the previous twenty-five years, was a terrible

---

[25] In *England's World Empire* by A. H. Granger, published in 1916, is given this statement by C. H. Norman: "...Nor is British Navalism innocuous in its spirit! Through that navalism, Britain has assailed nation after nation in Europe that has threatened her trade supremacy; and Germany, the latest comer, is being similarly handled. 'On the knee, you dog!' was a praise that rung unpleasantly through England not long ago ..."

disappointment; and we, who are now (in 1918) hopefully looking forward to a similar Congress at the end of the present war, cannot do better than to study the great failure of 1814, and take warning from it. The phrases which heralded the approaching Congress were curiously and disquietingly similar to those on the lips of our public men and journalists today (1918) when they speak of the 'settlement' before us. 'The Parliament of Man, the Federation of the World' ... seemed in 1814 on the eve of accomplishment. The work of the Congress was to be no less than 'the reconstruction of the moral order,' 'the regeneration of the political system of Europe, the establishment of 'an enduring peace founded on a just redistribution of political forces,' the institution of an effective and a permanent international tribunal, the encouragement of the growth of representative institutions, and, last but not least, an arrangement between the Powers for a gradual and systematic disarmament ... The Congress of Vienna was to inaugurate a New Era. (Pages 31-32.)

... the only man who at first voiced these aspirations of the world at large was the Russian Tsar, Alexander I., and such concessions to popular opinion as were made were due to what the English plenipotentiary, Lord Castlereagh, described as the 'sublime mysticism and nonsense' of the Emperor.

That history repeats itself, again and again, and again; may become apparent from the fact that one hundred years later Georges Clemenceau—an eminent servant of International Finance—termed Woodrow Wilson's Fourteen Points and "the subsequent addresses" as a joke on history. These Fourteen Points were completely washed out and eliminated before the end of the Peace Conference of 1919.

The British objectives in the Napoleonic War were stated in a few simple and forthright words in which the British Government declared that it was not its intent to fight the French people—only to rid Europe of the Scourge of Napoleon, bring peace to Europe and preserve the rights of small nations. These same words, with a mere change of names, have served to explain the British position in all the succeeding wars of the Balance of Power, including World War I and World War II.

Unfortunately, the exigencies of power politics after every cyclical war have been such that it was invariably deemed expedient to sacrifice some small nations for the general good, and a typical example is cited by Ford Madox Hueffer in *When Blood is Their Argument*, published in London in 1915: "I think the time has come when we may say that the one crime that this country (Britain) has committed against civilization was its senseless opposition to Napoleon. It was, to me, extraordinarily odd to hear the British Prime Minister the other day talk of the Campaign of 1815 as a war of Freedom. For, if you come to think of it, by the treaty after that war, Great Britain, the Holy Alliance and Metternich ... affirmed upon Poland the triple yoke of Austria, Russia and Prussia ..." There is a similar indictment by some British author of note on practically every war of the Balance of Power fought by Britain.

As to the fate of the working classes who fought the war with their blood and their life's savings in the case of a country which had achieved total victory after a long costly war, the *Illustrated Universal History of 1878* records: "Great Britain emerged from the long contest with France with increased power and national glory. Her Empire was greatly extended in all parts of the world; her supremacy on the sea was undisputed; her wealth and commerce were increased ... But with all this national prosperity, the lower classes of the English people were sunk in extreme wretchedness and poverty."

In *Old Diplomacy and New*, 1923, the British writer A. L. Kennedy states: "There is more than a grain of truth in the witticism that 'Conferences only succeed when their results are arranged beforehand." When the Financial Commission at Genoa met to discuss the stabilization of currencies, 250 delegates forced their way into the room. A sub-commission "No. 1" was formed for the transaction of the most important political business on which Germany was represented. But for ten days it was given no business to perform. The work was done in conversations between the principal Allied representatives meeting at Lloyd George's villa.

In his *Memoirs of the Peace Conference* Lloyd George records a memorandum which he had presented on March 25, 1919, for the consideration of the Peace Conference: "You may strip Germany of her colonies, reduce her armaments to a mere police force and her navy to that of a fifty-rate power; all the same in the end if she feels that she has been unjustly treated in the peace of 1919 she will find means of exacting retribution from her conquerors." There is every indication that Lloyd George considered the Peace Treaty as merely a temporary stop-gap to be renegotiated after ten or fifteen years because he made some contingent agreements of that length.

XIII. THE FIVE IDEOLOGIES OF SPACE AND POWER

By the tested and effective device of constant repetition, the international claque has manufactured into apparently accepted fact the falsehood that the United States has heretofore had no established foreign policy. That this is not true may be apparent from a consideration of the five great ideologies involved in the modern struggle for space and power, listed in the order of their presumed geographical scope. They are as follows:

1. The secret ideology of international finance, which has been described in comprehensive and precise detail hereinbefore, and which is aimed at eventual rule over all the world by the British Government. World rule by a closely knit and well-disciplined group of special privilege, secret mostly only in the United States as most European people have a fair conception of its existence and workings.

2. The ideology of Russia which was originally conceived in the Will of Peter the Great. A. H. Granger in *England's World Empire*, published 1916 (page 173) dwells on the fear of the Russian Pan-Slavic ideology which has overshadowed Europe for over a century, and he quotes the whole of this document which is directed at first eliminating the obstacle of Austria and Germany, then proposes the conquest of India and Persia, and ends with the words: "... which will ensure the subjugation of Europe." This fundamental scope has been broadened to encompass the entire world by the Bolshevist doctrine of world rule by the proletariat, with death to Capitalism and the International Capitalist."

3. The ideology of Japan, "Asia for the Asiatics," with its pretensions to almost half of the people of the world in a confederation dominated by Japan.

4. Pan-Germanism. German political control over the European continent, freedom from British restriction of the seas, and "the open door" in the trade and commerce of all the world.

5. Pan-Americanism, prerogative of the United States of political control of the Americas; the ideology of "America for the Americans," given early expression by the Monroe Doctrine.

Not only was Ideology No. 5 the expression of the established foreign policy of the United States from 1823 to its abandonment 75 years later by the adherents of the ideology of world rule by international finance, in order to ally the United States with the wider scope of Ideology No. 1; but it is still the fundamental ideology of those in favor of that theory of geopolitical thought which proposes isolation from the entanglements of Europe and Asia.[26]

---

[26] The expression of isolation by the Monroe Doctrine was reiterated by Secretary of State Root in 1906, in replying to a petition requesting the United States to take action to prevent the persecution of the Armenians by the Turkish Government: "By the unwritten law of more than a century, we are," he said, "debarred from sharing in the political aims, interests, or responsibilities of Europe, just as by the equally potential doctrine, now nearly a century old, the European powers are excluded from sharing or interfering in the political concerns of the

The first four of these ideologies all overlap and clash in their scope; and even the total destruction of any one would still leave a fair balance among the other three, which would restrain any one of them from exposing itself in an attack upon the Americas and the United States; particularly, if the United States could achieve real unity in the Americas. But the abandonment by the United States of its own ideology No. 5 to align itself with Ideology No. 1 with the avowed purpose of totally destroying Ideologies No. 3 and No. 4, will leave only the world embracing and absolutely opposed Ideologies No. 1 and No. 2 to possibly engage in a duel to the death with the aid of such subjugated peoples as each can wheedle or compel to join its forces. Such a duel seems inevitable in view of the deep animosities and the explosive economic pressures already existing.

That those in control of American foreign affairs do not propose to retain any allegiance to Ideology No. 5, or of making it an ideology within an ideology, and to evidently give the British Government assurance of this fact, seems indicated by the delegation of American purchases and of American finances in South America to British deputations and commissions. It would seem impossible as participants of Ideology No. 1 to maintain the iron tariff wall permitted us under the policy of isolation, which has been the principal bulwark of a scale of wages and a scale of life far above those of other countries, regardless of its condemnation at times due to misuse by selfish interests.

Of the five great ideologies of the world, only the Pan-American ideology ever substantially attained its objectives. It is the oldest of these modern ideologies except for that part of the Russian ideology expressed in the Will of Peter the Great, and that part of Ideology No. 1 laid down early in the history of the British oligarchy in the following rules of empire:

1. Gain and hold territories that possess the largest supplies of the basic raw materials.

2. Establish naval bases around the world to control the sea and commerce lanes.

3. Blockade and starve into submission any nation or group of nations that opposes this empire control program.

Ideology No. 1 did not arise until the 1890's and was the expression of the vision of Cecil Rhodes of a one-government warless world. It caught the fancy of many other dreamers and idealists who saw in it a solution of the periodical wars of the world, and failed to see in it the seed of gigantic wars of the future in the opposition of powerful races who would decline to recognize the fantastic doctrine of the racial superiority of the Anglo-Saxon and of his pre-ordained destiny to rule all the races of the earth. This doctrine was an integral part of Ideology No. 1 and was definitely expressed by one of its leading American proponents, the late William Allen White, newspaper publisher, in these words: "It is the destiny of the pure Aryan Anglo-Saxon race to dominate the world and kill off or else reduce to a servile status all other inferior races."

---

sovereign states of the Western Hemisphere." Secretary Olney had previously held in his note to Lord Salisbury during the Venezuela boundary dispute in 1895-6, that: "American non-intervention in Europe implied European non-intervention in America."

Only a very limited number of the British ruling class can make any pretensions of being "pure Aryan Anglo-Saxons," as the average Englishman is a mixture of all the races on earth, of all the oppressed peoples and fugitives who crossed the waters of the British Channel to the new free land beyond over a period of a thousand years; and of the British nobility itself a large proportion is Jewish. The Anglos and the Saxons were Germans, and more of their descendants and relatives remained in Germany than migrated to England. The Merriam-Webster dictionary defines an Anglo-Saxon as a member of the mixed race which forms the English nation. Few people can trace all branches of their ancestry very far, and those that can trace it back to some worthy individual in any branch are content to stop there and to accept that as the answer to their own pretensions; and when we note that Adolph Hitler was still a 23-year-old common laborer on building construction at a time when the words of Mr. White received wide acclaim in Britain and America, we can reasonably ask who started all this hokum of the master race.

The American pilgrims and partners who entered the new secret ideology in 1897 knew that they were renouncing and abandoning the established isolationism of "America for the Americans," for a presumably bigger and better ideology, despite the fact that for another 45 years the pretension of Pan-Americanism was kept up, until the recent acquisition of absolute control over American foreign affairs made possible the deft substitution of global Ideology No. 1.

The Monroe Doctrine was promulgated in 1823 at a time when the newly formed British-French alliance of the international bankers was faced with a rising discontent in the vast Mohammedan world and when their fleets were needed to protect their holdings in the Near-east, the Middle-east and the Far-east. Its inception was greeted with derision by the British press, but no immediate overt move resulted, because an uprising in the Greek Christian provinces of Turkey, nominal protector of Mohammedanism had provided a suitable cause for intervention, and it was urgent to overcome the menace of the Mussulman first.

Due to her sympathy with the suppressed Greek Christians, Russia entered the war against Mohammedanism and on October 20, 1827, the allied British-French-Russian fleet destroyed the allied Mohammedan fleet at the Battle of Navarino. Having initiated Russia into the war with Turkey and Egypt, Britain and France withdrew from the conflict, and after Russia had defeated Turkey two years later, curtailed her victory to such an extent that Turkey emerged out of the conflict as a British ally.

This initiated the long-drawn friction with Russia which ended in the great Crimean War, in which Russia was totally defeated and disarmed in the Black Sea area in 1856, and (in the opinion of many prominent British statesmen and writers) the Russian influence in the power politics of Europe removed for one hundred years.

Thus the British interest had been actively engaged in other parts of the world for 33 years after the Monroe Doctrine had been initiated, but now they were able to turn their attention at last to America. A close business relationship had grown up between the cotton-growing aristocracy of the southern states and cotton manufacturing England, and the southern states were swarming with British agents. Soon a great conspiracy arose among southern politicians, which erupted with the secession of South Carolina from the Union on December 20, 1860, followed by six more states in about one month. The conspirators raised armies and seized forts, arsenals, mints, ships and other National property. Members of the Cabinet actively engaged in crippling the Union, injuring the public credit and working to bankrupt the nation, with the apparently passive assent of President Buchanan.[27]

It was in this situation that the Republican dark-horse candidate Abraham Lincoln, victor in a four-cornered slave and anti-slave race for the Presidency, came into office on March 4, 1861. There had been a lot of bloodshed before Lincoln was inaugurated, but it is part of the American Fable that the first shot of the Civil War was fired at Fort Sumter on April 12, 1861. In December, 1861, a large British, French and Spanish expeditionary force was landed at Vera Cruz in defiance of the Monroe Doctrine. This, together with direct British aid to the Confederacy, and the fact that the Confederate army was far better trained and armed than the Federal forces at the outset of the war, brought the fortunes of the North to a very low ebb; and every indication at this stage was that Britain was preparing to enter the war. In this extremity, President Lincoln appealed to Britain's perennial enemy, Russia, for aid. When the document with the urgent appeal was given to Alexander II, he weighed it unopened in his hand and stated:

Before we open this paper or know its contents, we grant any request it may contain. On the day on which your President was inaugurated, we, Alexander II of Russia, signed the protocol which liberated twenty-three million serfs. Abraham Lincoln, President of the United States, has freed four million slaves. Therefore, whatever he asks of Russia, Russia will grant, for Alexander II will not be a factor in the enslavement of any man.

Unannounced, a Russian fleet under Admiral Lisiviski steamed into New York harbor on September 24, 1863, and anchored there; while the Russian Pacific fleet under Admiral Popov arrived at San Francisco on Oct. 12th. Of this Russian action, Gideon Wells said: "They arrived at the high tide of the Confederacy and the low tide of the North, causing England and France to hesitate long enough to turn the tide for the North."

As a matter of fact, Russian interest had made the entire matter a subject of the Concert of Europe, and Britain had already been obliged to withdraw from the Mexican venture and leave the same to Napoleon III by the dangerous reaction in Europe, and the rising tide of Liberalism and anti-Imperialism at home. The imperialistic aspirations of Napoleon III were shortly after drastically snuffed out by Bismarck, to be followed by 43 years of relative peace in Europe. The British interference had caused a furious resentment in the United States, immortalized by the words of the song: "In every battle kill our soldiers by the help they give the foe;" and when a demand for payment of direct and contingent damages due to this interference was rejected by Britain in 1869, war again was close. The controversy dragged out, however, and did not again break out until February 1872, when a Court of Arbitrations met and the British Arbitrator, Sir Alexander Cockburn, violently objected to the consideration of claims for indirect or contingent damages. After several months of futile argument, the United States gave up this part of its claims, and on September 6, 1872, was awarded very nominal damages of $15,500,000.

---

[27] Illustrated Univ. History, 1878— page 504.

Upon demand of the United States, Napoleon III withdrew his troops from Mexico shortly after the end of the Civil War. The Mexican Emperor placed on the throne created by Napoleon, Archduke Maximilian of Austria, was executed June 19, 1867.

An interesting sidelight on the relationship between certain members of the British and Southern aristocracies and elite of Civil War days, appears from the large part played by Joseph E. Wheeler, renowned Confederate and Spanish-American War cavalry general, in his activities in the subsequent subversion of the now firmly established and invincible ideology of the Monroe Doctrine and Pan-Americanism to Ideology No. 1. Joe Wheeler was the principal organizer of the Pilgrim secret society of International Finance, as related by Sir Harry Brittain in his "Pilgrim Partners."

The argument was expressed by Chauncey M. Depew, founder vice-president of the Pilgrims, that incontrollable overproduction would inevitably lead America back to stagnation and poverty, a very potent and fearful prospect at a time when it was just barely creeping out of the horror of the giant depression of the 1890's, but for its entry in what is herein indicated for purpose of brevity as Ideology No. 1.

In denial, former Congressman Towne in his speech "Lest We Forget," condemned American participation in the grand plan of International Finance to immediately eliminate Germany and Russia from the markets of the Far East with the aid of Japan. He said of the theory of remediless overproduction which supplied the justification of this intrigue:

> When men freeze at the mouth of a coal mine and starve in front of a bake shop, when the per capita consumption of wheat decreases as population multiplies, when millions of our citizens lack roof and raiment, to say that there is an overproduction of the necessaries of life is both an economic absurdity and an arraignment of our American civilization at the bar of humanity and justice.

At about the same time the Rev. Henry Van Dyke stated in a sermon:

> ... if Americans do not thirst for garrison duty in the tropics they must be bought or compelled to serve ... to willfully increase our need of military force by an immense and unnecessary extension of our frontier of danger is to bind a heavy burden and lay it upon the unconscious backs of future generations of toiling men ... If we go in among them we must fight when they blow the trumpet.

Further comment on the desperate expedient adopted by the exponents of the "Full Dinner Pail" to fulfill their campaign promise and to overcome the terrible depression of the 90's appears in an article written by the late Samuel Gompers, President of the American Federation of Labor. In this article, he stated: "A 'foreign war as a cure for domestic discontent' has been the device of tyrants and false counselors from time immemorial, but it has always lead to a Waterloo, a Sedan, to certain decadence and often utter ruin."

The above statements are to be found among over thirty great speeches and articles against the great intrigue of 1897 in William J. Bryan's *Republic or Empire?* published in 1899. The American statesmen and educators whose they are, proved to have been great and true prophets in the crucible of 45 years; but they are prophets without honor in their own country, for to revive their words is to expose facts that those in interest want forgotten.

There is no interval in American history as obscure as that between the secret agreement of 1897 and the tipping of the scales in favor of the British-French division of Africa by Theodore Roosevelt at the Conference of Algeciras in 1906. The second Hay-Pauncefote Treaty, one of the greatest political horse-trades of history, was concluded November 18, 1901, in order to obtain the British-French "permission" to build the Panama Canal. Writers and historians of this era are, in general, very vague as to the nature of the deal by which the noxious British restrictions, among other prohibiting the fortification and defense of the Canal Zone, were eliminated from the first treaty of Feb. 5, 1900, which the U. S. Senate had rejected.

John K. Turner in *Shall It Be Again?* published 1922, covers the fact that our presidents employed secret diplomacy in precisely the same manner as our allies and enemies employed it. There is little question that the two presidents who have deplored secrecy and hypocrisy the loudest—Theodore Roosevelt and Woodrow Wilson—were among the most prolific users of secret diplomacy.[28]

In accordance with the British rule of Empire: "Establish naval bases around the world to control the sea and commerce lanes," Britain maintains a mighty array of island approaches to the Americas; and while the United States is now permitted air bases on some of these islands, these air bases, constructed at immense cost, must all be returned to become the property of the "Crown" or "City" after the war is over. Despite her rebuff in America after the Civil War, Britain has tolerated, but never accepted, the ideology of Pan-Americanism and the Monroe Doctrine. She has insisted on her full rights as the dispenser of the "Freedom of the Seas," and therefore building of the Panama Canal required a "material quid pro quo" for the interests of the British-French Financial oligarchy, which in all probability involved our entry into Ideology No. 1, support of their contentions at Algeciras, participation in World War I, and many more things.

---

[28] In *From Isolation to Leadership*, published 1918, John Holladay Latane, Professor of American History in the Johns Hopkins University, states in regard to the Conference at Algeciras in 1906, (page 76):

"The facts in regard to America's part in this conference have never been fully revealed. There is nothing in any published American document to indicate that the participation of our representatives was anything more than casual. Andre Tardieu, the well-known French publicist, who reported the conference and later published his impressions in book form, makes it evident that President Roosevelt was a positive factor in the proceedings. He states that at a critical stage of the conference the German Kaiser sent several cablegrams to President Roosevelt urging him to modify his instructions to Mr. White.

"There can be no doubt that our participation in the Moroccan conference was the most radical departure ever made from our traditional policy of isolation. Roosevelt's influence was exerted for preserving the balance of power in Europe. As we look back upon the events of that year we feel, in view of what has happened that he was fully justified in the course he pursued. Had his motives for participating in the conference been known at the time, they would not have been upheld either by the Senate or by public opinion. There are many serious objections to secret diplomacy, but it cannot be done away with even under a republican form of government until the people, are educated to a fuller understanding of international politics."

An illusion has been fostered that some nations have certain established rights in their ideological aims and position, while others are law breakers. To give body to this allusion, there is usually added positive reference to International Law. Prof. Edwin J. Clapp developed in his *Economic Aspects of the War*—mentioned hereinbefore—that there is no such thing as International Law. International Law had consisted of the interpretation of the successive interlocking international agreements made by the nations of the world in meetings assembled under the provisions of the Concert of Europe. The Concert of Europe operated from about 1813 until it was laid to its final rest in the waters of Manila Bay on the morning of May 1, 1898, by International Finance, after it already had been reduced previously to a rather feeble shadow by the same forces. International Finance thereafter salvaged as many of the interpretations of the Concert of Europe as were useful, and added other desirable interpretations by "Order-in-Council," as needed, as largely developed by Prof. Clapp.

Arthur Kitson, eminent British engineer, scientist, author and inventor—Chairman of the Committee of Science and Arts of Franklin Institute of Philadelphia for ten years, and author since 1894 of a number of profound works attacking the fallacy of the "Money Power" and of "Economic Depressions" and of that menacing over-production of food and merchandise side by side with the most dire want condemned by former Congressman Charles A. Towne forty-five years ago as an "economic absurdity," in an article in the New Britain Magazine of London, of June 20, 1934—cited a devastating assertion by David Lloyd George that "Britain is the slave of an international financial bloc." Kitson also quoted words written by Lord Bryce that: "Democracy has no more persistent or insidious foe than the money power ..." pointed out Mr. Winston Churchill, as one of the supporters of International Finance; and stated: "Questions regarding the Bank of England, its conduct and its objects, are not allowed by the Speaker" (of the House of Commons). Mr. Kitson stated further: "Democracy in this country has become a farce! The real governing power is not at Westminster or at Downing Street, but rests partly in Threadneedle Street and partly in Wall Street, New York! There sits every day in the Bank of England premises, during banking hours, a representative of the Federal Reserve Board of New York for the purpose of advising and even instructing the Governor of the Bank regarding his policies. When the Governor and Deputy-Governor were invited to testify before the recent MacMillan Committee, the Governor introduced Mr. Sprague — his American adviser!"

This American ascendancy in the affairs of the British Empire has so far cost the American people a vast sum of money, but this money seems to be in the nature of a purchase of an interest in that Empire, for exuberant American post-war planners are openly making plans which seem to proclaim them the successors of those controlling the British Empire, themselves the jugglers of world power. This would make certain that the American people would not only be the principal participants in the major wars of the world, but would also take a part in all the minor wars of the British Empire and the world; that borrowing the words of the English Professor Cramb: "Scarcely a sun will set in the years to come, which will not look upon some American's face dead in battle— dead not for America—dead to satisfy the ambitions of power-crazed men."

Mr. Haxey in his "England's Money Lords M.P." covers at some length the Anglo-German Fellowship and its high Tory members, among who is listed Sir Harry Brittain of the Pilgrims. Lord Mount Temple, son-in-law of the great Jewish financier Sir Ernest

Cassel, was at one time a Chairman of this organization. Another member, Lord Redesdale, father-in-law of Sir Oswald Mosley, stated in 1936 that he was one of those who considered it high time that some arrangement should be made whereby Germany should have some of her Colonial territory restored to her. Many highly placed Germans were close to these high members of International Finance and Conservatism and this secret organization may well be prepared to function in any situation where the upstart amateur American planners in their delusions of grandeur forget their junior status in the organization of the master planners of an eventual British dominated world. As developed by Prof. Spykman on page 103 of *America's Strategy in World Politics*, the game of the balance of power permits no enduring friendships. He concludes that British tactics have invariably made the friend of today the opponent of tomorrow. The possibility of the Anglo-German Fellowship taking over from the Pilgrims may not be too remote with only a slight shift in British home politics.

The post-war plans of other countries with large natural resources, particularly those of China and Russia as now indicated, are being shaped to follow the American plan of prosperity by keeping out the goods of other countries in order to encourage their own industry and wealth by the aid of a high tariff wall or some equivalent measure; then to use every possible means of outselling other lands in foreign markets. China, free after 100 years of British over lordship and encirclement, will be a mighty competitor with her intelligent and industrious population. Her bankers and businessmen rank among the most able in the world. Her tariff wall has always been among the highest, but heretofore a large part of the customs has been in British hands, and British agents have disbursed the funds they collected under the provisions of that part of the *Laws of England* (Vol. 23, p. 307, par 641) quoted in the footnotes of Chapter V.

According to an article "How Fast Can Russia Rebuild: 1". by Edgar Snow in the Saturday Evening Post of February 12, 1943, Russia has made some far-reaching post-war plans which apparently do not include any market in Russia for American made goods; which do definitely propose to equal and surpass the United States in every line of production before 1960. They plan to sell these goods in the same markets for which the United States is fighting, and it would seem that the Commissar of the Russian Foreign Trade Monopoly may have a considerable edge over American private enterprise.

In attempting to meet this foreign competition the United States would be unable to take independent action as a member of Ideology No. 1. It would have to consult and await the views of its British and other associates, and abide by the decision of other peoples. So handicapped, the crash of the American standard of living to the common level, conjectured as a possibility by Professor Usher in *The Challenge of the Future*, published in 1916, is moving into the range of nearby probability; and many of the startling postulates advanced by Professor Usher in his works of 1913, 1915 and 1916, have already moved into the realm of fact.

The American standard of living was well illustrated in a discourse entitled "What the Machine Has Done to Mankind" presented at the 1937 Annual Meeting of the Western Society of Engineers. There, James Shelby Thomas stated that with only 7% of the population of the world we produce half of the food crops of this planet, that half of the world's communication system belongs to us, that we use half of the world's coffee and tin and rubber, ¾ of its silk, 1/3 of the coal and 2/3 of all the crude oil in the world.

Thomas then goes on to defend the cause of the machine against those that blame on it some of the ills of the world.

The American people lead the world in science and invention, but their geopolitical sense has not kept in step with developments. There is cause to fear that in that respect the United States is in the precarious predicament of the prehistoric dinosaur whose body grew too large for its head. Instead of ascribing the marvelous prosperity of the United States to its self-sufficiency and its isolation from the wars and the crushing burden of armaments and taxation that have kept the people of Europe in endless and hopeless poverty, a false theory has been created that this prosperity depends on eliminating other peoples from the markets of the world; a resurrection of the barbarous conceptions of biblical times in which conquering hosts put whole peoples to the sword.

It is said that only a few dozen men in the world know the nature of money; and therefore these few men are allowed to practice the manipulation of money and of that mysterious commodity known as credit as a mystic rite. This, despite the fact that their machinations cause recurrent giant depressions in which many of the life savings of the people are lost, and cause recurrent gigantic bloodshed in which the people must sacrifice their lives to protect the manipulators from the fury of those nations and peoples who have been their victims. This, despite the fact that eminent students of high business, financial and social position, such as Vincent C. Vickers and Arthur Kitson, have condemned this money system as a fraud, have condemned the men who manipulate it as super-criminals and traitors to their own lands and peoples, and have condemned the recurring economic depressions and wars as the deliberate products of the money power.

The deranged conception that in order for a nation to retain its prosperity and to escape return to stagnation and poverty, it must always continue to sell more than it buys, most certainly demands that some other nation or nations must always buy more than they sell. Once these other nations have exhausted their surplus gold and credits this process must end, and the account must be added up and balanced. To keep up American-British preponderance of sales, the process was artificially extended and aggravated by the extension of immense credits by International Finance to those countries drained of gold, adding an immense interest burden to their already seriously strained economy, and thus paving the way to repudiation, anarchy and dictatorship as a release from an impossible dilemma.

The power of International Finance rests upon the doctrine of government advanced by Niccolo Machiavelli, which holds that any means, however unscrupulous, may be justifiably employed in order to maintain a strong central government. This doctrine has always been used as a vindication and the mandate of imperialists and dictators, and it cannot gain a foothold unless the forces of freedom have become undermined and are no longer able to offer open opposition.[29]

---

[29] In a lengthy, well-detailed article "Let's Quit Pretending" in the *Saturday Evening Post* of December 18, 1943, Demaree Bess described the extent of the deceptions and the contradictions by which "propagandists" and the Government have kept the American people in the dark as to their foreign position over a period of years. He described how far the American Government was actively engaged in war with unconditional commitments to foreign governments and foreign political factions months before Pearl Harbor. He dwelt also

The people could regain their power by voting into office men definitely on record in opposition to International Finance. The power of International Finance could then be curbed by prohibiting any interchange of international values or credits by any private agency, and the prohibition of any intercourse or dealings by any government representative with any private agency, such as the Bank of England, in any foreign country. Foreign trade could be conducted under the supervision of a Commission formed of representatives of all nations, operating a central bank dealing only in credits arising out of commodity sales and purchases, permitting no interchange of gold or paper credits except under its strict supervision. By this means no nation would be able to sell more values than they are able to buy. The United States would not be affected very adversely, as will be readily apparent from an examination of foreign trade statistics over the past 45 years. In short, our foreign trade was never very important, and would actually profit by trade with a revived Europe. Nations with large populations and small natural resources and territory, being obliged to import heavily, would also be able to sell in proportion, thus overcoming a large part of the lack in self-sufficiency. Debtor nations to be permitted excess sales to liquidate their obligations, and their creditors to be penalized equivalent values in sales until the debts are liquidated. Other affairs between nations to be subject to a semi-formal organization such as the late Concert of Europe, electing its own temporary presiding officers and allowing no man, or nation, or group of nations a definite ascendancy; and subjecting each representative to qualification as to personal connection with any power or pressure group.

As matters stand now, with the end of the war considered by many as a near-by possibility, there is little talk of a "Peace Conference" or of some world organization, such as the League of Nations of the last war, to take over after the war. It appears that the end of the war is to find the defeated in the position of apprehended criminals coming up to the bar to hear their sentence from the lips of the dictators of the "United Nations," with subsequent events in the hands of "Post-War Planners."

In the penetrating classic, *The American Commonwealth*, published in 1888, James Bryce stated: "The day may come when in England the question of limiting the at present all but unlimited discretion of the executive in foreign affairs will have to be dealt with, and the example of the American Senate will then deserve and receive careful study." A little reflection will indicate that the contrary has occurred, that the United States has become a subject of the "Laws of England."

---

on the fears of many Americans that a "bad mess" may result in this country out of the expenditure of American lives and money to bring about a world such as is apparently in the making.

XIV. CONCLUSION

The foregoing matter of the first edition was written about two years ago and the "One World" camarilla has since advanced very close to its planned objective as may be apparent from a copy of the "Articles of Agreement of the International Monetary Fund and International Bank for Reconstruction and Development," adopted at Bretton Woods, New Hampshire, July 22, 1944. It appeared in *International Conciliation, No. 413* dated September, 1945, a booklet issued by the Carnegie Endowment for International Peace with a preface by Dr. Nicholas Murray Butler. The following sentences were selected from Article IX, Sections 1 to 9:

> The fund shall possess full juridical personality. Shall have immunity from judicial process.
>
> Property and assets of the Fund, wherever located and by whomever held, shall be immune from search, requisition, confiscation, expropriation, or any other form of seizure by executive or LEGISLATIVE ACTION.
>
> The archives shall be held inviolable.
>
> ... all property and assets shall be free from restrictions, regulations, controls, and moratoria of any nature.
>
> The officers and personnel shall be immune from legal processes, immigration restrictions, alien registration requirements, and national service obligations; shall be immune from taxation and customs duties, immune from liability for taxes and duties.
>
> No taxation of any kind shall be levied on any obligation or security, dividend or interest of the Fund.

This is obviously merely a precise rewording of the ambiguous provisions of the "Laws of England" which, as variously developed hereinbefore, have placed the Bank of England over and above LEGISLATIVE ACTION heretofore, and made of it a sovereign world supergovernment; with the House of Commons prohibited even from discussing its activities, while the House itself was subject to the orders of "the executive" as to the legislation required by "The City."

Thus the denizens of The City, who have heretofore been obliged to exist in furtive secrecy in the dark recesses of the Bank of England, are now able to abandon their lair to move into the magnificent structure of "One World" omnipotence erected by their henchmen, to rule their world realm in recognized and sublime dignity.

The British economy is burdened with numerous vested privileges which entitle their "proprietors" to everlasting perquisites out of the public funds. This "system" is recognized and supported by the British Labor Party, whose leadership is patently fraudulent and is neither Liberal or Labor, as is apparent from its naive proposal to buy the now empty shell of the Bank of England from its owners with money to be procured from the people of the United States. That even the administration of the British public treasury admittedly comes into this category of private perquisite should be quite significant.

[Editor's Note: The Bank of England was nationalized in 1946 but these vested perquisites of the British ruling class blanket the earth, and are asserted with such nonchalant and brazen affronts as to overawe dispute into dumbfounded inaction, and they include practically every basic commodity of world commerce and industry, be it international news, shipping and port rights, canal tolls, coaling monopolies, cartel control over rubber (to all appearance even to its manufacture in this country), colonial trade restrictions, or dictatorial disposition over vast segments of colonial empire.]

The weapons of the "system" are bully and bluff, bribery and besmear and the bewilderment of the public by being able through control or intimidation of public sources of information to accuse each of the successive challengers of "One World" of its own ideology of world rule and exploitation and to convict them of its own lies and crimes.

The modern dictators were the deliberate creations of international finance to plunge the world into that chaos out of which alone it would to possible to fashion "One World." It was first necessary to make the people of all the world tractable and obedient to these plans in a successive process, involving in their planned turn the people of the United States. The method by which this could be achieved was indicated 25 years ago by a leading financial organ in these words: "When through process of law, the common people have lost their homes, they will be more tractable and more easily governed through the influence of the strong arm of Government, applied by the general power of wealth under control of leading financiers." The structure of world supergovernment revealed hereinbefore in documented step by step detail receives almost daily verification in the news of greedy Imperialistic contest for the loot made possible by American victory. The mask of sanctimonious hypocrisy usually assumed in these grabs has been largely dropped in the need for haste to beat Communism or Nationalism to the plunder in most of the lands of the world.

The Chicago Tribune of December 1, 1945, on its front page carried the inside story of Senator Moore of Oklahoma. The fact is made public that the mystic British Government owns vast holdings in 80 of the largest American industrial corporations, among which are listed 434,000 shares of General Motors and 315,000 shares of Standard Oil of Indiana. At a moment when market has reached a 14 year peak, the "smart" money of the foreign clique which engineered the market excess of 1929 and thereby broke the back of the American economy, again overhangs the market.

The American public was blindly led to the slaughter like so many sheep being driven up the ramp at the abattoir, with endless years of ruin and fear to follow for the millions. Its government is now likewise being deliberately led into economic disaster, for history records that every excess is followed by reaction in direct proportion to its extremity.

Lord Keynes is termed the world's most influential living economist and the key man of Britain's treasury, in an article by Noel F. Busch in the September 17, 1945, issue of *Life*. Mr. Busch records that, as economic adviser to the Chancellor of the Exchequer, he had come to Washington to obtain a satisfactory substitute for Lend-Lease. Lord Keynes, who is a Cambridge neighbor of Lord Rothschild, also a director of the Bank of England, and the chief financial adviser of David Lloyd George in drafting the financial clauses of the Versailles Treaty, is credited with being indirectly responsible for the New Deal policy of endless spending, and is revealed as the originator of the Bretton Woods plan.

The financial clauses of the Versailles Treaty are perhaps the most fantastically unreal parts of this most perfidious instrument ever devised, and from a practical standpoint comprise merely so much gibberish. It is then significant to note that the leading protagonist of these clauses is described 25 years later as being consistently inconsistent in his economic concepts, with a remarkable facility to contradict himself whenever this seems appropriate. It is further developed that Keynes, who is a director also of a number of leading financial corporations of "The City," should not alone be blamed for the 1929 American market crash, which it is indicated he naturally foresaw a long time in advance, and out of which he personally profited immensely. On December 9, 1945, Representative White of Idaho, cited voluminous statistics showing Great Britain has nearly 50 billion dollars worth of assets, among them 2½ billion dollars invested in American industry. There is no indication of any comparable American holdings of British industry; nevertheless, the British Government demanded and was awarded several billions of dollars on a plea of poverty, backed up with a threat of economic reprisal. The British Government had already been given about 30 billion dollars, much of it for non-war purposes and for reasons that were obviously incorrect and spurious, to the stage where the American economy is apparently out of control and rapidly moving to destruction.

Rep. White developed that while this lend-lease was under way to an allegedly bankrupt British Government, that British Government was able, by a financial mumbo-jumbo that does not permit the right hand to know what the left hand is doing, to purchase 600 million dollars of American gold; in addition, it was lend-leased 300 million ounces of silver. Neither International Finance or any other system of finance disposes over any mystical or magical formula, unless the periodical watering and unwatering of money values can be rated as such; and all these mysterious financial convolutions in the end boil down to the simplest of simple arithmetic: the continued plunder of the American economic system with the planned purpose of its destruction.

Two interesting accounts appeared on the front page of the Chicago Tribune of December 6, 1945. In one, Maj. Gen. Patrick J. Hurley, former special ambassador to China, charges career men in the state department with sabotaging American foreign policy by fighting for the imperialistic designs of Great Britain, Holland and France—nations, as developed hereinbefore, whose financial systems are dominated by The City. The other account is of the first dinner meeting of the Pilgrim Society since the outbreak of the war, in which it is identified as a "hands across the sea organization." It recounts that both Labor Prime Minister Attlee and the lord high chancellor of the Laborite government, Lord Jowitt, were among the speakers; and that Lord Jowitt had stated he had greeted the Japanese attack on Pearl Harbor, in which 3,000 Americans died, with "thank God for that." Prime Minister Attlee lauded the United States "for having conquered all and given great satisfaction to everybody here."

It is likely that this dinner meeting was held at the ultra exclusive club of the Conservatives, the renowned Carlton Club, traditional meeting place of the Pilgrims. According to accounts, this club purveys the very finest in service of any club in all the world. It seems strange to find alleged Laborites and Liberals as honored guests at this rededication function of their alleged opponents. The same newspaper in the same issue of December 6, 1945, entitles its leading editorial, "Senators Who Lied." It develops that Senators Connally and Vandenberg welshed three months later on the pledges they and their fellow delegate, John Foster Dulles, associate of the American Pilgrim president, Dr. Nicholas Butler, on the board of the Carnegie Endowment for International Peace, had made to the American people at San Francisco.

On December 10, 1945, General Hurley charged that the United Kingdom Commercial Corporation, a profit-making corporation owned by the British government, was selling American lend-lease supplies in 18 countries and keeping the money. This charge was termed "utterly fantastic" by Dean Acheson, Undersecretary of State, who stated further that Gen. Hurley never had understood the lend-lease system in the Middle East. Mr. Hurley testified in a hearing of the Senate Foreign Relations Committee on this date in part, as follows: "The British corporation was selling American automobile tires. I required the corporation to put the money in the bank to pay for them. And I am told the money was given back to the corporation later by Mr. Acheson."

General Hurley is an eminent attorney, soldier and statesman, who was awarded the distinguished service medal as a general officer in World War I, and who served as Secretary of War in the last Republican administration. His charge, in effect, of treachery and treason, was insolently and contemptuously dismissed as mere exaggeration and lack of ordinary intelligence. Franklin D. Roosevelt asserted that economists have revised their fundamental conceptions every few years to conform to the trend of economic tides. But our leading legal lights have moved with the celerity of weather vanes in revising their conceptions and interpretations and application of basic Constitutional law in order to remain compatible with their status on the public payroll. It would seem that the weasel worded interpretations of leading jurists threaten to undermine and bring discredit, not only to its practitioners, but to the entire American legal structure. The Constitution of the United States is written in plain words, and these words were intended to apply in their broadest meaning. It is not written in legal terminology, and does not require and should not tolerate the layer upon layer of pseudo legal inhibitions with which it has been encrusted, with each successive layer drawing increasing sustenance from preceding layers; to the end, that the Internationalist clique is now able to nullify any part of it at will. Opposed by only 7 votes, the United States Senate, whose members are incidentally largely lawyers, voted to surrender part of the functions of the Senate and to set aside part of the Constitution of the United States, that Constitution which alone is authority for the existence of a Senate, and to delegate these functions to a foreign organization of world government, which by the provisions cited previously, herein proposes thereafter to be no longer subject to any legislative action.

Members of the Congress have been subject to an intensive process of intimidation. Leading Nationalists were nearly all Republicans and many of them were already eliminated in 1932 to 1936. The lot of the transgressor against the plans of the "One Worlders" has been a hard and unhappy one since then. More of the most outstanding Nationalists were eliminated by lavish use of the taxpayer's money for vicious smear campaigns. The American people have been literally drugged by propaganda. Big lies have been exposed, but have been simply wiped out by bigger lies. Of these bigger lie such as his "Give us the tools" and other monstrous exaggerations, Winston Churchill has nonchalantly observed that he lied because it was necessary. The International clique would obviously attempt to frustrate counter attack on their astonishing and complicated pseudo legal structure of encroachment, by guiding this attack into the glove of procrastination, indirection, capriciousness and pure duplicity which has become a mark of American legal procedure in matters of this kind, and which made even the conviction of city gang leaders operating with the connivance of their own legal talent nearly impossible. This would mean that the finely limned maze of legal duplicity designed by them would have to be laboriously retraced and unsnarled, with scant chance of success.

American jurisprudence has become a ponderous and pompous tool of frustration of justice, in which legal technicalities permit the introduction of vast masses of matter unrelated to the direct issue and so permit the issue to be submerged. As officers of the court, the legal fraternity is accustomed to glibly interject its own versions to obscure the real issue. Practiced observation indicates that no matter how obviously unreal they are, they seldom meet with rebuke from the court. It deliberately insults and belittles the public in the role of witness and puts on a show of extravagant professional superiority, not assumed by the members of any learned profession, in what can be termed pure judicial arrogance. The abominations of mass trials which the legal profession has tolerated with but slight protest can well be laid on its doorstep. To cut this Gordian knot of organized and disorganized frustration, and to reduce this complex situation to its least common denominator, it would seem that the Constitution of the United States speaks for itself directly and needs no interpretations or interpreters; that the morning after the people have awakened to their peril and have elected a Congress of American Nationalists, these things and secret world orders will have ceased. The fantastic structure of world-wide plunder and exploitation of humanity, masquerading as world law and order, is becoming more exposed day by day as its organizers climb further out on a limb, and it would then only await orderly disposition. The principal purpose of the League of Nations was to validate Internationalist plunder with a spurious seal of world law and to gain time for its proponents to prepare for the inevitable World War II. The United Nations Organization is a product of the same group, in fact of many of the same men, and its purpose is precisely the same and to prepare for the inevitable World War III. The presumption with which the henchmen of this racket are forcing their agents into control of still not fully subdued sovereign nations of Europe, Asia and South America, provides only a superficial preview of the endless bloody pacification that lies ahead, in which the money of the American taxpayer and the blood of American boys is to carry a large part of the cost.

The same group has succeeded in erasing even the memory of the Concert of Europe from the public mind, despite the fact that it functioned up to 1898 and that its agreements were still used as the basis for the Conference at Algeciras in 1906. In its approximately 85-year life it had erected an imposing structure of International Law. When the International clique sabotaged and destroyed this legitimate and effective structure of world law and order, they destroyed its International Law. The Internationalist pretension that laws substituted by them largely through the device of the "Order-in-Council" constitute International Law rests on pure deceit. The former precisely worded agreements between the nations made under the auspices of the Concert of Europe, blanketed the world. This machinery of arbitration was first undermined by secret bribery, then gradually disintegrated and demolished by "The City" through conspicuous and flagrant purchase of votes and general intimidation of the minor nations. "The City" administered the coupe de grace to the Concert of Europe with the formation of the overwhelming British-French-Dutch-Japanese-American imperialistic combine of 1897, which awarded the Philippine Islands and permission to build the Panama Canal to America as her quid pro quo. Thus did International Finance degrade the world back to the law of the jungle. Then, to cover up, it immediately organized the abortive and make-believe Hague World Court in 1899 as a stopgap to confound humanity until its forces could be aligned for the now imminent and inevitable World War. The decisive moment for this conflict came when the control of Italy had been bought for its agents, and Italy could be removed from its Triple Alliance with Germany and Austria-Hungary. The hallucination that Britain and its allies were then the innocent victims of an unprovoked and unanticipated attack is a triumph of the propaganda machine of "The City" and its almost absolute control over world news and sources of public information.

The utterly spurious nature of the Hague Court is readily evident from the few piddling and immaterial issues that were allowed to enter its hallowed portals for disposition in the period from 1899 to 1914, while none of the victims of the rampant British Imperialistic expansion of this period, and not one of the earth-shaking conflicts just prior to World War I, could gain a hearing. The United States has been tricked into a position of boundless peril and foreign nations will continue to take advantage of its fallacious position by shameless and insolent demands for huge subsidies in the guise of loans; actually little more than blackmail of American power politicians, certain to lose their voice in world politics like did Mr. Wilson after World War I, unless they continue to give.

Great nations and great civilizations have been spent into cataclysm and chaos in the past, and we can read with foreboding the words of James J. Hill, railway empire builder, delivered in an address at Chicago on October 7, 1908, in which he said in part:

> I need not remind you that our public credit, though vast, is not inexhaustible. Many of us have seen the day when it was strained to the breaking point. None of us knows when we may again need to rely upon it and when its strength or weakness will determine whether the nation is to live or to die. Of all our resources, perhaps, this one should be guarded with most jealous care; first because we can never know in advance where exhaustion begins. The earth and its products tell us plainly about what we may expect of them in the future; but credit is apparently unlimited at one moment and in collapse at the next. The only safe rule is to place no burdens upon it that may be avoided; to save it for days of dire need....

> Search history and see what has been the fate of every nation that abused its credit. It is the same, only more awful in its magnitude and its consequences, as that of the spendthrift individual. And it will profit us nothing to conserve what we have remaining of the great national resources that were the dower of this continent unless we preserve the national credit as more precious than them all. WHEN IT SHALL BE EXHAUSTED THE HEART OF THE NATION WILL CEASE TO BEAT.

The End

INDEX

PAWNS

IN THE

GAME

William Guy Carr

1956

PAWNS IN THE GAME

by Commander William Guy Carr

Library of Congress Catalog Information

LC control no.: 57042895

Author: Carr, William Guy (1895-1959).

Main title: Pawns in the game.

Edition: 2d ed.

Published/Created: [Willowdale, Ont., National Federation of Christian Laymen] 1956.

Description: 198 p. 22 cm.

Subjects: World politics.

               Illuminati.

LC classification: D445 .C28 1956

CONTENTS

About the Author

At the early age of twelve the author was thoroughly indoctrinated into the Bolshevik ideology by two revolutionary missionaries who travelled on the same ship with him out to the Orient in 1907. Unlike many others, he didn't swallow the bait they offered him "hook, line, and sinker." He decided to keep an open mind, and to investigate matters thoroughly, before reaching any conclusions. His investigations and studies of all angles of the International Conspiracy have taken him to nearly every country in the world.

Commander Carr has had a distinguished naval career. During World War One he served as Navigating Officer of H.M. Submarines. In World War Two he was Naval Control Officer for the St. Lawrence, then Staff Officer Operations at Shelbourne, N. S., then Senior Naval Officer at Goose Bay, Labrador. As an Officer on the staff of Commodore Reginald Brock he organized the 7th Victory Loan for the twenty-two Royal Canadian Naval Training Divisions.

As an author he has previously published the seven books listed below. Some were specially bound for inclusion in The Royal Library, The Library of The Imperial War Museum, and the Sir Millington Drake Library (which is bequeathed to Eton College), and the Braille Library for the Blind. Several of his books have been published in European languages.

Books previously published by same author.

By Guess and by God

Hell's Angels of the Deep

High and Dry

Good Hunting

Out of the Mists

Checkmate in the North

Brass Hats and Bell-Bottomed Trousers

Commander Carr is known to many Canadians who have attended his public lectures. He toured Canada for the Canadian Clubs in 1930-31. He warned people of the existence of an International Conspiracy. He foretold that the conspirators would, unless checked, drag the world into another Global War. In the years between 1931 and 1939 he addressed Social and Service Clubs all over Ontario. In 1944 and 1945 he was sent on another lecture tour of Canada by The Naval authorities. He explained why it would be necessary to win the Peace, if the fruits of military victory were not to be thrown away again.

Commander Carr is determined to inform as many people as possible regarding the Evil Forces which adversely affect all our lives, and the lives of our children. His book will be an eye-opener to parents, clergymen, teachers, students, statesmen, politicians, and labour leaders.

From Carr's Biography on Wikipedia.

William Guy Carr, Commander R.C.N., born William James Guy Carr, lived from June 2, 1895 to October 2, 1959.

Born in Formby, Lancashire, England, Carr was educated in Scotland, and went to sea at the age of fourteen. He served as Navigating Officer of H.M.S. Submarines during World War One, and as Naval Control Officer and Senior Naval Officer in World War Two. In World War II he was Naval Control Officer for the St. Lawrence, then Staff Officer Operations at Shelburne, Nova Scotia, then Senior Naval Officer at Goose Bay, Labrador. He served at the same time in the Canadian Intelligence Service. As an Officer on the staff of Commodore Reginald W. Brock he organized the 7th Victory Loan for the twenty-two Royal Canadian Naval Training Divisions.

His experiences in the submarine fleet in the First World War became the subject of *By Guess and By God* (1930), prefaced by his superior, Admiral S.S. Hall of the Submarine Service. Going through several printings, it was followed by sequels, including *Hell's Angels of the Deep* (1932). In 1931, he started giving conferences in different Canadian clubs on the topic of "International conspiracy" which was subdivided in two main subjects: "International communism" and "International capitalism", both controlled by the Illuminati and what he called the "International bankers."

In the 1950s, after he retired from the Navy, Carr's writings turned essentially to conspiracy themes from a firmly Christian standpoint. With his *Pawns in the Game* (1955) and *Red Fog over America* (1955) he became one of the most famous post-war conspiracy theorists, with 500,000 copies sold of *Pawns in the Game* before his death.

Publisher's Note to the Original Edition

Here is a TRUE story of international intrigue, romances, corruption, graft, and political assassinations, the like of which has never been written before. It is the story of how different groups of atheistic, materialistic men have played in an international chess tournament to decide which group would win ultimate control of the wealth, natural resources, and manpower of the entire world. It is explained how the game has reached the final stage. The International Communists and the International Capitalists (both of whom have totalitarian ambitions) have temporarily joined hands to defeat Christian democracy. The cover design shows that all moves made by the International Conspirators are directed by Satan, and while the situation is decidedly serious, it is definitely not hopeless. The solution is to end the game the International Conspirators have been playing right now, before one or another totalitarian-minded group imposes their ideas on the rest of mankind. The story is sensational and shocking, but it is educational because it is the TRUTH. The author offers practical solutions to problems so many people consider insoluble.

The Publisher

INTRODUCTION

The International Conspiracy

If what I reveal surprises and shocks the reader, please don't develop an inferiority complex, because I am frank to admit that although I have worked since 1911, trying to find out *why the Human Race can't live in peace and enjoy the bounties and blessing God provides for our use and benefit in such abundance,* it was 1950 before I penetrated the secret that the wars and revolutions which scourge our lives, and the chaotic conditions that prevail, are nothing more or less than the effects of the continuing Luciferian conspiracy. It started in that part of the universe we call heaven when Lucifer challenged the Right of God to exercise supreme authority. The Holy Scriptures tell us how the Luciferian conspiracy was transferred to this world in the Garden of Eden. Until I realized that our struggle is not with flesh and blood, but with the spiritual forces of darkness who control all those in high places on this earth (Eph. 6:12) the pieces of evidence gathered all over this world just didn't fit together and make sense. (I am not ashamed to admit that *The Bible* provided the answer to the question quoted above.)

Very few people seem able to appreciate that Lucifer is the brightest and most intelligent of the heavenly host and, because he is a pure spirit, he is indestructible. The scriptures tell us his power is such that he caused one-third of the most intelligent of the heavenly host to defect from God, and join him, because he claimed that God's Plan for the rule of the universe is weak and impractical, being based on the premise that lesser beings can be taught to know, love, and wish to serve Him voluntarily out of respect for his own infinite perfections. The Luciferian ideology states that might is right. It claims beings of proven superior intelligence have the right to rule those less gifted because the masses don't know what is best for them. The Luciferian ideology is what we call totalitarianism today.

The Old Testament is simply the history of how Satan became prince of the world, and caused our first parents to defect from God. It relates how the synagogue of Satan was established on this earth; it tells how it has worked since to prevent God's Plan for the rule of the universe being established on this earth. Christ came to earth when the conspiracy reached the stage that, to use his own words, Satan controlled all those in high places. He exposed the synagogue of Satan (Rev. 2:9, 3:9) he denounced those who belonged to it as sons of the devil (Lucifer), whom he castigated as the father of lies (John 8:44) and the prince of deceit (2 Cor. 11:14). He was specific in his statement that those who comprised the synagogue of Satan were those who called themselves Jews, but were not, and did lie (Rev. 2:9, 3:9). He identified the Moneychangers (Bankers) as the Scribes and Pharisees and Illuminati of his day. What so many people seem to forget is the fact that Christ came on earth to release us from the bonds of Satan with which we were being bound tighter and tighter as the years rolled by. Christ gave us the solution to our problem when he told us we must go forth and teach the truth, regarding this conspiracy (John 8. 31:59), to all people of all nations. He promised that if we did this, knowledge of the truth would set us free (Matt. 28:19). The Luciferian Conspiracy has developed until it is in its semi-final stage (Matt. 24, 15:34) simply because we have failed to put the mandate Christ gave us into effect.

In 1784 "an Act of God" placed the Bavarian government in possession of evidence which proved the existence of the continuing Luciferian Conspiracy. Adam Weishaupt, a Jesuit-trained professor of canon law, defected from Christianity, and embraced the Luciferian ideology while teaching in Ingolstadt University. In 1770 the money lenders (who had recently organized the House of Rothschild), retained him to revise and modernize the age-old "protocols" designed to give the Synagogue of Satan ultimate world domination so they can impose the Luciferian ideology upon what remains of the Human Race, after the final social cataclysm, by use of satanic despotism. Weishaupt completed his task on May 1st, 1776.

The plan required the destruction of ALL existing governments and religions. This objective was to be reached by dividing the masses, whom he termed Goyim (meaning human cattle) into opposing camps in ever increasing numbers on political, racial, social, economic and other issues. The opposing sides were then to be armed and an "incident" provided which would cause them to fight and weaken themselves as they destroyed National Governments and Religious Institutions.

In 1776 Weishaupt organized the Illuminati to put the plot into execution. The word Illuminati is derived from Lucifer, and means "holders of the light." Using the lie that his objective was to bring about a one-world government to enable men with proven mental ability to govern the world, he recruited about two thousand followers. These included the most intelligent men in their fields of arts and letters, education, the sciences, finance and industry. He then established Lodges of the Grand Orient to be their secret headquarters.

Weishaupt's revised plan required his Illuminati to do the following things to help them accomplish their purpose.

(1) Use monetary and sex bribery to obtain control of people already occupying positions in high places in the various levels of ALL governments and other fields of human endeavour. Once an influential person had fallen for the lies, deceits, and temptations of the Illuminati they were to be held in bondage by the application of political and other forms of blackmail and threats of financial ruin, public exposure, physical harm and even death to themselves and their loved ones.

(2) Illuminati on the faculties of colleges and universities were to recommend students possessing exceptional mental ability belonging to well-bred families with international leanings for special training in internationalism. This training was to be provided by granting scholarships to those selected. They were to be educated (indoctrinated) into accepting the "idea" that only a One-World Government can put an end to recurring wars and tribulations. They were to be at first persuaded and then convinced that men of special ability and brains had the RIGHT to rule those less gifted, because the Goyim (masses of the people) don't know what is best for them physically, mentally and spiritually. Today three such special schools are located in Gordonstoun, Scotland; Schloss Salem, Germany; and Anavryta, Athens, Greece. Prince Philip, the husband of Queen Elizabeth of England, was educated at Gordonstoun at the instigation of Lord Louis Mountbatten, his uncle, who became Britain's Admiral of the Fleet after World War Two.

Influential people trapped into coming under the control of the Illuminati, and students who had been specially educated and trained, were to be used as agentur and placed behind the scenes of ALL governments as "Experts" and "Specialists" so they could advise the top executives to adopt policies which would in the long run, serve the secret plans of the One Worlders and bring about the ultimate destruction of the governments and religions they were elected or appointed to serve.

The Illuminati were to obtain control of the Press and all other agencies which distribute information to the public. News and information was to be slanted so that the Goyim would come to believe that a One-World Government is the ONLY solution to our many and varied problems.

Because Britain and France were the two greatest powers at the end of the 18th Century, Weishaupt ordered the Illuminati to foment the Colonial Wars to weaken the British Empire and organize the Great Revolution to weaken the French Empire. The latter he scheduled should start in 1789.

A German author named Zwack put Weishaupt's revised version of the age-old conspiracy into book form and named it *Einige Original-Scripten*. In 1784 a copy of this document was sent to the Illuminists Weishaupt had delegated to foment the French revolution. The courier was struck dead by lightning as he rode through Ratisbon on his way from Frankfurt to Paris. The police found the subversive documents on his body and turned them over to the proper government authorities.

After careful study of the plot, the Bavarian Government ordered the police to raid Weishaupt's newly organized lodges of the Grand Orient and the homes of some of his most influential associates, including the castle of Baron Bassus-in-Sandersdorf. Additional evidence thus obtained convinced the authorities the documents were a genuine copy of a conspiracy by which the synagogue of Satan, who controlled the Illuminati AT THE TOP, planned to use wars and revolutions to bring about the establishment of one or another kind of One-World Government, the powers of which they intended to usurp as soon as it was established.

In 1785, the Bavarian Government outlawed the Illuminati and closed the lodges of the Grand Orient. In 1786, they published the details of the conspiracy. The English title is *The Original Writtings of the Order and Sect of The Illuminati*. Copies of the conspiracy were sent to the heads of church and state. The power of the Illuminati was so great that this warning was ignored, as were the warnings Christ had given the world.

The Illuminati went underground. Weishaupt instructed his Illuminists to infiltrate into the lodges of Blue Masonry and form a secret society within secret societies.

Only masons who proved themselves Internationalists, and those whose conduct proved they had defected from God, are initiated into the Illuminati. Thus the conspirators used the cloak of philanthropy to hide their revolutionary and subversive activities. In order to infiltrate into masonic lodges in Britain, Illuminists invited John Robison over to Europe. He was a high-degree mason in the Scottish Rite, professor of natural philosophy at Edinburgh University, and Secretary of The Royal Society of Edinburgh. John Robison did not fall for the lie that the objective of the one-worlders was to form a benevolent dictatorship. He kept his reactions to himself, however, and was entrusted with a copy of Weishaupt's Revised Conspiracy for study and safe keeping.

Because the heads of church and state in France were advised to ignore the warnings given them, the revolution broke out in 1789. In order to alert other governments to their danger, in 1798 John Robison published a book, entitled *Proofs of a Conspiracy to Destroy All Governments and Religions*.[1] But his warnings have been ignored, as were the others.

Thomas Jefferson had become a student of Weishaupt's. He was one of his strongest defenders when he was outlawed by his government. Jefferson infiltrated the Illuminati into the newly organized Lodges of The Scottish Rite in New England. Realizing this information will shock many Americans, I wish to record the following facts:

In 1789, John Robison warned masonic leaders the Illuminati had infiltrated into their lodges. On July 19th, 1798, David Pappen, President of Harvard University, issued the same warning to the graduating class and lectured them on the influence illuminism was having on American politics and religion.

INSIGNIA OF THE ORDER OF ILLUMINATI THAT ILLUMINIST JEFFERSON MADE THE REVERSE OF U. S. SEAL

The insignia of the Order of Illuminati was adopted by Weishaupt at the time he founded the Order, on May 1, 1776. It is that event that is memorialized by the MDCCLXXVI at the base of the pyramid, and not the date of the signing of the Declaration of Independence, as the uninformed have supposed.

The significance of the design is as follows: the pyramid represents the conspiracy for destruction of the Catholic (Universal Christian) Church, and establishment of a "One World" or *UN* dictatorship, the "secret" of the Order, the eye radiating in all directions, is the "all-spying eye" that symbolizes the terroristic, Gestapo-like, espionage agency that Weishaupt set up under the name of "Insinuating Brethren", to guard the "secret" of the Order and to terrorize the populace into acceptance of its rule. This "Ogpu" had its first workout in the Reign of Terror of the French Revolution, which it was instrumental in organizing. It is a source of amazement that the electorate tolerates the continuance of use of this insignia as part of the Great Seal of the U.S.

"*Annuit Coeptis*" means "our enterprise (conspiracy) has been crowned with success". Below, "*Novus Ordo Seclorum*" explains the nature of the enterprise: it means "a New World Order". It should be noted that this insignia acquired Masonic significance only after merger of that Order with the Order of Illuminati at the Congress of Wilhelmsbad, in 1782.

Benjamin Franklin, John Adams (Roosevelt's kinsman) and Thomas Jefferson, ardent Illuminists, proposed the above as the reverse of the seal, on the face of which was the eagle symbol, to Congress, which adopted it on June 20, 1782. On adoption of the Constitution, Congress decreed, by Act of September 15, 1789, its retention as seal of the United States. It is stated however, by the State Department in its latest publication on the subject (2860), that "the reverse has never been cut and used as a seal", and that only the obverse portion bearing the eagle symbol has been used as official seal and coat of arms. It first was published on the left of the reverse of the dollar bills at the beginning of the New Deal, 1933, by order of President F. D. Roosevelt.

What is the meaning of the publication at the outset of the New Deal of this "Gestapo" symbol that had been so carefully suppressed up to that date that few Americans knew of its existence, other than as a Masonic symbol?

It can only mean that with the advent of the New Deal the Illuminist-Socialist-Communist conspirators, followers of Professor Weishaupt, regarded their efforts as beginning to be crowned with success. In effect, this seal proclaims to the One Worlders that the entire power of the U.S. Government is now controlled by the Illuminati's agentur, and is persuaded or forced to adopt policies which further the secret plans of the conspirators to undermine and destroy it together with the remaining governments of the so-called 'Free World,' ALL existing religions, etc., so that the Synagogue of Satan will be able to usurp the powers of the first world government to be established and then impose a Luciferian totalitarian dictatorship upon what remains of the Human Race.

In 1826, Captain Wm. Morgan decided it was his duty to inform other Masons and the general public the TRUTH regarding the Illuminati, their secret plans and intended purpose. The Illuminati obtained the services of Richard Howard, an English Illuminist, to carry out their sentence, "That Morgan be EXECUTED as a traitor." Captain Morgan was warned of his danger. He tried to escape to Canada but Howard caught up with him near the border. He was murdered near the Niagara Gorge. Research proved that one Avery Allyn made a sworn affidavit in the City of New York to the effect that he heard Richard Howard report to a meeting of Knights Templars in St. John's Hall, New York, how he had "Executed" Morgan. He told how arrangements had then been made to ship Howard back to England.

Very few people today know that general disapproval and disgust over this incident caused nearly 40% of Masons belonging to the Northern Jurisdiction of the United States to secede. I have copies of minutes of a meeting held to discuss this particular matter. The power of those who direct the Luciferian conspiracy against God and Man can be realized by the ability of their agentur to prevent such outstanding events of history being taught in our public schools.

In 1829, the Illuminati held a meeting in New York which was addressed by a British Illuminist named Wright. Those in attendance were informed that the Illuminati intended to unite the Nihilist and Atheist groups with all other subversive organizations into an international organization to be known as Communism. This destructive force was to be used to enable the Illuminati to foment future wars and revolutions. Clinton Roosevelt (a direct ancestor of F.D.R.), Horace Greeley, and Chas. Dana were appointed a committee to raise funds for this new venture. The fund they raised financed Karl Marx and Engels when they wrote *Das Kapital* and *The Communist Manifesto* in Soho, England.

In 1830, Weishaupt died. He carried the deception that the Illuminati were dead to his own deathbed where, to convince his spiritual advisers, he pretended to repent and rejoin the Church.

According to Weishaupt's revised version of the Age-Old conspiracy, the Illuminati were to organize, finance, direct and control ALL international organizations and groups by working their agentur into executive positions AT THE TOP. Thus it was that while

Karl Marx was writing *The Communist Manifesto* under direction of one group of Illuminists, Professor Karl Ritter of Frankfurt University was writing the antithesis under direction of another group, so that those who direct the conspiracy AT THE TOP could use the differences in these two ideologies to start dividing larger and larger numbers of the Human Race into opposing camps so they could be armed and then made to fight and destroy each other, together with their political and religious institutions. The work Ritter started was continued by the German so-called philosopher Friedrich Wilhelm Nietzsche (1844-1900) who founded Nietzscheism.

Nietzscheism was developed into Fascism and later into Naziism and used to enable the agentur of the Illuminati to foment World Wars One and Two.

In 1834 the Italian revolutionary leader Giuseppe Mazzini was selected by the Illuminati to be director of their revolutionary programme throughout the world. He held this post until he died in 1872.

In 1840, General Albert Pike was brought under the influence of Mazzini because he became a disgruntled officer when President Jefferson Davis disbanded his auxiliary Indian troops on the grounds they had committed atrocities under the cloak of legitimate warfare. Pike accepted the idea of a one-world government and ultimately became head of the Luciferian Priesthood. Between 1859, and 1871, he worked out the details of a military blueprint for three world wars and three major revolutions which he considered would further the conspiracy to its final stage during the twentieth century.

Most of his work was done in the 13-room mansion he built in Little Rock, Arkansas, in 1840. When the Illuminati, and the lodges of the Grand Orient, became suspect, because of Mazzini's revolutionary activities in Europe, Pike organized the New and Reformed Palladian Rite. He established three supreme councils; one in Charleston, S.C., another in Rome, Italy and another in Berlin, Germany. He had Mazzini establish twenty-three subordinate councils in strategic locations throughout the world. These have been the secret headquarters of the world revolutionary movement ever since. Long before Marconi invented wireless (radio), the scientists who were of the Illuminati had made it possible for Pike and the Heads of his councils to communicate secretly. It was the discovery of this secret that enabled intelligence officers to understand how apparently unrelated "incidents" took place simultaneously throughout the world which aggravated a situation and developed into a war or revolution.

Pike's plan was as simple as it has proved effective. He required that Communism, Naziism, Political Zionism, and other International movements be organized and used to foment the three global wars and three major revolutions. The First World War was to be fought so as to enable the Illuminati to overthrow the powers of the Tzars in Russia and turn that country into the stronghold of Atheistic-Communism. The differences stirred up by agentur of the Illuminati between the British and German Empires were to be used to foment this war. After the war ended, Communism was to be built up and used to destroy other governments and weaken religions.

World War Two was to be fomented by using the differences between Fascists and Political Zionists. This war was to be fought so that Naziism would be destroyed and the power of Political Zionism increased so that the sovereign state of Israel could be established in Palestine. During World War Two, International Communism was to be built up until it equalled in strength that of united Christendom. At this point it was to be contained and kept in check until required for the final social cataclysm. Can any informed person deny Roosevelt and Churchill did not put this policy into effect?

World War Three is to be fomented by using the differences the agentur of the Illuminati stir up between Political Zionists and the leaders of the Moslem world. The war is to be directed in such a manner that Islam (the Arab World including Mohammedanism) and Political Zionism (including the State of Israel) will destroy themselves while at the same time the remaining nations, once more divided against each other on this issue, will be forced to fight themselves into a state of complete exhaustion physically, mentally, spiritually and economically. Can any unbiased and reasoning person deny that the intrigue now going on in the Near, Middle, and Far East isn't designed to accomplish this devilish purpose?

On August 15, 1871, Pike told Mazzini that after World War Three is ended, those who aspire to undisputed world domination will provoke the greatest social cataclysm the world has ever known. We quote his own written words (taken from the letter catalogued in the British Museum Library, London, England):

> We shall unleash the Nihilists and Atheists, and we shall provoke a formidable social cataclysm which in all its horror will show clearly to the nations the effect of absolute atheism, origin of savagery and of the most bloody turmoil. Then everywhere, the citizens, obliged to defend themselves against the world minority of revolutionaries, will exterminate those destroyers of civilization, and the multitude, disillusioned with christianity, whose deistic spirits will be from that moment without compass (direction), anxious for an ideal, but without knowing where to render its adoration, will receive the true light through the universal manifestation of the pure doctrine of Lucifer brought finally out in the public view, a manifestation which will result from the general reactionary movement which will follow the destruction of christianity and atheism, both conquered and exterminated at the same time.

When Mazzini died in 1872, Pike made another Italian revolutionary leader, named Adriano Lemmi, his successor. Lemmi was later succeeded by Lenin and Trotsky. The revolutionary activities of all these men were financed by British, French, German, and American international bankers. The reader must remember that the International Bankers of today, like the Money-Changers of Christ's day, are only tools or agents of the Illuminati.

While the general public has been lead to believe that Communism is a movement of the workers (soviets) to destroy Capitalism, *Pawns In The Game* and *The Red Fog Over America* prove that both British and American Intelligence Officers obtained authentic documentary evidence which proved that internationalist capitalists operating through their international banking houses had financed both sides in every war and revolution fought since 1776. Those who today comprise *The Synagogue of Satan* direct our governments, whom they hold in usury, to fight the wars and revolutions so they further Pike's plans to bring the world to that stage of the conspiracy when Atheistic-Communism and the whole of Christendom can be forced into an all-out war within each remaining nation as well as on an international scale.

There is plenty of documentary evidence to prove that Pike, like Weishaupt, was head of the Luciferian Priesthood in his day. In addition to the letter he wrote Mazzini in 1871, another he wrote to the heads of his Palladian Councils July 14th, 1889, fell into hands other than intended. It was written to explain the Luciferian dogma, concerning worship of Satan and worship of Lucifer. In it, he said in part:

> That which we say to the crowd is 'we worship God'. But it is the God that one worships without superstition. The religion should be, by all us initiates of the high degrees, maintained in the purity of the Luciferian doctrine...Yes! Lucifer is God. And unfortunately Adonay (the name given by Luciferians to the God we worship) is God also...for the absolute can only exist as two gods. Thus, the doctrine of Satanism is a heresy: and the true, and pure philosophical religion is the belief in Lucifer, the equal of Adonay: but Lucifer, God of Light, and God of Good, is struggling for humanity against Adonay the God of Darkness and Evil.

Propaganda put out by those who direct the Luciferian conspiracy has caused the general public to believe that all who oppose Christianity are Atheists. This is a deliberate lie circulated to hide the secret plans of the High Priests of the Luciferian Creed who direct the Synagogue of Satan so that the human race still find it impossible to establish on this earth God's plan for the rule of the universe, as he explained it to our first parents in the Garden of Eden, told in Genesis. The High Priests of the Luciferian Creed work from the darkness. They remain behind the scenes. They keep their identity and true purpose secret, even from the vast majority of those they deceive into doing their will and furthering their secret plans and ambitions. They know that the final success of their conspiracy to usurp the powers of world government depends upon their ability to keep their identity and TRUE purpose secret until no cunning or power can prevent them crowning THEIR leader King-despot of the entire world. The Holy Scriptures predicted what Weishaupt and Pike planned would be put into effect until the Spiritual forces of evil controlled this earth. Revelations chapter 20 tells us how, after these things we relate have come to pass, Satan will be bound for a thousand years. What the term a thousand years means in measure of time as we know it I don't pretend to know. As far as I am concerned, study of the Luciferian conspiracy, in the light of knowledge contained in the Holy Scriptures, has convinced me that the binding of Satan and the containment of Satanic forces upon this earth can be brought about more speedily if the WHOLE TRUTH concerning the existence of the continuing Luciferian conspiracy is made known as quickly as possible to ALL the people of ALL remaining nations.

Research dug up letters from Mazzini which revealed how the High Priests of the Luciferian Creed keep their identity and true purpose secret. In a letter Mazzini wrote to his revolutionary associate, Dr. Breidenstine, only a few years before he died he said, "We form an association of brothers in all points of the globe. We wish to break every yoke. Yet, there is one unseen that can be hardly felt, yet it weighs on us. Whence comes it? Where is it? No one knows...or at least no one tells. This association is secret even to us the veterans of secret societies."

In 1925, his Eminence Cardinal Caro y Rodriguez, Archbishop of Santiago, Chile, published a book, *The Mystery of Freemasonry Unveiled*, to expose how the Illuminati, the Satanists, and the Luciferians had imposed a secret society upon a secret society. He produces a great deal of documentary evidence to prove that not even 32nd and 33rd-degree Masons know what goes on in the Lodges of the Grand Orient and Pike's New and Reformed Palladian Rite and the affiliated Lodges of Adoption in which female members of the conspiracy are initiated. On page 108 he quotes the authority Margiotta to prove that before Pike selected Lemmi to succeed Mazzini as Director of the World

Revolutionary Movement, Lemmi was a rabid and confirmed Satanist. But after he had been selected he was initiated into the Luciferian ideology.

The fact that the High Priests of the Luciferian Creed on this earth introduced the worship of Satan in the lower degrees of both Grand Orient Lodges and the councils of the Palladian Rite and then initiated selected individuals to the FULL SECRET that Lucifer is God the equal of Adonay, has puzzled many historians and research workers. The Holy Scriptures mention Lucifer only a few times—Isa. 14, Luke 10:18, Rev. 9:1-11. The Luciferian Doctrine however states definitely that Lucifer led the Heavenly revolt, that Satan is the oldest son of God (Adonay) and the brother of St. Michael who defeated the Luciferian conspiracy in Heaven. The Luciferian teachings also claim that St. Michael came on earth in the person of Jesus Christ to try to repeat what he had done in Heaven...and failed. Because Lucifer, Satan, the Devil—call him what you may—is the father of lies, it would appear that those spiritual forces of darkness deceive as many as possible so-called intellectuals into doing their will here as they did in heaven.

Without getting into controversy, it should be easy for the average Christian to realize that there are TWO supernatural powers. One we refer to as God to whom the Scriptures give many names, and the other, the Devil, who also seems to have many names. The important thing to remember is that according to Revelations there is to be a final judgement. Satan will break or be released from the bonds with which he is bound for a thousand years. He will again create chaos on this earth. Then Christ will intervene on behalf of the elect and God will divide the Sheep from the Goats. We are told that those who defect from God will be ruled in utter chaos and confusion by Lucifer, Satan, or the Devil, for all eternity and will hate their ruler, themselves, and each other because they will realize they were deceived into defecting from God and losing his love and friendship for ever.

Once a person reads *Pawns In The Game* and *The Red Fog Over America*, it will be easy to realize that the struggle going on is NOT of a worldly or temporal nature. It originated in that part of the universe we designate "The Celestial World"; its purpose is to win the souls of men away from God Almighty.

Learned theologians have stated that Lucifer, Satan, or simply "The Devil" knows he *did* wrong and knows that he *was* wrong. Knowing he is wrong he still is determined to drag as many souls as possible into hell with him to share his misery. This being a fact, our duty is clear: We have to make known the TRUTH in this regard to as many others as quickly as possible so they can avoid the snares and pitfalls set by those who serve the devil's purpose. We must penetrate the lies and deceits of those who wander about the world seeking the ruin of souls. Wars and revolutions give the devil his greatest harvests of human souls, because "so many are called and so few are chosen" (Matt. 20:16, 22:14). We so often hear what is going on in the world today referred to as "A war for the minds of men." That is only a half truth and is worse than a whole lie.

Weishaupt's plot requires:
1. Abolition of ALL ordered national governments.
2. Abolition of inheritance.
3. Abolition of private property.
4. Abolition of patriotism.
5. Abolition of the individual home and family life as the cell from which all civilizations have stemmed.

6. Abolition of ALL religions established and existing so that the Luciferian ideology of totalitarianism may be imposed on mankind.

The headquarters of the conspiracy in the late 1700s was in Frankfurt, Germany, where the House of Rothschild had been established and linked together other international financiers who had literally "sold their souls to the devil". After the Bavarian Government's exposure in 1786, the High Priests of the Luciferian Creed established their headquarters in Switzerland; since World War Two the headquarters have been in the Harold Pratt Building, New York. The Rockefellers have replaced the Rothschilds as far as the manipulation of finances is concerned.

In the final phase of the conspiracy, the government will consist of the king-despot, the Synagogue of Satan, and a few millionaires, economists, and scientists who have proved their devotion to the Luciferian cause. All others are to be integrated into a vast conglomeration of mongrelized humanity, by artificial insemination practiced on an international scale. On pages 49-51 of *The impact of Science on Society,* Bertrand Russell says that ultimately less than 30 percent of the female population and 5 percent of the male population will be used for breeding purposes. Reproduction will be strictly limited to the type and numbers required to fill the needs of the state.

Because the rulings of the courts are so much in the public mind today, I will conclude my introduction by quoting from a lecture given to the members of the Grand Orient Lodge of Paris, France, by a top executive of Pike's Palladian Rite, at the turn of the present century. He said:

> Under our influence the execution of the laws of the Goyim has been reduced to a minimum. The prestige of the law has been exploded by the liberal interpretations introduced into this sphere. In the most important and fundamental affairs and questions judges decide as we dictate to them: see matters in the light where with we enfold them for the administration of the Goyim, of course through persons who are our tools though we do not appear to have anything in common with them. Even Senators and the higher administration accept our council...

Can any thinking person deny that the conspiracy as revised by Weishaupt in the latter 1700s, and the plans drawn up by Pike in the latter 1800s, have matured exactly as intended? The empires of Russia and Germany have been destroyed. Those of Britain and France reduced to third-class powers. The crowned heads have fallen like over-ripe fruit. The world's population has twice been divided into opposing camps as the result of propaganda put out by the Illuminati. Two world wars have seen Christians kill each other off efficiently by the tens of millions without any person engaged having the slightest personal animosity towards the other. Two of the major revolutions, those of Russia and China, are accomplished facts. Communism has been built up until it is equal in strength to the whole of Christendom. Intrigue now going on in the East and Middle East is fomenting World War Three. After that, *unless stopped right now* by sheer weight of informed public opinion, will come the final social cataclysm, then absolute physical, mental, and spiritual slavery will follow.

Can any informed person deny that Communism is being *tolerated* in the remaining so-called "free countries"? The British special branch of intelligence, the Canadian R.C.M.P., and the U.S. FBI could arrest every Communist leader within twenty-four hours of the order being given, but they are not allowed to act. *Why?* The answer is simple. Communism is being "contained" on the national and international levels of government on the "*advice*" of the Illuminati's agentur who give a great many utterly unconvincing excuses for the present policy of Britain, Canada, and the United States towards national and international Communism. If the FBI or the R.C.M.P. act, then the Judges of the Supreme Courts of both countries find reason in law why those arrested should be set free. *Such action would be utterly ridiculous if Communism wasn't being contained for use in the final social cataclysm.*

Is it not time Christians woke up to the realization of their danger? Is it not time parents refused to allow their children to be used as cannon fodder to serve the Luciferian cause? Is it not time we became "Doers" of the *word* of God instead of "Hearers" only?

The Federation of Christian Laymen, of which I have the honor to be president, has made available all the knowledge obtained to date dealing with the various aspects of the conspiracy. We have published *Pawns In The Game* and *Red Fog Over America* in book form, and other pamphlets. We keep those who have read our books up to date concerning the progress of the conspiracy by publishing a monthly news letter, entitled *News Behind The News*. Our predictions of forthcoming events are based on our knowledge of the continuing conspiracy. They have come true to such an amazing extent that we have aroused the interest of thinking people throughout the world. We invite you to join us. Make yourselves fully acquainted with the various aspects of the conspiracy, then pass that knowledge on to others. Do this and the power of informed public opinion will become the greatest power on earth.

I urge you to organize Christian Civic Leagues or similar groups. Use them as study groups. Use them to elect men who are loyal citizens. But before you select a candidate for public office, make sure he is fully informed regarding all aspects of the International Conspiracy on the municipal, state, and federal levels of government. All one worlders won't serve the Synagogue of Satan, knowingly. It is our duty to make them acquainted with the truth. Christian civic leagues should be non-partisan, and non-denominational. Their purpose should be to put God back into politics so we may establish government in accordance with His Plan for the rule of the universe as explained to us in The Scriptures and by God's only Son Jesus Christ. Only then will his will be done here as it is in heaven. In my humble opinion, not until this is done will God intervene on our behalf and the words of The Lord's Prayer be accomplished.

Signed:

William Guy Carr

Clearwater Fla. Oct. 13th, 1958

[1.] It was printed in London for T. Madell Jr. and W. Davies, Strand, and W. Creeck, Edinburgh. Copies are in museums and two are privately owned by friends of the author in America.

CHAPTER ONE

The World Revolutionary Movement (WRM)

In order to understand the *Causes* in the past, which have produced the *Effects* we experience today, especially in regard to the unsatisfactory state of national and international affairs, history must be studied because history does repeat itself. History repeats itself because there has been perfect continuity of purpose in the struggle which has been going on since the beginning of Time between the forces of Good and Evil to decide whether the Rule of Almighty God shall prevail, or whether the world shall literally go to the Devil. The issue is just as simple as that. It is a fact that both the forces for *Good*, and the forces for *Evil*, have been divided and split into factions. These factions often oppose each other in an effort to reach a common goal—this makes a study of the subject complicated. These differences in opinion have been produced by propaganda, which is used more often for spreading lies and half-truths than it is used as a medium for telling the plain, unvarnished truth regarding any given event or subject.

War-mongers have used propaganda to divide human beings into opposing camps on political, social, economic and religious issues so they could stir them up into such a state of emotionalism that they will fight and kill each other. In order to discover the *causes* which have produced the *effects* we experience today, all available evidence must be studied carefully. Truths must be separated from falsehoods, and fiction from fact. Past events must be studied to see how they have affected and influenced conditions existing today.

The human race is divided into two main camps as far as religion is concerned. Those in one camp believe in the existence of a God. Those in the other camp deny the existence of a Supreme Being of any kind. This fact is of major importance, because it will be proved that all wars and revolutions have been the result of one group or another trying to force their ideologies upon the people of the entire world.

The conception of GOD varies with different sects. Theism teaches that God is a personal being and the author and ruler of the universe. Pantheism identifies God with the universe but not as a personal Being. Pantheists believe in the doctrine of the universal Presence of the Divine Spirit in nature. A kind of Pantheism has found its way into many religious and philosophical systems—Buddhism and Hinduism both partake of this doctrine. Belief in a personal God includes belief in a celestial world, belief in the soul and life in the celestial world after the death of our mortal bodies. People who believe in a personal God must of necessity believe in the existence of Satan—a personal Devil.

A study of comparative religions proves that, as far as it is possible to probe back, even the members of isolated tribes have always had a religious instinct which caused them to discuss and ponder the questions: "Why were we born?" "For what purpose do we live?" "What ends do we serve?" "Whither do we go when we die?" Even the most backward tribes of Central Africa and Australia seem to have had no doubts regarding the existence of God, a spiritual world and another existence for their own souls after the death of their mortal bodies.

A study of comparative religions also indicates that most, if not all, religions (which teach belief in a Supreme Being) started out on a more or less uniformly high level in which the worship and love of Almighty God, respect for our elders and parents, love for our neighbours, *i.e.* benefactors, and the offering of prayers for deceased relatives and friends formed the basic principle. Evil men, actuated by motives of selfishness and greed and the desire for power, caused nearly all religions to deteriorate to the levels we find at them today. Some religions deteriorated as far as having priests sacrifice human beings as their offerings to God. Even Christianity, which is one of the most recent religions, deteriorated. Christianity has been split up into many factions (denominations) and it would require a great deal of imagination to picture the vast majority, who profess to be Christians today, as true soldiers, or followers, of Jesus Christ.

Generally speaking, Christianity has deteriorated in regard to the practice of good works. This becomes a matter of major importance when we study the struggle going on between the forces of Good and Evil today, because the practice of good works created neighbourliness, and brought about unity in the Christian Fold. The real definition of the word "neighbour" is a person who has proved himself your benefactor, a person upon whom you can rely, a person who, you are certain, wouldn't do you any harm under any circumstances; that man or woman is your neighbour. The Scriptures tell us we must love our neighbour as ourselves for God's sake. The only way to make good neighbours is to perform good works unselfishly. Lack of individual good works means lack of unity and lack of the proper community spirit. Today we have adopted the cold cheque-book type of doing good works. We leave the performance to professional Social Welfare Workers. This has justified the use of the term, "As cold as professional charity." It is well to remember that even government Social Security legislation does not relieve individuals of the duties of neighbourliness. Prayer without good works availeth a man nothing. In Christian weakness and disunity lies the atheistic strength.

For one reason or another, many Christian denominations are fast losing their hold upon the youth of the so-called Free Nations. Each person lost to the Christian belief usually turns to secularism and often ends up as a "Fellow Traveller" in one or another of the atheistic ideologies of Communism or Naziism.[1]

The vast majority of professed Christians are not real "Soldiers of Jesus Christ" whereas every card-bearing member of either the Communist or Nazi parties must swear to give unlimited obedience to the leaders, to devote every waking hour to the furtherance of the *Cause*, and contribute one tenth of his, or her, income, towards financing the party's activities.

While Christians are hopelessly divided into approximately 400 denominations, Communists and Nazis are all solidly united as anti-Christians. A continuation of this state of affairs cannot help but enable the leaders of one or another atheistic group winning world domination. When they do so, they will enslave—body, soul and mind— all who refuse to accept their heathen ideology. The Illuminati will then impose the despotism of Satan.

There is a great similarity in the beliefs of those who worship a Supreme Being, regarding the origin of Man. The majority believes that "The Great Father" peopled this world for the purpose of giving the less culpable of those who followed Lucifer during the heavenly revolution another chance to decide, of their own free will, whether they will accept God's authority, and give Him unlimited obedience or, literally, go to the Devil. It is such beliefs that sustain such despised sects as Doukhobors in their passive resistance to man-made laws which they consider are contrary to God's Divine Laws. It is well to remember that the name Lucifer means *Holder of the Light*—a very brilliant being, the "Brightest" of the Angels. Notwithstanding these special gifts and privileges, he revolted against the supremacy of Almighty God.

Most people, other than Atheists and Darwinists, accept the story of the Creation. There are however, a great many different opinions regarding the story of Adam and Eve and the Garden of Eden. Many students of Comparative Religion argue that it is likely God created many worlds, and many Adams and Eves, and placed them in locations where they could reproduce their kind and populate the planets upon which they lived.

The fact that human beings are placed on this earth by a method and process of birth, which prevents them having any knowledge of a previous existence, fits in with this theory. All we know, regarding the period before Creation, is what has been revealed to us as told in the Scriptures. It really doesn't matter a great deal if there was one or many Adams and Eves. The important thing to remember is the fact that all human beings have been given a *Free Will* and must decide for themselves whether they believe in a God and a Devil, or if they believe in the atheistic-materialistic ideology. Each and every human being must make up his, or her, mind one way or the other. If a person believes there is a God, and a Devil, then that person must decide which he is going to serve. An Atheist, if he joins either of the totalitarian ideologies serves *the Party* and *the State*. He must give unlimited obedience to the head of the Party and the State. The penalty for diversion is suffering, imprisonment, and possibly death.

Belief in the existence of God automatically includes belief in supernaturally Good and Evil Spirits which can influence men's minds for Good or Evil purposes. It is the struggle going on for the possession of men's souls that causes the conditions which prevail upon this earth today. The power of the Devil was dramatically emphasized when he tempted Christ himself, while he was in the desert preparing himself for his ministry.

Atheists, on the other hand, do not believe in the existence of Supernatural Beings. They argue that God has never been proved to exist. There are many groups of Atheists: True Communists, Grand Orient Masons, Free Thinkers, Members of the League of the Godless, Illuminatists, Nihilists, Anarchists, True Nazi,[2] and the Mafia. Many Godless people subscribe to various forms of Secularism, even if they fight shy of becoming active in the Atheistic Communists and Nazi groups.[3]

Most Atheists base their beliefs on the principle that there is only one reality— MATTER—that the blind forces of MATTER (sometimes referred to as ENERGY) evolve into vegetable, animal, and man. They deny the existence of a soul, and the possibility of life, in another world, after the death of our mortal bodies.

Evidence will be produced to prove that Modern Communism was organized in the year 1773 by a group of International Money-Barons who have used it since, as their manual of action, to further their secret plans to bring about a Totalitarian Godless State. Lenin made this clear in his book *Left Wing Communism*. On page 53, he said: "Our theory (Communism) is not a dogma (Settled Doctrine), it is a manual of action." Many modern leaders have said and done the same things as Lucifer did during the heavenly revolution. There is no appreciable difference between *Red* and *Black Atheism*. The only difference is in the plans used by the opposing leaders to ultimately win undisputed control of the world's resources, and bring into being their ideas for a Totalitarian, Godless, Dictatorship.

Karl Marx (1818-1883) was a German of Jewish descent. He was expelled from Germany, and afterwards from France, for his revolutionary activities. He was given asylum in England. In 1848, he published the *Communist Manifesto*. Marx admitted this long-range plan, to turn the world into an International of Soviet Socialist Republics, may take centuries to accomplish.

Karl Ritter (1779-1859) was a German Professor of History and Geopolitical science. He wrote the antithesis to Karl Marx's *Communist Manifesto*. He also drew up a plan by which he maintained the Aryan Race could first dominate Europe and then the entire world. Certain Atheistic leaders of the Aryan Group adopted Karl Ritter's plan. They organized Naziism to further their secret ambitions to obtain ultimate control of the World and turn it into a Godless State, under their conception of a totalitarian dictatorship. This small group of men knew they must either join up with, or destroy, the power and influence of the International Bankers. It is doubtful if more than a mere handful of the top level leaders of the Communist and Fascist movements know their organizations are being used to further the secret ambitions of the Illuminati which are the High Priests of Satanism.

According to the leaders of both atheistic groups, the State must be Supreme. This being so, the Head of the State is God on Earth. This belief brings into actual practice the deification of man.

Much more is generally known about Karl Marx and Communism than about Karl Ritter and Naziism. Ritter was for many years Professor of History at Frankfurt University, Germany. Afterwards he taught Geography at the Berlin University. In educational circles he was considered one of the greatest authorities on History, Geography, and Geopolitical Science. Because the "Aims and Objects" of the Leaders of the Aryan Party have always been kept secret, Karl Ritter's connection with the Leaders and Naziism is very little known. Intelligence Officers connected with the British Government unearthed his connection with the Aryan War Lords when studying Political Economy, Geopolitical Science, and Comparative Religions, in German universities.[4] This information was passed on to the proper authorities but, as so often happens, political leaders and diplomats, either failed to realize the significance of what they were told or wished to ignore it.[5]

Karl Ritter's study of History convinced him that a very small group of wealthy, and influential, international Bankers, who gave allegiance to no country but meddled in the affairs of all, had, in 1773, organized Grand Orient Freemasonry for the purpose of using *The World Revolutionary Movement* to further their secret ambitions. Their Long-Range Plan was for their group to gain ultimate control of the wealth, natural resources, and manpower of the entire world. Their ultimate objective was to form a Totalitarian Dictatorship based on their theories of Atheistic dialectical and historical materialism. Ritter claimed that most, if not all, of the International Bankers were of Jewish descent, regardless of whether or not they practiced the Jewish faith.

In his antithesis to Karl Marx's *Communist Manifesto* he dealt with the dangers to be faced if this group of men were allowed to continue to control and direct the policies of International Communism. He offered the German Aryan War-Lords very concrete and practical suggestions for defeating the conspiracy of the International Money-Barons.[6] Professor Ritter gave the Aryan War-Lords an alternative Long-Range Plan by which they could gain ultimate control of the world's resources for the Aryan races.

To offset the plans of the International Money-Barons, Karl Ritter advised the Leaders of the Aryan Groups to organize Naziism and use Fascism (*i.e.* National Socialism) as their manual of action to further their secret ambitions for world conquest. Professor Ritter also pointed out that because the International Bankers intended to use all phases of Semitism to further their plans, the Aryan Leaders should use all phases of anti-semitism to further their *Cause*.

Karl Ritter's Long-Range Plan for ultimate world conquest included the following suggestions:

The subjugation of all European countries by Germany. To achieve this end he suggested the German military Junkers be encouraged and assisted to obtain control of the Government so they could engage in a series of *Military Adventures*, interspersed with economic *wars*, the objective being to weaken the economy and manpower of the European nations to be subjugated.[7] Karl Ritter stated that it was NOT absolutely essential to the success of his Long-Range Plan that each *Military Adventure* end in a clear-cut victory, provided the other nations involved were left in such a weakened condition that their recovery economically, and in strength of man-power, took longer than that of Germany. Karl Ritter stressed the importance of convincing the German people that they were physically and mentally superior to the Semitic races. From this thought Aryan propagandists developed the idea of *The German Master Race*. They did this to counter the Propaganda of the International Bankers which claimed the Semitic Race is to be God's Chosen People and Divinely chosen to inherit the earth. The Aryan leaders promulgated the doctrine that "Their Race" was *The Master Race* on this Earth. Thus millions of people were divided into opposing camps.

Karl Ritter recommended a financial policy which would prevent the International Bankers obtaining control of the economy of Germany and her Satellite States as they had obtained economic control in England, France, and America.

1. He recommended the organization of a Nazi Fifth Column to counteract the Communist Underground organization. Its objective was to persuade the upper and middle classes of the countries they planned to subjugate to accept Fascism as the only antidote to Communism. German Fifth Columnists were to condition people in other countries to welcome the German Armies as their Military Protectors against threatened Communist aggression. Karl Ritter warned the leaders of the Aryan Group that a Military Invasion of another country should NEVER be undertaken until the Fifth Column and propaganda machines had thoroughly paved the way, and convinced the majority of the people to accept their armed intervention as the act of Saviours or Crusaders, and not as aggressors.[8]

2. Karl Ritter cold-bloodedly recommended the total destruction of Communism and the extermination of the Jewish Race as essential to obtaining ultimate control of International Affairs by the Aryan Leaders. He justified this drastic stipulation on the facts of history which he claimed proved that Communism was being used by the International Jewish Bankers to further their own selfish materialistic ambitions.

There were many more items making up the overall *Long-Range Plan* but in this chapter it is sufficient to produce enough evidence to unlock the door, behind which the secret plans of two small groups of totalitarian-minded, atheistic-materialistic men were hidden. The study of Comparative Religions, Geo-political Science, and Political Economy, and years of intensive research, revealed the truth that many millions of human beings have been used as *Pawns in the Game* by the leaders of the two atheistic totalitarian-minded groups who will continue playing their hideous game of International Chess until one or the other is eliminated. Evidence will be produced to show how this game has been conducted in the past, and what moves are likely to be made in the near future, to enable one group to win the game.

The followers of all religions that teach the existence of God and life in a hereafter believe in the love and worship of God, and charity towards all men of good will. Sincere believers will suffer any hardship, and make any sacrifice, in order to ensure their eternal salvation. The followers of Atheism are taught to HATE all who refuse to accept their materialistic creed. The determination of the leaders of both Atheist groups, to achieve world domination, permits them to conceive the most diabolical conspiracies, and perpetrate all kinds of crime, from individual assassinations to genocide. They foment wars in order to weaken nations they still have to subjugate.

The study of Comparative Religions shows also that Communism and Naziism are utterly incompatible with all religions that believe in the existence of an Almighty God. Experience, and history, proves that those who believe in God, and those who deny His existence, are in such contradiction that neither can survive the triumph of the other. Atheistic leaders in subjugated countries may, for a time, tolerate religions which teach belief in God, but they only allow the priests to function on the social periphery. They take good care that the priests do not have the opportunity to influence the social and political behaviour of their congregations. Evidence proves that the ULTIMATE objective of both major Atheistic Ideologies is to obliterate from the minds of mankind, by persecution and a systematically applied program of continuous *brain-washing*, all knowledge of a Supreme Being, the existence of a soul, and hope of life in a hereafter. These being facts, any talk of coexistence is either utter nonsense or propaganda.

The trouble today is the continuation of the Heavenly Revolution. If God has placed human beings on this earth so they may know Him, love Him, and serve Him in this life in order to be happy with Him forever in the next world, then it is logical to reason that the only way in which Lucifer could hope to win back the souls in dispute would be to inoculate them with the doctrine of Atheistic-Materialism.

Undoubtedly, many people will ask, "But how could the Devil inoculate the minds of men with Atheistic and other evil ideas?" That question can be answered in this way: If HUMAN Beings can establish radio and television stations, from which one individual can influence millions of others by broadcasting his opinions on any given subject over the invisible airwaves, then why shouldn't it be possible for CELESTIAL Beings to broadcast their messages to us? No brain specialist has dared to deny that in the brain of each individual there is some kind of mysterious receiving set. Every hour of every day Human Beings are saying, "I was inspired to do this," or, "I was tempted to do that." Thoughts, be they good or evil, must originate somewhere, from some "cause," and be transmitted to the human brain. The body is only the instrument which puts the dominating thought for "Good" or for "Evil" into effect.

One fundamental fact which all people who believe in the existence of God must never forget is this: If we are on this earth for a period of trial, if we have been given our Free

Will, it is to enable us to decide whether we want to go to God or want to go to the Devil. Therefore, if the Devil did not have the opportunity to influence the minds of men, there would be no test.

If Almighty God sent his prophets and His son Jesus Christ to show us clearly what is *Good* and what is *Evil*, then why wouldn't the Devil send his false Christs and his false prophets to try and prove to us that *Evil* is *Good* and that *Good* is *Evil?*

The simplest way to understand what is going on in the world today is to study the events of History as the moves being made in a continuing game of International Chess. The leaders of the Illuminati have divided the people of the world into two main camps. They used Kings and Queens, Bishops and Knights, and the masses of the world's population, as pieces in their games. The ruthless policy of the leaders is to consider all other human beings as EXPENDABLE, providing the sacrifice of a *Major* piece, or a million *Pawns*, places them a move nearer their ultimate totalitarian goal: the despotism of Satan.

Professor Ritter is reported to have said the present phase of this game started in the Counting House of Amschel Mayer Bauer, alias Rothschild, located at Frankfurt-on-the-Main in Germany, when thirteen Gold and Silversmiths decided they must remove all the Crowned Heads of Europe, destroy all existing governments, and eliminate all organized religions, before they could secure absolute control of the wealth, natural resources, and man-power of the entire world, and establish a Satanic Despotism.[9] Dialectical and historical materialism was to be used to further these plans.

Strange though it may seem, history will prove that leaders of both the Semitic and Anti-Semitic groups have on occasion joined forces to fight against a common enemy such as the British Empire, or the Christian religion. And while the masses fought, the Illuminati, who constitute the *Secret Power* behind the World Revolutionary Movements, jockeyed for the best position from which they would derive the greatest future benefit. The leaders of both Communism and Naziism have crossed and doublecrossed each other, but it is doubtful if many of the leaders realized, before it was too late, that even they were only tools controlled by the Agentur of the Illuminati who use all that is evil to further their ends. When the *Secret Powers* heading either group even suspect that one of their "tools" know too much, they ordered him *liquidated*. Evidence will be produced to prove that the leaders of these two groups of totalitarian-minded men have instigated many individual assassinations, and caused many revolutions and wars, in which tens of millions of human beings have been killed, while millions have been wounded and rendered homeless. It is difficult to discover a military leader who can justify the decision to drop atomic bombs on Hiroshima or Nagasaki where, in the twinkling of an eye, approximately 100,000 people were killed, and twice the number seriously injured. The Japanese Military forces had already been defeated. Surrender was only a matter of hours or days away when this diabolical act was perpetrated. The only logical conclusion is that *The Secret Powers*, who—it will be proved—influence and control the policies of most national Governments, decided that this most modern of all lethal weapons had to be demonstrated to remind Stalin what would happen if he became too obnoxious. This is the only excuse which provides even the resemblance of justification for such an outrage against humanity.

But the atomic bomb and the hydrogen bomb are no longer the world's most lethal weapons. Nerve gas, now being stockpiled by both Communist and Non-Communist nations, is capable of wiping out all living creatures in a country, a city, or a town. The extent of destruction of all human life in a nation can be adjusted to the military and economic requirements of those who decide to use nerve gas to reach their goal. Nerve gas is said to be highly concentrated fluorine in its gaseous form. It is the most penetrating and deadly gas ever discovered by man. It is colourless, odourless, tasteless as well as economical to produce. One single drop, even when heavily diluted with water or oil will, if it comes in contact with a living body, cause paralysis of the breathing apparatus and death. In a few minutes it will penetrate even through rubber clothing such as is worn by firemen when on duty. Nerve gas will not seriously damage inanimate objects.

Within a few days after the nerve gas had been applied, it would be safe for the invading force to enter the contaminated areas again. They would be areas of the dead, but all buildings and machinery would be intact. The only known antidote to nerve gas is the drug Atropine. To be effective, it must be injected into the veins of victims immediately, and repeatedly, after they have been contaminated. This means of defence is not practical for densely populated areas. Both Communist and Anti-Communist governments have nerve gas. The knowledge that both sides have this gas in quantity may cause both sides to hesitate to use it. But it is a well-known fact that desperate and ruthless men will resort to any extremes to gain their objectives. And, as will be proved, they have never hesitated to sacrifice millions upon millions of human beings—men, women and children—if by doing so they advance themselves only one step nearer to their ultimate goal.

We may well ask the question, "How is the struggle now going on upon this earth going to end?" It is doubtful if there is a single living being who hasn't asked this question. It is a question young married couples anxiously ask each other when they debate if they should allow their connubial bliss to bring more children into this hate-dominated world. The most complete answer is to be found in the Gospel of Saint Matthew, Chapter XXIV, verses 15 to 34. At that time Jesus said to His disciples:

> When you shall see the abomination of desolation, which was spoken of by Daniel the Prophet, standing in the Holy Place (he that readeth let him understand), then they that are in Judea, let them flee to the mountains, and he that is on the house top let him not come down to take anything out of his house, and he that is in the field let him not go back to get his coat. And woe to them that are with child, and give suck in those days. But pray that your flight be not in winter or on the sabbath, for there shall be great tribulation such as hath not been from the beginning of the world until now, neither shall be, and unless those days shall be shortened NO FLESH SHOULD BE SAVED, but for the sake of the elect, those days shall be shortened.

Christ then proceeded to deal with the problem of the false leaders and the anti-Christs who he foretold would use propaganda to befuddle men's thinking. He said:

> Then if any man shall say to you *Lo, here is Christ* or *There* do not believe him, for there shall arise false Christs and false prophets who shall show great signs and wonders in so much as to deceive (if possible) even the elect. Behold I have told it to you beforehand. If therefore they shall say to you *Behold, he is in the desert* go ye not out. *Behold he is in the closet* believe it not. For as lightning cometh out of the East and appeareth even unto the West, so shall also the coming of the Son of Man be. Wheresoever the body shall be, there shall the eagles be gathered together. And immediately after the tribulations of those days, the sun shall be darkened, and the moon shall not give her light, and the stars shall be moved, and the powers of heavens shall be shaken.[10] And then shall appear the sign of the Son of Man in heaven, and then

shall the tribes of the earth mourn, and they shall see the Son of Man coming in the clouds of heaven, with much power and majesty, and He shall send His angels with a trumpet, and a great sound and they shall gather together His elect from the four winds, from the farthest part of the heavens to the utmost bounds of them. And from the fig tree learn this parable, when the branch thereof is now tender, and the leaves come forth, you know that summer is nigh. So you also, when you shall see all these things, know ye that it is nigh even at the doors. Amen I say to you that this generation shall not pass till all these things shall be done.

The branch is indeed now tender, many leaves have budded out, we need only one more war in which both sides use atomic and hydrogen bombs, and nerve gas, and we shall have inflicted upon ourselves the abominations of desolation which shall reduce the human race to such chaotic conditions that Divine intervention will be our only salvation. Today it is common practice for people, especially those who act willfully or unwillfully, as the agents of the Evil Powers, to blame God for the sorry mess in which we find ourselves. The intelligent person will admit that God cannot be blamed. He gave us our Free Will; He gave us the Commandments as our guide. He gave us Christ as a teacher and living example. If we obstinately refuse to accept the teachings and example of Christ, if we also refuse to obey the Commandments of God, how can we reasonably blame any agency other than ourselves for allowing the Forces of Evil to gain supremacy in this World of ours? Edmund Burke once wrote: "All that is necessary for the triumph of Evil, is that good men do nothing." He wrote a great truth.

The study of comparative religions, in relation to the conditions we are experiencing in the world today, brings the unbiased student to the conclusion that those human beings who worship God, and believe in another life after the death of our mortal bodies, enjoy a religion of Love and Hope. Atheism is a religion of Hate and blackest Despair. Yet, never before in the history of the world, has such a determined effort been put forth to introduce secularism into our lives as since 1846, when C.J. Holyoake, C. Bradlaugh, and others asserted their opinion "THAT HUMAN INTEREST SHOULD BE LIMITED TO CONCERNS OF THE PRESENT LIFE." These advocates of secularism were the predecessors of the most recent flock of false Christs and false Prophets--Karl Marx, Karl Ritter, Lenin, Stalin, Hitler and Mussolini. These men did deceive millions upon millions of people by working great signs and wonders. They deceived many professing Christians who should have known better.

---

[1] The terms Nazi & Naziism are used to indicate and identify the extremist members of the "Right Wing" parties who gave allegiance and loyalty to the totalitarian-minded Aryan War Lords who plotted to use Fascism to further their secret plans and ambitions in exactly the same way as the "International Group" consisting of bankers, monopolists and certain politicians have used Communism and all other groups "Left" of centre to further their secret plans and Totalitarian ambitions.

[2] The terms "True Communist" and "True Nazi" are used to identify the leaders and agents of the two totalitarian ideologies who have been initiated into the Satanic ritual of Illuminism in Grand Orient Freemasonry or the Pagan Aryan Rites used by German Nazi Military Grand Orient Lodges.

[3] The reader must realize the difference between Naziism and Fascism because, contrary to what anti-Fascist propaganda has led so many people to believe, the Fascist Movement, as

started in Italy in 1919, was intended to be a Christian Crusade to combat the Atheistic ideology of Karl Marx and to support "Nationalism" as against "Internationalism" as planned by the leaders of both German Nazi War Lords and the International Bankers, Industrialists and politicians.

4. The Aryan Nazi War Lords must not be confused with the more moderate Junkers who were young Germans who took military training to protect what they considered "Germany's National" Political and economic rights as threatened by International minded groups.

5. One of Britain's greatest Intelligence Officers is Godfather to my daughter Eileen. I have known him intimately since October 1914. I served with him, on occasions, in both World Wars. He and I both investigated this angle of Naziism independently but when we checked our evidence we found we were very close to complete agreement.

6. The term "International Money-Barons" is used to define the International Group of men who control International Banking, Industries, and Trade and Commerce. They are the men who have used Communism to destroy constituted authority, and existing political and religious institutions, in order that they may ultimately usurp undisputed control of the World's resources for themselves.

7. This is an illustration of how the Anti-Communist extremists also use the "Joint Stock Company Principle" and use others to serve their purpose while the actual directors and Instigators remain hidden and unknown to the general public.

8. When Hitler acted contrary to the fundamental principles laid down by Karl Ritter, the German Generals who belonged to the Hard Core of the Nazi Leaders tried to have him assassinated, regardless of the fact that they had originally set him up as the Instrument of their Will.

9. Not all Goldsmiths were Jewish. Only some turned to the practice of usury. One of the richest Goldsmiths is that of the London City Company dating from 1130.

10. The Greek word for Heavens is "Ouranor" from which the Planet Uranus and metal Uranium are named. This predicts the "A" and "H" bombs.

CHAPTER TWO

The English Revolution, 1640-1660

The Forces of Evil realize that in order to win undisputed control of the material assets of the world, and establish an Atheistic Materialistic Totalitarian Dictatorship, it is necessary to destroy all forms of constitutional government and organized religion. In order to do this, the Forces of Evil decided they must divide the peoples of the world against each other on various issues. Dating back into antiquity, the Aryan and Semitic races were driven into enmity against each other to serve the secret ambitions of their atheistic-materialistic leaders. Had the people of the Aryan and Semitic races remained steadfast to their belief in God, and faithful to His commandments, the Forces of Evil could never have accomplished their evil purpose.

The term Aryan actually denotes the lingual groups otherwise known as Indo-European or Indo-Germanic. It comprises two groups: the Western or European, and the Eastern or Armenian. The Aryan languages show a common origin by their vocabulary, system, and inflections. Actually the word Aryan means "An honourable Lord of the Soil." Thus it is that most leaders of the Aryan group in Europe were Landed Barons who maintained strong armed forces to protect their properties. From amongst these Barons came the Aryan War Lords. They in turn organized Naziism, and used Fascism, and all anti-semitic groups right of centre to serve their purpose, and further their secret plans for world domination.

The Chief Divisions of the Aryan groups are the Teutonic, the Romanic, and the Slavic races, who settled in Western Europe. The Turks, the Magyars, the Basques, and the Finns are non-Aryan races. The common ancestors of the Aryan groups dwelt among the Pamirs at a period of remote antiquity.

On the other hand, the Semitic groups are actually divided into two sections. One includes the Assyrian, the Aramaean, the Hebrew, and Phoenician groups. The other section includes the Arabic and Ethiopian groups. The Arabic is the most copious group, and the Aramaean the poorest. The Hebrews occupy an intermediary position.[1]

Today the term Jew is used very loosely to define people who have at one time or another embraced the Jewish Faith. Many of these are not actually Semitic in racial origin. A great number of people who accepted the Jewish Faith are descendants of the Herodians who were Idumeans of Turkish-Mongol blood. They are actually Edomites.[2] The important fact to remember is that among the Jewish leaders, in exactly the same way as among the Aryan leaders, there always has been a small, hard core of men who have been, and still are, Illuminists or Atheists. They may have given lip-service to the Jewish or Christian religions to suit their own purpose, but they never believed in the existence of God. They are Internationalists now. They give allegiance to no particular nation although they have used, on occasion, nationalism to further their causes. Their only concern is to gain greater economic and political power. The ultimate objective of the leaders of both groups is identical. They are determined to win, for themselves, undisputed control of the wealth, natural resources, and manpower of the entire world. They intend to turn the world into *their* conception of a Totalitarian-Godless Dictatorship.

The Non-Semitic and the Turk-Finnish races infiltrated into Europe from Asia sometime around the first century after the advent of Christ. They took the land route north of the Caspian Sea. These peoples are referred to in history as Khazars. They were a pagan people. They settled in Eastern Europe and established the powerful Khazar Kingdom. They expanded their domains by military conquests until, by the end of the 8th century, they occupied the greater portion of Eastern Europe west of the Ural Mountains, and North of the Black Sea. The Khazars ultimately accepted Judaism as their religion in preference to Christianity or Mohammedanism. Synagogues, and schools for teaching Judaism, were built throughout their Kingdom. At the peak of their power, the Khazars were collecting tribute from twenty-five conquered races.

The Great Khazar Kingdom flourished for almost five hundred years. Then, towards the end of the 10th century, the Khazars were defeated in battle by the Varangians (Russians) who swept down upon them from the North. The conquest of the Khazars was completed by the end of the 13th century. The revolutionary movement inspired by the Khazar-Jews went on within the Russian Empire from the 13th century until the Red October Revolution of 1917. The conquest of the Khazars in the 13th century explains how so many people, now commonly referred to as Jews, remained within the Russian Empire.

There is one other important fact which sheds light on the subject of Aryanism and Semitism. The Finns, and other groups generally classified as Varangians (Russians), were of non-Aryan origin and the German people generally speaking have treated them as enemies.

One act of Christ has a great deal of importance in the study of the World Revolutionary Movement. Christ was considered by many a radical who based his reform movement on the worship of Almighty God, obedience to constituted authority, and love of one's neighbours. The story of the life of Christ shows that he loved *all* people except one particular group. He hated the moneylenders with an intensity that seems strange in a man of so mild a character. Jesus repeatedly admonished the moneylenders for their practice of usury. He publicly denounced them as worshippers of Mammon. He said they were of the Synagogue of Satan. (Rev. 2:9). He emphatically expressed His extreme hatred of the moneylenders when he took a whip and drove them out of the Temple. He admonished them in these words: "This Temple was built as the house of God...But you have turned it into a den of thieves." By performing this act of vengeance on the moneylenders, Christ signed his own death warrant.

It was the Illuminati, and the false priests and elders in their pay, who hatched the plot by which Christ would be executed by the Roman soldiers. It was they who supplied the thirty pieces of silver used to bribe Judas. It was they who used their propagandists to misinform and mislead the Mob. It was the agents of the Illuminati who led the Mob when they accepted Barabbas and screamed that Christ be crucified. It was the illuminati who arranged matters so that THE ROMAN SOLDIERS ACTED AS THEIR EXECUTIONERS. Then, after the foul deed had been done, and they had had their revenge, the conspirators stepped into the background and let their guilt rest on the masses of the Jews and their children. History proves they had a fiendish reason for putting the guilt for the death of Christ on the Jewish people. History proves that they intended to use the hate engendered amongst the Jewish people as the result of persecution, to serve their vile purposes, and further their secret totalitarian ambitions. Christ knew all these things. He made His knowledge known in the most dramatic manner possible. As He hung dying on the Cross He prayed to His Heavenly Father and He said: "Father forgive them for they know not what they do." Surely He was praying for the Mob? He was asking forgiveness for the men who had been USED by the Illuminati to be the INSTRUMENT of their revenge. History proves the International Moneylenders have been using the Mob to further their secret ambitions ever since. In the Lenin Institute in Moscow the professors who lecture to aspiring revolutionary leaders from all over the world invariably refer to the Masses as "The Mob." The Illuminati direct all evil forces.

Study of the World Revolutionary Movement (WRM) from the time of Christ to the present day proves that it is unjust to blame the whole Jewish Race for the crimes committed against humanity by a small group of false priests and moneylenders. These men always have been, and still are, *The Secret Power* behind Internationalism. They use Communism today as their manual of action to further their secret plans for ultimate world domination.

Study of history will prove that it is equally unjust to blame the whole German and Italian people for the crimes against humanity committed by the small group of Aryan War Lords who organized Naziism, in the hope that they could defeat International Communism and Political Zionism and give them world domination by military conquest. History proves clearly that the leaders of the two opposing groups have divided the masses of the people regardless of race, colour, or creed, into two opposing camps and then used them all as pawns in the game of International Chess. They play to decide which group will ultimately defeat the other and establish, once and for all, undisputed control over the world, its wealth, its natural resources, its man-power, and its religion. It must be remembered that as the purpose of the Devil is to win men's souls away from God, Satan uses both "Red" Communism and "Black" Naziism to influence the minds of men so that they will embrace EITHER Atheistic ideology. Those who accept EITHER Atheistic ideology sell their souls to the Devil.

Historical events prove the continuity of the evil purpose of the Illuminati. Many theologians agree that this perfect continuity of their Long-Range Plans is positive evidence that they are, as Christ named them, "Of the Synagogue of Satan." Theologians base their opinion on the theory that nothing human could have such a continuing record of evil down through the ages of time. The continuity of evil is the exact opposite of the Apostolic succession of the Roman Catholic Church. In this, as in many other things, we are forcibly reminded of the actual power of the supernatural forces to influence our individual lives, national policy, and international affairs. Arguments of this kind regarding evil-minded Jews are equally applicable to evil-minded Aryans, and evil-minded men of all races, colour and creeds.

History proves that Seneca (4 B.C. to 65 A.D.) died because he, like Christ, tried to expose the corrupt practices and evil influence of the moneylenders who had infiltrated into the Roman Empire. Seneca was a famous Roman philosopher. He was chosen tutor to Nero who became Emperor of Rome. For a long time, Seneca was Nero's best friend, and most trusted advisor. Nero married Poppaea who brought him under the evil influence of the moneylenders. Nero became one of the most infamous rulers the world has ever known. His licentious conduct and depraved habits developed in him a character so base that he lived only to persecute and destroy everything that was good. His acts of revenge took the form of atrocities usually committed in public upon the victims of his wrath. Seneca lost his influence over Nero but he never stopped publicly denouncing the moneylenders for their evil influence and corrupt practices. Finally the moneylenders demanded that Nero take action against Seneca who was very popular with the people. So as not to arouse the wrath of the people against himself, and the moneylenders, Nero ordered Seneca to end his own life.

This is the first recorded case in which the moneylenders made a person commit suicide because he had become troublesome to them, but it was by no means the last. History records dozens of similar suicides, and murders which were made to appear as accidents or suicides.

One of the most notorious in recent years was that of James V. Forrestal. In 1945, Forrestal had been convinced that the American Bankers were closely affiliated with the International Bankers who controlled the Banks of England, France and other countries. He was also convinced, according to his diaries, that the International Money-Barons were the Illuminati and directly responsible for the outbreak of World Wars One and Two. He tried to convince President Roosevelt, and other Top-Level Government officials, of the truth. Either he failed, and committed suicide in a fit of depression, or he was murdered to shut his mouth forever. Murder, made to appear like suicide, has been accepted policy in the top levels of international intrigue for many centuries.[3]

Justinian I (Flavius Anicius Justinus, 483-565 A.D.) wrote his famous book of law, *Corpus Juris Civilis*. He tried to put an end to the illegal methods of traffic and trade indulged in by certain Jewish merchants. By engaging in illegal trade and wholesale smuggling, the Jewish merchants, who were only agents of the Illuminati, obtained unfair advantage over their Gentile competitors. They put them out of business. The book of law, written by Justinian, was accepted as the text book of law right down to the 10th century. Even today it is considered the most important of all documents of jurisprudence. But the moneylenders were able to offset the good Justinian tried to do.[4] Funk & Wagnall's *Jewish Encyclopedia* has this to say about the Jews in those days: "They enjoyed full religious liberty...Minor offices were open to them. The trade in slaves constituted the main source of livelihood for the Roman Jews, and decrees against this traffic were issued in 335, 336, 339, 384 A.D., etc."

There is the story in black and white. But history reveals that the Jewish merchants and moneylenders did not confine their illegal activities to the slave trade. It is recorded that they engaged in every form of illegal traffic including the drug trade, prostitution, wholesale smuggling of liquors, perfumes, jewels, and other dutiable goods. In order to protect their illegal trade and traffic, they bribed and corrupted officials; by use of drugs, liquors and women, they destroyed the morals of the people. History records that Justinian, although Emperor of the Roman Empire, wasn't strong enough to put a stop to their activities.[5]

Edward Gibbon (1737-1794) deals with the corrupting influence of the Jewish merchants and moneylenders. He credits them with contributing greatly to "The Decline and Fall of the Roman Empire." He wrote the book with that title. Gibbon gives considerable space to the part Poppaea, Nero's wife, played in bringing about the conditions which started the people of Rome reeling drunkenly towards their own destruction. With the fall of the Roman Empire, Jewish predominance was established. The nations of Europe entered into what historians name "The Dark Ages".

The Encyclopedia Britannica has this to say on the subject: "There was an inevitable tendency for them [the Jewish merchants and moneylenders] to specialize in commerce for which their acumen, and ubiquity, gave them special qualifications. In the Dark Ages the commerce of Western Europe was largely in their hands, in particular, the Slave Trade."

Jewish control of trade and commerce, both legal and illegal, grew tighter and tighter. It spread far and wide, until every European country's economy was more or less in their hands. Evidence in the form of Polish and Hungarian coins bearing Jewish inscriptions gives some indication of the power they exerted in financial matters during those days. The fact that the Jews made a special effort to issue and control currency, supports the opinion that the moneylenders had adopted the slogan, "Let us issue and control the money of a nation and we care not who make its laws" long before Amschel Mayer Bauer (1743-1812) used the slogan to explain to his co-conspirators the reason the Jewish moneylenders had obtained control of the Bank of England in 1694.[6]

The barons, who were the leaders of Aryanism, determined they would break the Jewish control of trade, commerce and money in Europe. It was with this purpose in mind that in 1095 they obtained the support of certain Christian rulers to start The Crusades or Holy Wars.[7] Between 1095 and 1271, eight Crusades were organized. Officially, the Crusades were military expeditions undertaken to ensure the safety of Pilgrims who wished to visit the Holy Sepulchre and set up Christian Rule in Palestine. In actual fact they were wars fomented for the purpose of dividing the population of Europe into two camps: one camp pro-Jewish and the other Anti-Jewish. In more recent years, the Secret Powers divided the white race into Semitic and Anti-Semitic groups. Some of the Crusades were successful, some were not. The net result was that, in 1271, Palestine still remained in the hands of the "Infidels," although the countries of Christendom had spent MILLIONS IN MONEY and treasure to finance the Crusades and sacrificed MILLIONS OF HUMAN LIVES fighting those Holy Wars. Strange to relate, the Jewish moneylenders grew richer and stronger than ever.

There is one phase of the Crusades which must not be overlooked when the "Causes" are being studied in relation to the "Effects" they produced in later years. In 1215, the Roman Catholic Hierarchy held the Fourth Lateran Council. The main topic under consideration was Jewish aggression in all the countries of Europe. During this period of history, the Rulers of the Church and the Rulers of the State worked in unity. The rulers of the Church, after due deliberation, expressed themselves in favor of continuing the Crusades. They also drew up, and passed Decrees, designed to put an end to usury and the Jewish moneylender's practice of using unethical methods in traffic and trade to obtain unfair advantage over Gentile competitors, and to curb corrupt and immoral practices. To achieve this purpose, the dignitaries attending the Fourth Lateran Council decreed that in the future the Jews be restricted to living in their own quarters. Jews were absolutely prohibited from hiring Christians as their employees. This decree was passed because Jewish moneylenders and merchants operated on the Joint Stock Company principle. They employed Christians to act as their *front* men while they hid in the background directing operations. This was convenient because, when anything went wrong, the Christian *front* men got the blame, and the punishment, while they got off scot-free. In addition, by the Decrees, Jews were absolutely prohibited from employing Christian females in their homes and establishments. This decree was passed because evidence was produced to prove that young females were systematically seduced, and then turned into prostitutes; their masters used them to obtain control over influential officials. Other decrees made it unlawful for Jews to engage in many commercial activities. But even the power of the Church, supported by most Christian officials of the State, could not make the Money-Barons amenable to the law. All the decrees accomplished was to intensify the hatred the Illuminati had for the Church of Christ, and they started a continuing campaign to separate the Church from the State. To achieve this purpose they introduced the idea of secularism amongst the laity.

In 1253, the French government ordered the Jews expelled because they refused to obey the law. Most of the Jews who were expelled went over to England. By 1255, the Jewish moneylenders had obtained absolute control of many Church dignitaries and most of the nobility.[8] That the moneylenders, the Rabbis, and Elders belonged to the Illuminati was proved by evidence given during the investigation ordered by King Henry III into the *ritual* slaying of St. Hugh of Lincoln in 1255. Eighteen Jews were proved to have been the culprits. They were tried, found guilty, and executed. In 1272, King Henry died. Edward I became King of England. He determined that the Jewish leaders must give up the practice of usury. In 1275, he had Parliament pass the *Statutes of Jewry*. They were designed to curb the power Jewish usurers were exerting over their debtors, both Christians and fellow Jews. The *Statutes of Jewry* were probably the first legislation in which *The Commons* in Parliament had an active part. They cannot be classified as Anti-Semitic because they actually protected the interests of honest and law-abiding Jews.[9]

But, as had happened so often before, the Jewish moneylenders thought that the power they could exert over both the Church and the State would permit them to defy the king's decree in the same way as they had set at nought those passed by the Lateran Council. They made a grave mistake. In 1290, King Edward issued another decree. *All* Jews were expelled from England. This was the start of what historians call *The Great Eviction*.

After Edward I started the ball rolling, all the Crowned Heads of Europe followed his example. In 1306, France expelled the Jews. In 1348, Saxony followed suit; .in 1360, Hungary; in 1370, Belgium; in 1380, Slovakia; in 1420, Austria; in 1444, The Netherlands; in 1492, Spain.

The expulsion of the Jews from Spain has special signification. It throws light on the Spanish Inquisition. Most people have the idea the Inquisition was instituted by Roman Catholics to persecute Protestants who had broken away from the Church. As a matter of fact the Inquisition, as introduced by Pope Innocent III, was a means of unmasking heretics and infidels who were masquerading as Christians for the purpose of destroying the Christian Religion from within.[10] It didn't make the slightest difference to the Inquisitors whether the accused was Jew or Gentile, black or white. The terrible ceremony of the "*Auto-da-Fé*" or "Act of Faith" was specially designed to be used in connection with the execution of all convicted heretics, and infidels, when Torquemada (1420-1498) was Grand Inquisitor.[11]

It is these hidden incidents which reveal so much truth. It was in Spain, during the 14th century, that the Jewish moneylenders first succeeded in having the loans that they made to the State secure by the right to collect the taxes levied upon the people. They used such cruelty, when demanding their *Pound of Flesh*, that it only required the inflammatory oratory of the priest Fernando Martenez to produce mass action which ended in one of the bloodiest massacres recorded in history. Here again is a perfect example of how thousands of innocent Jews were victimized, for the sins and crimes committed against humanity by just a few.[12]

In 1495, Lithuania expelled the Jews; in 1498, Portugal; in 1540, Italy; in 1551, Bavaria. It is important to remember that during the general evictions, certain wealthy and influential Jews managed to obtain sanctuary in Bordeaux, Avignon, certain Papal States,

Marseille, Northern Alsace, and part of northern Italy. But, as stated in the *Encyclopedia Britannica*, "The masses of the Jewish people were thus to be found once more, in the East and in the Polish and Turkish Empires." The few communities suffered to remain in Western Europe were meantime subjected at last to all the restrictions which earlier Ages had usually allowed to remain as an ideal, so that, in a sense, the Jewish *Dark Ages* may be said to begin with the Renaissance. This admission would indicate there is some justification for the claim made by certain historians that not until the Western European nations wrested economic control from the Jewish moneylenders did the rebirth of western civilization occur.

Following the Great Eviction, the Jews again resumed living in Ghettos or Kahals. Thus, isolated from the masses of the population, the Jews were under the direction and control of the Rabbis and Elders, many of whom were influenced by the Illuminati and the wealthy Jewish moneylenders who remained in their various sanctuaries. In the Ghettos, agents of the Illuminati inspired a spirit of hatred and revenge in the hearts of the Jewish people against those who had evicted them. The Rabbis reminded them that, as the chosen people of God, the day would come when they would have their revenge and inherit the earth.

It should be mentioned that most Jews who settled in Eastern Europe were restricted to living within the "Pale of Settlement" located on the western borders of Russia and extending from the shores of the Baltic Sea in the north, to the shores of the Black Sea in the South. Most of them were Khazar Jews.[13] The Khazar Jews were noted for their Yiddish culture, their rapacious practices in financial matters, and their lack of ethics in commercial transactions. They should not be confused with the Biblical Hebrews who are mild mannered and, generally speaking, pastoral people.

Within the Ghettos, in an atmosphere of hatred, the desire for revenge was developed by the agents of the Illuminati. They organized these negative conditions into the World Revolutionary Movement, based on *Terrorism*. From its very inception the international-minded Money-Barons, and their High Priests, designed, financed, and controlled the World Revolutionary Movement. They used it as the instrument by which they would obtain their revenge on the Christian churches, and the Crowned Heads of Europe.

History proves how the Money-Barons developed the revolutionary movement into International Communism as we know it today. They organized individual acts of terrorism into a disciplined revolutionary movement. They then planned systematic infiltration of the Jews back into the countries from which they had been expelled. Because their reentry was illegal, the only method by which infiltration could be accomplished was to establish Jewish *Undergrounds*. Because the Jews who infiltrated into the *Undergrounds* of the European cities could not obtain lawful employment, they were supplied with funds with which to develop the *Black Market* system. They indulged in every kind of illegal traffic and trade. Working on the principle of the Joint Stock Co., the identity of the Money-Barons who owned and controlled this vast underground system always remained secret.[14]

Count de Poncins, Mrs. Nesta Webster, Sir Walter Scott, and many other authors and historians have suspected that the Illuminati and a group of Internationalists were *The Secret Power* behind the World Revolutionary Movement, but it was not until recently that sufficient evidence was pieced together to prove that what they suspected was an actual fact. As the events of history are unrolled in their chronological sequence, it will be seen how the Illuminati used the Semitic groups and the Aryan groups to serve their purpose, and involved millions upon millions of people in revolutions and wars to further their own secret and selfish ambitions. William Foss and Cecil Gerahty, who wrote *The Spanish Arena,* said:

> The question of who are the leading figures behind the attempt of the JOINT STOCK COMPANY domination of the world, and how they obtain their ends, is beyond the scope of this book. But it is one of the important *Livres à faire* yet to be written. IT WILL HAVE TO BE WRITTEN BY A MAN OF THE HIGHEST COURAGE WHO WILL COUNT HIS LIFE AS NOTHING COMPARED WITH ENLIGHTENING THE WORLD AS TO WHAT THE SATANIC SELF-APPOINTED PRIESTHOOD WOULD ORDAIN.

How successful the plan–to infiltrate back into the countries from which they had been expelled–turned out to be can best be judged by the following records. The Jews were back in England in 1600; they were back in Hungary in 1500. They were expelled again in 1582; they were back in Slovakia in 1562 but were expelled again in 1744. They were back in Lithuania in 1700. Regardless of how many times they were expelled, there always remained the Jewish underground from which the revolutionary activities of the *Secret Powers* were conducted.

Because King Edward I of England had been the first to expel the Jews, the Jewish Money-Barons in France, Holland, and Germany decided it would be poetic justice if they tried out their planned revolutionary technique in England first. They used their underground agents, or *Cells*, to cause trouble between the king and his government, employers and labour, ruling class and workers, Church and State. The plotters injected controversial issues into politics and religion to divide the people into two opposing camps.[15] First they divided the people in England into Catholics and Protestants; then they divided the Protestants into Conformists and Non-Conformists.

When King Charles I was brought into disagreement with his Parliament, a Jewish Money-Baron in Holland, named Manasseh Ben Israel, had his agents contact Oliver Cromwell. They offered him large sums of money if he would carry out their plan to overthrow the British Throne. Manasseh Ben Israel and other German and French moneylenders financed Cromwell. Fernandez Carvajal of Portugal, often referred to in history as *The Great Jew*, became Cromwell's Chief Military Contractor. He reorganized the *Round Heads* into a model army. He provided them with the best arms and equipment that money could buy. Once the conspiracy was under way, hundreds of trained revolutionaries were smuggled into England and were absorbed into the Jewish *Underground*. The same thing goes on in America today.

The head of the Jewish underground in England at that time was a Jew named De Souze. The Great Jew, Fernandez Carvajal, had used his influence to have De Souze appointed Portuguese Ambassador. It was in his house, protected by diplomatic immunity, that the leaders of the Jewish revolutionary underground remained hidden and worked out their plots and intrigue.[16]

Once the revolution had been decided upon, the Jewish plotters introduced Calvinism into England to split Church and State, and divide the people. Contrary to general belief, Calvinism is of Jewish origin. It was deliberately conceived to split the adherents of the Christian religions, and divide the people. Calvin's real name was Cohen! When he went from Geneva to France to start preaching his doctrine, he became known as Cauin. Then in England it became Calvin. History proves that there is hardly a revolutionary plot that wasn't hatched in Switzerland; there is hardly a Jewish revolutionary leader who hasn't changed his name.

At the B'nai B'rith celebrations held in Paris, France, in 1936, Cohen, Cauvin, or Calvin, whatever his name may have been, was enthusiastically acclaimed to have been of Jewish descent.[17]

In addition to the religious controversy, the revolutionary leaders organized armed mobs to aggravate every situation injected into politics and labour by their masters. Isaac Disraeli, 1766-1848, a Jew, and father of Benjamin Disraeli who afterwards became Lord Beaconsfield, deals with this angle of the British Revolution in detail in his two-volume story *The Life of Charles II.* He remarks that he obtained considerable information from the records of Melchior de Salem, a Jew, who was French Envoy to the British Government at that time. Disraeli draws attention to the great similarity, or pattern, of the revolutionary activities which preceded both the British and the French revolutions. In other words, the handiwork of the secret and real directors of the World Revolutionary Movement (WRM) could clearly be seen in both—a fact which we will proceed to prove.

The evidence which ABSOLUTELY convicts Oliver Cromwell of participating in the Jewish Revolutionary Plot was obtained by Lord Alfred Douglas, who edited a weekly review, *Plain English,* published by the North British Publishing Co. In an article which appeared in the issue of September 3, 1921, he explained how his friend, Mr. L.D. Van Valckert of Amsterdam, Holland, had come into possession of a missing volume of records of the Synagogue of Mulheim. This volume had been lost during the Napoleonic wars. The volume contains records of letters written to and answered by the Directors of the Synagogue.

They are written in German. One entry, dated June 16th, 1647, reads:

> From O.C. (*i.e.* Olivier Cromwell) to Ebenezer Pratt.

> In return for financial support will advocate admission of Jews to England. This however impossible while Charles living. Charles cannot be executed without trial, adequate grounds for which do not at present exist. Therefore advise that Charles be assassinated, but will have nothing to do with arrangements for procuring an assassin, though willing to help in his escape.

In reply to this dispatch the records show E. Pratt wrote a letter dated July 12th, 1647 addressed to Oliver Cromwell.

> Will grant financial aid as soon as Charles removed, and Jews admitted. Assassination too dangerous. Charles should be given an opportunity to escape.[18] His recapture will then make trial and execution possible. The support will be liberal, but useless to discuss terms until trial commences.

On November 12th that same year, Charles was given the opportunity to escape. He was of course recaptured. Hollis and Ludlow, authorities on this chapter of history, are both on record as considering the flight as the stratagem of Cromwell. After Charles had been recaptured, events moved apace. Cromwell had the British Parliament purged of most members he knew were loyal to the king. Notwithstanding this drastic action, when the House sat all night on December 5th, 1648, the majority agreed, "That the concessions offered by the king were satisfactory to a settlement."

Any such settlement would have disqualified Cromwell from receiving the blood-money promised him by the International Money-Barons through their agent, E. Pratt, so

Cromwell struck again. He ordered Colonel Pryde to purge Parliament of those members who had voted in favour of a settlement with the King. What then happened is referred to, in school history books, as *Pryde's Purge.*[19] When the purge was finished, fifty members remained. They are recorded as *The Rump Parliament.* They usurped absolute power. On January 9th, 1649, "A HIGH COURT OF JUSTICE" was proclaimed for the purpose of putting the king of England on trial. Two-thirds of the members of the Court were "Levellers" from Cromwell's Army. The conspirators couldn't find an English lawyer who would draw up a criminal charge against King Charles. Carvajal instructed an alien Jew, Isaac Dorislaus, Manasseh Ben Israel's Agent in England, to draw up the indictment upon which King Charles was tried. Charles was found guilty of the charges levelled against him by the International Jewish moneylenders, not by the people of England. On January 30th, 1649, he was publicly beheaded in front of the Banqueting House at Whitehall, London. The Jewish moneylenders, directed by the High Priests of the Synagogue of Satan, had had their revenge because Edward I had expelled the Jews from England. Oliver Cromwell received his Blood-Money just as Judas had.

History proves that the International Jewish moneylenders had a purpose other than revenge for getting rid of Charles. They removed him to obtain control of England's economy and government. They planned to involve many European countries in war with England. Great sums of money are needed to fight wars. By loaning the Crowned Heads of Europe the money required to fight the wars they fomented, the Internationalists were able to rapidly increase the National Debts of all European Nations.

The chronological sequence of events, from the execution of King Charles in 1649 to the institution of the Bank of England in 1694, shows how the National Debt was increased. The International Bankers used intrigue and cunning to throw Christians at each others' throats.

1649 Cromwell, financed by Jews, waged war in Ireland. Captures Drogheda and Wexford. British Protestants blamed for persecution of Irish Catholics.

1650 Montrose in rebellion against Cromwell. Captured and executed.

1651 Charles II invades England. Defeated and flees back to France.

1652 England involved in war with Dutch.

1653 Cromwell proclaims himself Lord Protector of England.

1654 England involved in more wars.

1656 Trouble started in American Colonies.

1657 Death of Cromwell—Son Richard named Protector.

1659 Richard, disgusted with intrigue, resigns.

1660 General Monk occupies London, Charles II proclaimed King.

1661 Truth revealed regarding intrigue entered into by Cromwell and his cohorts Ireton and Bradshaw causes serious public reaction. Bodies are exhumed and hung from gallows on Tyburn Hill, London.

1662 Religious strife is engendered to divide members of the Protestant denominations. Nonconformists to the established Church of England are persecuted.

1664 England is again involved in war with Holland.

1665 A great depression settles over England. Unemployment and shortages of food undermine the health of the people and the Great Plague breaks out.[20]

1666 England involved in war with France and Holland.

1667 Cabal agents start new religious and political strife.[21]

1674 England and Holland make peace. The men directing international intrigue change their characters. They become matchmakers. They elevate plain Mr. William Stradholder to the rank of Captain-General of the Dutch Forces. He became William Prince of Orange. It was arranged that he meet Mary, the eldest daughter of the Duke of York. The Duke was only one place removed from becoming King of England.

1677 Princess Mary of England married William Prince of Orange. To place William Prince of Orange upon the Throne of England it was necessary to get rid of both Charles II, and the Duke of York, who was slated to become James II.

1683 The Rye House Plot was hatched. The intention was to assassinate both King Charles II and the Duke of York. It failed.

1685 King Charles II died. The Duke of York became King James II of England. Immediately a campaign of *L'Infamie* was started against James II. The Duke of Monmouth was persuaded, or bribed, into leading an insurrection to overthrow the king. On June 30th, the Battle of Sedgemoor was fought. Monmouth was defeated and captured. He was executed July 15th. In August, Judge Jeffreys opened what historians have named *The Bloody Assizes*. Over three hundred persons concerned in the Monmouth Rebellion were sentenced to death under circumstances of atrocious cruelty. Nearly one thousand others were condemned to be sold as slaves. This was a typical example of how the Secret Powers, working behind the scenes, create conditions for which other people are blamed. Others are aroused to take active opposition against those they blame. They in turn are liquidated. King James still had to be disposed of before William of Orange could be placed on the throne to carry out their mandate. Every person in England was bewitched and bewildered. They were not allowed to know the truth. They blamed everyone and everything except the "Secret Powers" who were pulling the strings. Then the conspirators made their next move.

1688 They ordered William Prince of Orange to land in England at Torbay. This he did on November 5th. King James abdicated. He fled to France. He had become unpopular by reason of the campaign of *L'Infamie*, intrigue and his own foolishness and culpability.

1689 William of Orange and Mary were proclaimed King and Queen of England. King James did not intend to give up the Throne without a fight. He was a Catholic, so the Secret Powers set up William of Orange as the Champion of the Protestant Faith. On February 15th, 1689, King James landed in Ireland. The Battle of The Boyne was fought by men of definite, and opposing, religious convictions. The Battle has been celebrated by Orangemen on the 12th of July ever since. There is probably not one Orangeman in ten thousand who knows that all the wars and rebellions fought from 1640 to 1689 were fomented by the International moneylenders for the purpose of putting themselves in position to control British politics and economy. Their first objective was to obtain permission to institute a Bank of England and consolidate and secure the debts Britain owed them for loans made to her to fight the wars they instigated. History shows how they completed their plans.

In the final analysis, none of the countries and people involved in the wars and revolutions obtained any lasting benefits. No permanent or satisfactory solution was reached regarding the political, economic, and religious issues involved. The only people to benefit were the small group of moneylenders who financed the wars and revolutions, and their friends and agents, who supplied the armies, the ships, and the munitions.

It is important to remember that as soon as the Dutch General was sitting upon the throne of England, he persuaded the British Treasury to borrow £1,250,000 from the Jewish bankers who had put him there. The school book history informs our children that the negotiations were conducted by Sir John Houblen and Mr. William Patterson on behalf of the British Government with moneylenders WHOSE IDENTITY REMAINED SECRET.

Search of historical documents reveals that in order to maintain complete secrecy, the negotiations regarding the terms of the loan were carried on in a church. In the days of Christ, the moneylenders used the Temple. In the days of William of Orange they desecrated a church.

The international moneylenders agreed to accommodate the British Treasury to the extent of £1,250,000, providing they could dictate their own terms and conditions. This was agreed to. The terms were in part:

1. That the names of those who made the loan remain secret and that they be granted a Charter to establish a Bank of England.[22]

2. That the directors of the Bank of England be granted the legal right to establish the Gold Standard for currency by which —

3. They could make loans to the value of £10 for every £1 value of gold they had on deposit in their vaults.

4. That they be permitted to consolidate the national debt, and secure payment of amounts due as principal and interest by direct taxation of the people.

Thus, for the sum of £1,250,000, King William of Orange sold the people of England into economic bondage. The Jewish moneylenders gained their ambitions. They had usurped the power to issue and control the currency of the nation. And, having secured that power, they cared not who made the laws.

Just what the acceptance of the Gold Standard meant is best illustrated by citing a simple transaction. The directors of the Bank of England could loan £1,000 for every £100 worth of gold they had on deposit as security. They collected interest on the full £1,000 loan. At 5 per cent this amounted to £50 a year. Therefore at the end of the first year the bankers collected back 50 per cent of the amount they had originally put up to secure the loan. If a private individual wished to obtain a loan, the bankers made him put up security, in the form of property, stocks, or bonds, much in excess of the value of the loan he required. If he failed to meet payments of principal and interest, foreclosure proceedings were taken against his property, and the moneylenders obtained many times the value of the loan.

The international bankers never intended that England be allowed to pay off the national indebtedness. The plan was to create international conditions which would plunge ALL nations concerned deeper and deeper into their debt.[23]

As far as England is concerned, in only four years, 1694 to 1698, the national debt was increased from one to sixteen million pounds sterling. This debt accumulated because of wars. It is interesting to note that John Churchill, 1650-1722, became the leading military figure during this period of English history. Because of his military genius, and his services to Britain, he was created the first Duke of Marlborough.[24]

The Secret Power behind the World Revolutionary Movement pulled the necessary strings and brought about The Wars of the Spanish Succession. In 1701, the Duke of Marlborough was made Commander-in-chief of the armed forces of Holland. No less an authority than the Jewish Encyclopedia records the fact that FOR HIS MANY SERVICES THE DUKE OF MARLBOROUGH RECEIVED NOT LESS THAN £6,000 A YEAR FROM THE DUTCH JEWISH BANKER, SOLOMON MEDINA.

The events leading up to the French Revolution show how between 1698 and 1815 the National Debt of Britain was increased to £885,000,000. By 1945 the British National Debt had reached the astronomical figure of £22,503,532,372, and for the years 1945-46 the carrying charges alone amounted to £445,446,241.

[1.] See *Pears Cyclopedia*, pages 514 and 647.

[2.] See *Jewish Encyclopedia* Vol. 5, p. 41: 1925. It states, "Edom is in Modern Jewry". Also Professor Lothrop Stoddard the eminent Ethnologist states: "The Jews' own records admit that 82 per cent of those who subscribe to the Political Zionist movement are Ashkenazim, so-called Jews, but not Semitic. There are many different opinions on these racial matters.

[3.] *The Forrestal Diaries*, Viking press, New York, 1951.

[4.] Some readers claim Justinian had no such purpose. I claim knowledge of wrong spurs men to create corrective legislation and laws.

[5.] The same evil influences are responsible for the same evil conditions which exist in all big cities today.

[6.] Bauer is the Jewish Goldsmith who established "The House of Rothschild" in Frankfurt-on-the-Main. He and his *confrères* plotted the French Revolution of 1789.

[7.] Because hate and revenge are the Stock-in-Trade of the forces of evil, they will use any pretext to foment wars and revolutions even to using the name of God, whom they hate.

[8.] The book *Aaron of Lincoln*. Shapiro-Valentine & Co. gives interesting information regarding this period of history. Valentine's *Jewish Encyclopedia* has this to say. "Their numbers and prosperity increased. Aaron of Lincoln (whose house still stands to this day) became the richest man in England. His financial transactions covering the whole country and concerning many of the leading Nobles and Churchmen.... On his death his properties passed to the Crown, and a special branch of the Exchequer had to be created to deal with the estates.

[9.] The Statutes of Jewry were printed in detail as appendix 1 in *The Nameless War* by Captain A.H.M. Ramsay. Because the Jews were being evicted from all European countries, Chemor, Rabbi of Arles in Provence, sought advice from the Sanhedrin, then located in Constantinople. His appeal was dated Jan. 13th, 1489. The reply arrived back November 1489. It was signed V.S.S. -V.F.F. Prince of the Jews. It advised the Rabbis to use the tactics of "The Trojan Horse" Christian and make their sons priests, laymen, lawyers, and doctors, etc. so they could destroy the Christian structure from within.

10. *The Encyclopedia Britannica* on page 67, Vol. 13, 1947 has this to say: "The 14th Century was the Golden Age of the Jews in Spain. In 1391, the preaching of a Priest of Seville, Fernando Martenez, led to the first general massacre of the Jews who were envied for their prosperity and hated because they were the king's tax collectors.

11. This is dealt with more fully in the chapters on Spain.

12. H.G. Wells defines the differences very clearly in his *Outline of History*, pages 493-494.

13. It does even today. Illegal entry into the United States and into Palestine has reached unprecedented numbers since the end of World War Two. Evidence will be produced to prove the Underground is invariably associated with the Anti-Social characters who constitute the Underworld.

14. Sombirt's work, *The Jews and Modern Capitalism*, and the *Jewish Encyclopedia*, bear out the above statement.

15. This policy has been common practice ever since. The Soviet Embassies in every country have been turned into the Headquarters of intrigue and espionage as further evidence will prove.

16. This fact was commented upon in the Catholic Gazette in February of that year.

17. Charles was in custody at this time.

18. It is important to note that school history books make no mention of the two opposing groups of men who have been the "Secret Power" behind International Affairs who made history. This policy seems to have been by tacit agreement.

19. The outbreak of the Great Fire of London, known as *The Great Cleaner*, ended the plague.

20. The word Cabal is closely related to the Cabala, a mysterious Hebrew theosophy dating back into antiquity, but which became very active during the 10th and succeeding centuries. Cabala was announced as "a special revelation" which enabled Rabbis to explain to the Jewish people the hidden meanings of the sacred writings.

21. *Pears Cyclopedia* (57th edition, page 529) says, "Cabalism was later carried to great excess." Cabalist leaders pretended to read signs and evidence in letters and forms and numbers contained in the Scriptures. The French named this mysterious rite "Cabale." They used this term to designate any group of political or private intriguers. The English adopted the term Cabal because the chief personages concerned with Cabalistic intrigue in England were Clifford, Ashley, Buckingham, Arlington, and Lauderdale, in that order. The first letter of their names spells Cabal! Cabalists were the instigators of various forms of political and religious unrest during the unhappy reign of Charles II.

22. The identity of the men who control the Bank of England still remains a secret. The Macmillan Committee appointed in 1929 to throw light on the subject failed completely. Mr. Montague Norman, the official Head of the Bank of England was most evasive and non-committal in any answer he made to the committee. For further particulars read Facts about the Bank of England by A.N. Field, p. 4.

23. If such a policy is carried to its logical conclusion, it is only a matter of time before the international moneylenders control the wealth, natural resources, and man-power of the entire world. History shows how rapidly they have progressed toward their goal since 1694.

24. The duke is the direct ancestor of Sir Winston Churchill, the Prime Minister of England today... i.e. 1954—Churchill is self-acknowledged as having been the foremost Zionist of this era. He is the man most responsible for influencing the United Nations to create the State of Israel.

CHAPTER THREE

The men who caused the French Revolution of 1789

In the previous chapter, evidence was given to prove how a small group of foreign moneylenders, operating through their English agents, remained anonymous while they secured control of that nation's economy for the modest sum of £1,250,000. Evidence will now be produced to identify some of these International Jewish moneylenders and prove that they, or their successors, plotted, planned and helped finance the Great French Revolution of 1789, exactly the same way as they plotted, planned and financed the English Revolution of 1640-1649. In succeeding chapters, evidence will be produced to prove that the descendants of these same International Jewish Financiers have been *The Secret Power* behind every war and revolution from 1789 onwards.

The Jewish Encyclopedia says *Edom is in modern Jewry*. This is a very important admission, because the word *Edom means Red*. History reveals that a Jewish goldsmith, Amschel Moses Bauer, tired of his wandering in Eastern Europe, decided in 1750 to settle down in Frankfurt-on-the-Main in Germany. He opened a shop, or Counting House, in the Judenstrasse district. Over the door of his shop he placed as his sign of business *A RED SHIELD*. It is of the greatest importance to remember that the Jews in Eastern Europe, who belonged to the revolutionary movement based on *terrorism*, had also adopted *The Red Flag* as their emblem because it represented *blood*.

Amschel Moses Bauer had a son born in 1743, and he named him Amschel Mayer Bauer. The father died in 1754 when his son was only eleven years of age. The boy had shown great ability, and extraordinary intelligence, and his father had taught him everything possible about the rudimentary principles of the money-lending business. It had been the father's intention to have his son trained as a Rabbi, but his own death intervened.

A few years after his father's death, Amschel Mayer Bauer was employed by the Oppenheimer Bank as a clerk. He soon proved his natural ability for the banking business, and was rewarded with a junior partnership. Later he returned to Frankfurt where he secured control and ownership of the business which had been established by his father in 1750. The Red Shield was still proudly displayed over the door. Knowing the secret significance of the Red Shield, Amschel Mayer Bauer decided to adopt it as the new family name. "Red shield" in German was written *Rothe Schild*, and thus *The House of Rothschild* came into being.

Amschel Mayer Bauer lived until 1812. He had five sons. All of them were specially trained to become Captains of High Finance. Nathan, one of the sons, showed exceptional ability and, at the age of twenty-one, went to England with the definite purpose of securing control of the Bank of England. The purpose was to use this control to work in conjunction with his father and other brothers to set up and consolidate an International Banking Monopoly in Europe.

The combined wealth of the International Banking Pool could then be used to further the secret ambitions his father had made known to all his sons. To prove his ability, Nathan Rothschild turned £20,000, with which he had been entrusted, into £60,000 in three years.

In studying the World Revolutionary Movement, it is important to remember that *The Red Flag* was the symbol of the French Revolution and every revolution since. More significant still is the fact that when Lenin, financed by International Bankers, overthrew the Russian Government and established the first Totalitarian Dictatorship in 1917, the design of the flag was a Red Flag, with a Hammer and Sickle, and *the star of Judea* imposed.

In 1773, when Mayer Rothschild was only thirty years of age, he invited twelve other wealthy and influential men to meet him in Frankfurt. His purpose was to convince them that if they agreed to pool their resources, they could then finance and control the World Revolutionary Movement and use it as their *Manual of Action* to win ultimate control of the wealth, natural resources, and man-power of the entire world.

Rothschild revealed how the English Revolution had been organized. He pointed out the mistakes and errors that had been made. The revolutionary period had been too long. The elimination of reactionaries had not been accomplished with sufficient speed and ruthlessness. The planned reign of terror, by which the subjugation of the masses was to be accomplished speedily, had not been put into effective operation. Even after all these mistakes had been made, the initial purpose of the revolution had been achieved. The bankers who instigated the revolution had established control of the national economy and consolidated the national debt. By means of intrigue carried out on an international scale, they had increased the national debt steadily by loaning the money to fight the wars and rebellions they had fomented since 1694.

Basing his arguments on logic and sound reasoning, Mayer Rothschild pointed out that the financial results obtained as the result of the English Revolution would be as nothing when compared to the financial rewards to be obtained by a French Revolution, provided those present agreed to unity of purpose and put into effect his carefully thought-out and revised revolutionary plan. The project would be backed by all the power that could be purchased with their pooled resources. This agreement reached, Mayer Rothschild unfolded his revolutionary plan. By clever manipulation of their combined wealth, it would be possible to create such adverse economic conditions that the masses would be reduced to a state bordering on starvation by unemployment. By use of cleverly conceived propaganda it would be easy to place the blame for the adverse economic conditions on the King, His Court, the Nobles, the Church, Industrialists, and the employers of labour. Their paid propagandists would arouse feelings of hatred and revenge against the ruling classes by exposing all real and alleged cases of extravagance, licentious conduct, injustice, oppression, and persecution. They would also invent infamies to bring into disrepute others who might, if left alone, interfere with their overall plans.[1]

After the general introduction to build up an enthusiastic reception for the plot he was about to unfold, Rothschild turned to a manuscript and proceeded to read a carefully prepared plan of action. The following is what I have been assured is a condensed version of the plot by which the conspirators hoped to obtain ultimate undisputed control of the wealth, natural resources, and man-power of the entire world.

1. The speaker started to unfold the plot by saying that because the majority of men were inclined to *evil* rather than to *good,* the best results in governing them could be obtained by using violence and terrorism and not by academic discussions. The speaker reasoned that in the beginning human society had been subject to brutal and blind force which was afterwards changed to LAW. He argued that LAW was

FORCE only in disguise. He reasoned it was logical to conclude that, "*By the laws of nature right lies in force.*"

2. He next asserted that political freedom is an *idea* and not a *fact*. He stated that in order to usurp political power all that was necessary was to preach "Liberalism" so that the electorate, for the sake of an idea, would yield some of their power and prerogatives which the plotters could then gather together into their own hands.

3. The speaker asserted that the *Power of Gold* had usurped the power of liberal rulers even then (1773). He reminded his audience that there had been a time when FAITH had ruled but stated that once FREEDOM had been substituted for FAITH, the people did not know how to use it in moderation. He argued that because of this fact it was logical to assume that they could use the idea of FREEDOM to bring about "CLASS WARS." He pointed out that it was immaterial to the success of his plan whether the established governments were destroyed by internal or external foes because the victor had of necessity to seek the aid of "Capital" which "*is entirely in our hands.*"[2]

4. He argued that the use of any and all means to reach their final goal was justified on the grounds that the ruler who governed by the moral code was not a skilled politician because he left himself vulnerable and in an unstable position on his throne. He said, "*Those who wish to rule must have recourse to cunning and to make-believe because great national qualities like frankness and honesty, are vices in politics.*"[3]

5. He asserted: "*Our right lies in force. The word RIGHT is an abstract thought and proves nothing. I find a new RIGHT...to attack by the RIGHT of the strong, and to scatter to the winds all existing forces of order and regulation, to reconstruct all existing institutions, and to become* the sovereign Lord of all those who left to us the RIGHTS to their powers by laying them down *voluntarily in their 'Liberalism.'*"

6. He then admonished his listeners with these words: "*The power of our resources must remain invisible until the very moment when it has gained such strength that no cunning or force can undermine it.*" He warned them that any deviation from the *Line* of the strategical plan he was making known to them would risk bringing to naught "THE LABOURS OF CENTURIES".

7. He next advocated the use of "Mob Psychology" to obtain control of the masses. He reasoned that the *might* of the Mob is blind, senseless, and unreasoning, ever at the mercy of suggestion from any side. He stated: "Only a despotic ruler can rule the Mob efficiently, because without absolute despotism there can be no existence for civilization which was carried out NOT by the masses, but by their guide, whosoever that person might be." He warned, "The moment the Mob seizes FREEDOM in its hands it quickly turns to anarchy."

8. He next advocated that the use of alcoholic liquors, drugs, moral corruption, and all forms of vice, be used systematically by their "Agenturs"[4] to corrupt the morals of the youth of the nations. He recommended that the special 'agenturs' should be trained as tutors, lackeys, governesses, clerks and by our women in the places of dissipation frequented by the Goyim.[5] He added: "*In the number of these last I count also the so-called society ladies who become voluntary*

followers of the others in corruption and luxury. We must not stop at bribery, deceit, and treachery when they should serve towards the attainment of our end."

9. Turning to politics he claimed they had the RIGHT to seize property by any means, and without hesitation, if by doing so they secured submission, and sovereignty. He pronounced, *"Our STATE, marching along the path of peaceful conquest, has the RIGHT to replace the horrors of wars by less noticeable and more satisfactory sentences of death necessary to maintain the 'terror' which tends to produce blind submission."*

10. Dealing with the use of slogans, he said: *"In ancient times we were the first to put the words 'Liberty', 'Equality' and 'Fraternity' into the mouths of the masses...words repeated to this day by stupid pollparrots; words which the would-be wise men of the Goyim could make nothing of in their abstractness, and did not note the contradiction of their meaning and inter relation."* He claimed the words brought under their direction and control *"legions... who bore our banners with enthusiasm."* He reasoned that there is no place in nature for "Equality," "Liberty" or "Fraternity." He said, *"On the ruins of the natural and genealogical aristocracy of the Goyim we have set up the aristocracy of MONEY. The qualification for this aristocracy is WEALTH which is dependent upon us."*

11. He next expounded his theories regarding war. In 1773, he set down a principle which the governments of Britain and the United States publicly announced as their joint policy in 1939. He said it should be the policy of those present to foment wars but to direct the peace conferences so that neither of the combatants obtained territorial gains. He said the wars should be directed so that the nations engaged on both sides would be placed further in their debt, and in the power of "our" Agenturs.

12. He next dealt with administration. He told those present that they must use their wealth to have candidates chosen for public office who would be *"servile and obedient to our commands, so they may readily be used as Pawns in our game by the learned and genious men we will appoint to operate behind the scenes of government as official advisers."* He added, *"The men we appoint as 'Advisers' will have been bred, reared, and trained from childhood in accordance with our ideas to rule the affairs of the whole world."*

13. He dealt with propaganda, and explained how their combined wealth could control all outlets of public information, while they remained in the shade and clear of blame, regardless of what the repercussions might be due to the publication of libels, slanders, or untruths. The speaker said, *"Thanks to the Press we have got gold in our hands, notwithstanding the fact that we had to gather it out of the oceans of blood and tears... But it has paid us even though we have sacrificed many of our own people. Each victim on our side is worth a thousand Goyim."*

14. He next explained the necessity of having their 'Agentur' always come out into the open, and appear on the scene, when conditions had reached their lowest ebb, and the masses had been subjugated by means of want and terror. He pointed out that when it was time to restore order they should do it in such a way that the victims would believe they had been the prey of criminals and irresponsibles. He

said, "*By executing the criminals and lunatics after they have carried out our preconceived 'reign of terror', we can make ourselves appear as the saviours of the oppressed, and the champions of the workers.*" The speaker then added, "*We are interested in just the opposite...in the diminution, the killing out of the Goyim.*"

15. He next explained how industrial depressions and financial panics could be brought about and used to serve their purpose, saying, "*Enforced unemployment and hunger, imposed on the masses because of the power we have to create shortages of food, will create the right of Capital to rule more surely than it was given to the real aristocracy, and by the legal authority of Kings.*" He claimed that by having their agentur control the "Mob," the "Mob" could then be used to wipe out all who dared to stand in their way.

16. The infiltration into continental Freemasonry was next discussed extensively. The speaker stated that their purpose would be to take advantage of the facilities and secrecy Freemasonry had to offer. He pointed out that they could organize their own Grand Orient Lodges within Blue Freemasonry, in order to carry on their subversive activities and hide the true nature of their work under the cloak of philanthropy. He stated that all members initiated into their Grand Orient Lodges should be used for proselytizing purposes and for spreading their atheistic-materialistic ideology amongst the Goyim. He ended this phase of the discussion with the words: "*When the hour strikes for our sovereign Lord of all the World to be crowned, these same hands will sweep away everything that might stand in his way.*"

17. He next expounded the value of systematic deceptions, pointing out that their *agentur* should be trained in the use of high-sounding phrases and popular slogans. They should make the masses the most lavish of promises. He observed: "*The opposite of what has been promised can always be done afterwards... that is of no consequence.*" He reasoned that by using such words as *Freedom* and *Liberty*, the Goyim could be stirred up to such a pitch of patriotic fervour that they could be made to fight even against the laws of God, and Nature. He added, "*And for this reason, after we obtain control the very NAME OF GOD will be erased from the 'Lexicon of life.'*"[6]

18. He then detailed the plans for revolutionary war, the art of street fighting, and outlined the pattern for the "Reign of Terror" which he insisted must accompany every revolutionary effort, "*Because it is the most economical way to bring the population to speedy subjection.*"

19. Diplomacy was next discussed. After all wars secret diplomacy must be insisted upon "*in order that our agentur, masquerading as 'political', 'financial', and 'economic' advisers, can carry out our mandates without fear of exposing who are 'The Secret Power' behind national and international affairs.*" The speaker then told those present that by secret diplomacy they must obtain such control "*that the nations cannot come to even an inconsiderable private agreement without our secret agents having a hand in it.*"

20. Ultimate World Government the goal. To reach this goal the speaker told them: "*It will be necessary to establish huge monopolies, reservoirs of such colossal*

riches, that even the largest fortunes of the Goyim will depend on us to such an extent that they will go to the bottom together with the credit of their governments ON THE DAY AFTER THE GREAT POLITICAL SMASH." The speaker then added, "*You gentlemen here present who are economists just strike an estimate of the significance of this combination.*"

21. Economic war. Plans to rob the Goyim of their landed properties and industries were then discussed. A combination of high taxes and unfair competition was advocated to bring about the economic ruin of the Goyim, as far as their national financial interests and investments were concerned. In the international field he felt they could be encouraged to price themselves out of the markets. This could be achieved by the careful control of raw materials, organized agitation amongst the workers for shorter hours and higher pay, and by subsidizing competitors. The speaker warned his co-conspirators that they must arrange matters, and control conditions, so that "*the increased wages obtained by the workers will not benefit them in any way.*"

22. Armaments. It was suggested that the building up of armaments for the purpose of making the Goyim destroy each other should be launched on such a colossal scale that in the final analysis "*there will only be the masses of the proletariat left in the world, with a few millionaires devoted to our cause...and police, and soldiers sufficient to protect our interests.*"

23. The New Order. The members of the One-World Government would be appointed by the Dictator. He would pick men from amongst the scientists, the economists, the financiers, the industrialists, and from the millionaires because "*in substance everything will be settled by the question of figures.*"

24. Importance of youth. The importance of capturing the interest of youth was emphasized with the admonition that "*Our agenturs should infiltrate into all classes, and levels of society and government, for the purpose of fooling, bemusing, and corrupting the younger members of society by teaching them theories and principles we know to be false.*"

25. National and International Laws should not be changed but should be used as they are, to destroy the civilization of the Goyim "*merely by twisting them into a contradiction of the interpretation which first masks the law and afterwards hides it altogether. Our ultimate aim is to substitute ARBITRATION for LAW.*"

The speaker then told his listeners, "You may think the Goyim will rise upon us with arms, but in the WEST we have against this possibility an organization of such appalling terror that the very stoutest hearts quail...the 'Underground'...The Metropolitans...The subterranean corridors...these will be established in the capitals and cities of all countries before that danger threatens."

The use of the word "WEST" has great significance. It makes it plain that Rothschild was addressing men who had joined the World Revolutionary Movement which was started in the Pale of Settlement in the "EAST." It must be remembered that before Amschel Moses Bauer settled down in Frankfurt, Germany, he had followed his trade as a gold and silversmith, travelling extensively in the "East" of Europe, where he had undoubtedly met the men his son Amschel Mayer addressed after he developed from a moneylender into a banker and established the House of Rothschild in the Judenstrasse, where the above meeting is said to have taken place in 1773.

As far as can be ascertained, the original plan of the conspiracy ended at the point where it terminated above. I am satisfied that the documents which fell into the hands of Professor S. Nilus in 1901, and which he published under the title "The Jewish Peril" in 1905 in Russia, were an enlargement of the original plot. There appears to be no change in the first section, but various additions disclose how the conspirators had used Darwinism, Marxism, and even Nietzche-ism. More important still, the documents discovered in 1901 disclose how Zionism was to be used. It must be remembered that Zionism was only organized in 1897.

This matter is referred to later, when the intrigue leading up to the abdication of King Edward VIII is explained. The translation Mr. Victor Marsden made of *The Jewish Peril* was published by The Britons Publishing Society, London, England, under the title *The Protocols of The Learned Elders of Zion* in 1921. This book is also discussed. It appears logical to say that the discovery of the later document confirms the existence of the earlier one. Little, if anything is changed, but considerable material is added, probably due to the rapid development of the international conspiracy. The only point upon which there seems to be grounds for disagreement is in regard to the titles chosen by Prof. Nilus and Mr. Marsden for their books. Mr. Marsden definitely states the contents of his book are the Protocols of the meetings of the Learned Elders of Zion, whereas it would appear it was a plot presented to moneylenders, goldsmiths, industrialists, economists, and others, by Amschel Mayer Rothschild, who had graduated from moneylender to banker.

Once the spirit of revolt against constituted authority had been aroused within the hearts and minds of the masses, the actual revolutionary effort would be carried out under the impetus of a preconceived Reign of Terror. The Reign of Terror would be conceived by the leaders of the Jewish Illuminati. They in turn would have their agents infiltrate into the newly organized French Freemasonry and establish therein Lodges of Grand Orient Masonry, to be used as the revolutionary underground, and as their instrument for proselytizing the doctrine of atheistic dialectical and historical materialism. Rothschild ended his discourse by pointing out that if proper precautions were taken, their connection with the revolutionary movement need never be known.

The question may well be asked: "How can it be proved these secret meetings were held?"And "If they were held, how is it possible to prove what matters were discussed at such meetings?" The answer is simple. The devilish plot was made known by "An Act of God."

In 1785, a courier was galloping madly on horseback from Frankfurt to Paris carrying detailed information regarding the World Revolutionary Movement in general and instructions for the planned French Revolution in particular. The instructions originated with the Jewish Illuminati in Germany, and were addressed to the Grand Master of the Grand Orient Masons in France. The Grand Orient Lodges had been established as the revolutionary underground by the Duc D'Orleans after he, as Grand Master of French Masonry, had been initiated into the Jewish Illuminati in Frankfurt by Mirabeau. The courier was struck by lightning while passing through Ratisbon, and killed. The documents he carried fell into the hands of the police, who turned them over to the Bavarian Government. A record of historical events told in chronological order connects

Georgian London

Lodge &c News

Crut Wells

Masquerade Otartull

3,689
_____

White
Enamel Paint
Urban Brown
_____

2,000   300 ⟩ Amazon
·1,000   300 ⟩ Ebay
  Saving   MrByrnes
_____

Elephant

Chris Punkido · Case ·
Haircut · Dye - Church ·

Above Earthly Vibration

(Christ)mas Gift

CHARITY

(Forward More of Limit)

Mary, Norlia
Kidma, jester, Pio

Man m Iron, Lady m 1 gain

John
Paul Genette

Eddie G.
702 340 8255

the House of Rothschild with the Jewish Illuminati in Frankfurt and the Illuminati within French Free Masonry known as the Grand Orient Lodges, as will be shown.

It has been recorded how the Jewish Rabbis claimed the power to interpret the secret and hidden meanings of the writings of Holy Scripture by special revelation obtained through the Cabala. Claiming to have such powers was of little avail unless they had an organization, or instrument, in their hands to put the inspiration they claimed to have received into effect. The moneylenders, certain High Priests, Directors, and Elders decided to organize a very secret society to serve their evil purpose — they named it "The Illuminati." The word Illuminati is derived from the word Lucifer, which means Bearer of the Light, or Being of extraordinary brilliance. Therefore the Illuminati was organized to carry out the inspirations given to the High Priests by Lucifer during the performance of their Cabalistic Rites. Thus Christ is proved justified when he named them of the Synagogue of Satan. The Supreme Council of the Jewish Illuminati numbered thirteen. They were, and still remain, the executive body of The Council of Thirty-Three. The heads of the Jewish Illuminati claim to possess superlative knowledge in everything pertaining to religious doctrine, religious rites, and religious ceremonies. They were the men who conceived the Atheistic-materialistic ideology which in 1848 was published as "The Communist Manifesto" by Karl Marx. Marx was the nephew of a Jewish Rabbi, but he disassociated himself officially from the Jewish High Priesthood when designated to perform his important duties, putting into practice once again the Joint Stock Co. principle of operation.

The reason the Supreme Council numbered thirteen was to remind the members that their one and only duty was to destroy the religion founded by Christ and his twelve Apostles.[7] To ensure secrecy and avoid the possibility of Judas-like betrayal, every man initiated into the Illuminati was required to take an oath of Unlimited Obedience to the head of the Council of Thirty-Three, and to recognize no mortal as above him. In an organization, such as the Illuminati, this meant that every member acknowledged the head of the Council of Thirty-Three as his God upon this earth. This fact explains how high-level Communists, even today, swear on oath that they do not give allegiance to Russia. They don't. They give allegiance only to the head of the directors of the World Revolutionary Movement.

The Supreme Council decided they would use the Lodge in Ingoldstadt (now Ingolstadt) to organize a campaign by which the agents or Cells of the Illuminati would infiltrate into Continental Freemasonry and, under the cloak of social enjoyment and public philanthropy, organize their revolutionary underground. Those who infiltrated into Continental Freemasonry were ordered to establish Lodges of the Grand Orient and use them for proselytism so they could quickly contact non-Jews of wealth, position, and influence connected with both Church and State. Then, by using the age-old methods of bribery, corruption and craft, they could make them become willing, or unwilling, disciples of Illuminism. They could make them preach the inversion of the Ten Commandments of God. They could make them advocate atheistic-materialism.

Once this policy had been decided upon, agents of the Supreme Council contacted the Marquis of Mirabeau as the most likely person in France to serve their ends. He belonged to the nobility. He had great influence in court circles, being an intimate friend of the Duc D'Orleans, whom they had decided they would use as Front Man to lead the French

Revolution. But more important still, the Marquis of Mirabeau was devoid of morals, and his licentious excesses had led him heavily into debt.

It was a simple matter for the moneylenders to have their agents contact Mirabeau, the famous French orator. Under the guise of friends and admirers, they offered to help him out of his financial difficulties. What they actually did was lead him down the "Primrose Path" into the very depths of vice and debauchery, until he was so deeply in their debt that he was forced to do their bidding. At a meeting to consolidate his debts, Mirabeau was introduced to Moses Mendelssohn, one of the big Jewish financiers who took him in hand. Mendelssohn in due time introduced Mirabeau to a woman, famous for her personal beauty and charm but without moral scruples.

This stunning Jewess was married to a man named Herz, but, to a man like Mirabeau, the fact that she was married only made her more desirable. It wasn't long before she was spending more time with Mirabeau than with her husband. Heavily in debt to Mendelssohn, tightly ensnared by Mrs. Herz, Mirabeau was completely helpless. He had swallowed their bait hook, line, and sinker. But, like good fishermen, they played him gently for a time. If they exerted too great a pressure, the leader might break and their fish might get away. Their next move was to have him initiated into Illuminism. He was sworn to secrecy and unlimited obedience under pain of death. The next move was to lead him into compromising situations which mysteriously became public. This method of destroying a man's character became known as the practice of *L'Infamie*. Because of scandals and organized detraction, Mirabeau was ostracized by many of his social equals. His resentment produced a desire for revenge, and thus he embraced the revolutionary Cause.

Mirabeau's task was to induce the Duc D'Orleans to lead the Revolutionary Movement in France. It was implied that once the King had been forced to abdicate, the Duke would become the Democratic Ruler of France. The real plotters of the French Revolution were careful not to let either Mirabeau or the Duc D'Orleans know that they intended to murder the King and Queen, as well as thousands of the nobility. They made Mirabeau and the Duc D'Orleans believe that the purpose of the revolution was to free politics and religion from superstition and despotism. Another factor which made the men who were The Secret Power behind the revolutionary movement decide that the Duc D'Orleans should be their Front man was the fact that he was Grand Master of French Freemasonry.

Adam Weishaupt was given the task of adapting the ritual and rites of Illuminism for use of initiation into the Grand Orient Masonry. He also lived in Frankfurt, Germany. Mirabeau introduced the Duc D'Orleans and his friend Talleyrand to Weishaupt who initiated them into the secrets of Grand Orient Masonry. By the end of 1773, Philippe, Duc d'Orleans, had introduced the Grand Orient Ritual into French Freemasonry. By 1788, there were more than two thousand lodges in France affiliated with Grand Orient Masonry, and the number of individual adepts exceeded one hundred thousand. Thus the Jewish Illuminati under Moses Mendelssohn was introduced into Continental Freemasonry by Weishaupt under the guise of Lodges of the Grand Orient. The Jewish Illuminati next organized secret revolutionary committees within the lodges. Thus the revolutionary underground directors were established throughout France.

Once Mirabeau had succeeded in having the Duc D'Orleans amalgamate the Blue or National freemasonry in France with the Grand Orient rites, he led his friend down the same "Primrose Path" which had led to his own social ostracism. In exactly four years, the Duc D'Orleans was so heavily in debt that he was PERSUADED to engage in every form of illegal traffic and trade to recuperate his losses. But in some mysterious manner his ventures always seemed to go wrong, and he lost more and more money.

By 1780 he owed 800,000 livres. Once again the moneylenders came forward and offered him advice in regard to his business transactions and financial aid. They very nicely manoeuvred him into the position of signing over to them his palace, his estates, his house, and the Palais Royal as security for their loans. The Duc D'Orleans signed an agreement under which his Jewish financiers were authorized to manage his properties and estates so as to ensure him sufficient income to meet his financial obligations and leave him a steady and adequate income.

The Duc D'Orleans had never been too bright in regard to financial matters. To him, the agreement he signed with his Jewish Bankers appeared to be a sound financial deal. They had offered to manage his business affairs and turn them from a dismal failure into a great financial success. What more could he want? It is doubtful if the Duc D'Orleans even suspected that there was a catch. It is doubtful if he even suspected he had sold himself body and soul to the Agents of the Devil... But he had done so. He was completely in their hands.[8]

The Secret Powers directing the French Revolution appointed Choderlos de Laclos to manage the Palais Royal and the Duc D'Orleans' estates. De Laclos is thought to have been a Jew of Spanish origin. When he was appointed manager of the Palais Royal, he was acclaimed as the author of *Les Liaisons Dangereuses* and other pornographic works. He publicly defended his extreme immorality on the grounds that he studied the politics of love in all its varied aspects because of his love of politics.

It matters little who Choderlos de Laclos was; it is what he did that is of importance. He turned the Palais Royal into the greatest and most notorious house of ill fame the world has ever known. In the Palais Royal he established every kind of lewd entertainment, licentious conduct, shameless shows, obscene picture galleries, pornographic libraries, and staged public exhibitions of the most bestial forms of sexual depravity. Special opportunities were provided for men and women who wished to indulge in every form of debauchery. The Palais Royal became the centre in which details of the campaign for the systematic destruction of the French religious faith and public morals were conceived and carried out. This was done on the Cabalistic theory that the best revolutionary is a youth devoid of morals.

Associated with de Laclos was a Jew from Palermo named Cagliostro, alias Joseph Balsamo. He turned one of the Duc's properties into a printing house from which he issued revolutionary pamphlets. Balsamo organized a staff of revolutionary propagandists. In addition to literature they organized concerts, plays, and debates calculated to appeal to the very lowest instincts of human nature and further the revolutionary cause. Balsamo also organized the spy-rings which enabled the men who were The Secret Power behind the revolutionary movement to put into operation their plan of *L'Infamie* to be used for systematic character assassination.

Once enticed into the web spun by de Laclos and Balsamo, men and women could be blackmailed into doing their bidding. Thus it was that the Duc D'Orleans' estates were turned into the Centre of Revolutionary Politics while—under the guise of Lecture Halls, Theatres, Art Galleries, and Athletic Clubs—the gambling rooms, brothels, and wine and drug shops did a roaring trade. In this revolutionary underworld, potential leaders were first ensnared. Their consciences were at first deadened by evil associations, and then killed by indulgence in evil practices. The estates of the Duc D'Orleans were turned into factories in which the Secret Power behind the World Revolutionary Movement manufactured the "pieces" they intended to use in their game of International Chess. Scudder, who wrote *Prince of the Blood,* says of the Palais Royal: "It gave the police more to do than all other parts of the city." But as far as the public was concerned, this infamous place was owned by the Duc D'Orleans, the cousin of the king. Only a mere handful of men and women knew that the moneylenders controlled it and used it to create a revolutionary organization which was to be the instrument of their revenge and their manual of action to further their secret aims and ambitions.

After the secret documents found on the body of the courier had been read by the police, the documents were passed on to the Bavarian Government. The Bavarian Government ordered the police to raid the headquarters of the Illuminati. Further evidence was obtained which exposed the wide-spread ramifications of the World Revolutionary Movement. The Governments of France, England, Poland, Germany, Austria and Russia were informed of the International Nature of the revolutionary plot, but as has happened repeatedly since, the governments concerned took no serious action to stop the diabolical conspiracy. Why? The only answer to this question is this: The power of the men behind the world revolutionary movement is greater than the power of any elected government. This fact will be proven time and time again as the story unfolds.

The malevolent men who plot and plan the WRM have another advantage over decent people. The average person, who believes in God and finds pleasure and enjoyment in the beautiful things with which God has blessed us, just cannot bring himself or herself to believe a diabolical plan of hatred and revenge could be conceived by human beings. Although all Christians believe most sincerely that the Grace of God enters their own souls as the result of attending their religious services, receiving the Sacraments, and saying their prayers, they cannot make themselves believe that through the ceremonies and Rites of the Illuminati, be it the Semitic Cabala or the Aryan Pagan Grand Orient type, the Devil does inoculate his evil influence and powers into the hearts and souls of the men and women who accept, as their religion, Satanism or atheism, and put the theories of their High Priests into practice.

A few illustrations will be given to show how individuals and governments have remained just as stupid and naïve in regard to warnings given them concerning the evil mechanism of the real leaders of the World Revolutionary Movement.

After various governments failed to act on the information made known by the Bavarian police in 1785, the sister of Marie Antoinette wrote her personal letters warning her of the revolutionary plot, the connection of the International Bankers, the part Freemasonry was destined to play, and her own danger. Marie Antoinette (1755-1793) was the daughter of the Emperor Francis I of Austria. She married Louis XVI of France. She just couldn't bring herself to believe the terrible things her own sister told her were being plotted by the Illuminati. To the repeated warnings sent by her sister, Marie Antoinette wrote long letters in reply. In regard to her sister's claim that evidence had been obtained that the Illuminati operating under the guise of Philanthropic Freemasonry planned to destroy both the Church and State in France, Marie Antoinette replied: "I believe that as far as France is concerned, you worry too much about Freemasonry. Here it is far from having the significance it may have elsewhere in Europe."

How wrong she proved to be is a matter of history. Because she refused consistently to heed her sister's repeated warnings, she and her husband died under the guillotine.

Between 1917 and 1919, the British Government was given full particulars regarding the international bankers who were at that time The Secret Power behind the WRM. The information was submitted officially by British Intelligence Officers, American Intelligence Officers and confirmed by Mr. Oudendyke and Sir M. Findlay. Mr. Oudendyke was the representative of the Netherlands Government in St. Petersburg (now Leningrad) at the time. He looked after Britain's interests after The Mob had wrecked the British Embassy and killed Commander E.N. Cromie. This aspect of the WRM is dealt with in detail in subsequent chapters on Russia.

The majority of students of history believe Marie Antoinette was a woman who entered fully into the spirit and gaiety of the French Court. It is generally accepted as a fact that she engaged in many affairs *d'amour* with her husband's close friends, and indulged in reckless extravagances. That is the picture Balsamo and his propagandists painted of her. The fact that they made their *L'Infamie* stick enabled them to have the mob demand her life. But their version of the conduct of Marie Antoinette is a pack of lies, as historians have proved. The fortitude with which she bore the sufferings inflicted upon her by her enemies, the dignity with which she met her fate and the resignation and courage with which she offered up her life on the scaffold, cannot be reconciled with the characteristics of a wanton woman.

In order to defame Marie Antoinette, Weishaupt and Mendelssohn thought up the idea of the Diamond Necklace. At the time, the financial resources of France were at their lowest ebb, and the government of France was begging the International Money-Barons to grant them further credit. A secret agent of the arch-conspirators ordered a fabulous diamond necklace to be made by the Court Jewellers. The order for this necklace, the estimated value of which was a quarter of a million livres, was placed in the name of the Queen. When the Court Jewellers brought the Diamond Necklace to the Queen for her acceptance, she refused to have anything to do with it. She disclaimed all knowledge of the transaction. But the news of the fabulous necklace leaked out as the plotters intended it should. Balsamo put his propaganda machine into operation. Marie Antoinette was deluged with criticism, her character was smeared, and her reputation dragged in the mire by a whispering campaign of character assassination. And, as usual, nobody could ever put a finger on the person or persons who started the slanders. After this build-up, Balsamo uncorked his own special master-piece. His printing presses turned out thousands upon thousands of pamphlets which claimed a secret lover of the Queen's had sent the necklace as a mark of appreciation for her favours.

But those who operated *L'Infamie* thought up even more diabolical slanders to circulate regarding the Queen. They wrote a letter to Cardinal Prince de Rohan to which they forged the signature of the Queen. In the letter he was asked to meet her at the Palais Royal about midnight to discuss the matter of the diamond necklace. A prostitute from the Palais Royal was engaged to disguise herself as the Queen, and involve the Cardinal. The incident was played up in newspapers and pamphlets, and the foulest innuendoes were circulated involving two of the highest personages of both Church and State.

History records that after the diamond necklace had served its foul purpose it was taken over to England and taken apart. A Jew named Eliason is said to have retained the majority of the valuable diamonds used in its original composition.

Another piece of evidence which connects the English Jewish moneylenders with the plot to bring about the French Revolution was unearthed by Lady Queensborough, author of *Occult Theocrasy*. While doing some research work, she read a copy of *L'Anti-Semitisme*, written by a Jew named Bernard Lazare and published in 1849. With the leads obtained from this book, Lady Queensborough claims Benjamin Goldsmid, his brother Abraham, their partner Moses Mecatta, and his nephew Sir Moses Montifiore, were Jewish financiers in England who were definitely affiliated with their continental Jewish brethren in the plot to bring about the revolution in France. Further evidence was found to tie Daniel Itsig of Berlin, his son-in-law David Friedlander, and Herz Gergbeer of Alsace in with the Rothschilds and the plot. Thus are revealed the men who at that time constituted the Secret Power behind the World Revolutionary Movement.

Knowledge of the methods these men used to manoeuvre the French Government into financial difficulty is of importance, because it set the pattern they followed in America, Russia, Spain and other countries afterwards.

Sir Walter Scott, in Vol. II of *The Life of Napoleon*, gives a clear story of the initial moves. He then sums up the situation with these words: "These financiers used the Government (French) as bankrupt prodigals are treated by usurious moneylenders who, feeding the extravagance with one hand, with the other wring out of their ruined fortunes the most unreasonable recompenses for their advances. By a long succession of these ruinous loans, and various rights granted to guarantee them, the whole finances of France were brought to a total confusion."[9]

After the Government of France was forced into the position of seeking huge loans because of debts incurred in fighting wars to further the secret ambitions of the International Conspirators, they very kindly offered to supply the money providing they could write the terms of the agreement. On the surface, their terms were most lenient. But again they had placed a mole or snake in the grass, in the person of one M. Necker. He was to be appointed to the French King's Council as his Chief Minister of Financial Affairs. The Jewish financiers pointed out that this financial wizard would pull France out of her monetary troubles in less than no time at all. What he actually did during the next four years was to involve the French Government so badly with the Jewish financiers that the National Debt increased to £170,000,000.

Captain A.H.M. Ramsay sums up the situation aptly in *The Nameless War*. He says: "Revolution is a blow struck at a paralytic...When the debt-grip has been firmly established, control of every form of publicity and political activity soon follows, together with a full grip on industrialists, both management and labour. The stage is then set for the revolutionary blow. The grip of the right hand of finance establishes the paralysis, while the revolutionary left hand that holds the dagger and deals the fatal blow. Moral corruption facilitates the whole process."

While Balsamo's propaganda sheets damned the higher officials of both Church and State, special agents of the Illuminati organized the men who were to be used as leaders in the Reign of Terror planned to accompany the revolutionary effort. Among these leaders were Robespierre, Danton, and Marat. To conceal their real purpose, the men who were to release the prisoners and lunatics to create the necessary atmosphere for instituting the preconceived Reign of Terror, met in the Jacobean Convent. Within the walls of the sacred edifice the details of the bloody plan were worked out. The lists of reactionaries marked down for liquidation were compiled. It was explained that while the criminals and lunatics ran wild terrorizing the population by committing mass murders and publicly performing rapes, the organized underground workers, under direction of Manuel, Procurer of the Commune, would round up all the important political figures, heads of the clergy, and military officers known to be loyal to the King.[10] The men who were to emerge from the Jewish organized underground were formed into Jacobin Clubs. Under leaders who were well versed in the duties required of them to direct the "Reign of Terror," they conducted the mass atrocities so they would serve the purpose of their hidden masters, and move them further towards their ultimate goal.

[1.] These were the original theories on which Class War was ultimately organized.

[2.] This statement in the original documents should convince all but the biased that the speaker was not a Rabbi or Elder of the Jews nor was he addressing Elders and Rabbis because it was the Goldsmiths, the moneylenders and their affiliates in commerce and industry who in 1773 had the wealth of the world in their hands as they have it still in their hands in the 20th Century.

[3.] The Red Fog explains how this theory has been put into effect in America since 1900.

[4.] The word "agentur" means the complete organized body of agents: spies, counter-spies, blackmailers, saboteurs, underworld characters, and everything and every body outside the LAW which enables the international conspirators to further their secret plans and ambitions.

[5.] The word "Goyim" means all others than their own group. The unimportant people.

[6.] The "Lexicon of Life" he referred to, was Almighty God's plan of creation.

[7.] There were also twelve tribes of Israel, which could have some bearing on the matter of numbers.

[8.] The same Evil Geniuses used their agents to involve William Pitt in debt and forced him to resign as Prime Minister of England because during the early part of his ministry he obstinately refused to allow England to become involved in wars they planned to further their own secret plans and ambitions. Pitt had learned a great deal regarding the part the International Money-Barons played in International Affairs when Chancellor of the Exchequer and Prime Minister, from about 1783 to 1801.

[9.] Because of his alleged anti-semitic utterances, Sir Walter Scott's important works consisting of a total of nine volumes dealing with many phases of the French Revolution have been given the silent treatment by those who control the publishing houses as well as the biggest portion of the press. They are almost unattainable except in Museum Libraries and are never listed with his other works.

[10.] Sir Walter Scott — *Life of Napoleon*, Vol. 2, P. 30 says "The demand of the Communauté de Paris, now the Sanhedrin of the Jacobin, was of course, for blood."

CHAPTER FOUR

The Downfall of Napoleon

The international bankers planned the French Revolution so they could become *The Secret Power* behind the governments of Europe, and further their Long-Range Plans.

With the outbreak of the revolution, the Jacobins took over control. They were men who had been hand picked by the Illuminati and Grand Orient Masonry. They used the Duc D'Orleans to serve their purpose right up to the time he was required to vote for the death of his cousin the King. The Duc believed he would be made the constitutional monarch, but the Jacobins had other instructions. Once he had voted for the death of the King, and assumed the blame, he left the real plotters free from suspicion. Then those who comprised *The Secret Power* behind the revolution ordered him *liquidated* also. They switched the full force of their propaganda, and *L'Infamie*, against him. In an unbelievably short time, he was on his way to the guillotine. While riding over the cobblestones on the death-cart he heard himself reviled and execrated by all classes of the people.

Once Mirabeau realized what a terrible instrument of vengeance he had helped to bring into being, he repented. Wild and dissolute as he had been, he just couldn't stomach witnessing the terrible and shocking atrocities which the Jacobins were systematically perpetrating on all those who were *Fingered* for outrage and death by their secret masters. Mirabeau was actually opposed to any violence being done to the King. His personal plan had been to reduce Louis XVI to a Limited Monarch, and then have himself appointed his chief advisor. When he realized that his Masters were determined to kill the King, he tried to arrange for Louis to escape from Paris so he could place himself under the protection of his loyal Generals who still commanded his army. When his plans were betrayed to the Jacobins, Mirabeau was ordered liquidated also. In his case, a public execution could not be arranged because his enemies did not consider they had time to frame charges against him and make them stick, so he was poisoned. His death was made to look like suicide. A book was written about The Diamond Necklace already referred to. In it is the significant remark, "Louis was not ignorant of the fact that Mirabeau had been poisoned."

Danton and Robespierre were the two devils incarnate who stepped up the *Reign of Terror* designed by the Illuminati to give them revenge upon their enemies, and to remove personages they considered obstacles in their path. Yet, when they had served their purpose, their two chief executioners were arrested and charged with their many infamies and then executed.[1]

Lafayette was a Mason. He was a good man. He joined the revolutionary forces because he honestly believed revolutionary action was necessary to bring about much needed reforms speedily. But Lafayette never thought for a moment he was leading the people of France from their old oppression into a new subjection. When he tried to save the King, he was packed off to fight a war in Austria. Since the French Revolution of 1789, up to the revolutions going on today, the Secret Power behind them has used many Duc D'Orleans, Mirabeaus and Lafayettes. Although the men have borne different names, they have all been used as tools and played similar parts. They have been used to foment the revolutions and, after having served their purpose, they have been liquidated by the very men they served. Their deaths are always so arranged that they die under a blanket of guilt which should rightfully have covered the shoulders of the men who still remain *The Secret Power* behind the scenes in International Intrigue.

Sir Walter Scott understood a great deal about how *The Secret Power* behind the French Revolution worked. Any person who reads his *Life of Napoleon* will sense that the author thought he detected the Jewish origin of the plots.[2]

Sir Walter points out that the real key figures in the revolution were mostly *foreigners*. He observed that they used typically Jewish terms such as *Directors* and *Elders*, in their work. He points out that a man named Manuel was in some mysterious manner appointed Procurer of the Commune. Sir Walter states that this one man was responsible for the arrest and detention, in prisons all over France, of the victims of the pre-arranged massacres which took place in September 1792. During the massacres, 8,000 victims were murdered in the prisons of Paris alone. Sir Walter also noted that the *Communauté de Paris* (the Paris County Council) became the SANHEDRIN of the Jacobins who cried for blood and more blood. Scott relates that until they had served their purpose, Robespierre, Danton, and Marat shared the high places in the SYNAGOGUE of the Jacobins. (Author's emphasis) It was Manuel who sparked the attack against King Louis and Marie Antoinette, attacks that finally led them to the guillotine. Manuel was well supported by a man named David who, as a leading member of the Committee of Public security, tried Manuel's many victims. David's voice always called for blood and death.

Sir Walter records that David used to preface his "bloody work of the day" with the professional phrase: "*Let us grind enough of the Red.*" It was David who introduced The Cult of the Supreme Being. The heathen ritual was Cabalistic mummery which was substituted for every external sign of rational devotion. Scott also mentions that Choderlos de Laclos, thought to have been of Spanish origin, was manager of the Palais Royal which played such a devilish part in the preparations for the outbreak of the Revolution. Another matter of importance is this: After Robespierre had been ordered liquidated two men named Reubel and Gohir were appointed Directors of The Council of Elders. With three others they became the actual government of France for a time. The five men referred to were known as the *Directoires*. It is a very remarkable fact that Sir Walter Scott's *Life of Napoleon* (in nine volumes) which reveals so much of the real truth is practically unknown.

Mention must be made of G. Renier's *Life of Robespierre*. He writes as if some of the secrets were known to him. He says: "From April 27th to July 28th, 1794 (when Robespierre was defeated), the reign of terror was at its height. It was never a dictatorship of a single man, least of all Robespierre. Some 20 men shared in the power." Then again: "On July 28th Robespierre made a long speech before the Convention...a Philippic against ultra-terrorists...during which he uttered vague and general accusations." Robespierre is quoted to have said, "I dare not name them at this moment and in this place. I cannot bring myself entirely to tear asunder the veil that covers this profound mystery of iniquity. But I can affirm most positively that among the authors of this plot are the agents of that system of corruption and extravagance, the most powerful of all the means invented by the Foreigners for the undoing of the Republic: I mean the impure apostles of Atheism, and the immorality that is its base." Mr. Renier added: "Had he (Robespierre) not spoken these words he might still have triumphed."

Robespierre had said too much. He was deliberately shot in the jaw to silence him effectively until he could be dragged to the guillotine the following day. Thus another

Mason who knew too much was disposed of. As the events which led up to the Russian and Spanish revolutions are reviewed, it will be shown that the Hidden Revolutionary Section of the Illuminati within the Grand Orient Lodges of Continental Freemasonry was the instrument of the men who constituted *The Secret Power behind the World Revolutionary Movement*. Thousands of individuals are publicly blamed, and many organizations brought into disrepute, simply because it was within the power of the secret leaders of the WRM to saddle them with the blame for their crimes and thus conceal their own identity. There are not many people living today who know that Robespierre, Marat and Danton, were only the instruments used by the thirteen directors of the Illuminati who plotted and directed the Great French Revolution. It was the men behind the scenes who preconceived the pattern of The Reign of Terror as the means of gratifying their desire for revenge. Only during a Reign of Terror could they remove human obstacles from their path.

Having run out of victims, the men who directed the French Revolution decided to engage in international intrigue again. For the purpose of increasing their economic and political power Anselm Mayer Rothschild trained his son Nathan Mayer for the special purpose of opening up a House of Rothschild in London, England. His intention was to consolidate, more strongly than ever, the connections between the men who controlled the Bank of England and those who controlled the Banks of France, Germany and Holland. Nathan undertook this important task at the age of 21. He tripled his fortune. The Bankers then decided to use Napoleon as the Instrument of their will. They organized the Napoleonic Wars to topple several more of the Crowned Heads of Europe.

After Napoleon swept over Europe, he pronounced himself Emperor in 1804. He appointed his brother Joseph as King of Naples; Louis, King of Holland; Jerome, King of Westphalia. At the same time Nathan Rothschild arranged matters so that his four brothers became the kings of finance in Europe. They were *the Secret Power* behind the newly established thrones. The international moneylenders set up headquarters in Switzerland. It was agreed between them that, in their interests, and for their security, Switzerland should be kept neutral in all disputes. In their Swiss headquarters at Geneva they organized the different combines and cartels on an international scale. They arranged things so that no matter who fought who, or who won and who lost, the members of the International Moneylenders Pool made more and more money. This group of men soon obtained control of the munitions plants, the ship-building industry, the mining industry, chemical plants, drug supply depots, steel mills, etc. The only fly in the ointment was the fact that Napoleon grew more and more egotistical until he finally had the temerity to denounce them publicly. Thus he also decided his own fate. It was not the weather, nor the cold, that turned his victorious invasion of Russia into one of the most tragic military defeats the world has ever known. The failure of munitions and supplies to reach his armies was due to the sabotaging of his lines of communications.

The secret strategy used to defeat Napoleon, and force his abdication, has been accepted as essential for all revolutionary efforts since that date. It is very simple. The leaders of the revolutionary movement arrange to place their agents secretly in key positions in the departments of supply, communication, transport and intelligence, of the armed forces they plan to overthrow. By sabotaging supplies, intercepting orders, issuing contradictory messages, tying up or misrouting transports, and by counter-intelligence work, revolutionary leaders have discovered they can create utter chaos in the most efficient military organization on land, at sea, or in the air. Ten *Cells* secretly placed in key positions are worth ten thousand men in the field. The methods used to bring Napoleon to ruin in the early part of the nineteenth century were used to bring about the defeat of the Russian Armies in the war with Japan in 1904; and again to cause mutiny in the Russian Armies in 1917; and mutiny in the German Army and Navy in 1918.

Communist infiltration into key positions was the real reason the German Generals asked for, and were granted, an Armistice in November 1918. The same methods were used to destroy the effectiveness of the Spanish Army, Navy and Air Force in 1936. Exactly the same tactics were used to bring about the defeat of Hitler after his victorious advances into Russia in World War Two. Thus history repeats itself, because the same powers use the same methods over and over again. But most important of all, it was the descendants of the men who brought about Napoleon's downfall who brought about the defeat of China's National Forces in 1945 and onwards. Mysterious orders were given that caused millions upon millions of dollars worth of arms and ammunition to be dumped into the Indian Ocean when they should have gone to Chiang Kai-Shek. The true story of the manner in which British and American politicians betrayed our anti-Communist Chinese and Korean allies will prove that it was the agents of the International Bankers, manoeuvring to let Communism obtain control of Asia, who deceived and ill-advised our top-level statesmen. Communism is today what it always has been since 1773—the instrument of destruction and the manual of action used by the international arch-conspirators to further their own secret plans by which, in the final analysis, they intend to obtain control of the wealth, natural resources, and manpower of the entire world.

History records how Napoleon was forced to abdicate in Paris in 1814, then sent into exile on St. Elba; he escaped and tried to make a come-back, but he was playing against men who use loaded dice. Nathan Rothschild and his international clique had backed Germany to defeat Napoleon. They had planned to make money regardless of the outcome of the struggle. When the Battle of Waterloo was about to be fought, Nathan Rothschild was in Paris. He had obtained, as his place of residence, a palace which overlooked that occupied by Louis XVIII.

He could, when he wished, look right into the window of the palace occupied by the aspirant to the throne of France. He had arranged also to have agents on the field of battle despatch to him by carrier pigeon information regarding the fighting. Nathan Rothschild also arranged to have false information sent to England by carrier pigeons regarding the results of the battle. Once he was sure Wellington had been victorious, he had his agents inform the British public that Wellington had been defeated and that Napoleon was on the rampage again. The fact that carrier-pigeons played such an important role in this conspiracy gave birth to the expression, "A little bird told me." (If a person in England asks another, "Where did you get that information?" the person questioned will most likely say, "Oh! A little bird told me," and let it go at that).

Nathan Rothschild's little birds told lies of such magnitude regarding the battle of Waterloo that the people of Britain went into a panic. The bottom dropped out of the stock market. English pounds could be bought for a "Song" or a shilling. Values of everything fell to an all time low. Nathan chartered a small vessel for the sum of £2,000 to take him from France to England. Upon arrival he and his financial associates bought up all the stocks, bonds, shares, other properties, and securities they could get their hands on. When the truth regarding Wellington's victory became known, values returned to normal. The International moneylenders made astronomical fortunes.

Why they were not assassinated by some of the people they ruined is beyond comprehension. As a token of their joy and gratitude for the marvellous feat of arms performed by Wellington and Blücher, the Rothschilds LOANED England £18,000,000 and Prussia £5,000,000 of this ill-gotten gain, TO REPAIR THE DAMAGES OF WAR. When Nathan Rothschild died in 1836, he had secured control of the Bank of England and the National Debt which, after his big financial killing in 1815, reached £885,000,000.

It is most unlikely that one Freemason in a thousand knows the TRUE story of how the heads of the Grand Orient Illuminati infiltrated their agents into Continental Freemasonry. Because the facts related are the truth, the Grand Masters of English Freemasons have warned their Brother Masons that they must have no truck with Grand Orient Masons or affiliate with them in any way. The fact that The Revolutionary Illuminati established itself within Continental Freemasonry caused Pope Pius IX to publicly denounce Communism, and prohibit Catholics from becoming Masons. To convince any reader who may still have doubts regarding the part Freemasonry played in the French Revolution, part of a debate will be quoted, which took place on the subject in the French Chamber of Deputies in 1904. The Marquis of Rosanbe, after some searching questions related to proving French Freemasonry was the author of the French Revolution, said: "We are then in complete agreement on the point that Freemasonry was the only author of the revolution, and the applause which I receive from the *Left*, and to which I am little accustomed, proves gentlemen, that you acknowledge with me that it was Masonry which made the French Revolution?"

To this statement M. Jumel, a well-known Grand Orient Mason, replied: "We do more than acknowledge it...we proclaim it".[4]

In 1923 at a big banquet attended by many men prominent in International Affairs, some of whom were connected with the League of Nations organization, the President of the Grand Orient gave this toast: "To the French Republic, daughter of French Freemasonry. To the universal republic of to-morrow, daughter of universal Masonry."[5]

To prove that The Grand Orient Freemasons have controlled French politics from 1923 onwards a brief review of historical events will be given. The most important victory the International Bankers gained, after their agents had acted as advisors to the political leaders who devised and finally ratified the infamous Treaty of Versailles, was to have M. Herriot elected to power in France in 1924. Every political policy dictated by the heads of Grand Orient Freemasonry in 1923 was put into effect by the Herriot Government within a year.

1.   In January 1923, the G.O.L. (Grand Orient Lodges) decreed the suppression of the embassy to the Vatican. The French Parliament carried out this order on October 24th, 1924.

2.   In 1923, the G.O.L. demanded the triumph of the idea of Laicity (this is the primary principle essential to the establishment of the Grand Orient's ideology of an Atheistic State) Herriot made his public ministerial declaration in favour of this policy June 17th, 1924.

3.   On January 31st, 1923, the G.O.L. demanded a full and complete amnesty for condemned persons and traitors. Several prominent Communist leaders were to

benefit, amongst them André Marty, who afterwards became notorious as the organizer of the International Brigades which fought on the Communist side in Spain 1936-39. The Chamber of Deputies voted for a general Amnesty July 15th, 1924, and thus turned loose on an unsuspecting society a number of International Gangsters whose master was the Supreme Council of Grand Orient Masonry, the Illuminati.

4. In October 1922, the G.O.L. had started a campaign to popularize the idea that diplomatic relations be opened with the SOVIET Government as established in Moscow. This movement didn't get very far until after the election of M. Herriot to power. This Friendship with Russia campaign was started in France when the *Bulletin Officiel de la Grande Loge de France* published an article on the subject in the October issue of 1922 on page 286. Political relations were established with the Communist Revolutionary Leaders by Herriot on October 28th, 1924.[6] The same forces of evil are advocating the recognition of Red China today.

One of the leaders of the Grand Orient at this time was Leon Blum. He was being primed to become a political instrument ready to do the bidding of his leaders. High-ranking members of the Military Lodges in Spain who defected (after they found out they were being used as tools by leaders of the WRM), disclosed that every Grand Orient Mason was required to take an oath of UNLIMITED OBEDIENCE to the head of the Council of Thirty-Three and to recognize no human as above him. An oath of this kind taken by an avowed atheist literally means that he recognized the State as above everything else, and the head of the State as his God. A great deal of detail about Grand Orient intrigue in France and Spain from 1923 to 1939 is told in *The Spanish Arena,* written by William Foss and Cecil Gerahty and published by The Right Book Club, London, England, in 1939. To establish continuity of the International Banker's plot, it is sufficient to touch on just a few highlights.

Leon Blum was born in Paris in 1872 of Jewish parents. He was noted for the part he played in the Dreyfus affair. He was elected French Premier in June 1936 and remained in office until June 1937. His supporters managed to get him back into politics as Vice-Premier June 1937 to January 1938. He was re-elected Premier in March 1938, but remained only for one month. Mendes-France is being used the same way today.

During the whole of this time, Leon Blum's task was to mold French governmental policy so that it would aid the plans of the leaders of the WRM in regard to Spain. In order to throw suspicion away from themselves, the arch-conspirators made it appear that it was Franco and his military associates who were the planners and plotters of the events which led up to the Civil War in Spain. It is now proved that Stalin, and his revolutionary experts the Comintern, were the conspirators who carried out the plans of *The Secret Power* behind the WRM. They planned to duplicate what they had achieved in both the French Revolution in 1789, and the Russian Revolution in 1917. As early as 1929, M. Gustave pointed out in his paper *La Victoire* the truth regarding Leon Blum and his associates. He had the courage to declare: "The Collectivist Party of Leon Blum, the second branch of Freemasonry...is not only anti-religious, but a party of class-war, and of social revolution."

Leon Blum put into effect the plans of the leaders of the WRM to supply Spanish *Loyalists* with arms, munitions, and finances. He was instrumental in keeping the

Pyrenees open but he followed a one-sided policy of non-intervention...It only applied to the Nationalists of Franco's forces.

Evidence is produced, in the chapters dealing with the revolution in Spain, to prove that the French and Spanish Grand Orient Lodges were the line of communications between the directors of the WRM and their agents in Moscow, Madrid and Vienna.[7]

Should the reader think too much importance is being placed on the influence Grand Orient Masonry has on International Affairs, A.G. Michel—the author of *La Dictature de la Franc-Maçonnerie sur la France*—there gives evidence to prove that the Grand Orient of France decreed in 1924, to make The League of Nations "An international tool for Freemasonry." Trotsky wrote in his book *Stalin*: "Today there is a Tower of Babel at the service of Stalin, and one of its principal centres is Geneva, that hot-bed of intrigue."

The importance of what Trotsky says lies in the fact that the accusations he made regarding the evil influence of Grand Orient Masons within the League of Nations applies equally to the bad influence they have in the United Nations today. The student who studies today's happenings in the United Nations will see their handiwork especially in regard to strange policies which just don't make sense to the average man-in-the-street. But these strange policies become extremely clear if we study them to see how they will further the long-range plan of the WRM. To do this we only have to remember one or two important facts: First, that the Illuminati consider it necessary to destroy all existing forms of constitutional government, regardless of whether they be monarchy or republic; Second, that they intend to introduce a World Dictatorship just as soon as they consider they are securely in position to usurp absolute control. M.J. Marques-Rivière[8] had this to say: "The centre of the International Freemasons is at Geneva. The offices of the International Masonic Association are at Geneva. This is the meeting place of delegates of nearly all the forms of Masonry throughout the world. The interpretation of the League and the I.M.A. is easy, apparent and confessed."

One can well understand the exclamation in 1924 by Brother Barcia, Past Grand Master of the Spanish Grand Orient, at the Convent of the Grand Orient when he returned from Geneva: "I have assisted at the work of the commissions. I have heard Paul-Boncour, Jeuhaux, Loucheur, de Jouvenal. All the French had the same spirit. Beside me were representatives of American Freemasons, and they asked each other: 'Are we in a secular assembly or a Masonic Order? ... Brother Joseph Avenal is the Secretary-General of the League.' "

It is well to remember that the International Illuminati chose Geneva as their headquarters nearly a century before the above event was recorded. They had, in accordance with their policy, kept Switzerland a neutral nation in all international disputes because they had to have one place where they could meet and instruct their agents who were doing their bidding and carrying out their secret policies. The United States Government refused to join the League of Nations. Certain interests promoted the *Isolationist Policy*. The Secret Powers were determined to exploit those who honestly support the idea of a One World form of Super-government to assure peace and prosperity. They determined to wreck the League of Nations and substitute The United Nations. World War Two gave them this opportunity. In 1946, the remnants of the League of Nations were picked up and used in the quilted pattern of the United Nations, which included the U.S.S.R. and the U.S.A. as the two most powerful members. The fact that the United Nations gave Israel to the Political Zionists, which they had been after for half a century, and on the advice of these same men, turned over China, Northern Korea, Manchuria, Mongolia, the Dutch East Indies, and parts of Indo-China, to Communist leaders, proves how successfully the Secret Powers laid, and carried out, their plans. It must be remembered that Lenin predicted that the forces of Communism would, in all probability, sweep over the western world from the East. People, who study the MERCATOR'S PROJECTION of the world, fail to understand how the nations of the Far East could sweep over the nations of the Western world like a tidal wave. To those who study Global War, Lenin's statements are as clear as crystal. What is even more important: when Lenin had outlived his usefulness he died, or was removed. Few people can understand how it was that Stalin—by a few ruthless, murderous moves—removed all those who, by reason of their activities in the Russian Revolution, were considered better qualified for leadership in the U.S.S.R., and usurped power for himself.

Those who study the WRM from the evidence presented in this book will understand why Stalin was chosen to follow Lenin. The old Joint Stock Company principle was being put into effect again. American and British Intelligence Officers had exposed the part the International Bankers had played in the Russian Revolution, to their Governments. In April 1919, the British Government had issued a *White Paper* on this subject. It was quickly suppressed, but a certain amount of damage had been done. The International Bankers had been accused of financing International Jewry to put their plans for an International Dictatorship into effect. The International Bankers had to find some means of countering these impressions and ideas. The true picture of their utter ruthlessness is seen when it is pointed out that Stalin, a Gentile, was chosen by the International moneylenders, and that, acting on their instructions, he put Trotsky out of the way and proceeded to liquidate hundreds of thousands of Russian Jews in the *purges* which put him in power, following Lenin's death. This should prove to sincere but misguided people everywhere, that the International Bankers, and their carefully selected agents and friends, don't consider the MASSES of the people of any race, colour, or creed, as anything other than expendable pawns in the game. It is true that many Jews became Communists and followers of Karl Marx. They worked and fought to bring into being Karl Marx's published theories for an International of Soviet Socialist Republics. But they, like many Gentiles, were deceived. By the time Stalin was firmly seated in Moscow as the head agent of the International Bankers, it was difficult to find any members of the First and Second Internationals alive. The manner in which the Arch-conspirators used Grand Orient Masons, and then had them liquidated as soon as they had served their purpose, is just another illustration of the ruthlessness of those whose only god is Satan.

Further evidence will be produced to prove that the International Bankers are not interested in anything else other than obtaining for their own small and very select group, ultimate undisputed control of the wealth, natural resources, and man-power of the entire world.[9] The only honest thought in any of their minds is that they obviously believe that they are so superior in mental ability to the rest of mankind that they are better able than any other group of individuals to manage the World's affairs. They are convinced that they can work out a plan of world government that is better than God's plan. For this reason, they are determined to ultimately obliterate from the minds of all human beings all knowledge of God and of His Commandments and substitute their own *New Order* based on the theory that the State is Supreme in all things and the Head of the State is, therefore, God Almighty upon this earth. The attempted deification of Stalin is proof of this statement. Once people become convinced of this great truth they will realize that men of all races, colours, and creeds have been used, and are still being used, as "Pawns in the Game."

---

1. Protocols of Zion Number 15 reads, "We execute Masons in such wise that none save the brotherhood can ever have a suspicion of it," and again "In this way we shall proceed with those GOY masons who get to know too much." E. Scudder, in his *Life of Mirabeau* says, "He (Mirabeau) died at a moment when the revolution might still have been checked."

2. My investigations prove that the men who have constituted The Secret Powers behind the scenes of International Intrigue and directed the WRM and the Nazi plan for World Conquest, have not all been of Semitic origin or members of the Jewish religion. I feel certain they were all of the Illuminati, regardless of racial origin. Money-Barons, Industrial Monopolists, Grasping Politicians, never hesitated to blame Jews and Gentiles alike, for the crimes they committed against humanity.

3. The volumes are never mentioned or reprinted with his other works. They are almost unobtainable. As the story of The Secret Power unfolds, the reader will realize the importance of this significant fact which illustrates how the channels of publicity are controlled. (Note to 2010 edition: recently they have been reprinted, and can also be viewed on the Internet.)

4. This was quoted in the Convent du Grand Orient 1923, p. 402. The Illuminati control masonry.

5. Henry Delassus' passage quoted in *La Conjuration Anti-Chrétienne* Vol. I, p. 146, re-quoted in *The Spanish Arena*, p. 143.

6. A.G. Michel in *La Dictature de la Franc-Maçonnerie la France* requoted in the Spanish Arena, p. 143.

7. All political events which have occurred in France from the outbreak of World War Two to the recent refusal by Mendes-France to agree to the E.D.C. must be studied, with due regard to the Long Range Plan of the Illuminati whose agents, the grand Orient Freemasons, are members of all levels of the French government, and all political parties. At the last check more than one hundred members of the French Parliament were Grand Orient Masons.

8. J. Marques-Rivière is the author of *Comment la Franc-Maçonnerie fait une Révolution.*

9. The reason the International Bankers backed Political Zionism from 1914 to date is explained in another chapter dealing with events which led to World War Two. It is sufficient to say here that the International Bankers were interested in securing control of the Five Trillion Dollars worth of minerals and oil which had been discovered in Palestine by Cunningham-Craig, consulting Geologist to the British Government and others, prior to 1918. These geological reports were kept secret. In 1939, Cunningham-Craig was recalled from Canada to make another survey in the Middle East. He died under mysterious circumstances immediately after he had completed his task. Today, (1954), arrangements are being made quietly by the big money people to exploit these resources.

CHAPTER FIVE

Monetary Manipulation

When the Rothschilds obtained control of the Bank of England, following Nathan's spectacular financial "killing" in 1815, he and his associates insisted that Gold be made the only base for the issuance of paper money. In 1870, the European Bankers experienced a little annoyance in their control system due to the fact that in America a considerable amount of silver coin was used. The European Bankers decided that silver must be demonetized in the United States. At that time England had much gold and very little silver; America had much silver and very little gold.[1] The bankers on both sides of the Atlantic knew that while this difference continued, they could not obtain absolute control of the economy of the nation, absolute control being essential for the success of big scale manipulation.

The European International Bankers sent Ernest Seyd over to America and placed at his disposal in American banks $500,000 with which to bribe key members of the American legislature. In 1873, at the instigation of the bankers, their agents introduced a "Bill" innocently named "A Bill to reform Coinage and Mint Laws." It was cleverly drafted. Many pages of writing concealed the real purpose behind the Bill. The Bill was sponsored by none other than Senator John Sherman, whose letter to the House of Rothschild has already been referred to. Sherman was supported by Congressman Samuel Hooper. After Senator Sherman gave a very plausible, but misleading, report regarding the purpose of the Bill, it was passed without a dissenting vote. Three years passed before the full import of the Bill began to be realized. It was a camouflaged Bill to demonetize silver. President Grant signed the Bill without reading the contents after he had been assured it was just a routine matter necessary to make some desirable reforms in the coinage and monetary laws. According to the Congressional Record, none but the members of the Committee which introduced the Bill understood its meaning.

The International Bankers considered the passage of the Bill so essential to their plans to obtain absolute control of the monetary system of the United States, that Ernest Seyd was instructed to represent himself as an expert on coining of money. After organizing the formation of a committee favourable to his master's objectives, he sat in with the committee, in a professional advisory, capacity, and helped draft the Bill in accordance with the Rothschilds' instructions.

Congressman Samuel Hooper introduced the Bill in the House on April 9th, 1872. He is recorded as saying: "Mr. Ernest Seyd, of London, a distinguished writer, has given great attention to the subject of mints and coinage. After examining the first draft of the Bill, he furnished many valuable suggestions which have been incorporated in the Bill." Mr. John R. Elsom in his book, *Lightning over the Treasury Building*, on page 49 declares: "According to his (Seyd's) own statement, made to his friend Mr. Frederick A. Lukenback, of Denver, Colorado, who has, under oath, given us the story, he (Seyd) said 'I saw the Committee of the House and Senate and paid the money, and stayed in America until I knew the measure was safe.' "

In 1878, a further withdrawal of currency and restricting of credits caused 10,478 business and banking failures in the United States. In 1879, the issuance of more coin at the insistence of Congress halted the artificially created recession and reduced business failures to 6,658. But in 1882, the "Secret Power" behind International affairs issued orders that there was to be no more pussy-footing. They reminded their banking associates in the States that sentiment has no place in business. These admonishments produced results as spectacular as they were drastic. Between 1882 and 1887 the per capita money in circulation in the United States was reduced to $6.67. This action increased the total business failures from 1878 to 1892, to 148,703 while proportionate foreclosures were made on farms and private dwellings. Only the bankers and their agents, who made the loans and took foreclosure proceedings, benefited.

It would appear that the International bankers were deliberately creating conditions of poverty and despair in the United States in order to produce conditions which would enable their instrument the *World Revolutionary Party* to recruit revolutionary forces. This accusation is supported by a letter issued to all American Bankers, by the American Bankers Association. It has been proved that this association was intimately affiliated with Rothschild's European Monopoly, if not actually controlled by the House of Rothschild, at that time. The letter reads:

March 11, 1893.

Dear Sir:

The interests of the National Banks require immediate financial legislation by Congress. Silver certificates, and Treasury notes, must be retired, and national bank notes, upon a gold basis, made the only money. This will require the authorization of new bonds in the amount of $500,000,000 to $1,000,000,000 as the basis of circulation. You will at once retire one-third of your circulation and will call one-half of your loans. Be careful to create a money stringency among your patrons, especially among influential business men. The life of the National Banks, as fixed and safe investments, depends upon immediate action as there is an increasing sentiment in favour of government legal tender and silver coinage.

This command was obeyed immediately and the panic of 1893 was created. William Jennings Bryan tried to counteract the bankers' conspiracy, but once again the public believed the false accusations circulated in the Press by the bankers' propagandists. The man in the street blamed the government. The average citizen never even suspected the part the bankers had played in creating chaos in order to feather their own nests. William Jennings Bryan was unable to do anything constructive. His voice, like the voices of many other honest and loyal citizens, was a voice crying in the wilderness.

In 1899, J.P. Morgan and Anthony Drexel went to England to attend the International Bankers' Convention. When they returned, J.P. Morgan had been appointed head representative for the Rothschild's interests in the United States. He was probably chosen as Top-man because of the ingenuity he had shown when he made a fortune selling his government Union Army rifles which had already been condemned.[2]

As the result of the London Conference, J.P. Morgan & Co. of New York, Drexel & Co. of Philadelphia, Grenfell & Co. of London, Morgan Harjes & Co. of Paris, M.M. Warburgs of Germany & Amsterdam, and the House of Rothschild were all affiliated.

The Morgan-Drexel combination organized the Northern Securities Corporation in 1901 for the purpose of putting the Heinze-Morse group out of business. The Heinze-Morse controlled considerable banking, shipping, steel and other industries. They had to be put out of business so the Morgan-Drexel combination could control the forthcoming Federal election.

The Morgan-Drexel combination succeeded in putting in Theodore Roosevelt in 1901. This delayed the prosecution which had been started against them by the Justice Department because of the alleged illegal methods used to rid themselves of competition. Morgan-Drexel then affiliated with Kuhn-Loeb & Co. To test their combined strength, it was decided to stage another financial "killing." They created "The Wall Street Panic of 1907." The public reaction to such methods of legalized gangsterism was sufficient to make the Government take action, but the evidence which follows clearly proves how the public was betrayed.

The Government appointed a *National Monetary Commission*. Senator Nelson Aldrich was appointed head of the commission. He was charged with the duty of making a thorough study of financial practices, and then formulating banking and currency reforms by submitting the necessary legislation to Congress. Aldrich, it was discovered afterwards, was financially interested with the powerful Rubber and Tobacco Trusts. He was just about the last man in the Senate who should have been entrusted with such a task. Immediately after his appointment, Aldrich picked a small group of trusted lieutenants and they all departed for Europe. While in Europe they were given every facility to study the way the international bankers controlled the economy of European countries. After Aldrich had spent two years, and over $300,000 of the American tax-payers' money, in Europe, he returned to the U.S.A. All the public received for their money was to be told by Aldrich that he hadn't been able to arrive at any definite plan which would prevent recurring of these financial panics that had upset business, created unemployment, and destroyed many small fortunes in the U.S.A. since the Civil War. Aldrich was so close to the Rockefellers that J.D. Jr. married his daughter Abby.

Prior to the tour of Europe, Aldrich had been advised to consult Paul Warburg. Paul Moritz Warburg was a unique character. He had arrived in the U.S.A. as a German immigrant about 1902. It turned out afterwards that he was a member of the European Financial House of M.M. Warburg & Co. of Hamburg and Amsterdam. This company was, as we have seen, with the House of Rothschild. Paul Warburg had studied International finance in Germany, France, Great Britain, Holland and other countries before entering America as an immigrant. The U.S.A. proved to be his land of golden opportunity because in no time at all he purchased a partnership in Kuhn-Loeb & Co. of New York. He was voted a salary of $500,000 a year. One of his new partners was Jacob Schiff who had previously purchased into the firm with Rothschild gold. Jacob Schiff is the man, evidence will prove, who financed the Terrorist Movement in Russia from 1883 onwards to 1917.

Schiff hadn't done too badly for himself and his backers. He had managed to achieve undisputed control over the transportation, the communication systems, and the supply lines in the United States. As has been proved, control of these is absolutely essential for successful revolutionary effort in any country.[3]

On the night of November 22nd, 1910, a private railway coach was waiting at the Hoboken, New Jersey, Railway Station. Senator Aldrich arrived with A. Piatt Andrew, a professional economist and treasury official, who had been wined and dined in Europe. Shelton, Aldrich's private secretary, also turned up. He was followed by Frank Vanderlip, president of the National City Bank of New York; this Bank represented the Rockefeller

Oil Interests and the Kuhn-Loeb railway interests. The directors of the National City Bank had been publicly charged with helping to foment a war between the U.S.A. and Spain in 1898. Regardless of the truth or otherwise, of the charges, the fact remains that the National City Bank owned and controlled Cuba's sugar industry when the war ended. Others who joined Aldrich were H.P. Davison—the senior partner of J.P. Morgan & Co., and Charles D. Norton—the president of Morgan's First National Bank of New York. These last three had been accused in the American legislature of controlling the entire money and credit of the U.S.A. Last to arrive were Paul Warburg and Benjamin Strong. Warburg was so wealthy and powerful by this time that he is said to have inspired the famous comic strip ("Orphan Annie") in which *Warbucks* is featured as the most wealthy and influential man in the world—a man who can, when he so wishes, use superhuman or supernatural powers to protect himself and his interests. Benjamin Strong came into prominence during the preliminary manipulations of high finance which led to the Wall Street Panic of 1907. As one of J.P. Morgan's lieutenants he had earned a reputation for carrying out orders without question and with ruthless efficiency.

Aldrich's private coach was attached to the train. Newspaper reporters learned of this gathering of the men who controlled America's oil, finances, communications, transportations and heavy industries. They began to swarm down upon the private car like locusts...but they couldn't get anyone to speak. Mr. Vanderlip finally brushed off the reporters' demands for information with the explanation "We are going away for a quiet week-end."

It took years to discover what happened that quiet week-end. A secret meeting was held on Jekyll Island, Georgia. This hideaway was owned by J.P. Morgan and a small group of his financial affiliates. The business discussed at the meeting referred to was, "Ways and means to ensure that proposed legislation to curb financial racketeering and monetary manipulation in the U.S.A. be sabotaged and legislation favourable to those attending the secret meeting be substituted." To achieve these two important objectives was no easy task. Mr. Paul Warburg was asked to suggest solutions. His advice was accepted.

Subsequent meetings were held by the same group to iron out details in New York. The conspirators named their group the *First Name Club* because, when meeting together, they always addressed each other by their first names, to guard against strangers becoming interested should they hear the surnames of national and international financiers being spoken. To make a long story short, Aldrich, Warburg and Company drew up the monetary legislation which Aldrich ultimately presented as the work of his special committee. He had it passed by Congress in 1913 under the title "The Federal Reserve Act of 1913". The vast majority of American citizens honestly believed that this act protected their interests, and placed the Federal Government in control of the nation's economy.

Nothing is further from the truth. The Federal Reserve System placed the affiliated bankers in America and Europe in position to bring about and control World War One. This statement will be proved. World War One was fought to enable the International Conspirators to bring about the Russian Revolution in 1917.

These facts illustrate how history does repeat itself and why. By means of similar plots and intrigue, the International Bankers had brought about the English Revolution in 1640-1649, and the Great French Revolution of 1789.[4]

In 1914, the Federal Reserve System consisted of twelve banks which had bought $134,000,000 worth of Federal Reserve Stock. According to Congressional Record of May 29th, 1939; they had made a profit of $23,141,456,197. In 1940, the assets of the Federal Reserve were shown as five billion dollars. In 1946, they were declared to be forty-five billion dollars. The bankers made forty billion dollars profit out of their transactions in World War Two.

The majority of citizens in the United States believe that the Federal Reserve System benefits the people of the Nation as a whole. They think the Federal Reserve System protects the depositors' money by making bank failures impossible. They think that profits made by the Federal Reserve Banks benefit the National Treasury. They are wrong on all suppositions.

What the majority of the people think is exactly what the Federal Reserve System was originally intended to accomplish, but the legislation drawn up on Jekyll Island, Georgia in 1910, and passed by the American Congress in 1913, did not benefit the people or the government of the U.S.A. It benefited only the American Bankers, who were interlocked with the International Bankers of Europe.

The President of the United States nominates four of the men who are charged with the responsibility of operating the Federal Reserve System. They are paid $15,000 a year for their services. Congressional records will prove that the member banks shared illegally the profits made right from its inception. It wasn't until 1922 that the original Act was amended so the bankers could take the profits legally.

Regarding the delusion that the Federal Reserve System protects people who deposit their money for safe-keeping in American Banks against possible bank failures, statistics show that since the Federal Reserve System came into operation in 1913, over 14,000 banks have failed. Millions upon millions of dollars, the depositors' hard-earned money, were lost. As money or wealth is indestructible, generally speaking, somebody got what the others lost. That is what we term "Smart Business" today.

---

[1] It was to aggravate this situation that agents of the International Conspirators in America organized the gangs of stage-coach and train-robbers to intercept shipments of gold being sent from various mines to the U.S. Treasury during this period. This connection between international Bankers and the Underworld will be proved to exist even today.

[2] Gustavus Myers deals with J.P. Morgan's and his father's connections with the House of Rothschild in much greater detail. All Americans who wish to stop history repeating itself should read how they were sold down the river in the middle of last century. It is explained in another Chapter how the International Bankers met in one section of London and planned policy while the revolutionary leaders met in another and worked out the details of intrigue which would put the wars and revolutions planned by the master-minds into effect.

[3] Investigations in several countries already subjugated prove that the Financial Tycoons who owned and controlled the transportation systems on land and sea, and affiliated industries deliberately brought about conditions which led to general strikes immediately prior to the date set for a revolutionary effort to take place. It must be obvious that these international Tycoons cannot form dictatorships as they did in Russia until existing governments and institutions have been overthrown. This book proves how this purpose was achieved in Russia.

[4] For full details of the Federal Reserve Conspiracy, read the book of that title written by Eustace Mullins and published by Common Sense, Union, New-Jersey, 1954.

CHAPTER SIX

Events Preceding the Russian Revolution

The invasion of Russia in 1812 by Napoleon shook the Russian people to the core. Tzar Alexander I set about the task of organizing a recovery programme. In the hope that he could bring about a united effort throughout the Russian Empire, he relaxed many of the restrictions which had been imposed on the Jews when they were confined to the Pale of Settlement in 1772. Special concessions were made to the artisans and professional classes. A determined effort was made to establish Jews in agriculture. Under Alexander I they were given every encouragement to assimilate themselves into the Russian way of life.

Nicholas I succeeded Alexander I in 1825. He was less inclined to favour the Jews, because he viewed their rapid inroads into the Russian economy with alarm. His government viewed with great displeasure the determination of the Jews to maintain their separate culture, language, mode of dress, etc.

In order to try to assimilate the Jews into the Russian society, Nicholas I, in 1804, made it compulsory for all Jewish children to attend Public School. Nicholas thought that if the young Jews could be convinced that they would be welcomed into Russian society it would go a long way to eliminate misunderstandings. His avowed purpose was to offset the one-sided story of religious persecution which was drilled into their minds from early infancy.

The net results of the Russian experiment didn't turn out as expected. Education for non-Jewish children was not compulsory. The Jews became the best educated segment in Russia.[1]

Alexander II followed Nicholas I to the throne of Russia in 1855. Benjamin Disraeli referred to Alexander II as "the most benevolent prince that ever ruled over Russia." Alexander devoted his life to improving the conditions of the peasants, poorer classes, and the Jews. In 1861, he emancipated 23,000,000 serfs. This unfortunate class had been *forced* to work on the land. They were *literally* slaves. They could be transferred from one owner to another in all sales, or leases, of landed estates.

Many Jews, who had taken advantage of the compulsory education, entered universities. They found themselves severely handicapped after graduation when seeking employment. To correct this injustice, Alexander II ruled that all Jewish graduates be allowed to settle and hold government positions in Greater Russia. In 1879, Jewish apothecaries, nurses, mid-wives, dentists, distillers and skilled craftsmen were permitted to work and reside anywhere in Russia.

But the Jewish revolutionary leaders were determined to continue their movement for Popular World Revolution. Their terrorist groups committed one outrage after another. They worked to enlist the support of disgruntled Russian intellectuals and to plant the general idea of violent revolution in the minds of the industrial working population. In 1866, they made their first attempt on the life of Alexander II. They tried to murder him a second time in 1879. In some miraculous manner both attempts failed. It was then decided a very special effort had to be made to remove Alexander. His benevolent rule was completely upsetting their claim that "much needed reforms can only be brought about speedily by revolutionary action." The conspirators hatched their next plot against the life of Alexander II in the home of the Jewess Hesia Helfman. The Tzar was murdered in 1881.

While the Revolutionary Forces within Russia were trying to embarrass the government in every way possible, and committing all kinds of outrages, including assassination, the "Secret Powers" behind the WRM from their headquarters in England, Switzerland and the United States were trying once again to involve Britain in war with Russia. In such a war, neither Empire could make any appreciable gains. The final outcome of such a war would be to weaken both Empires materially and leave them easier prey for revolutionary action afterwards.

In the Nineteenth Century, October issue, 1881, Goldwyn Smith, professor of modern history at Oxford University wrote: "When I was last in England we were on the brink of war with Russia, which would have involved the whole Empire — the Jewish interests throughout Europe, with the Jewish Press of Vienna as its chief organ, was doing its utmost to push us in." [2]

The assassination of the Russians' "Little Father" in 1881 caused wide-spread resentment which was expressed by a spontaneous outbreak of violence against the Jewish population in many parts of Russia. The Russian Government passed "The May Laws." These were harsh laws passed because the Russian officials who sponsored them argued that "if the Jews could not be satisfied and reconciled by the benevolent policy of Alexander II then it was obvious that they would be satisfied with nothing less than the absolute domination of Russia." Once again the whole Jewish Race was being punished for the sins of a few self-appointed revolutionary leaders.

On May 23rd, 1882, a Jewish delegation, headed by Baron Ginzberg,[3] called on the new Tzar Alexander III and officially protested the May Laws. The Tzar promised a thorough investigation into the whole matter concerning the conflict between the Jewish and non-Jewish factions of the Empire's population. On September 3rd he issued this statement:

> For some time the government has given its attention to the Jews, and their problems and their relations to the rest of the inhabitants of the Empire with a view to ascertaining the sad conditions of the Christian population brought about by the conduct of the Jews in business matters. During the last twenty years the Jews have not only possessed themselves of every trade and business in all its branches but also of a great part of the land by buying or farming it. With few exceptions they have, as a body, devoted their attention not to enriching, or benefiting the country, but to defrauding the Russian people by their wiles. Particularly have the poor inhabitants suffered, and this conduct has called forth protests from the people as manifested in acts of violence against the Jews. The government, while on one hand doing its best to put down these disturbances, and to deliver the Jews from oppression and slaughter, on the other hand thought it a matter of urgency, and justice, to adopt the stringent measures to put an end to oppression as practiced by the Jews on the other inhabitants, and to rid the country of their malpractices, which were, as is well known, the original cause of the anti-Jewish agitations.

The May Laws had been passed by the Government not only as an act of resentment because of the assassination of Tzar Alexander II, but also because Russian economists had been urgently warning the Government that the national economy was in danger of being ruined if measures were not taken to curb the illegal activities of the Jews. The economists pointed out that while the Jews only represented 4.2 per cent of the whole population, they had been able to entrench themselves so well in the Russian economy that the nation was faced with economic disaster. How correct the economists proved to be is shown by the action taken after Baron Ginzberg's deputation failed to have the May Laws rescinded. The International Bankers imposed economic sanctions against the Russian Empire. They almost reduced the nation to bankruptcy. They exercised an embargo on Russian trade and commerce. In 1904, after they involved the Russian Empire in a disastrous war with Japan, the English Banking House of Rothschild repudiated its promise of financial aid and tried to render the Russian Empire bankrupt, while Kuhn-Loeb & Co. New York extended to Japan all the credit for which they asked.

Encyclopedia Britannica, page 76, Vol. 2 — 1947 says this of the May Laws:

> The Russian May Laws were the most conspicuous legislative monument achieved by modern anti-semitism...Their immediate results were a ruinous commercial depression which was felt all over the empire and which profoundly affected the national credit. The Russian Minister was at his wits end for money. Negotiations for a large loan were entered into with the House of Rothschild and a preliminary contract was signed when the Finance Minister was informed that unless the persecutions of the Jews were stopped, the great banking house *would be compelled* to withdraw from the contract...In this way antisemitism, which had already so profoundly influenced the domestic policies of Europe, set its mark on the International relations of the Powers, for it was the urgent need of the Russian Treasury, quite as much as the termination of Prince Bismarck's secret treaty of mutual neutrality, which brought about the Franco-Russian Alliance.

Many orthodox Jews were worried because of the ruthless terrorism being practised by their compatriots. They knew that a similar policy was being carried out in France, Germany, Spain and Italy. The less radical Jews worried because they feared a continuation of such terrorism would result in such a wave of anti-semitism that it could quite possibly end with the extermination of the Jewish race. Their worst fears were confirmed by a German Jew, Theodore Herzl, who informed them of Karl Ritter's anti-semitic policy and warned them that it was rapidly being spread throughout Germany. He suggested the organization of a Jewish *Back to Israel* Movement on the part of orthodox Jews. This was the beginning of the Zionist movement.[4]

After Tzar Alexander III had issued his verdict blaming AVARICIOUS Jews as the cause of the Empire's unrest and economic ruin, the leaders of the revolutionaries organized "The Social Revolutionary Party." An utterly ruthless man named Gershuni was appointed organiser of the Terrorist Groups. A tailor named Yevno Azev was appointed to organize the "Fighting Sections." The leaders of the Social Revolutionary Party also emphasized the importance of enlisting Gentiles in the movement. Gentiles, who passed the tests to which they were submitted, became full members. It was this decision that brought Alexander Ulyanov into the party. Before the revolutionary leaders would admit him into full membership, he was ordered to take part in the plot to assassinate Tzar Alexander III. The attempt on the Tzar's life failed. Alexander Ulyanov was arrested. He was tried and condemned to death. His execution caused his younger brother, Vladimir, to dedicate himself to the revolutionary cause. Vladimir rose in power until he became leader of the Bolshevik Party. He assumed the name of Lenin. He ultimately became the first Dictator of the U.S.S.R.

Between 1900 and 1906, in addition to causing serious labour trouble and creating terrible misunderstanding between all levels of Russian society, the Revolutionary Party rubbed the sore of religious bigotry until it developed into a festering boil. This boil was brought to a head by the hot applications of wholesale murders and assassinations. The boil burst in the form of the revolution of 1905.

The official assassinated by the Social Revolutionaries Terrorist Section was Bogolepov, Minister of Education in 1901. This assassination was perpetrated to register Jewish resentment against the educational clause in the previously-referred-to May Laws. This clause limited the number of Jews attending state-supported schools, and universities, to a number in ratio to the Jewish population as compared to the whole Russian population. This measure was passed because the State financed schools had become flooded with Jewish students. A group of young Jews who had "suffered" when boys (because of the educational clause in the May Laws of 1882) were given the task of murdering the Minister of Education. They had to prove their courage and ability to qualify them for duty with the Terrorist section of the Social Revolutionary Party.

Next year (1902) Sipyagin, Minister of the Interior, was assassinated to emphasize Jewish resentment against the May Law which had reversed the policy of Alexander II, and prohibited Jews from living outside the Pale of Settlement. Jews who had been evicted from their homes in Greater Russia under the May Law as children were chosen to carry out this "Execution." They made no mistake.

In 1903, Bogdanovich—Governor of Ufa—was assassinated; in 1904 Vischelev von Plehve, the Russian Premier was killed; in 1905 the first full-scale Russian Revolution broke out. The Grand Duke Sergius, uncle of the Tzar, was assassinated on February 17th. In December, 1905, General Dubrassov suppressed the revolutionaries, but in 1906 he was assassinated by the Terrorist Section.

After the Tzar had blamed the Jews for the unsatisfactory state of affairs in Russia, Baron Ginzberg was instructed to work to bring about the destruction of the Russian Empire. It was agreed that to start the Russo-Japanese War, the Rothschild interests in Europe would pretend to be friendly with Russia. They would finance the war on Russia's behalf while secretly the Rothschild's partners, Kuhn-Loeb & Co. of New York, would finance the Japanese government. The defeat of Russia was to be made certain by the Rothschilds withdrawing financial aid when it was most needed. Chaos and confusion was to be created within the Russian armed forces in the Far East by sabotaging the lines of transport and communication crossing Siberia. This caused both the Russian Army and Navy to run short of supplies and reinforcements.[5]

Then again, a Russian Naval Officer bound from the Baltic to Port Arthur in the Far East, ordered his ships to fire on a British Trawler Fleet fishing on the Dogger Bank in the North Sea. No logical reason was ever forthcoming to explain this wanton act of cruelty and mass murder against a supposedly friendly power. Public reaction in England was such that war was narrowly averted. Because of this incident, many British Naval Officers and British Merchant Officers volunteered their services to Japan.

The Japanese government was financed by international loans raised by Jacob Schiff (New York). Schiff was senior partner in Kuhn-Loeb & Co. He cooperated with Sir Ernest Cassels (England) and the Warburgs (Hamburg). Jacob Schiff justified his action of financing the Japanese in the war against Russia in a letter he wrote to Count Witte, the Tzar's emissary who attended the Peace negotiations held at Portsmouth, U.S.A. in 1905:

> Can it be expected that the influence of the American Jew upon public opinion will be exerted to the advantage of the country which systematically degraded his brethren-in-race?...If the Government, now being formed, should not succeed in assuring safety, and equal opportunity throughout the Empire, to the Jewish population, then indeed the time will have come for the Jews in Russia to quit their inhospitable fatherland. While the problem with which the civilized world will then be faced will be enormous, it will be solved, and you, who are not only a far-seeing statesman, but also a great economist, know best that the fate of Russia, and its doom, will then be sealed.

The hypocrisy of Jacob Schiff can be better appreciated when it is explained that from 1897 he had financed the Terrorists in Russia. In 1904, he helped finance the revolution that broke out in Russia in 1905. He also helped to organize on an international basis the financing of the Russian Revolution which broke out early in 1917, and gave him and his associates their first opportunity to put their Totalitarian Theories into effect.[6]

The Russo-Japanese War was fomented by the international bankers in order to create the conditions necessary for the success of a revolutionary effort to overthrow the power of the Tzars. The plans of the International Bankers were upset when the Jewish-led Mensheviks started a revolution independently in Russia in 1905. When the International Bankers withheld financial support the revolution failed right at the moment it appeared to have reached the pinnacle of success.

Because the Jewish-dominated Mensheviks acted on their own initiative, the International Bankers decided that Lenin would conduct *their* revolutionary programme in Russia from that date onwards.

Lenin was born in the city of Simbirsk, located on the banks of the river Volga. He was the son of a government official who had the title of "Actual State Counselor." This title was not inherited, but had been awarded to his father for outstanding service as a school supervisor. Lenin received a university education and was admitted to the practice of Law but he never set himself up in business. Jewish students had persuaded him that it was time to overthrow the power of the privileged classes and time that the masses ruled their own countries. It was while Lenin was toying with the idea that "necessary reforms could only be brought about speedily by revolutionary action" that his brother was arrested by the police and executed.

Lenin was quickly recognized as an intellectual. He was associating with the leaders of the Revolutionary Party when in his early twenties. It has been previously stated that the wealthy direct influential international moneylenders had helped finance and direct the revolutionary activities within the Pale of Settlement. Lenin wanted to find out all he could about the people who directed the various national revolutionary groups which were united in the common cause of Popular Revolution. In 1895, at the age of twenty-five, he went to Switzerland and joined Plekhanov who had fled there from Russia to escape the fate of Lenin's older brother Alexander.

While in Switzerland, Lenin and Plekhanov, who were Gentiles, joined forces with Vera Zasulich, Leo Deutch, P. Axelrod, and Julius Tsederbaum, who were all Jews. They formed a Marxist Movement on a worldwide scale which they named the "Group for the Emancipation of Labour." Tsederbaum was a young man like Lenin. He had earned a reputation in "The Pale of Settlement" as a ruthless terrorist and accomplished agitator. He changed his name to Martov. He became leader of the Mensheviks. Lenin ruled the Bolsheviks in Russia.

The abortive revolutionary attempt by the Mensheviks in 1905 convinced Lenin that the only way to have a successful revolution was to organize an International Planning Committee which would first plan and then direct any agreed-upon revolutionary effort. Lenin brought into being the *Comintern*, as the Central International Revolutionary Planning Committee. The International Bankers picked him as their top-level agent in Russia. Lenin had made a serious study of the Great French Revolution. When he learned that the *Secret Power* which had brought about the French Revolution was still in active operation, he threw in his lot with them. His plan was to let the members of the Comintern think they were the *Brains*, but to influence their thinking, so that they furthered the Long-Range Plans of the International Bankers. If the day came when the revolutionary leaders couldn't be controlled, they could always be liquidated. Evidence will be given to show how this actually happened.

Having decided his own policy, Lenin returned to Russia with Martov to organize his Money-Raising Campaign which consisted of blackmail, bank robbery, extortion, and other kinds of illegal practices. Lenin argued that it was only logical to take money from the people whose government they plotted to overthrow. He made it a principle of his party that all young people who aspired to membership should, like his older brother Alexander, be tested for physical courage and mental alertness. Lenin insisted that part of every young revolutionary's training should include robbing a bank, blowing up a police station, and liquidating a traitor or spy.

Lenin also insisted that the revolutionary *leaders*, in all other countries, should organize an underground system. In discussing this matter and writing about it, Lenin declared, "everything legal and illegal which furthers the revolutionary movement is justified." He warned, however, that "the legal party should always be in control of the illegal." This practice is in force today, particularly in Canada and the United States. Communists who openly acknowledge their membership in the Labour Progressive Party take great care not to get involved in a criminal way with the illegal activities of the Communist party's underground organization. But the "Apparatus" secretly directs operations and benefits financially as a result.

It is a fact that few of the early leaders of Communism were members of the proletariat. Most of them were well-educated intellectuals. In 1895, they caused a series of strikes. Some of these were successfully turned into riots. Thus they brought about one of the fundamental principles of revolutionary technique "developing a minor disturbance until it became a riot, and brought the citizens into actual physical conflict with the police."

Lenin, Martov, and a number of other revolutionaries were arrested and sentenced to prison. Lenin finished his prison term in 1897.

It is not generally known that in those days in Russia, political offenders exiled to Siberia were not imprisoned if they had not been convicted of any other *criminal* offence. Therefore, Lenin took his beautiful young Jewish wife, and her Yiddish speaking mother, into exile with him. During his term of exile, Lenin drew an allowance of seven rubles and forty kopecks a month from the Russian Government. This was just about enough to pay for room and board. Lenin worked as a bookkeeper to earn extra money. It was while in exile that Lenin, Martov, and an accomplice named Potresov, decided upon their release to publish a newspaper for the purpose of combining the brains and energies of the entire revolutionary movement which at that time was broken up into many factions.

In February 1900, Lenin finished his exile. He was granted permission to return to Switzerland for a visit. He joined the other revolutionary leaders and the agents of the *Secret Powers*. They approved his idea, and *Iskra* (The Spark) was published. The editorial board consisted of the older revolutionary leaders—Plekhanov, Zasulich and Axelrod — with Lenin, Potresov and Martov representing the younger members. Lenin's wife was secretary of the board. Trotsky joined the editorial staff two years later. For a while the paper was actually printed in Munich, Germany. The editorial board met in London.[7] In 1903, it was moved back to Geneva. The copies were smuggled into Russia and other countries by way of the underground system organized by the Grand Orient Masons. Because the paper was named *Iskra*, the revolutionaries who subscribed to the Party Line, as defined by the editorial board, became known as Iskrists.

The paper called for a Unification Congress to take place in Brussels in 1903 for the purpose of uniting various Marxist groups. The Russian Social Democrats, Rosa Luxemberg's Polish Social Democrats, the group for the Emancipation of Labour, and the Maximalist group, were represented. Early in August, the Belgium police took action, and the delegates moved over to London *en masse*. This Congress is of historical importance because during this Congress the ideological split developed between the Iskrists. Lenin became leader of the Bolshevik (or majority group) while Martov became leader of the Mensheviks (or minority group).

When the Mensheviks pulled off the abortive revolution in Russia in 1905, Trotsky proved himself a leader of ability. It is difficult for the uninitiated to understand just what caused the effort to fold up, because the revolutionaries had control of St. Petersburg from January to December 1905. They formed the Petersburg Soviet. Lenin and many of his top-level revolutionary leaders stayed aloof. They let the Menshevik Party handle this revolution.

Lenin had been in Geneva consulting with the *Secret Powers* when the revolution broke out following the Bloody Sunday tragedy in St. Petersburg in January 1905. He didn't return to Russia until October. The Bloody Sunday tragedy was blamed on the intolerance of the Tzar. However, many who investigated the happenings found ample evidence to convince them that the Bloody Sunday incident had been planned by the Terrorist Group for the purpose of arousing anger and hatred in the hearts of the non-Jewish workers against the Tzar. The incident enabled the leaders of the revolutionary movement to enlist the support of thousands of non-Jewish men and women who, until that sad day, had remained loyal to the Tzar, and spoken of him as "The Little Father." Bloody Sunday is of great historical importance.

In January 1905, Russia was at war with Japan. Transportation on the railway across the Russian wastelands from west to east had been broken down. Reinforcements and supplies had failed to get through to the eastern front due to sabotage. On January 2nd, the Russian people were shocked with the news that Port Arthur had fallen to the Japanese. They had lost the war against what they had considered a very second-class power.

The Imperial Government, in its attempt to gain the favour of the industrial population, had adopted the policy of encouraging the formation of legal trade unions. Known revolutionaries had to be barred from membership. One of the most active leaders in organizing the Legal Trade Unions was the Russian Orthodox Priest, Father Gapon. The liberal reforms, obtained by non-radical citizens, didn't please the leaders of the revolutionary party who claimed that "necessary reforms could only be brought about speedily by revolution." Father Gapon had won so much respect he was welcomed by the Tzar and his ministers any time he wished to discuss a weighty labour problem.

On January 2nd, when the bad war news swept the Empire, organized labour disturbances broke out in St. Petersburg's huge Putilov Works. A strike was called, but because of the general situation, Father Gapon said he would settle the matters in dispute by direct appeal to the Tzar. The idea appealed to the majority of the workers, but the "Radicals" opposed it. However, on Sunday afternoon January 22nd, 1905, thousands of workmen, accompanied by their wives and children, formed into a procession to accompany Father Gapon to the palace gates. According to the authentic reports, the procession was entirely orderly. Petitioners carried hastily made banners expressing loyalty to the "Little Father." At the palace gates, without the slightest warning, the procession was thrown into utter confusion by a withering volley of rifle and machine gun fire. Hundreds of workers and their families were slaughtered. The square in front of the Palace was turned into a space of agonized chaos. January 22nd, 1905 has been known as "Bloody Sunday" ever since. Was Nicholas II responsible? It is a proven fact that he was not in the Palace, or in the city, at the time. It is known that an officer of the guard ordered the troops to fire. It is quite possible he was a "Cell" carrying out the terrorist policy of his superiors. This act was the "spark" that touched the "tinder" provided by the revolutionary leaders. The "blaze" of a full-scale revolution followed.

Regardless of who was responsible, tens of thousands of previously loyal industrial workers joined the Socialist Revolutionary Party, and the movement spread to other cities. The Tzar tried to stem the tide of rebellion. Early in February he ordered an investigation into the St. Petersburg events, by the Shidlovsky Commission. In August he announced provision had been made for the establishment of a democratic representative legislature. This became the Duma. He offered amnesty to all political offenders. It was under this amnesty that Lenin, and his Bolshevik leaders, returned to Russia in October from Switzerland and other countries abroad. But nothing the Tzar did could stem the tide of revolution.

On October 20th, 1905, the Menshevik-led all-Russian Railway Union went on strike. On October 25th general strikes were effective in Moscow, Smolensk, Kursk, and other cities. On October 26th the Revolutionary Petersburg Soviet was founded. It assumed the functions of a national government. The Soviet government was dominated by the Menshevik faction of the Russian Social-Democratic Labour Party although the Social Revolutionary Party had representation. The first President was Menshevik Zborovisk. He was quickly displaced by Georgi Nosar. He in turn was superseded by Lev Trotsky who became President on December 9th, 1905. On the 16th of December, a military force arrested Trotsky and 300 members of the Soviet government. There wasn't a single prominent Bolshevik amongst those arrested. This should prove that Lenin was acting for, and protected by, the Secret Powers which operate behind the government.

The revolution wasn't quite over. On December 20th a Jew named Parvus assumed control over a new Soviet Executive. He called a general strike in St. Petersburg and 90,000 workers responded. The next day 150,000 workers went on strike in Moscow.

Open insurrection broke out in Chita, Kansk and Rostov. On December 30th the troops and government officials, who had remained loyal to the Tzar, in some *miraculous* manner regained control. They put an end to the revolution.[8] Tzar Nicholas II kept his promise. The Duma was formed and an elected legislature established.

In 1907, the Fifth Congress of the Russian Social Democratic Labour Party was held in London. Lenin with 91 delegates represented the Bolshevik party; the Mensheviks led by Martov had 89 delegates; Rosa Luxemburg led her Polish Social democrats with 44 delegates; the Jewish Bund led by Rafael Abramovitch had 55; the Lettish Social Democrats, led by Comrade Herman (Danishevsky) made up the remainder. All told there were 312 delegates of which 116 were or had been workers.

This Congress had been called for the purpose of holding a postmortem on the abortive Russian Revolution of 1905. Lenin blamed the failure of the revolutionary effort on lack of cooperation between the Mensheviks and other group leaders. He told the 312 delegates that the Mensheviks had run the whole show and made a mess of things generally. He called for unity of policy and unity of action. He argued that revolutionary action should be planned well in advance, and the element of surprise used to full advantage.

Martov hit back at Lenin. He accused him of failing to give the Menshevik revolutionary effort the support he should have. He accused him particularly of withholding financial assistance. Martov and the other Jewish groups led by Ross, Luxemberg and Abrahamovitch were annoyed that Lenin had been able to finance the attendance of the largest number of delegates. They accused him of financing his Bolshevik party by robbery, kidnappings, forgery and theft. They reprimanded him for refusing to contribute a fair proportion of his ill-gotten gains to the central unifying organization. One big laugh was created when one of the Mensheviks accused Lenin of marrying off one of his top officials to a rich widow in order to enrich his party treasury.

Lenin is alleged to have admitted he had done this for the good of the Cause. He maintained that the official he had married off to the widow was a fine, strong, healthy specimen of humanity. He thought the widow would agree she had gotten full value for her money. It was at this Congress that Stalin, then a very minor character, became attached to Lenin. The Congress finally agreed to closer cooperation between the leaders of the various revolutionary groups and decided who should edit their revolutionary newspapers. They put great emphasis upon propaganda. At this Congress they laid the foundation for a reorganization of their propaganda machine with the understanding that all publications should adopt the same editorial policy "The Party Line."

In 1908, the Bolsheviks started publishing the *Proletarie*. Lenin, Dubrovinsky, Zinoviev and Kamenev were the editors. The Mensheviks published *Golos Sotsial-Demokrata*. Plekhanov, Axelrod, Martov, Dan and Martynov (Pikel) were the editors. All editors were Jewish except Lenin and Plekhanov. Trotsky started a semi-independent publication known as The Vienna *Pravda*.

In 1909, Lenin won the unconditional support of two Jewish leaders, Zinoviev and Kamenev. They became known as "The Troika" and this friendship endured until Lenin's death in 1924.

After the Fifth Congress of the Russian Social Democrats Labour Party held in London in 1907, Lenin decided to find out how courageous and trustworthy his new disciple

Stalin was. He also wished to convince the leaders of the other revolutionary groups that he was financially independent. To accomplish this dual purpose, he instructed Stalin to rob the Tiflis Bank. Stalin picked as his accomplice an Armenian named Petroyan, who afterwards changed his name to Kamo. They discovered the Bank was going to transfer a large sum of money from one place to another by public conveyance. They waylaid the conveyance. Petroyan tossed a bomb. Everything, and everyone, in the conveyance was blown to smithereens, except the strong box containing the cash—250,000 rubles. Thirty people lost their lives. The loot was turned over to Lenin. Stalin had proven himself as a potential leader.

The Bolsheviks encountered difficulty using the stolen rubles for party purposes because most of the currency consisted of 500 ruble notes. Lenin conceived the idea of distributing the 500 ruble notes among trustworthy Bolsheviks in various countries. They were instructed to get rid of as much of the money as they could on a given day. This directive was carried out, but two of Lenin's agents fell foul of the police during the transaction. One was Olga Ravich, who afterwards married Zinoviev, Lenin's great friend. The other was Meyer Wallach, whose real name was Finklestein. He afterwards changed his name again to Maxim Litvinov. He became known throughout the world as Stalin's Commissar of Foreign Affairs from 1930 to 1939.[9]

After the revolution of 1905 had ended, Tzar Nicholas II set about making many radical reforms. He planned turning the Russian absolute monarchy into a limited monarchy such as is enjoyed by the British people. After the Duma began to function, the Premier, Peter Arkadyevich Stolypin, became a great reformer. He dominated Russian politics and drafted the "Stolypin Constitution" which guaranteed civil rights to peasants who were about 85 per cent of the entire Russian population. His land reforms granted financial assistance to the peasants so they could purchase their own farms. His idea was that the logical way to defeat those who advocated the communal way of life was to encourage individual ownership.

But the revolutionary leaders wanted to usurp political and economic power. They were not the least bit satisfied with reforms. In 1906, the Terrorist Group attempted to assassinate Stolypin. They destroyed his home with a bomb. Several more plots were hatched to do away with the most progressive premier the Russians could have hoped to have. On a dark September night, in 1911, the Great Emancipator was shot to death in cold blood while attending a gala performance at the Kiev theatre. The assassin was a Jewish lawyer named Mordecai Bogrov.

In 1907, the International Bankers organized the Wall Street Panic in order to reimburse themselves for the money spent in connection with the Russian wars and revolutions. They were also financing the preliminary stages of the Chinese revolution that broke out in 1911.

Many of Stolypin's proposed reforms were carried out after his death. In 1912, an industrial insurance law gave all industrial workmen compensation for sickness and injury to the extent of two-thirds of their regular pay for sickness, and three-fourths, for accidents. Newspapers of the revolutionary parties were given legal status for the first time since they had been printed. Public schools were expanded. The election laws were revised in order to give more representative government. In 1913, the government of the Tzar of Russia granted a general amnesty for all political prisoners. Immediately after they were released from prison, they began to plot with renewed energy the overthrow of the Russian Government. Terrorists advocated the liquidation of the Royal Family. But the reforms had appealed to the vast majority of the Russian people. The revolution in Russia looked like a dead issue for the time being. Those who directed the World Revolutionary Movement decided they would give Russia a rest for the time being. They concentrated their efforts in other countries. Portugal and Spain came in for attention.

Because of the Red Fog created by Communist propaganda, and an organized campaign of *"L'Infamie"* carried on in Russia—as it had been carried on in France and England prior to those revolutions—it is difficult for the average person to believe that the Russian Tzars and Nobles were anything else than big bearded monsters who enslaved the peasants, raped their young women, and speared babies on the points of their swords while galloping through villages on horse back. In order to prove that the last of the Tzars was a reformer we will quote Bertram Wolfe, because Bertram Wolfe was anti-Tzarist and pro-revolutionary. Wolfe says on page 360 of his book *Three who made a Revolution*:

> Between 1907 and 1914 under Stolypin's land reform laws, 2,000,000 peasants and their families receded from the village mir and became individual proprietors. All through the war (1914 -1917) the movement continued so that by January 1st, 1916, 6,200,000 peasant families out of approximately 16,000,000 who had become eligible, had made application for separation. Lenin saw the matter as a race with time between Stolypin's reforms and the next revolutionary upheaval. Should the upheaval be postponed for a couple of decades the new land measures would transform the countryside so it would no longer be a revolutionary force. How near Lenin came to being right is proved by the fact that in 1917, when he called upon the peasants to *Take the Land* they already owned more than three-fourths of it.

It is unfortunately true that Rasputin did exert an evil influence upon certain men and women of the Russian Imperial Court. I know, from ladies attached to the Court at that time, that Rasputin exercised a tremendous influence over the Empress because her young son suffered from hemophilia and Rasputin was the only man who could stop the bleeding.

Rasputin definitely had mesmeric powers which are not uncommon amongst certain of the Russian people. He seemed able to place the Empress under his influence, not as a lover, but for the purpose of making her force the Tzar to do what Rasputin decided he wanted him to do. It is not an exaggeration to say that Rasputin, because of the power he exerted on the Tzar through the Queen, virtually ruled Russia to the dismay of the Russian people.

It is also true that Rasputin introduced into Court Circles men and women who practised the pagan rites which were secretly carried on in the Palais Royal prior to the outbreak of the French Revolution in 1789. These ritualistic orgies were based on the ridiculous assumption that people could not be saved until they had plumbed the depths of degradation in sin. He introduced subversives right into the Royal Household and they obtained information that enabled their masters to blackmail many influential people into doing their bidding. Rasputin was undoubtedly of the Illuminati and the Synagogue of Satan.

[1.] This fact had a great deal to do with the eventual destruction of Tzarist power which ended with the murder of Tzar Nicholas II, and his whole family, in the house in Ekaterinburg on July 17th, 1918 by a man named Yorovrest. Ekaterinburg was afterwards renamed Sverdlovsk in honour of the Jew Yakov Sverdlov who was president of the Soviet Republic at the time of the executions. Illuminati symbols were formed on the walls of the death cellar.

[2.] This is another illustration of how even a Professor of History can fall into the Anti-Semitic pitfalls set by the conspirators. Admittedly the majority of people believe that all the International Bankers and Tycoons are Jews, but this is incorrect. The majority are not Jews, either by blood, racial descent or religion. They actually foster Anti-Semitism because they can use all Anti-movements to further their diabolical plans.

[3.] Ginzberg was the official representative in Russia of the House of Rothschild.

[4.] The Zionist Movement was in turn controlled by the International Bankers and also used to further their secret plans and ambitions. Read *The Palestine Plot* by B. Jensen.

[5.] My father, Captain F.H. Carr, was one of the British officers who served with the Japanese in 1904 and 1905. I have in my possession a very beautiful ivory carving of a Japanese wood-cutter enjoying a smoke after his lunch. This museum piece was presented to my father by the Japanese government in appreciation of services rendered. My father gave me a great deal of valuable information regarding the behind-the-scene intrigue which led to the Russian-Japanese War.

[6.] François Coty in *Figaro*, Feb. 20th, 1932, said: The subsidies granted the Nihilists at this period (i.e. 1905 to 1914 – author) by Jacob Schiff were no longer acts of isolated generosity. A veritable Russian Terrorist organization had been set up in the U.S.A. at his expense, charged to assassinate Ministers, Governors, Heads of Police, etc.

[7.] Because the Rothschild's influence was so great with the Bank of England's directors, and because the directors of the Bank of England could control the policy of the British government, revolutionaries have always been able to find asylum in England when barred by every other country. Karl Marx and Engels are typical examples.

[8.] Had Lenin and the International Bankers intervened on behalf of the Mensheviks at this time nothing could have defeated the revolutionary efforts. There is no possible explanation for them allowing the Government Forces to regain control except that they had secret plans which they were not then ready to put into effect. That they were preparing for World War One and wished Russia to remain a Monarchy until after the war broke out seems to be the only logical conclusion, and future events would indicate this was their plan.

[9.] This "Gangster" played an important part in International affairs in England and Germany, in the League of Nations and the United Nations right up to the time of his death.

CHAPTER SEVEN

The Russian Revolution — 1917

In January 1910, nineteen leaders of the World Revolutionary Movement met in London. This meeting is recorded as "The January Plenum of the Central Committee." Ways and means were discussed to bring about greater unity. Lenin was again pressed to give up his policy of financial independence. He responded by burning the Five Hundred Ruble notes left over from the Tiflis bank robbery. Lenin was convinced it was just about impossible to cash the notes without getting caught by the police.

The Plenum decided to accept the newspaper Sotsial Demokrata as the general party publication. The Bolsheviks appointed Lenin and Zinoviev, and the Mensheviks, Martov and Dan as editors. Kamenev was appointed to assist Trotsky in editing the Vienna *Pravda*. The Plenum also discussed the pattern the world revolutionary effort should take. The delegates considered the possible repercussions certain contemplated political assassinations would bring about. The policy of the party was set. The Central Committee was ordered to prepare the Temples and Lodges of the Grand Orient for action. The members were to be made active proselytizing their revolutionary and atheistic ideology.[1]

The Party Line was to unite all revolutionary bodies for the purpose of bringing all the big capitalistic countries into war with each other so that the terrific losses suffered, the high taxation imposed, and the hardships endured by the masses of the population, would make the majority of the working classes react favourably to the suggestion of a revolution to end wars. When all countries had been Sovietized, then the Secret Powers would form a Totalitarian Dictatorship and their identity need remain secret no longer. It is possible that only Lenin knew the secret aims and ambitions of the Illuminati who moulded revolutionary action to suit their purposes.

The revolutionary leaders were to organize their undergrounds in all countries so as to be ready to take over their nation's political system and economy; the International Bankers were to extend the ramifications of their agencies right around the world. It has been shown that Lenin became active in revolutionary circles in 1894. It has also been stated that he decided to throw in his lot with the International Bankers because he doubted the ability of the men who led the Jewish dominated national revolutionary parties to consolidate their victories when gained. In view of these statements it is necessary to review revolutionary events from 1895 to 1917.

The Empress of Austria was assassinated in 1898; King Humbert in 1900; President McKinley in 1901; the Grand Duke Sergius of Russia in 1905, and the King and Crown Prince of Portugal in 1908. To prove that the Illuminati acting through the Grand Orient Masons were responsible for these political assassinations, the following evidence is submitted.

The leaders of the World Revolutionary Movement, meeting in Geneva, Switzerland, thought it was necessary to remove King Carlos of Portugal so they could establish a Republic in Portugal; in 1907 they ordered his assassination. In December 1907, Megalhaes Lima—the head of Portuguese Grand Orient Masonry—went to Paris to lecture to the Masonic Lodges. His subject was "Portugal, the overthrow of the

Monarchy, and the need of a Republican form of government." A few weeks later, King Carlos and his son, the Crown Prince, were assassinated.

Continental Masons boasted of this success. Furnemont, Grand Orator of the Grand Orient of Belgium, said on February 12, 1911:

> Do you recall the deep feeling of pride which we all felt at the brief announcement of the Portuguese Revolution? In a few hours the throne had been brought down, the people triumphed, and the republic was proclaimed. For the uninitiated, it was a flash of lightning in a clear sky... But we, my brothers, we understood. We knew the marvellous organization of our Portuguese brothers, their ceaseless zeal, their uninterrupted work. We possessed the secret of that glorious event.[2]

The leaders of the World Revolutionary Movement and the top-level officials of continental Freemasonry met in Switzerland in 1912. It was during this meeting that they reached the decision to assassinate the Archduke Francis Ferdinand in order to bring about World War One. The actual date on which the murder was to be committed was left in abeyance because the cold-blooded plotters did not consider the time was quite ripe for his murder to provide the maximum political repercussions. On September 15th, 1912, the *Revue Internationale des Sociétés Secretes*, edited by M. Jouin, published the following words on pages 787-788:

> Perhaps light will be shed one day on these words spoken by a high Swiss Freemason. While discussing the subject of the heir to the throne of Austria he said: 'The Archduke is a remarkable man. It is a pity that he is condemned. He will die on the steps of the throne.'

Light was shed on those words at the trial of the assassins who murdered the heir to the Austrian throne and his wife on June 28th, 1914. This act of violence committed in Sarajevo, was the spark that touched off the blaze that was developed into World War One. Pharos' shorthand notes of the Military Trial are most enlightening. They provide further evidence that the international bankers used the Grand Orient Lodges to bring about World War One, as they used them in 1787-1789 to bring about the French Revolution. On October 12, 1914, the president of the military court questioned Cabrinovic, who threw the first bomb at the Archduke's car.

> The President: Tell me something more about the motives. Did you know, before deciding to attempt the assassination, that Tankosic and Ciganovic were Freemasons? Had the fact that you and they were Freemasons an influence on your resolve?[3]
>
> Cabrinovic: Yes.
>
> The President: Did you receive from them the mission to carry out the assassination?
>
> Cabrinovic: I received from no one the mission to carry out the assassination. Freemasonry had to do with it because it strengthened my intention. In Freemasonry it is permitted to kill. Ciganovic told me that the Freemasons had condemned the Archduke Franz Ferdinand to death MORE THAN A YEAR BEFORE.

Add to this evidence the further evidence of Count Czernin, an intimate friend of the Archduke. He says in *Im Weltkrieg*: "The Archduke knew quite well that the risk of an attempt on his life was imminent. A year before the war he informed me that the Freemasons had resolved on his death."

Having succeeded in bringing about a World War, the leaders of the Revolutionary Movement proceeded to use the very fact to convince the industrial workers, and the men in the armed forces, that the war was a capitalistic war. They agitated. They criticized everything possible. They blamed the various governments for everything that went wrong. The International "Capitalists" were directed by the Illuminati who remained discreetly in the background, unsuspected and unharmed.[4]

Because Russia had only emerged from the disastrous war with Japan a few years previously, it was a comparatively simple matter for the trained agitators amongst the Mensheviks to create an atmosphere of doubt, suspicion, and unrest in the minds of the Russian workers, and finally amongst the troops in 1914-1916. By January 1917, the Russian Imperial Armies had suffered nearly 3,000,000 casualties. The cream of Russia's manhood had died.

Lenin and Martov were in Switzerland, the neutral ground upon which all international plots are hatched out. Trotsky was organizing the hundreds of ex-Russian revolutionaries who had found refuge in the United States. He was particularly active in New York's East Side.[5] The leaders of the Mensheviks were carrying on their subversive policy in Russia. Their first objective was to overthrow the power of the Tzar. Their opportunity came in January of 1917. Cleverly carried out sabotage in the communication systems, the department of transport, and the ministry of supply, resulted in a serious food shortage in St. Petersburg. This happened at the time when the population was swollen so far above its normal size, due to the influx into the city of industrial workers needed for the war effort. February 1917 was a bad month. Food rationing was introduced. On March 5th, general unrest was evident. Bread lines were growing. On March 6th, the streets became crowded with unemployed. Cossack troops were brought into the city. The Tzar was still at the front visiting the troops.[6]

On March 7th, the Jewish leaders of the Menshevik party organized the women to put on street demonstrations as a protest over the bread shortage.[7] On March 8th, the women staged the demonstration. The revolutionary leaders then took a hand. Selected groups staged diversionary demonstrations. Gangs appeared here and there singing revolutionary songs and raising Red Flags. At the corner of Nevsky Prospekt and the St. Catherine Canal, the Mounted Police and Cossacks dispersed the crowds without inflicting any casualties. The crowds who gathered around those who raised the Red Flags and cried out for revolution weren't even fired on. It looked as if definite orders had been given to avoid, at all cost, a repetition of what happened on Bloody Sunday, 1905.[8]

On March 9th, the Nevsky Prospekt from Catherine Canal to Nikolai Station was jammed with milling crowds which became bolder under the urgings of agitators. Cossack cavalry cleared the street. Some were trampled but the troops only used the flat of their sabres. At no time were firearms used. This tolerance infuriated the revolutionary leaders and the agitators were directed to increase their efforts to bring the people into physical conflict with the police and troops. During the night the revolutionary leaders set up machine-guns in hidden positions throughout the city.

On March 10th, an unfortunate incident provided the tiny spark necessary to kindle the revolutionary tinder which had been piled up, and soaked with inflammable oratory. A big crowd had gathered about Nikolai station. About two in the afternoon a man, heavily dressed in furs to protect himself from the cold, drove into the square in his sleigh. He was impatient. He ordered his driver to go through the crowd. He misjudged the temper of the crowd.

The man was dragged from the sleigh and beaten. He regained his feet and took refuge in a stalled street car. He was followed by a section of the mob and ONE of them, carrying a small iron bar, beat his head to a pulp. This single act of violence aroused the blood-lust in the crowd and they surged down Nevsky smashing windows. Fights broke out.

The disorder spread until it became general. The revolutionary leaders by pre-arrangement fired on the mob from their hidden positions. The mob attacked the police. They blamed the police for firing on them. They slaughtered every policeman to a man.[9] The inmates of the prisons and jails were then released to stir up the blood-lust. Conditions necessary for the Reign of Terror were introduced.

On March 11th, the depredations of the recently released criminals led to wide-spread rioting. The Duma still tried to stay the rising tide of revolt. They dispatched an urgent message to the Tzar telling him the situation was serious. The telegram explained at considerable length the state of anarchy which then existed. Communist "Cells" within the communication systems sent another message. The Tzar, upon reading the telegram he did receive, commanded the dissolution of the Duma. Thus he deprived himself of the support of the majority of the members who were loyal to him.

On March 12th, the President of the dissolved Duma sent a last despairing message to the Tzar. It concluded with the words, "The last hour has struck. The fate of the fatherland and the dynasty is being decided." It is claimed the Tzar never received this message. This control of communication systems by "Cells" placed in key positions was used widely during the next few months.[10]

That same day, several regiments revolted and killed their own officers. Then, unexpectedly, the garrison of St. Peter and St. Paul fortress surrendered, and most of the troops joined the revolution. Immediately after the surrender of the garrison, a Committee of the Duma was formed consisting of 12 members. This provisional government survived until overthrown by Lenin's Bolsheviks in November, 1917. The revolutionary leaders, who were for the most part Mensheviks, organized the Petersburg Soviet. They agreed to allow the Provisional Government to function because it had the resemblance of rightful authority.

St. Petersburg was only one city in a vast Empire. There was no way of knowing accurately just how the citizens in other cities would behave. Kerensky, the Socialist, was a very strong man. He was referred to as the *Napoleon of Russia*.

Through the good auspices of the international bankers, M.M. Warburg & Sons, Lenin was put in communication with the German military leaders. He explained to them that the policy of both Kerensky's Provisional Government, and the Menshevik revolutionary Soviet, was to keep Russia in the war against Germany.[11]

Lenin undertook to curb the power of the Jewish revolutionary leaders in Russia. He promised to take the Russian Armies out of the war against Germany, providing the German government would help him overthrow the Russian Provisional Government and obtain political and economic control of the country. This deal was agreed to and Lenin, Martov, Radek and a party of 30-odd Bolsheviks were secretly transported across Germany to Russia in a sealed railway compartment. They arrived in St. Petersburg on April 3rd. The Warburgs of Germany and the international bankers in Geneva provided the necessary funds.

The Russian Provisional Government signed its own death warrant in 1917 when, immediately after it was formed, it promulgated an order granting unconditional amnesty to all political prisoners. The amnesty included those in exile in Siberia, and those who had sought refuge in countries abroad. This order enabled over 90,000 revolutionaries, most of them extremists, to re-enter Russia. Many of them were trained leaders. Lenin and Trotsky enlisted this vast influx of revolutionaries into their Bolshevik Party.

No sooner was Lenin back in Russia than he used propaganda to attack the Provisional Government which had granted him and his followers pardon. At the beginning of April, the Petersburg Soviet (meaning Workers' Council) was dominated by the Mensheviks. The Essars (S.R.'s, Social Revolutionaries) came second, and the Bolsheviks, for once, were the minority group. The policy of the Provisional Government was to continue the war effort because the majority of Russians considered the totalitarian ambitions of the German "Black" Nazi War Lords a direct threat to Russian sovereignty. This policy was vigorously supported by Tcheidze who had assumed the presidency of the Petersburg Soviet in the absence of Martov. Vice-president Skobelev of the Soviet, who was also a member of the Provisional Government, also supported the war effort because he thought that if the revolutionaries could help bring about the defeat of Germany's armed forces, they might be able to help the German and Polish revolutionary groups overthrow the German Government in the hour of its defeat.

Lenin's one objective at that time was to obtain leadership. He attacked the policy of the Provisional Government. He accused its members of being instruments of the bourgeois. He openly advocated its immediate overthrow by violent means. He didn't want to antagonize the Menshevik members of the Petersburg Soviet at this time. Lenin instructed his Bolshevik agitators to preach the destruction of the Provisional Government to factory workers and military garrisons but to use the slogan, "All power to the Soviets"—meaning all power to the workers' councils.

Amongst the thousands of revolutionaries who returned to Russia following the general amnesty, was Trotsky. He took back with him, from Canada and the United States, several hundred revolutionaries who had previously escaped from Russia. The vast majority were Yiddish Jews from the East End of New York.[12]

These revolutionaries helped put Lenin into power. Once these revolutionaries had served their purpose, most of them were condemned to exile or death. It was only a comparatively short time before all original members of the First International were either dead, in prison, or in exile. The history of the Lenin and Stalin Dictatorships should convince any unbiased person that the masses of the world's population, regardless of colour, or creed have been used as *Pawns in the Game* of international chess played by the "Red" international bankers and the "Black" Aryan Nazi War Lords as directed by the Illuminati.

Further proof that the international bankers were responsible for Lenin's part in the Russian Revolution is to be found in a "White Paper" published by authority of the King of England in April 1919 (Russia No. 1).The international bankers, through the directors of the Bank of England, *persuaded* the British Government to withdraw the original document and substitute another in which all reference to international Jews was removed.[13]

François Coty in *Figaro,* February 20th, 1932 states:

"The subsidies granted to the Nihilists in Russia and elsewhere at this period by Jacob Schiff were no longer acts of isolated generosity. A veritable Russian Terrorist organization had been set up in the U.S.A. at his expense, charged to assassinate ministers, governors, heads of police, etc." The Illuminati who use Communism and Naziism to further their secret totalitarian ambitions organize revolutionary action in three steps or movements.[14]

1. The change-over of the existing form of government (regardless of whether it be a monarchy, or a republic) into a socialist state by constitutional means if possible.

2. The change-over of the Socialist State into a Proletarian Dictatorship by revolutionary action.

3. The change-over from a Proletarian Dictatorship to a Totalitarian Dictatorship by purging all influential people who may be opposed.

After 1918, all Russian Jews were either revolutionary Jews, clinging tenaciously to the Marxian theories, and working for the establishment of an international of Soviet Socialist Republics (Trotskyites), or they favoured returning to Palestine (The Zionists). Miss B. Baskerville, in her book *The Polish Jew*, published in 1906, has this to say about the Ghettos on pages 117-118:

Social-Zionism aims at converting the Zionists to socialism before they go to Palestine in order to facilitate the establishment of a Socialist Government...in the meantime they do their best to overthrow those European Governments which do not attain to their political standard...their programme which is full of Socialistic ideas...includes the organization of strikes, acts of terror, and the organizers being very young, acts of folly as well...

The *Secret Power* behind the WRM also controls political Zionism, yet the vast majority of the Jews who work for Zionism are absolutely ignorant that they also are being used as "Pawns in the Game" of International Chess.

[1.] The Atheistic Grand Orient Masons must not be confused with other European and American Freemasons, whose principles are above reproach, work philanthropic, and whose ritual is based on belief in The Great Architect of the Universe.

[2.] Note: *Bulletin du Grand Orient de Belgique 5910*, 1910, page 92.

[3.] Tankosic and Ciganovic were higher Masons than Cabrinovic. It had previously been brought out at the trial that Ciganovic had told Cabrinovic that the Freemasons could not find men to carry out the Archduke's murder.

[4.] It was indeed a Capitalistic war, but not the kind of Capitalistic war the workers were led to believe it was by propaganda put out by the press the international bankers controlled in every country of the world.

[5.] Police officials and debates in Congress show this illegal entry is going on today on an ever increasing scale. The underworld characters also find admittance to Canada very easy. The danger lies in the fact that the underworld and the revolutionary underground are interlocked. One could not and never has survived without the other. The men who are The

Secret Power direct both. The Aryan War Lords have used the Mafia, The International Tycoons, the Jewish terrorists. This explains gang wars.

6. The troops had one rifle to six men by Feb. 1917: one day's ammunition.

7. This move was almost identical with the plot to use men disguised as women in the march on the Tuileries.

8. One of the best works dealing with the events leading up to the Russian Revolution is *Behind Communism* by Frank Britton.

9. I have definite and authoritative evidence in my possession from people who were in St. Petersburg and in a position to know that the machine guns used were neither placed in their positions, nor fired by the police. The police had received definite orders that they were not to use drastic action.

10. Lenin, in order to break the spirit of the troops fighting the Germans at the front in November 1917, had messages sent to field officers which they accepted as coming from the Russian High Command. One General received orders to advance against the enemy, while two others, one on each flank of the General who was ordered to advance, were ordered to retire. It is little wonder that the troops turned on their own officers.

11. I have evidence to prove that the brother of Paul Warburg of New York was the German Army Intelligence Officer who negotiated with Lenin on behalf of the German High Command and arranged for his safe passage across Germany to Russia.

12. Father Denis Fahey C.S. Sp. in his book *The Rulers of Russia* pages 9-14 gives the names of all these revolutionary leaders, their nationality, racial origin, and the positions they were assigned to immediately Lenin had usurped power and Trotsky consolidated his position in Russia in November, 1917.

13. Captain A.H.M. Ramsay, member of Parliament for Midlothian and Peebleshire from 1931 to 1945, states on page 96 of his book, *The Nameless War*: "I was shown the Two White Papers...the original and the abridged issue, side by side. Vital passages had been eliminated from the abridged edition."

14. For further details regarding this matter, read *The Last Days of the Mevanovs*, by Thornton Butterworth, and *Les Derniers Jours des Romanoff*, by Robert Wilton, 15 years Russian correspondent for the *London Times*.

CHAPTER EIGHT

Political Intrigue: 1914–1919

The way international intrigue was used to depose the Right Honourable H.H. Asquith when he was Prime Minister of Great Britain in 1916 was explained to me by a man who was extremely well informed. I met him while he was serving as King's Messenger in 1917. We were in my room in a hotel when, during the course of conversation, I mentioned that I strongly suspected that a comparatively small group of extremely wealthy men used the power their wealth could buy to influence national and international affairs, to further their own secret plans and ambitions.

My companion replied: "If you talk about such things it is unlikely that you will live long enough to realize how right you are." He then told me how Mr. Asquith had been deposed in December 1916, and Mr. David Lloyd George, Winston Churchill, and The Rt. Hon. Arthur James Balfour were placed in power in England.

The story he told me had a remarkable similarity to the plot used by the *Secret Powers* who directed the campaign of *L'Infamie* immediately prior to the outbreak of the French revolution in 1789. It will be recalled a letter was used to lure Cardinal Prince de Rohan to the Palais Royal where he was involved with a prostitute disguised as Marie Antoinette. The alleged modern method is as follows:

Shortly after the outbreak of the war in August 1914, a small group of wealthy men authorized an agent to turn an old, but very spacious mansion, into a fabulous private club. Those who made it possible to finance such a costly undertaking insisted that their identity remain secret. They explained that they simply wished to show their deep appreciation to officers in the Armed Forces who were risking their lives for King and Country.

The club provided every kind of luxury, entertainment, and facilities for pleasure. The use of the club was usually restricted to commissioned officers on leave in London from active service. A new member had to be introduced by a brother officer. My companion referred to it as the "Glass Club".[1]

Upon arrival, officer guests were interviewed by an official. If he was satisfied with their credentials, they were told how the club functioned. The officer applying for admission was asked to give his word of honour that he would not mention the names of any persons he met during his stay at the club, or reveal their identity after he left the club. Having given this solemn promise, it was explained to the guest that he would meet a number of women well known in the best of London's society. They all wore masks. The officer was asked not to try to identify any of the ladies. He was sworn to keep their secret should he happen to identify any of them accidentally.

With the preliminaries over, the officer was shown to his private room. It was furnished in a most luxurious manner. The furnishings included a huge double bed, dressing table, wardrobe, cabinet with wines and liqueurs, a smoking humidor, and private toilet and bath. The new guest was invited to make himself at home. He was informed that he would receive a lady visitor. She would wear a brooch of costume jewelry with the number of his room. If, after getting acquainted, he wished to take her down to dinner that was his privilege.

The reception room, where guests and their hostesses mingled over cocktails before dinner, was like that of a King's palace. The dining room was large enough to accommodate fifty couples. The ballroom was such that many people dream about but few seldom see. Costly decorations were set off by luxurious drapes, subdued lighting, beautiful women gorgeously dressed, soft dreamy music; the smell of rare perfumes made the place an Arab's dream of heaven. The whole atmosphere of the club was such that the officers on leave relaxed at first and then set out to have a real Roman Holiday. There was nothing gross or vulgar about the "Glass Club". Everything about the place was beautiful, delicate, soft, and pliant...the exact opposite of the horrors, the violence, the brutality, of a modern war. Between dance numbers, entertainers gave performances which brought out the feelings of joy, fun and laughter. As the evening progressed, a long buffet was literally loaded with luscious dishes of fish and game. A bar provided every kind of drink from champagne to straight whisky. Between midnight and one a.m. five beautiful girls performed the Dance of the Seven Veils. The dance depicted a scene in a Sultan's Harem. The girls started the dance fully clothed, (even to the veil they wore to conceal the facial features) but, when the dance ended, the girls were entirely naked. They danced the final act in their lithe-nakedness, waving the flimsy veil around and about them in a manner which extenuated, rather than concealed, their physical charms. Couples, when tired of entertainment, dancing, and other people's company, retired to their private rooms.

The next day they could enjoy indoor swimming, tennis, badminton, billiards; or there was the card room which was a miniature Monte Carlo. About November 1916, a very high personage was lured into visiting the Club when he received a note saying that he would obtain information of the greatest importance to the British Government. He drove to the Club in his private car. He instructed his chauffeur to wait for him. After being admitted, he was taken to one of the luxuriously furnished bed-sitting rooms. A lady joined him. When she saw him she nearly fainted. It was his own wife. She was much younger than her husband. She had been acting as hostess to lonely officers on leave for a considerable time. It was a most embarrassing situation.

The wife knew nothing of the plot. She had no secret information to give. She was convinced that both she and her husband were philandering. She thought it was only this unfortunate chance meeting which had brought them face to face. There was a scene. The husband was informed regarding the part hostesses played at the Club. But his lips were sealed as if in death. He was a member of the Government. He couldn't afford to figure in a scandal.

Every employee in the club, both male and female, was a spy. They reported everything that happened at the club to their masters. The identity of those involved became known. The information thus obtained was printed for the record in what became known as "The Black Book". "The Black Book" recorded their sins of omission and commission, their peculiar vices, their special weaknesses, their financial status, the condition of their domestic relations, and the degree of affection they had for relatives and friends. Their connection with, and their influence over, influential men in politics, industry, and religion was carefully noted.

In November 1916, a member of Parliament tried to expose the real character of the "Glass Club". Three army officers, who had patronized the club, became suspicious that it was a vast espionage system after an attempt had been made to blackmail them into giving information that would have been valuable to the enemy. Their adventure involved an Australian lady, her chauffeur, and the wives and daughters of several highly placed government officials.[2]

The effort to make known the true facts was suppressed, but mention of "The Black Book" was made in Parliament and in the public press. The government's policy was said to be based on the contention that a scandal of such magnitude could prove a national calamity at a time when the armed forces at sea, on land, and in the air, were meeting severe reverses.

The *Liberal* press began to attack the Prime Minister. He was accused of harbouring men within his government who were unfit to hold office. He was accused of having had extensive dealings with German industrialists and financiers prior to the war. He was accused of being friendly towards the Kaiser. He was accused of being unable to make prompt and firm decisions. He was ridiculed as "Wait-and-see-Asquith." My companion told me that evidence against high officials involved in the "Glass Club" scandal caused the Government to resign. Thus, according to my companion, the British Empire was forced to change political Horses in the middle of a World War. When Mr. Asquith did resign in December 1916, he was superseded by a coalition government headed by David Lloyd George. Winston Churchill and Mr. Balfour were two of the more prominent members.

Shortly after hearing the above story, I was struck by the fact that the three army officers mentioned were reported in the official lists as "Killed in action". In war-time such a thing is quite possible. Next came a brief notice that the Australian lady and her chauffeur had been imprisoned under the Defence of the Realm Act. Then came an announcement that the member of parliament who was involved in the case had retired from public life. A few weeks later I was taken off duty as King's Messenger and appointed as Navigating Officer of British Submarines. We did lose 33 per cent of our officers and men but I was one of those to survive.

It was not until long after the war, when I was studying modern history and comparative religions that I began to realize the vast importance of political Zionism to those who planned to obtain undisputed control of the world's economy. The following historical events speak for themselves.

When war broke out in 1914, the Rt. Hon. H.H. Asquith was Prime Minister. He was an Anti-Zionist. The International Bankers decided that Asquith's Government had to go and be replaced by a coalition government in which David Lloyd George and Winston Churchill would wield great influence. Lloyd George had for years been Solicitor for the Zionist movement as planned and financed by the Rothschilds. Winston Churchill had been a supporter of political Zionism from the time he first entered politics.

In 1917, the International Bankers were supporting both the Bolshevik and Zionist movements. It would seem incredible that the British Cabinet didn't know what was going on, particularly when the British Government had had to intervene to get Trotsky and his revolutionary leaders released after they had been detained in Halifax while on their way from New York to Russia.

The overthrow of the Russian Empire was bound to cause the withdrawal of the mighty Russian Armies from the war on the side of the Allied Powers. The German Armies, which had been engaged on the Eastern Front, would be free to reinforce the Armies fighting against the allied forces on the Western Front. Despite this knowledge, nothing was done to prevent the plans of the International Financiers reaching maturity.

The British Government was aware of the serious conditions brewing in regard to Russia. This is proved by the fact that the matter was discussed by the cabinet and a decision was reached to send Lord Kitchener to Russia for the purpose of re-organizing the Russian military forces. Lord Kitchener sailed from Scapa Flow aboard the *HMS Hampshire*. She was mysteriously sunk during the night of June 5th, 1916. Lord Kitchener was lost with all but a dozen of the crew. The survivors drifted ashore on a life-raft. The British Government announced that the *HMS Hampshire* was sunk by a German U-boat or a German mine. This has been proved to be a lie.

I investigated this incident very thoroughly. In a previous book, *Hell's Angels of the Deep*, published in 1932, *I proved HMS Hampshire* had not been sunk by an enemy torpedo or mine. *HMS Hampshire* was sunk by either sabotage or due to an error of judgment on the part of her navigating officer. Judging all evidence available, I was convinced that *HMS Hampshire* sank after striking the submerged North Shoals Rocks. It is hard to believe that a skilled and experienced naval navigator committed such an error of judgment. I still believe that a saboteur probably tampered with the magnets in the steering compass. Gyro compasses were not then standard equipment and even ships that had them found the Sperry models very unreliable as I know from personal experience.

General Erich von Ludendorff (who was Chief of Staff and shared with General Hindenburg the leadership of Germany's military might), also studied the circumstances surrounding the loss of *HMS Hampshire* and Lord Kitchener's death. He states positively: "Action by German naval units, either U-boats or mine-layers, had nothing to do with the sinking of the ship." He said he had arrived at the conclusion that the death of Lord Kitchener was "An act of God," because had he lived, he would undoubtedly have reorganized the Russian Armies and trained them into the most formidable fighting force. The General then remarked: "Had he done this the Bolsheviks would have come into possession of one of the most formidable fighting machines the world has ever known. Such a force would have enabled Communism to sweep over the whole world."

I maintain that the International Bankers could not afford to have the Russian Armies reorganized until AFTER the Menshevik uprising, and after Kerensky's provisional government had been overthrown in 1917. It is very doubtful if Lenin and Trotsky could have accomplished what they did if Lord Kitchener had been able to reorganize, discipline and train the Russian armed forces in 1916. History also records that Winston Churchill and Lord Kitchener had quarreled seriously over military policy during 1914–1916. Lord Kitchener had bitterly opposed Churchill's idea of sending the Naval Division to Antwerp in 1914. He had also opposed Churchill's plan to capture the Dardanelles. Both ventures proved to be costly mistakes. The Dardanelles venture could have succeeded, and would probably have ended the war in 1916 if Churchill had waited until both army and naval forces were ready to cooperate jointly.

When Churchill insisted that the naval forces attack the Dardanelles alone, he notified the enemy of the intended strategy. After Churchill had committed the initial blunder, the army was ordered to participate. Lord Kitchener's objections were overruled. His advice was ignored. The allied military forces committed to the assault on the Dardanelles were insufficient in number, improperly trained, poorly equipped for such a task, and badly supported in regard to provisions, medical aid, and reinforcements. They were forced to attack first class troops whose leaders had been alerted to their danger. The allied military and naval forces were required to overcome military and naval obstacles that had not been in existence when Churchill ordered the first naval assault. The Dardanelles campaign was doomed to failure from the start.

The more we study the methods employed by the Secret Powers behind international affairs, the more obvious it is to see that they make private assassinations look like accidents or suicides, and sabotage look like carelessness, errors of judgment, and unintentional blunders committed due to excusable circumstances.

The only possible consideration that could justify the policy of the coalition government in 1916, in regard to Russia, was the fact that the government knew they could not obtain financial backing, or military aid from America until AFTER the Russian government had been overthrown. Such a statement seems preposterous, but it is supported by the following facts:

The Mensheviks started the Russian Revolution in February of 1917.

The Tzar abdicated on March 15th, 1917.

Jacob H. Schiff, senior partner of Kuhn-Loeb & Co. of New York, immediately removed the restrictions he had imposed extending financial aid to the Allies. Mortimer Schiff was then ordered by his father Jacob to cable Sir Ernest Cassels: "Because of recent action in Germany and developments in Russia we shall no longer abstain from Allied government financing."

On April 5th, the British government announced that it was sending Rt. Hon. Arthur James Balfour, the Foreign Secretary, to the United States, to notify the American bankers that the British government was prepared to officially endorse their plans for political Zionism provided they would bring America into the war on the side of the Allies. America came into the war. On June 7th, 1917, the first American troops landed in France.

On July 18th, 1917 Lord Rothschild wrote Mr. Balfour as follows:

> Dear Mr. Balfour:
>
> At last I am able to send you the formula you asked for. If His Majesty's government will send me a message in line with this formula, and they and you approve it, I will hand it to the Zionist Federation at a meeting to be called for that purpose.

The draft declaration was as follows:

> His Majesty's government accepts the principle that PALESTINE should be reconstituted as a national home for the Jewish people.[3]
>
> His Majesty's government will use its best endeavours to secure the achievement of this object, and will discuss the necessary methods and means with the Zionist organization.[4]

Mr. Balfour and the British government agreed to the terms dictated by Lord Rothschild and his Zionist confreres. This is proved by the fact that on August 28th, Sir Herbert Samuel (he was subsequently made a Viscount), Sir Alfred Mond (he was subsequently made a Lord), and Lord Rothschild persuaded the British cabinet to send Lord Reading to the U.S.A. as head of the Economic Mission. Lord Reading, when Sir Rufus Isaacs, had been mixed up in the Marconi scandal.

The details of the deal he negotiated with the U.S.A. government in September 1917 have never been made known. It is known, however, that the *deal* had to do with the Bank of England because it was completely reorganized, under American supervision, and physically rebuilt after 1919.[5]

In September, Jacob Schiff of Kuhn-Loeb & Co. wrote a long letter dealing with the Zionist question to a Mr. Friedman. In it, the following passages occur:

I do believe that it might be feasible to secure the goodwill of America, Great Britain and France,[6] in any event, towards the promotion of a large influx, and settlement of our people in Palestine...further it might be possible to obtain from the Powers the formal assurance to our people that they shall obtain autonomy in Palestine as soon as their numbers become large enough to justify this.

September 26th, 1917, Louis Marshall—legal representative of Kuhn-Loeb & Co—wrote his friend Max Senior, another leading Zionist, as follows:

Major Lionel de Rothschild, of the League for British Jews, informs me that his organization is in agreement with the American Jewish Committee...The Balfour Declaration, with its acceptance by the Powers, is an act of the highest diplomacy. Zionism is but an incident of a far-reaching plan: It is merely a convenient peg on which to hang a powerful weapon. All protests they (the opponents) may make would be futile. It would subject them individually to hateful and concrete examples of a most impressive nature. I would shrink from the possibilities which might result.

Here we have a blunt admission from Louis Marshall, that "Zionism is but an incident of a far reaching plan...it is merely a convenient peg on which to hang a powerful weapon." The far reaching plan referred to cannot be anything else than the Long-Range Plan to which continual reference has already been made. It is a plan by which the International Financiers intend to win ultimate undisputed control of the wealth, natural resources, and man-power of the entire world.

A few of the more important historical events which bear out the above statement are as follows:

On January 28th, 1915, Mr. Asquith, Prime Minister of England wrote in his diary:

I just received from Herbert Samuel a memorandum headed *The Future of Palestine*...He thinks we might plant in this territory about three or four million European Jews. It read almost like a new edition of *Tancred* brought up to date. I confess I am not attracted by this proposed addition to our responsibilities.

Thus Asquith proved himself Anti-Zionist.

Prominent Zionists owned most, if not all, of Britain's major war industries. For no good reason, in 1915-1916, Britain suddenly found herself short of chemicals needed in the manufacturing of explosives. Guns and munitions which had been promised our Russian allies failed to materialize. Shells for our guns were so scarce they had to be rationed. The Asquith government was accused of bungling the war effort. But let us examine the facts.

Sir Frederick Nathan was in charge of chemical production. Messrs. Brunner & Mond were credited with doing all they could to correct the critical situation which had arisen. Using GOVERNMENT FUNDS they constructed a large chemical factory at Silvertown. Sir Alfred Mond was appointed His Majesty's Commissioner of Works. He afterwards became head of the Jewish agency in Palestine.

Work on the factory was rushed ahead. The factory was brought into production in record time. Bouquets were passed around and honours bestowed upon the wealthy Zionist financiers who were supposedly doing so much for the British war effort. But as soon as the Silvertown factory came into production, it blew up with the loss of forty lives. Over eight hundred buildings and homes were demolished.[7]

Because of the failure of Britain to deliver arms and munitions to Russia as promised, severe military reverses were experienced on the Eastern Front. Newspapers reported Russian troops were fighting with sticks and bare fists until slaughtered by well-armed German troops. A letter written by Professor Bernard Pares (who was knighted afterwards) to Lloyd George would indicate that the guns and munitions promised the Imperial Russian government were deliberately withheld to create conditions favourable for the revolution then being planned in Geneva and New York by the international bankers. Professor Pares' letter, written in 1915, reads in part:

> I have to submit my strong opinion that the unfortunate failure of Messrs. Vickers-Maxim & Co. to supply Russia with munitions which were to have reached the country five months ago, is gravely jeopardizing the relations of the two countries, and in particular their cooperation in the work of the present war...I AM DEFINITELY TOLD THAT SO FAR NO SUPPLIES WHATEVER HAVE REACHED RUSSIA FROM ENGLAND.

David Lloyd George, at the time the letter was written, was Chancellor of the Exchequer and responsible for financing the war. Messrs. Vickers-Maxim &Co. was controlled by Sir Ernest Cassels, business associate of Kuhn-Loeb & Co. of New York, who in turn, were affiliated with the Rothschilds and the international bankers of England, France, Germany, etc.

When Professor Pare's letter was discussed by the cabinet, Lloyd George is alleged to have defended the government's policy by saying, "Charity should start at home. Our British soldiers fighting in France have only got four machine-guns to a battalion. They should be better armed before we export arms to Russia."

Lord Kitchener is reported to have replied, "I consider more than four machine-guns per battalion a luxury when our failure to deliver the arms we promised to Russia has resulted in the Russians having only ONE rifle available for every six men."

The agents of the international conspirators were ordered to smear Lord Kitchener; they circulated the story all over the world that Lord Kitchener stated that he considered more than four machine-guns to a battalion of British soldiers, fighting in France, a luxury. This smear and untruth has continued to this very day. It appeared in the biography of David Lloyd George recently published. It appeared in a review of the biography which appeared recently in the Toronto *Star Weekly*. I sent the editor of the *Star Weekly* the truth regarding this important historical event. He replied it was too much dynamite for him to handle. He informed me that he had handed my correspondence to the *Daily Star*. Needless to say, the TRUTH was never published.

This is a typical illustration of how the international conspirators smear the reputations of honest men, even dead men, in order to cover up their own wrong-doing. It illustrates perfectly how their agents use the world press to misinform the public so they will blame innocent men, and even their own governments, for the harm done as the result of their machinations.

To prove that Vickers-Maxim & Co. were under the influence of Kuhn-Loeb & Co. at this time, Boris Brazel Brasol says:

On February 4th, 1916 the Russian Revolutionary Party of America held a meeting in New York which was attended by 62 delegates...It was revealed that secret reports had just reached the Party from Russia designating the moment as favourable...the assembly was assured that ample funds would be furnished by persons in sympathy with the liberating of the people of Russia. In this connection the name of Jacob Schiff was repeatedly mentioned.[8]

Jacob Schiff was at that time senior member of Kuhn-Loeb & Co. of New York. Approximately 50 of the 62 people attending the meeting on Feb. 4th, 1916, were men who had taken an active part in the Russian Revolution in 1905. Once again they were to be used to foment revolutionary action, but Jacob Schiff had planned that the fruits of victory were to be usurped by Lenin, in the interests of the international bankers.

The *Encyclopedia of Jewish Knowledge* says of Zionism: "The World War forced the abandonment of Berlin as the centre of the organization and all authority was transferred to the Provisional Zionist Emergency Committee established in New York under the leadership of Justice L.D. Brandeis."

Jacob de Haas writing in his book *Louis Dembitz Brandeis* says:

The (Zionist) Transfer Department...its ramifications extended through all the war-zones occupied by the Allies, and throughout Turkey, Syria, Palestine, to Trans-Jordan and Baghdad, practically not a cent of the millions handled was lost...Starting by using the good offices of the U.S.A. Dept. of State (Foreign Office) as a means of communication and deposit, it became so successful, and so reliable, it was employed by the Treasury of the U.S.A. to deliver moneys, and messages, which the government could not handle successfully...Embassies in European capitals advanced cash on the requisition of the (Zionist) Executive Secretary in New York.

L. Fry has this to say in *Waters Flowing Eastward*, p. 51:

From then on their influence was felt more and more in POLITICAL circles in Europe and America. In particular, the Zionist Transfer Department as it was called, was in a position to transmit funds, and information, to subversive elements in enemy countries.

Next we find the Grand Orient Lodges back into the Picture of the WRM again. M. Erzberger says on pp. 145-146 of *My Experience in the World War*:

On March 16th, 1916, the Alliance Israelite paid the Grand Orient of Paris the sum of 700,000 francs, and in the archives of the Grand Orient of Rome it can be proved that on March 18, 1916 the transfer of one million lire to the Grand Orient of Rome took place. I am not so naive as to imagine that the 'Alliance Israelite' makes use of two Grand Orients solely for the purpose of sending one million lire to Italian Jews.

Telling of events AFTER Asquith had been deposed in 1916, A.N. Field says in *All These Things*, p. 104: "Jewish influence in British Politics became pronounced after the rise of Mr. Lloyd George".

L. Fry on page 55 of *Water Flowing Eastward* says:

The first official London meeting of...the Political Committee took place on Feb. 7th, 1917, in a house of Dr. Moses Gaster. There were present Lord Rothschild, James de Rothschild, (son of Edmund de Rothschild of Paris, former owner of the Rothschild colonies in Palestine) Sir Mark Sykes, – (whose house in Buckingham Gates was fully equipped as headquarters for the Zionist Cause with telegraphic apparatus, etc.), Sir Herbert Samuel, Herbert Bentwich, (later Attorney-General for Palestine) Harry Sacher, Joseph Cowen, Chaim Weizmann, and Nahum Sokolov.[9] The Zionist programme to serve as a basis for official negotiations covering the future mandates of Palestine, Armenia, Mesopotamia, and the kingdom of the Hedjaz, was discussed in detail.

J.M.N. Jeffries *op. cit.* p. 139 contributes this further information: "The minutes of this meeting were communicated forthwith in cipher to the Zionist organization of the United States...From now on the political Zionist organization in the United States began to take a hand in the shaping of British policy, and the ordering of British affairs."

To illustrate the power the international bankers exercise over the British government's affairs, Samuel Landman is quoted.[10] He says:

After an agreement had been arrived at between Sir Mark Sykes, Weizmann, and Sokolov, it was resolved to send a secret message to Justice Brandeis that the British cabinet would help the Jews to gain Palestine in return for active Jewish sympathy, and for support in the U.S.A. for the Allied Cause so as to bring about a radical Pro-ally tendency in the United States. This message was sent in cipher through the British Foreign Office. Secret messages were also sent to the Zionist leaders in Russia through General MacDonogh...Dr. Weizmann (one of the founders of political Zionism) was able to secure from the government the service of half a dozen younger Zionists for active work on behalf of Zionism. At that time conscription was in force, and only those engaged in work of national importance could be released from active service at the front. I remember Dr. Weizmann writing a letter to General MacDonogh (director of Military Operations) and invoking his assistance in obtaining the exemption from active service of Leon Simon, Harry Sacher, Simon Marks, Hyamson, Tolkowsky and myself. At Dr. Weizmann's request I was transferred from the War Office (M.I.9)...to the Ministry of Propaganda...and later to the Zionist office...about December 1916. From that time onwards, for several years, Zionism was considered an ally of the British government...Passport and travel difficulties did not exist when a man was recommended by our office. For instance, a certificate signed by me was accepted by the Home Office that an Ottoman Jew was to be treated as a friendly alien and not as an enemy, which was the case of Turkish subjects.

Study of the life of Disraeli reveals that he spent many Sunday evenings with the Rothschilds of London. It is revealed that while Kuhn-Loeb & Co. of New York was financing the Jewish revolutionaries in Russia, the London Rothschilds were the managers of the Tzarist administration in London. We also learn that the London Rothschilds were *Liberals* and that from 1840 to 1917 the *Liberal Press* controlled by the Rothschilds was consistently Anti-Russian. Disraeli informs us that in Germany the head men in politics and finance were considered reactionaries because they didn't allow the international bankers to do exactly as they wanted to do. Baron von Bleichroeder of Berlin and the Warburgs of Hamburg were the Rothschild representatives in Germany. In Russia, the Weinsteins of Odessa assisted the Ginzbergs in St. Petersburg to look after the Rothschild interests.

Another man who was very active on the part of the international bankers was Otto Kahn. He cleverly hid his true colours as a world revolutionary behind the national flags of the several countries in which he lived and pretended to be a Patriotic citizen. Mr. Otto Kahn was born in Germany. He migrated to the United States as Paul Warburg did. Like

Warburg he also became a partner in Kuhn-Loeb & Co. Kahn, upon arriving in America, obtained employment as a clerk with Speyer & Co. so as not to make matters too obvious. He later on married the granddaughter of Mr. Wolf, one of the founders of Kuhn-Loeb & Co. When Mrs. Kahn visited Moscow in 1931, she was officially received by the Soviet government which gave a grand dinner and several brilliant receptions in her honour. The Red armies of Stalin lined the roads as she passed along, and the soldiers presented arms as she passed by.[11]

On April 2nd, 1934, an article appeared in the *Daily Herald* in which Mr. Hannen Swaffer wrote: "I knew Otto Kahn, the multimillionaire, for many years. I knew him when he was a patriotic German. I knew him when he was a patriotic American. Naturally when he wanted to enter the (British) House of Commons, he joined the *Patriotic Party*." Mr. Otto Kahn would have become President of the English-speaking Union if his revolutionary activities had not been accidentally exposed when it was proved that his house was the meeting place for Soviet agents such as Nina Smorodin, Claire Sheridan, Louise Bryant, and Margaret Harrison.

In the summer of 1917 the problem of who was to finance Lenin and Trotsky during their joint revolutionary effort in Russia had to be solved. The international bankers decided that their representatives would meet in Stockholm, Sweden, because that country was neutral and comparatively free from international spies. Among those attending the meeting were men representing the banking interests in Britain, Germany, France, Russia, and the United States of America. Mr. Protopopoff, the Russian Minister of the interior was there, and so was Mr. Warburg of Hamburg. He was the brother of Paul Warburg who was a partner in the Kuhn-Loeb & Company of New York, who had drafted the legislation for the Federal Reserve System in 1910. It will be seen that in order to decide how finances should be arranged for Lenin and Trotsky to overthrow the Russian government, delegates attended from ALL warring nations. It was finally decided that Kuhn-Loeb of New York should place $50,000,000 to the credit of Lenin and Trotsky in the bank of Sweden.

Both British and American Intelligence officers reported these facts to their respective governments in 1917. Commander E.N. Cromie died fighting off a revolutionary mob which attacked the British Consulate in St. Petersburg. He held them off in order to give his confreres time to burn documents relating to this and other matters.[12]

The American government forwarded to the British government reports they had received from their intelligence officers. Mr. Oudendyke, the Netherlands Minister in Petrograd (who looked after the British interests in Russia after Commander Cromie was murdered) also warned the British government. His warning was published in April 1919 as part of a White Paper on the Bolshevik Revolution published by the King's Printer.

The plans Jacob Schiff had made to allow Trotsky, and his band of revolutionary leaders, to return to St. Petersburg from New York went awry when Trotsky was detained by Canadian government officials in Halifax, Nova Scotia, while en route. The power the international bankers exercise over constitutional governments is fully illustrated by the fact that immediately after they protested to the governments concerned, Trotsky and his whole gang of revolutionary gangsters were released and given safe conduct through the British Blockade Zone.

Further proof of the British politicians' complicity in the Russian Revolution of 1917 was obtained by D. Petrovsky who explains the part played by Sir G. Buchanan, the Ambassador.[13] Petrovsky proves that, although fully informed of all that was going on behind the scenes, Lloyd George's government aided the international bankers to put Trotsky and his revolutionary leaders into Russia while at the same time the German High Command aided the international bankers to get Lenin and his gang of revolutionary leaders from Switzerland to Petrograd. Lenin and his followers were provided with a private railway coach for their journey across Germany.

Mr. Petrovsky reveals that Milioukoff, who had been appointed Minister for Foreign Affairs by the Russian Republican government in the spring of 1917, was the man who negotiated this intrigue which involved both warring nations. It is also recorded that in appreciation for the cooperation given by the German General Staff, the government of Great Britain agreed to Milioukoff's request that M.M. Litvinov be released. He had been arrested by British Intelligence officers as a spy for Germany. The identification of M.M. Litvinov proves of great interest. He was born to parents whose name was Finklestein. When he joined the World Revolutionary Movement, he changed his name to Meyer Wallach. When he was closely associated with Lenin and his Bolshevik Party, he changed his name once again to Maxim Litvinov. He is the same man referred to as Litvinov the German Spy; he is the same man who had been arrested while trying to cash the five hundred ruble notes Stalin had obtained when he bombed and robbed the Tiflis bank.

Following his release by the British authorities, Litvinov returned to Russia. He aided Lenin to overthrow the Kerensky Provisional Government and the Menshevik Soviet established in St. Petersburg prior to October 1917. Litvinov was Stalin's Commissar for Foreign Affairs from 1930 to 1939. He was appointed a member of the Central Committee of the Communist Party in 1935. His ability as an assassin, receiver of stolen money, spy, international gangster, and leader of revolutionary efforts in several countries was acclaimed by the nations of the world when he was appointed President of the Council of the United Nations. Only an international group, such as the international bankers, could have saved this man's life, and assured him his liberty when he was carrying out the criminal aspects of international intrigue. Only the power and influence of the international bankers could have caused him to be elected president of the United Nations Council. This illustrates the fact that the Illuminati control those who control the United Nations.

Other evidence is available to prove that the international bankers of the United Kingdom, the United States, Germany and Russia worked together even after Germany and Britain were at war. It is contained in a pamphlet entitled *Trotsky* (Defender Publishers, Wichita, Kansas) which quotes a letter written by J.M. Dell to Lloyd George, personally. But why go on? It would take volumes to quote all the evidence to prove that the international bankers organized, financed, and directed the Russian Revolution in order to obtain control of a vast territory so that the Illuminati could try out their ideas for totalitarianism. Only by experimenting in an area as vast as the so-called U.S.S.R. could they find out mistakes and weaknesses by the process of trial and error. Until they had performed this experiment, which cost millions and millions of human lives, it would have been gross stupidity on their part to try to rule the whole world. Theirs has been a Long-Range Plan. It started 3,000 years ago. It was revised at the meeting in Bauer's

Goldsmith Shop in Frankfurt in 1773. *Unless united action is taken, it is likely to end when they take over economical and political control after World War Three.*

It will thus be seen that the Coalition Government which took over the prosecution of the war from Prime Minister Asquith in December 1916, made no effort to stop the international bankers from proceeding with their plans for the Russian Revolution, even when they knew its success would cause the Russian armies to be withdrawn from the war. Proof that the Zionists in both Britain and the U.S.A. agreed that the Russian Imperial government should be overthrown is to be found in the fact that immediately after Lenin announced that he had established his dictatorship in November 1917, Lloyd George also announced that the policy of the British government would be to back the Rothschild plan for the establishment of a national home for the Jewish people in Palestine. This proves Lloyd George held no resentment towards the international bankers for taking Russia out of the war as an ally of Britain.

The Jewish-dominated Menshevik revolutionaries in Russia had fought the abortive revolution in 1905. They also started the revolution in February 1917. Once again they met with great success during the first stages of the revolutionary effort. They actually established a Soviet in Petrograd. The international bankers didn't mind who carried the ball until it was near the goal, but as soon as the ball carrier got into position to score they stepped in and took over the play. Their goal was to bring about a totalitarian Dictatorship operated on the JOINT STOCK COMPANY PRINCIPLE: Lenin was made *Dictator*. They remained behind the scene. The Communist "Mob" was blamed for their crimes against humanity.

On July 17, 1917, the Bolsheviks under Lenin started an anti-government agitation in Russia. This resulted in an uprising by thousands of the city's inflamed worker-soldier population. This abortive revolt is known as "The July Days." Kerensky dealt with the situation firmly. The mobs were fired upon, several hundred people were killed, but order was restored. The Bolshevik leaders fled. Some were arrested. Lenin and Zinoviev hid in Sestroretsk. Trotsky, Kamenev, and Lunarcharsky were amongst those arrested. Stalin, who was at that time editor of Pravda, was not molested. After the revolt, Prince Lvov resigned and Kerensky—the Jewish Napoleon—became Prime Minister. Kerensky was a great orator. He tried to whip up enthusiasm for the war effort amongst the soldiers and workers. All Kerensky's oral efforts failed.

Kerensky's influence began to decline steadily. Lenin was busy. He called for the Sixth Congress of the Russian Social-Democratic Labour Party to be held August 8th to 16th. He came out of it leader of the unified revolutionary groups. Within a year, the united revolutionary party called itself The Communist Party. At the congress a secret committee was formed called the October Central Committee. It consisted of 26 members who were to plan the October Revolution and then direct the revolutionary effort in all its various phases. Stalin made the grade at last. He was elected to the presidium of the Sixth Party Congress. The majority of students believe Stalin wouldn't even have been given notice if many of the other experienced revolutionary leaders hadn't been in jail but the truth is that Lenin was acting as Chief Agent for the "Secret Powers." They had plans to use Stalin to supersede others.

The idea of the central committee to organize the October Revolution was to anticipate the provisional government's intention to call a general election in which the secret ballot would be used to elect a representative constitutional government to rule the Russian

Empire. Lenin felt that if his bid for power was to succeed he had to make it before the Constitutional Assembly met in January to arrange the nation-wide election. If this election was ever held, the people would have their own representatives in the government. He felt it would be harder to get the support necessary to overthrow a peoples' government than it would to overthrow the provisional government. In this he proved right.

Strange as it may seem, in the light of future events, Kamenev was released from prison on August 17th and Trotsky exactly a month later. By September 24th, Trotsky was elected president of the Petersburg Soviet in place of Cheidze. On September 26th, the Petersburg Soviet voted to transfer all military power to a Military Revolutionary Committee under the leadership of Trotsky. The real Lenin revolution was by now only a few days away. Lenin was proving what proper planning and timetable precision, backed by unlimited financial aid, could accomplish. He knew how to use the element of surprise advantageously. He rapidly convinced many leaders of other revolutionary groups that he was the man to direct the revolutionary war. He soon had everyone under discipline. The leaders were required to obey orders efficiently, and without question, or else.

The revolutionary leaders circulated an order that the second All-Russian Congress of the Soviets would meet November 7th. This was a "red" herring, drawn across the trail to make the general public believe that no revolutionary action was pending in the immediate future. On November 4th, however, the Military Revolutionary Committee arranged huge mass meetings preparatory for the actual revolt. The next day, November 5th, the garrison of Peter and Paul declared itself in alliance with the Bolsheviks. On November 6th, Kerensky made a desperate effort to forestall the revolution by ordering the arrest of the Military Revolutionary Committee. He banned all Bolshevik publications. He ordered fresh troops to replace the garrison of Peter and Paul. But Lenin had organized his Fifth Column too well; Kerensky's orders were never carried out. Officials he trusted let him down.

Lenin sneaked out of hiding. He joined the Military Revolutionary Committee in Smolny Institute as soon as he knew Kerensky's counter-revolutionary measures had failed. The Institute served as the revolutionary headquarters. At 2:00 A.M. November 7th, the order to begin the organized revolutionary effort was given. By noon, St. Petersburg was largely in Lenin's hands. At 3:00 P.M. he delivered a fiery speech to the Petersburg Soviet. By 9:00 P.M. Bolshevik troops were besieging the Winter Palace headquarters of the Provisional Government. At 11:00 P.M. the Second All-Russian Congress of Soviets met and the Bolsheviks had a clear majority. The Congress thus became the official government of Russia. Kamenev was elected the first president. Lenin became Premier. Trotsky became Commissar of Foreign Affairs. On November 21st, a Jew by the name of Sverdlov succeeded Kamenev. He had been in the Bolshevik Party only six months and was considered a very minor figure but, after being elected president, he quickly assumed absolute control of the Russian economy. He was a specially trained financial expert and agent of the Bankers. After they established control, Lenin and the communists outlawed gold as money, closed down private banks and issued interest-free, government-backed, paper currency.

Many things happen in revolutionary circles which never come to light. Sverdlov died, a very young man, only two years after he reorganized the Russian internal economy. He had served his purpose. He knew too much, so he died. Thus history repeats itself.

Bloody battles, which might better be described as wholesale massacres, and the ruthlessly conducted "Reign of Terror" proved the theory that utter ruthlessness and organized terror, in which physical sufferings are combined with mental anguish, and moral degradation, have definite economic value, because the Bolsheviks obtained undisputed control of Petersburg within a few days. Lenin didn't allow success to go to his head. The Russian Empire was large. He craftily allowed the elections, for which the provisional government had set up the machinery, to be held on November 25th.

The provisional government had planned that the convocation of the Assembly of freely elected representatives should be organized by a special commission. Lenin let everything go according to schedule and then he arrested the members of this special commission. He substituted for it a "Commissary for the Constitutional Assembly." The only difference between the one and the other was that Bolsheviks headed by Uritzky dominated the one Lenin had formed. By this move the Bolsheviks were in a position to exert authority over the newly elected Assembly as soon as it convened. When the Assembly did finally convene Sverdlov took charge of the proceedings *although he was not a delegate*. The Bolsheviks present resorted to tactics which kept the delegates in a constant uproar. They created utter confusion. After ten hours the Bolsheviks all walked out suddenly. Bolshevik troops walked in. They ejected the remaining delegates and locked the doors of the building. This was the end of Constitutional rule in Russia.

In March 1918, the Bolsheviks, who called themselves "The Russian Social-Democratic Labour Party" moved to Moscow and changed their name to the Communist Party. The second All-Russian Congress of Soviets now became the official governing body.

The Jewish-led Social Revolutionary Party did not want Lenin as Number One man in Russia. On August 30th, 1918, two Jewish members of this group tried to assassinate him. Lenin was wounded and Uritzky, whom Lenin had appointed head of his Cheka organization, was killed.

This incident gave Lenin the excuse for pulling out all stops. He turned on terrorism at full blast. Night raids became regular occurrences. No person knew, when he went to bed, if he would be alive in the morning. David Shub in his Pro-Marxist book *Lenin* says: "Little time was wasted sifting evidence, or classifying people rounded up, in these night raids...The prisoners were generally hustled to the old police station, near the Winter Palace and shot." Murder, torture, mutilation, rape, burning—these and all other outrages against human sentiment and decency, were the impregnable rocks upon which the so-called Soviet Socialist Republic was founded. Millions of Russian citizens died. It is estimated that more than 12,000,000 others were condemned to serve the State at forced labour until they were released by death.

And while the allies were half-heartedly fighting Bolshevism on four fronts, Lenin reorganized the WRM. In March 1919, he convened the Third International, with himself presiding. Zinoviev was elected president. The purpose of the meeting was to consolidate the revolutionary parties in every country in the world, and to arrange to provide the leaders with advice, financial aid, and any other assistance considered necessary to the success of Popular World Revolution.[14]

[1.] An exact duplicate of this club was organized just outside Montreal during World War Two.

[2.] This was in keeping with paragraph 8 of the plot exposed in Chapter 3.

[3.] Note the word used is "Palestine" not "Israel."

[4.] This letter was quoted by Mr. Stokes, M.P. in the British Parliament during the Palestine Debate, December 11, 1947.

[5.] Read *Programme for the Third World War*, by C.H. Douglas, Liverpool, 1944.

[6.] Mr. Cambon of the French Ministry of Foreign Affairs accepted the Balfour Declaration in regard to supporting Zionism at this time.

[7.] For further details of this aspect of the war read *The Brief for the Prosecution*, by C.H. Douglas.

[8.] Boris Brazel was author of *World at the Crossroads*, see p. 69.

[9.] This is the Sokolov who afterwards wrote *History of Zionism*.

[10.] He wrote *World Jewry* (London) February 22nd, 1936. It will be seen that a very similar situation was created by international intrigue at the beginning of World War II.

[11.] Read *All These Things* by A.N. Field.

[12.] Comdr. Cromie served in British Submarines at the same time as the author. His exploits on behalf of the Russians are recorded in *By Guess and by God*—a book published by the author in 1931.

[13.] *La Russie sous les Juifs*, pp. 20-28 and 34-35.

[14.] A great deal more information on the Russian angle can be obtained by reading *Behind Communism* by Frank Britton.

CHAPTER NINE

The Treaty of Versailles

It has been previously stated that the Treaty of Versailles was one of the most iniquitous documents ever signed by the representatives of so-called civilized nations. The injustice perpetrated upon the German people by the terms of the "Peace Treaty" made another world war inevitable.[1]

The circumstances surrounding the signing of the Armistice on November 11, 1918, must be understood. The German High Command did not ask for the Armistice because their armies were in danger of defeat. When the Armistice was signed, the German armies had never been defeated on the field of battle. The German High Command asked for an Armistice so that they could devote their efforts towards preventing a Communist Revolution. Rosa Luxemberg, and her Jewish-dominated Spartacus Bund, had planned to duplicate in Germany what Lenin had achieved in Russia exactly one year previously.

The Armistice was signed *as a prelude to a negotiated peace*. It is of the utmost importance to remember this fact because an Armistice entered into under those conditions is far different from unconditional surrender.

The events which caused the German High Command to realize their danger on the home front were as follows:

Rosa Luxemberg's revolutionaries infiltrated into the German High Seas fleet. They became very active in 1918. They spread rumours that the ships and their crews were to be sacrificed in an all-out battle with the combined British and American navies. The rumour-mongers stated that the purpose of the battle was to cripple the combined allied fleets to such an extent they would be unable to defend the British coasts against a military invasion planned to bring the German Warlords Victory. The Communist 'Cells' exhorted the German seamen to mutiny because they claimed that the planned invasion of Britain was doomed to failure due to the fact that British Scientists had developed a secret weapon. According to the rumour-mongers, invading craft could, by the use of chemicals fired from guns ashore or dropped from planes, be surrounded by a sea of flames. Fire, heat, and lack of oxygen would create conditions in which nothing human could survive. The subversives argued that the only way to avoid such a fate was to bring about a revolution to end the war. The German seamen mutinied on the 3rd of November, 1918.

On November 7th, a large body of marines deserted while on their way to the Western Front. They had been told that they were going to be used to 'Spear-head' the rumoured invasion of Britain. Meantime, uprisings had caused shut-downs in many German industrial centres. Subversives talked defeatism. Conditions deteriorated until, on November 9th, the Kaiser abdicated.

The Social Democratic Party immediately formed a Republican Government. The Armistice was signed November on 11th, 1918. The Communist leaders of the Spartacus Bund had placed their 'Cells' in key positions within the new government and throughout the armed forces. Their combined efforts created chaotic conditions everywhere. Rosa Luxemberg then played her trump card. She forced the Socialist government to order the immediate demobilization of the German armed forces. This action prevented the German

High Command from using their well-disciplined troops to prevent the pending revolution which broke out in January of 1919.

Before she usurped power in Germany, Rosa Luxemberg was promised the same financial assistance and military aid the international bankers had given to Lenin and Trotsky a year before. The initial stages of her revolutionary effort were financed by the fund they made available through the Soviet Ambassador Joffe. The revolutionary effort only failed to accomplish what Lenin had achieved in Russia when the promised aid failed to materialize after Rosa had launched her initial onslaught. Then she realized her Jewish Spartacus Bund had been betrayed by the very men she considered her friends and supporters. This incident alone should prove that "The Secret Power" behind the world revolutionary movement, is not concerned about the welfare of the Jews any more than it is about the Gentiles. The majority of the Directors of the WRM are men who descended from the Khazars, Tartars, and other Mongol-Asiatic non-semitic races. They adopted the Jewish religion to suit their own selfish purposes between the 7th and 8th centuries.[2] They have used Jews exactly as they have used Gentiles as "Pawns in the Game."

The purpose of the doublecross was twofold. The men who plot and plan the World Revolutionary Movement did not want Germany *sovietized* until *after* they had used the German people to fight another war against Britain. They calculated that a Second World War would render both Empires so utterly exhausted that they could then be easily subjugated by the resources of the U.S.S.R. they controlled under Lenin's dictatorship. In order to start a Second World War, they considered it was necessary to build up within Germany an intense anti-semitic hatred for the purpose of dividing Europe into two opposing camps—Fascist and Anti-Fascist. The plan required all communist countries to remain neutral, in a military sense, while their agents did everything possible to aggravate the adverse conditions the master-minds created.

After the Jewish-dominated revolution collapsed for want of aid, the German Aryan people took a full measure of revenge on the Jewish people. Thousands of Jews—men, women and children—were rounded up during the night and executed. Rosa Luxemberg, and her right hand man Karl Liebknecht, were captured and shot in the head like mad dogs by a German lieutenant. Thus, once again, a large number of Jews were made to pay the penalty for the crimes of a small group of international gangsters who used them as "Pawns in the Game" of international intrigue.

To prolong and intensify the hatred of the German people for the Jews, propaganda blamed the Jews for bringing about the military defeat of Germany's armed forces, and the unjust and humiliating terms enforced by the Treaty of Versailles. Propaganda strengthened the trend towards National-Socialism in Germany by representing Britain, France, and the United States as selfish capitalistic countries influenced and controlled by the international Jewish bankers. Thus the way was prepared for the advent of Hitler.

Soon after the Armistice was signed, the international bankers instructed Lenin to consolidate the Communist gain and to prepare to defend the Soviet States against capitalistic aggression. Lenin announced this as his policy. Trotsky disagreed bitterly. He advocated immediate revolution in all European countries which remained to be subjugated. He wanted to help Germany's Spartacus Bund in order to keep the revolutionary spirit alive.

Lenin insisted that their first duty was to establish the Communist sphere of influence in all countries of the world located between the 35th and 45th parallels of latitude in the Northern Hemisphere. Lenin stated he would only countenance revolutionary action in countries within those limits. The most important countries were Spain, Italy, Greece, certain sections of Asia-Minor (including Palestine), certain sections of China, and the area both sides of the border in Canada and the United States. Lenin warned the Third International that it was the duty of the revolutionary leaders in all those countries to organize their parties so as to be ready to take over their governments when outside forces created favourable conditions to revolt. Rosa Luxemberg's failure was cited as an example of what would happen if revolutionary action was taken independently.

Lenin's strategic plan is known in military circles as "The Musk Ox Plan" because these northern animals have been able to survive against the attacks of all their enemies by the simple expedient of forming a circle with their heads pointing out and their tails in. Calves are placed inside the circle. Wolves and bears could not attack the herd from flank or rear. If they attacked head-on they were gored to death or cut to ribbons by the razor-like hooves of the oxen.[3]

Lenin justified himself for abandoning Rosa Luxemberg on the grounds that he had thus been able to organize the Soviet armies to withstand the combined onslaught of the Capitalistic countries from 1919 to 1921. In 1921, Lenin informed the members of the Third International that Spain was to be the nest country *sovietized*. He blamed Rosa Luxemberg as being responsible for the wave of anti-Semitism which had swept over Germany. The Third International then despatched Karl Radek to lead Communism in Germany. He was instructed to use his own initiative as far as recruiting, organizing, and training the party was concerned, but he was warned not to take revolutionary action until ordered to do so by the Comintern. The Comintern was under control of Lenin, and therefore the international bankers.

Having settled internal conditions in Germany to suit their Long-Range Plans, the international gangsters next turned their attention to Palestine. Palestine occupied a central geographical position in their overall plans for world conquest. In addition to that, they knew that world famous geologists had located vast deposits of mineral wealth in the area around the Dead Sea.[4] They therefore decided to sponsor Political Zionism to further their two-fold purpose.

One: To force the nations of the world to make Palestine a National Home for the Jews so they would have a *sovereign state* which they would control by reason of their wealth and power. If their long-range plans matured to the extent of a third world war they could use their *sovereign state* to extend the control they exercised over the communized nations throughout the whole world. When this was accomplished they would be able to crown the head of the group "King of the Universe" and "God upon this Earth."[5]

Two: They had to secure control of the five trillion dollars worth of mineral wealth they knew was hidden in and around the shores of the Dead Sea. Events will show how they went about their dual purpose. After Britain, France and the United States had been committed to form a national home for the Jews in Palestine, by the Balfour Declaration in April 1917, Lord Allenby was ordered to drive the Turks out of Asia-Minor and occupy the Holy Land. The fact that Palestine was to be turned over to the Jews was not made known until *after* the Arabs had helped Allenby accomplish this task. The general impression was that Palestine would be a British Protectorate.

Immediately after Lord Allenby's triumphant entry into Jerusalem the international bankers "persuaded" the allied governments to appoint their political emissaries as a Zionist Commission. Officially, the members of this commission were sent to Palestine to act as liaison between the military Administration and the Jews. Their real purpose was to "advise" General Clayton so his military administration would further their secret plans. The Zionist Commission went into effect in March 1918.

Members of the Zionist Commission included:

Major Ormsby-Gore. He afterwards became Lord Harlich. He was a director of the Midland Bank, the Standard Bank of South Africa, and the Union Corporation.[6]

Major James de Rothschild, the son of Edmund de Rothschild of Paris, who had formerly owned the Rothschild Colonies in Palestine. Major de Rothschild afterwards became a Liberal member of the British parliament. He served in this capacity from 1929 to 1945. He was appointed parliamentary secretary in the Churchill-Labour Coalition Government.

Lieut. Edwin Samuel. He afterwards became Chief Censor for the British government during the Second World War. He was appointed Chief Director of Palestine Broadcasting after the State of Israel was established in 1948.[7]

Mr. Israel Sieff. He was a director of Marks and Spencer, the huge British departmental stores. He was a close associate of all the international bankers. He was appointed Chairman of the Political and Economic Planning Committee. He was a permanent member of the "Brain Trust" which "advised" successive British governments. His standing in Great Britain was very similar to that of Bernard Baruch in the United States of America from 1918 to date (1945). Mr. Sieff rendered the international bankers such outstanding service that he was made a commander of the Order of Maccabees.

Leon Simon. He was afterwards knighted, and placed in charge of the British General Post Office. He controlled all telegraph, telephone, and cable facilities.

The remaining members of the commission were Dr. Elder, Mr. Joseph Cowen, and Mr. Chaim Weizmann, all close friends of wealthy Zionists in America.[8]

Sir R. Storrs says the Zionist Commission was sent to Palestine *before* the Peace Conference started, in order to create an atmosphere favourable to establishing a national home for the Jews, and also to stimulate its financial supporters.

The international bankers dominated the conference which culminated in the Treaty of Versailles. This is proved by the fact that in January 1919 Mr. Paul Warburg (who drafted the Federal Reserve System in the U.S.A.), arrived in Paris to head the American delegation. His brother Max arrived to head the German delegation. Comte de St. Aulaire says: "Those who look for the truth elsewhere than in the official documents know that President Wilson, whose election had been financed by the Great Bank of New York (Kuhn-Loeb & Co.) rendered almost complete obedience to its beck and call."

Dr. Dillon states, "The sequence of expedients framed and enforced in this direction were inspired by the Jews (*i.e.* representatives of the international bankers) assembled in Paris for the purpose of realizing their carefully thought out programmes which they succeeded in having substantially executed."

The Mandate of Palestine was drafted by Professor Felix Frankfurter, the eminent American Zionist, who afterwards became Chief Adviser in the White House to President Roosevelt. He was assisted by the Right Honourable Sir Herbert Samuel, Dr. Jacobson,

Dr. Fiewel, Mr. Sacher, Mr. Landman, Mr. Ben Cohen, and Mr. Lucien Wolfe who exercised tremendous influence over Mr. David Lloyd George.[9] He was said to possess all the secrets of the British Foreign Office.[10]

At the preliminary conferences M. Mandel (whose real name was Rothschild) was private secretary to Mr. Clemenceau of France. Mr. Henry Morgenthau was on the U.S. delegation in a general supervisory capacity. He was the father of the man who afterwards became President Roosevelt's Financial Secretary. Another man affiliated with the international bankers was Mr. Oscar Strauss who took a leading part in forming the League of Nations and moulding its policies so that they fitted in with the International Gangsters' Long-Range Plan for ultimate world domination.

Mr. Lucien Wolfe says on page 408 of his *Essays in Jewish History*:

> A small group of other distinguished Jews appear as signatories of the Peace Treaty. The Treaty of Versailles is signed for France by Louis Klotz, (Editor: He was afterwards implicated in shady financial transactions and retired from public life) Baron Somino for Italy, and Edwin Montague for India.

Mr. Harold Nicolson, in his *Peace Making 1919-1944* (p. 243), states that Wolfe suggested to him that all Jews should have international protection while retaining all national rights of exploitation. M. Georges Batault says in *Le Problème Juif*, p. 38: "The Jews who surrounded Lloyd George, Wilson, and Clemenceau are to blame for creating a 'Jewish Peace.'" Once again the Jewish race is blamed for the sins of a few ruthless financiers.

In the spring of 1919, Béla Kun usurped power in Hungary. He tried to put Lucien Wolfe's ideas into practice. Béla Kun's dictatorship lasted only three months, but during that time tens of thousands of Christians were dispossessed and ruthlessly murdered. The victims included working men, army officers, merchants, land-owners, professional men and women, priests and laymen.

The *New International Year Book of 1919* says in part:

> The government of Béla Kun was composed almost exclusively of Jews, who held also the administrative offices. The Communists had united first with the Socialists, who were not of the extremely radical party, but resembled somewhat the Labour Parties, or Trade Union groups, in other countries. Béla Kun did not however select his personnel from among them, but turned to the Jews and constituted virtually a Jewish bureaucracy.

History records that after three months of systematic pillage, rape, and wholesale murder, Béla Kun was deposed. *Instead of being executed, he was interned in a lunatic asylum.* His release was arranged by agents of the powerful group he had served so well. He returned to Russia and was put in charge of the Cheka which terrorized the Ukrainians into subjection when Stalin was ordered to collectivize agriculture in the Soviets. Five million peasants were starved to death for refusing to obey the edicts. Over five million more were sent to forced labour in Siberia.

When Stalin tried to turn Spain into a Communist Dictatorship in 1936, Béla Kun was chosen to organize the *Reign of Terror* in Spain.

The power of the international bankers is well illustrated by an incident that happened during the preliminary conferences held in Paris in 1919. The negotiations tended to stray away from the policy set by the international bankers. Thereupon Jacob Schiff of New

York sent President Wilson, who was attending the Paris conference, a two-thousand-word cable. He "instructed" the president of the United States what to do in regard to the Palestine Mandate, German Reparations, Upper Silesia, The Sarre, The Danzig Corridor, and Fiume. The cablegram was dated May 28th, 1919. Schiff sent it in the name of the Association of the League of Free Nations.[11]

Upon receipt of the cablegram, President Wilson immediately changed the direction of the negotiations. Of this incident Comte de St. Aulaire said: "The Treaty of Versailles on these five questions was dictated by Jacob Schiff and his co-religionists."[12] It must be pointed out again that the rank and file of the Jewish people had absolutely nothing to do with framing the policy which the international bankers insisted Lloyd George, President Wilson, and Premier Clemenceau carry out.

As soon as the allied governments had been "persuaded" to make Palestine a British Protectorate, (as demanded in the cable), the international bankers instructed their agents that the terms of the Peace Treaty were to be made so severe that it would be impossible for the German people to tolerate them very long. This was part of the plan to keep the German people hating the British, French, Americans and the Jews so they would be ready to fight again to regain their legal rights.

Immediately after the Treaty of Versailles was signed, the phony Capitalist-Bolshevik war was started. This war enabled Lenin to justify his policy, by which he abandoned the German revolutionaries to their fate in order to consolidate the gains he had already made in Russia. The war against Bolshevism was never permitted to endanger Lenin's dictatorship. It was ended in 1921. The net result was that the Bolsheviks gained a tremendous amount of prestige, while the Capitalist countries lost a similar amount. This paved the way for the agents of the international bankers to suggest, in the interests of permanent peace, that the Soviet States be admitted to membership in the League of Nations.

The British government, always obedient to the "wishes" of the international bankers, was the first to comply with the new "request." France followed suit on October 28th, 1924. After the infamous Litvinov had worked on Henry Morgenthau and Dean Acheson—who were both dominated by Felix Frankfurter and Louis D. Brandeis—President Roosevelt recognized the Soviets on November 16th, 1933. The League of Nations accepted the Soviet States as members. From that day on, the League of Nations was nothing more or less than an instrument in the hands of Stalin. His agents moulded its policy and activities to suit the Long-Range Plans of those who direct the World Revolutionary Movement.[13]

Once the Communist countries were admitted into the League of Nations, the Grand Orient Masons—who were delegates or on the staff—took charge.[14]

Wickham Steed, former editor of the *Times*, London, was one of the best-informed men in the world. On more than one occasion, he discussed the fact that the international bankers dominated international affairs. He made this definite statement just after the Treaty of Versailles was signed: "I insisted that, unknown to him, the prime movers (to make the Allied Powers acknowledge the Bolshevik dictatorship) were Jacob Schiff, Warburg, and other international financiers, who wished above all to bolster up the Jewish Bolsheviks in order to secure a field for German and Jewish exploitation of Russia."[15]

Leo Maxse, writing in the August issue of the *National Review* 1919 stated: "Whoever is in power in Downing Street, whether Conservative, Radicals, Coalitionist, or Pseudo-Bolshevik, the international Jews rule the roost. Here is the mystery of the 'Hidden Hand' of which there has been no intelligent explanation." Once again the word "Jew" should have been "Banker" or "Gangster." It would be just as reasonable to blame all Roman Catholics for the crimes of a few Roman Mafia Chieftains who had given up the practice of their religion for many years.[16]

When Mr. Winston Churchill visited Palestine in March 1921, he was asked to meet a delegation of Moslem leaders. They protested that the ultimate objective of political Zionism was to give the natural resources of Palestine to the Jews. They pointed out that the Arabs had occupied Palestine for over a thousand years. They asked Churchill to use his influence to correct what they considered a great injustice. Churchill is recorded as saying in reply: "You ask me to repudiate the Balfour Declaration and to stop (Jewish) immigration. This is not in my power...and it is not my wish...We think it is good for the world, good for the Jews, good for the British Empire, and good for the Arabs also...*and we intend it to be so.*"[17]

When Churchill gave the Arabs his reply he was in all probability thinking of the threat issued by Chaim Weizmann who had been an agent of the international bankers for many years. Just a year before Churchill's visit to Palestine, Weizmann had made an official statement of policy which was published in *Jüdische Rundschau*, No. 4, 1920: He said "We will establish ourselves in Palestine whether you like it or not...You can hasten our arrival or you can equally retard it. It is however better for you to help us so as to avoid our constructive powers being turned into a *destructive power which will overthrow the world.*"

Weizmann's statement must be studied in conjunction with another declaration made by an international banker to a gathering of Zionists in Budapest in 1919. When discussing the probabilities of a supergovernment, he was quoted by Comte de St. Aulaire as saying:

> In the management of the New World we give proof of our organization both for revolution and for construction by the creation of the League of Nations, which is our Work. Bolshevism is the accelerator, and the League of Nations is the brake on the mechanism of which we supply both the motive force and the guiding power...What is the end? That is already determined by our mission.[18]

One world government.

The two statements combined show the international extent of their secret ambitions. Eight years after I had finished this chapter of the original manuscript, the following report came into my possession through Canadian Intelligence Service. Because the statements made at the Conference held in Budapest on January 12th, 1952, support my contentions made in 1944, and confirm the conclusions I had arrived at in 1924, I insert the report of the speech given in 1952 here verbatim. It was originally made available to an American publication *Common Sense* by Mr. Eustace Mullins, an authority on the Marxist conspiracy.[19]

> A report from Europe carries the following speech of Rabbi Emanuel Rabinovich before a special meeting of the Emergency Council of European Rabbis in Budapest, Hungary; January 12, 1952:

"Greetings, my children: You have been called here to recapitulate the principal steps of our new programme. As you know, we had hoped to have twenty years between wars to consolidate the great gains which we made from World War II, but our increasing numbers in certain vital areas is arousing opposition to us, and we must now Work with every means at our disposal to precipitate World War III *within five years.*

"The goal for which we have striven so concertedly for three thousand years is at last within our reach, and because its fulfillment is so apparent, it behooves us to increase our efforts, and our caution, tenfold. I can safely promise you that before ten years have passed, our race will take its rightful place in the world, with every Jew a king, and every Gentile a slave. (Applause from the gathering.) You remember the success of our propaganda campaign during the 1930's, which aroused anti-American passions in Germany at the same time we were arousing anti-German passions in America, a campaign which culminated in the Second World War. A similar propaganda campaign is now being waged intensively throughout the world. A war fever is being worked up in Russia by an incessant anti-American barrage, while a nationwide anti-Communist scare is sweeping America. This campaign is forcing all of the smaller nations to choose between the partnership of Russia or an alliance with the United States.

"Our most pressing problem at the moment is to inflame the lagging militaristic spirit of the Americans. The failure of the Universal Military Training Act was a great setback to our plans, but we are assured that a suitable measure will be rushed through congress immediately after the 1952 elections. The Russian, as well as the Asiatic peoples, are well under control and offer no objections to war, but we must wait to secure the Americans. This we hope to do with the issue of anti-Semitism, which worked so well in uniting the Americans against Germany. We are counting heavily on reports of anti-Semitic outrages in Russia to help whip up indignation in the United States and produce a front of solidarity against the Soviet power. Simultaneously, to demonstrate to Americans the reality of anti-Semitism, we will advance through new sources large sums of money to outspokenly anti-Semitic elements in America to increase their effectiveness, and we shall stage anti-Semitic outbreaks in several of their larger cities. This will serve the double purpose of exposing reactionary sectors in America, which can be silenced, and of welding the United States into a devoted anti-Russian unit.

"Within five years, this programme will achieve its objective, the Third World War, which will surpass in destruction all previous contests. Israel, of course will remain neutral, and when both sides are devastated and exhausted we will arbitrate, sending our Control Commission into all wrecked countries. This war will end for all time our struggle against the Gentiles.

"We will openly reveal our identity with the races of Asia and Africa. I can state with assurance that the last generation of white children is now being born. Our Control Commissions will, in the interests of peace, and wiping out inter-racial tensions, forbid the whites to mate with whites. The white women must cohabit with members of the dark races, the white men with black women. Thus the white race will disappear, for mixing the dark with the white means the end of the white man, and our most dangerous enemy will become only a memory. We shall embark upon an era of ten thousand years of peace and plenty, the Pax Judaica, and our race will rule undisputed over the world. Our superior intelligence will easily enable us to retain mastery over a world of dark peoples."

Question from the gathering:

"Rabbi Rabinovich, what about the various religions after the Third World War?"

Rabinovich:

"There will be no more religions. Not only would the existence of a priest class remain a constant danger to our rule, but belief in an after-life would give spiritual strength to irreconcilable elements in many countries, and enable them to resist us. We will, however, retain the rituals, and customs of Judaism, as the mark of our hereditary ruling caste, strengthening our racial laws so that no Jew will be allowed to marry outside our race, nor will any stranger be accepted by us.

"We may have to repeat the grim days of World War II, when we were forced to let the Hitlerite bandits sacrifice some of our people, in order that we may have adequate documentation and witnesses to legally justify our trial and execution of the leaders of America and Russia as war criminals, after we have dictated the Peace. I am sure you will need little preparation for such a duty, for sacrifice has always been the watchword of our people, and *the death of a few thousand Jews in exchange for world leadership is indeed a small price to pay.*

"To convince you of the certainty of that leadership, let me point out to you how we have turned all of the inventions of the white man into weapons against him. His printing presses and radios are the mouthpieces of our desires, and *his heavy industry manufactures the instruments which he sends out to arm Asia and Africa against him.* Our interests in Washington are greatly extending the Point Four Programme for developing industry in backward areas of the world, so that after the industrial plants and cities of Europe and America are destroyed by atomic warfare, the whites can offer no resistance against the large masses of the dark races, who will maintain an unchallenged technological superiority.[20]

"And so, with the vision of world victory before you, go back to your countries and intensify your good work, until that approaching Light when Israel will reveal herself in all her glorious destiny as the Light of the World." [The Illuminati or "Enlightened ones."]

This speech also confirms what I have contended in regard to the manner in which the Secret Powers have deliberately stirred up anti-Semitism to suit their purposes and also anti-Communism. It proves my contention that the Illuminati have used Communism, Zionism, and Fascism to further their secret ambitions. And they will, if they can, use Christian-Democracy against Communism to bring about the next phase of their long range plan: World War Three. But the most illuminating feature of the speech is the fact that it discloses the manner in which the Illuminati use a Jewish Rabbi to convince other co-religionists that they will be the governing class in the New World Order—a fact that past history would indicate is very doubtful. Satanism, not the Jews, will rule.

Under the terms of the Treaty of Versailles in 1919, the international bankers obtained control over Germany's military rearmament, and her economic recovery. This accomplished, they entered into the *Abmachungen* (agreements) with the German High Command. They agreed to have the Soviets secretly supply the German generals with all the arms and munitions they required for a modern army of several million. They also undertook to have the Soviet dictator place complete training facilities at the disposal of the Germans to enable them to train the number of commissioned and non-commissioned officers they would require to officer the new army they planned to bring into being when they considered the time was ripe.

The vast building projects required to put the terms of the *Abmachungen* into effect were financed by the international bankers.[21] They thus enabled both Communist and Fascist countries to build up their economy and war potentials. The international bankers enabled the German High Command to evade all the military restrictions placed upon them by the Treaty of Versailles.[22]

The vast Krupp Munitions and Armaments Plants built in the Soviets behind the Ural Mountains were named "Manych." The German armament firms were granted every concession they asked for. International intrigue on such a lavish scale could only mean one thing. Those involved were preparing for World War II. The governments of the so-called Allied nations were kept fully informed regarding what was going on behind the scenes, as I found out when I visited London during the conference on naval disarmament in 1930. This is only another proof that Disraeli spoke the truth when he said, "The governments elected do not govern."

Thus history reveals that from 1920 to 1934 the Secret Power directed international intrigue in such a manner that the leaders of *allegedly* Jewish-dominated Communism in Russia were working hand in glove with the leaders of *allegedly* Aryan-dominated Naziism in Germany. This phase of history is most complicated. It is difficult for the average citizen to understand.[23]

Communism and Naziism have several things in common. Both are atheistic creeds which deny the existence of Almighty God. They both advocate war, hatred, and force, as opposed to Christ's policy of peace, love, and teaching. The leaders of both atheistic-materialistic ideologies *must* therefore be agents of the Devil. They further the diabolical conspiracy to win the souls of men away from loyalty and obedience to Almighty God. They both use a form of Grand Orient Masonry for proselytizing purposes.[24]

The head of the Council of Thirty Three is the president of the top-executive Council of Thirteen, previously referred to. Because the initiating ceremonies of *all* Grand Orient Lodges require the candidate to swear he will acknowledge no other mortal as above the head of the organization, that *head* is automatically *God on Earth*. The international bankers have always been the top executives of the Grand Orient Masonry since 1770. Aryan War Lords have always been the top executive of the German Lodges. They select their own successors.

A review of history, 1914-1934, indicates:

1. That the international bankers fomented World War I to bring about conditions favourable for revolutionary action and thus enable them to obtain undisputed control of the Russian Empire.

2. To remove the Crowned Heads of Europe. These rulers had to be removed before either group could achieve their totalitarian ambitions.

3. To force the British and French governments to agree to establish *A National Home for the Jews in Palestine.*

The government of Britain was forced to aid the international bankers' plan for the Bolshevik revolution in Russia in 1917, in order to obtain their promise that they would bring America into the war on the side of the allies. It can be assumed that *S.S. Lusitania* was sunk to provide the necessary incident to justify the changer of American policy, just as Pearl Harbour was used as an excuse for America to enter World War II.

The original draft of the mandate on Palestine reads: "TO TURN PALESTINE INTO A NATIONAL HOME FOR THE JEWS". It was altered at the last minute to read "to establish a National Home for the Jew IN PALESTINE". This was done to conceal the secret ambitions of the Zionists.

The international bankers deliberately concealed the truth regarding the vast mineral deposits geologists had discovered in Palestine until *after* the governments of Britain, France, and the United States had agreed to their *Mandate of Palestine*.[25]

The international bankers used Zionism to obtain control of a centrally located Sovereign State from which they could extend the control they now exert over the USSR to cover the entire World.

The conspirators managed international affairs between 1921 and 1934 so that Europe was divided into two camps—Fascist and Anti-Fascist—in preparation for World War II.

[1.] The injustice perpetrated at Versailles was only exceeded by the agreements afterwards entered into at Tehran, Potsdam, and Yalta. It will be proved that the same evil influences were at work in all negotiations.

[2.] See the *Iron Curtain Over America* by Pro. John Beaty. Wilkinson Publishing Co., Dallas, Texas. pp. 15-16.

[3.] Time has shown how far this long range plan has matured, and it explains why China was turned over to the Communists.

[4.] This was Conningham-Craig, previously mentioned.

[5.] The Long-Range Plans published in Chapter 3 proves this is intended.

[6.] The directors of the Standard Bank helped bring about the Boer war in order to give them control of the gold and diamond fields in Africa.

[7.] It might have been more accurate to have given him the title of Chief Director of Propaganda for the International Bankers.

[8.] The importance of Palestine in the plans of those who direct the World Revolutionary Movement is such that several books have been written on the subject. People wishing to be better informed should read *Palestine, the Reality*, by J.M.N. Jeffries; *The Palestine Plot* by B. Jensen; *Zionism and Palestine* by Sir Ronald Storrs (who was first Governor of Jerusalem); *Geneva versus Peace* by Comte de St. Aulaire, (who was at one time ambassador to the Palace of St. James, England); *The Paris Peace Conference* by Dr. Dillon, London, 1919; *Brief for Prosecution* by Major C.H. Douglas.

[9.] Mr. L. Wolfe published *Essays in Jewish History* in 1934.

[10.] See *Jewish Guardian* June issue 1920. Also *The Surrender of an Empire* by Nesta H Webster, p. 357, 1933; and *The Palestine Plot* by B. Jensen, p, 60.

[11.] This league was financed, and dominated, by five American Bankers.

[12.] See *Geneva versus Peace*, p. 90.

13. For further particulars read *Moscow's Red Letter Day in American History* by Wm. La Varre, in the August 1951 edition of the *American Legion Magazine*. Also Trotsky's book entitled *Stalin* (1941).

14. Read *The Hidden Hand*, page 28, by Colonel A.H. Lane. Nahun Sokolov, who was President of the Executive Committee of the Zionist Congress, said on August 25th, 1952, "The League of Nations is a Jewish idea".

15. Read *Through Thirty Years* by Wickham Steed, London. Vol. 2, pp. 301-302.

16. It was the references to "The Secret Power" and "Hidden Hand" by Steed, De Poncin, Mrs. Webster, Maxse and others which caused me to investigate the matter in an effort to find the real answer.—Author.

17. The full significance of this declaration was not appreciated even by the author until 1954 when Prime Minister Churchill (during his visit to Bernard Baruch) stated, "I am a Zionist and have always promoted Zionism." He then followed this declaration by strongly advocating "Peaceful coexistence with the Communist Nations." As the Communist States are actually International Financiers Dictatorships it must be assumed that in 1921 as in 1954 Churchill secretly believed they are best fitted, and most able to rule under present-day conditions.

18. *Geneva versus Peace*, p. 83.

19. Mr. E. Mullins is author of *The Federal Reserve Conspiracy*. Published by *Common Sense*, New Jersey, U.S.A.

20. Study this statement in regard to the meeting of leaders of all 'Dark' and 'Black' races which met in Bandung in April 1956 and the policy of sending arms to Israel and Egypt.

21. This was prior to the advent of Hitler.

22. It will be proved that the German generals and top-level officials who negotiated the Abmachungen were the ones condemned to death at the Nuremberg Trials as War Criminals. They knew too much.

23. A great deal of light has, however, been thrown on this subject by Mr. Cecil F. Melville, who made a deep study of this particular phase of the World Revolutionary Movement, and wrote *The Russian Face of Germany*.

24. Note: The German Grand Orient Lodges have never admitted Jews to membership for the obvious reason that the Secret Powers could never have put into effect an international plot of the nature and proportions of the *Abmachungen*, had their policy been otherwise.

25. Note: The truth regarding value of mineral resources was not allowed to leak out until the United Nations had partitioned Palestine in 1948 in such a manner that over five trillion dollars worth of minerals are now known to be located in The State of Israel. Count Bernadotte of Sweden proposed that the Jews should give up the south, and receive West Galilee in the north. His plan was rejected; in September 1947, Count Bernadotte was assassinated by Jewish extremists.

CHAPTER TEN

Stalin

Stalin was born Joseph Vissarionovich Djugashvili, in the mountain village of Gori in the province of Georgia in 1879. His father was a peasant from the town Dido-Lilo. His mother, Ekaterina Geladze, was a devoutly religious woman whose forebears had been serfs in the village of Gambarouli.

Not a great deal is known about Stalin's father, except that he sometimes worked as a labourer and sometimes as a cobbler in a shoe factory in Adelkhanov. He is said to have been an easy-going individual who liked to drink a great deal. Stalin's mother, however, was a devoted mother and worked hard. She took in washing to earn extra money for her family's benefit. Her ambition was to see Stalin become a priest. She skimped and saved to provide him with the necessary education. Young Stalin attended the elementary school in Gori for four years and won a scholarship which entitled him to attend the Tiflis Theological Seminary. But Stalin wasn't cut out for a religious life. He was continually getting into trouble with the seminary authorities. He was expelled after completing four years of study. He then joined a group of young revolutionaries.

Stalin first married Ekaterina Svanidze, who bore him a son, Yasha-Jacob Djugashvili. This boy was never very bright. Even after his father became dictator, he worked as an electrician and mechanic.

Stalin's second wife was Nadya Allilyova, who bore him two children: Vasili, a son, and Svetlana, a daughter. Vasili became a major-general in the Soviet Air Force. He usually led the flying demonstrations on special occasions of state after his father became dictator. He was thrown into the discard after his father died.

Stalin and his second wife don't seem to have gotten along very well together. Stalin had an affair with a beautiful Jewess, Rosa Kaganovich. She is reported to have been living with Stalin when his second wife, Nadya, committed suicide.

It is believed that in addition to Stalin's love affairs, Nadya became more and more depressed as the result of the ruthless way in which Stalin slaughtered so many of her co-religionists whom he accused of being diversionists.

Rosa's brother, Lazar Kaganovich, was a great friend of Stalin's. He was made a member of the Politburo and retained his office until Stalin died. Kaganovich proved his ability as Commissioner for Heavy Industry when he developed the Donetz Basin Oil Fields and built the Moscow subway. Kaganovich's son, Mihail, married Stalin's daughter Svetlana.[1] What became of Svetlana's first husband remains a mystery. It would appear that Svetlana's first husband removed himself, or was removed, to allow Kaganovich's son to marry Stalin's daughter, just as Stalin's second wife removed herself or was removed, to allow Stalin to marry Kaganovich's sister, Rosa. It is reported that Stalin did marry Rosa after his wife's suicide.

Molotov, vice-premier to Stalin, was married to a Jewess, the sister of Sam Karp, owner of the Karp Exporting Co. of Bridgeport, Connecticut. Molotov's daughter was engaged (but apparently not married) to Stalin's son, Vasilli, in 1951, so the Politburo was to a certain extent "A Family Compact." (Both Stalin and Molotov named their daughters Svetlana, meaning "Light".)

As was mentioned previously, Stalin only became a member of the Upper Crust of the Russian revolutionary party because many of the better-known leaders were in jail during the preliminary phases of the Russian Revolution. Stalin never rose to any very exalted position in the Communist Party during Lenin's dictatorship. It was during Lenin's last illness that Stalin jockeyed for position, and then he moved out in front, to eliminate Trotsky and other Jewish contenders. Once he took over the leadership, he never relinquished it until his death.

How Stalin rose to power is an interesting story. Lenin suffered a paralytic stroke in May 1922, and this affected his speech and motor reflexes. In December of that year, he appointed a triumvirate composed of Zinoviev, Kamenev and Stalin to share the problems of government. Shortly afterwards, Lenin suffered another stroke and died. Trotsky has suggested, and his followers believe, that Stalin helped bring about Lenin's death, because he was irritated by Lenin's incapacity and prolonged illness.

When the triumvirate started to function in Moscow, the Politburo included Lenin, Zinoviev, Kamenev, Trotsky, Bukharin, Tomsky, and Stalin. Zinoviev and Kamenev had been Lenin's right-hand men from the day he became dictator. They naturally regarded themselves as the senior members of the triumvirate and logically his successors. Zinoviev treated Stalin in a circumspectly patronizing manner, and Kamenev treated him with a touch of irony.[2]

Zinoviev and Kamenev considered Trotsky as their real competitor for the dictatorship after Lenin died. In Trotsky's book, *Stalin*, he records that Stalin was used by both Zinoviev and Kamenev as a counterweight against him (Trotsky), and to a lesser extent by other members of the Politburo also. No member of the Politburo at that time thought Stalin would one day rise away above their heads.

Zinoviev was considered senior member of the triumvirate when he was delegated to give the opening address of the 12th Party Congress, a function Lenin had always reserved for himself on previous occasions. Zinoviev didn't go over too well. Stalin was quick to take advantage. Before the congress was over, Stalin had secured control over the Communist Party machine and held a dominant position in the triumvirate. This was the situation when Lenin died in 1924.

In April 1925, Stalin had Trotsky removed as war commissar. He then broke relations with Zinoviev and Kamenev and allied himself with Bukharin, Rykov, and Tomsky. Zinoviev, Kamenev and Trotsky then united forces in opposition to Stalin, but they had moved too late. In February, 1926, Stalin had Zinoviev expelled from the Politburo, then from the presidency of the Petersburg (Leningrad) Soviet, and finally from the presidency of the Third International. In October 1926, Stalin had Kamenev and Trotsky expelled from the Politburo. Next year, Stalin had his three enemies removed from the Central Committee of the Communist Party and shortly afterwards he had them weeded out of the party altogether.

In 1927, Trotsky tried to start a revolt against Stalin on the grounds that he was departing from the Marxian ideology and substituting an imperialistic totalitarian dictatorship for a genuine Union of Sovietized Socialist Republics. What everyone seems to have failed to realize was the fact that Stalin had been nominated to rule the Soviets by the international bankers. He had to purge Russia of all men who might obstruct their Long-Range Plans.

During the purge, several million people were slain and about an equal number sent to forced labour. Many men who had been leaders of the revolutionary movement, since the First International was formed, were hounded to death or imprisoned. Amongst the leaders Stalin purged were Trotsky, Zinoviev, Kamenev, Martynov, Zasulich, Deutch, Parvus, Axelrod, Radek, Uritzky, Sverdlov, Dan, Lieber, and Martov. About the only Jews close to Stalin at the time of his death were Kaganovich, his brother-in-law, and Rosa, his third wife.

Stalin continued to develop Lenin's policy to establish the Communist sphere of influence between the 35th and 45th parallels of latitude right around the northern hemisphere. Many revolutionary leaders in other countries became convinced that Stalin had developed personal Imperialistic ideas and was intent upon making himself ruler of a worldwide totalitarian dictatorship. They were right. Stalin took his orders, as Lenin had done, from the men who are "The Secret Power" behind the World Revolutionary Movement, until 1936 and then he began to ignore their mandates, as will be proved.

Stalin did not want to involve his armed forces in wars with other nations. His policy was to feed the revolutionary fires in all countries to the south between the 35th and 45th parallels of latitude. His policy paid off exceedingly well. At the time of his death, Communistic control had been established across half the territory in the Northern Hemisphere. About half the world's population had been subjugated.

Lenin had stated in 1921 that Spain was to be the next country Sovietized. Upon his death, Stalin accepted the subjugation of Spain as a pious legacy. Once Spain had been turned into a so-called proletarian dictatorship, it would be an easy matter to subjugate France and Britain. Germany would then be between the nut-crackers. If by some mischance the subjugation of Spain failed to materialize, then the incident could be used to help bring about World War II.

While preparing for the Spanish revolution, Stalin was ordered by the international bankers to take an active part in an economic war which was planned in 1918, immediately after the Armistice had been signed. Generally speaking, the people who had not been engaged in the actual fighting became prosperous during World War I. When the fighting ended, the people in the allied countries enjoyed two boom years. Then, after speculative investments had just about reached their peak, vast amounts of money were withdrawn from circulation. Credits were restricted. Calls were made on loans. In 1922-25 a minor depression was experienced.[3] This economic juggling was a preliminary experiment before the "Powers that be" brought about the great depression of 1930.

After 1925, financial policy was reversed and conditions steadily improved until prosperity in America, Britain, Canada, and Australia, reached an all-time record. Speculation in stocks, bonds and real estate went wild. Then, towards the end of 1929 came the sudden crash, the greatest depression ever known settled down over the free world. Millions of people were rendered destitute. Thousands committed suicide. Misgovernment was blamed for the economic upset which made paupers out of tens of millions of people, and *trillionaires out of three hundred who were already millionaires.*

In 1925, Stalin started his five-year industrial plans to increase the so-called Sovietized countries' internal recovery. The plan was to exploit the natural resources, manufacture raw materials into useful commodities, and modernize industrial and agricultural machinery. This vast Five-Year Plan was financed by loans from the international bankers. This programme, when added to the development of the Russian and German war potential under the Abmachungen (agreements) previously referred to, gave a great boost to the Soviet economy. The fact that the Rulers of Russia could use millions of men and women as slaves gave those who enslaved them an additional advantage over nations which employ paid labour, and maintain a high standard of living.

The next move was the collectivization of farms. For centuries, the serfs in Russia had been little better than slaves of the landed proprietors. Lenin had won their support by promising them even greater concessions than they had been granted under the benevolent rule of Premier Peter Arkadyevich Stolypin from 1906 to 1914, when over 2,000,000 peasant families seceded from the village *mir* and became individual land owners. By January 1st, 1916, the number had increased to 6,200,000 families.

But, in order to secure the loans they had made for the Abmachungen and industrial development programmes, the international bankers insisted that they control the import and export trade of the Sovietized nations. They also demanded the collectivization of farms as the only means to obtain greatly increased agricultural production.

History records what happened when Stalin enforced the edicts. He has always been blamed personally for the inhuman atrocities which made the peasants comply with the laws. Many versions of what happened have been given. The truth, as I reported it to American newspapers in 1930, has never been published to date. It is acknowledged that over 5,000,000 peasants were executed, or systematically starved to death, because they refused to obey, or tried to evade the edicts. Over 5,000,000 more were sent to forced labour in Siberia. A fact not generally known is that the grain which was confiscated from the Russian farmers was pooled together with a vast quantity of grain purchased by the agents of the international bankers in other countries except Canada and the United States. In addition to this corner on grain, the international bankers bought up huge supplies of processed and frozen meats in the Argentine and other meat producing countries. Canada and the United States could not find a market for their cattle, or their grain.

During the period of 1920-1929, the international bankers subsidized shipping in most countries except Britain, Canada, and the United States. As the result of this commercial piracy, it became impossible for ships owned in Britain, Canada, and the United States to compete with ships owned by other countries. Thousands of ships were tied up idle in their home ports.

Export trade fell off to an all-time low.

The falling off of exports from the allied nations was accompanied by increasing the importation of cheaply manufactured goods from Germany, Japan, and central European countries. To enjoy reasonable prosperity, five out of every eight wage-earners in Canada must obtain their pay directly or indirectly as a result of the export trade. When the export trade falls off, a recession immediately follows, due to loss of purchasing power among five-eighths of the population. This immediately affects those who earn their living by rendering services of one kind or another. If the export trade remains down, then the recession deteriorates into a depression.

To make absolutely sure that the skids were completely knocked from under the economic structures of allied countries, the men who had cornered grain and meats began to dump their supplies on the markets of the world at prices below the cost of production in Canada, America and Australia. This action brought about a situation in which the granaries of the countries allied together in World War I were bursting with grain they couldn't sell, while the people of other countries were starving to death for want of bread and meat. Britain needs to earn £85,000,000 a year from her ocean services in order to offset her unfavourable annual trade balance each year. The British economy was given a severe jolt when unfair competition made it impossible for her to earn this money. The British people were forced to buy their bread and meat in the cheapest markets. This artificially produced economic mess-up was used by the men who mastermind international intrigue to cause grave misunderstanding between different units of the British Commonwealth of Nations and thus weaken the bonds of Empire.[4]

As the result of this economic war, the shipping, industrial, and agricultural activities of the allied or capitalistic countries were brought to a virtual standstill, while the Soviet States and the Axis Powers worked at full capacity. Once again, it must be remembered that the men who plot and plan the World Revolutionary Movement always work on the fundamental principle that wars end depressions and pave the way for revolutionary action in countries that still remain to be subjugated. This being a fact, it was essential to the furthering of their Long-Range Plans to arrange international affairs so they could bring about World War II when they wished to do so. As Spain had been indicated by Lenin and Stalin as holding a key position, the manner in which Spain was used will be studied next.

---

[1] The marriage of Svetlana Stalin to Mihail Kaganovich was reported in the *Associated Press*, July 15th, 1951.

[2] Note: *Stalin*, by Trotsky, page 337 (ibid page 48).

[3] This is explained in Chapters 1 and 2 of *The Red Fog*.

[4] This phase of history is dealt with more extensively elsewhere.

CHAPTER ELEVEN

The Spanish Revolution

The Long-Range Plan for the ultimate subjugation of Spain started, as in other countries, early in the Christian era. In an attempt to crush the power of the Christian Church in Spain, the moneylenders sent their agents to infiltrate into the congregations and pose as Christians.[1] This placed them in positions to destroy the church organizations from within. This conspiracy became obvious, and in the 13th century Pope Innocent III instituted the Inquisition. The purpose of the Inquisition was to ferret out and question infidels suspected of masquerading as Christians. Spain had been exceptionally kind to the Jews. They were allowed to hold office and acted as tax-collectors. But, as happened in every other country in Europe, the crimes of the atheistic moneylenders and their agents were charged against the whole Jewish population. Between 1475 and 1504, during the reign of Isabella and Ferdinand, the Inquisition was used extensively to locate and destroy all traitors who plotted to overthrow the power of the Church and State. The Inquisitors under Torquemada discovered the subversive underground to be so widespread and well-organized that in 1492, Spain followed the example of other European countries and expelled all the Jews. This task provided the opportunity for some extremists to organize mob violence against the Jews, and several extensive and regrettable massacres took place. These illegal killings were condemned publicly by the Church authorities in Rome.

After the international bankers reorganized during the 1600s, their agents infiltrated the Spanish Treasury Department. They were exceptionally active during both the English and the French revolutions, trying to destroy the Spanish economy in order to prepare the way for revolutionary efforts in that country also.

It is worthwhile to study the political intrigue that went on in Spain from 1839 to 1939 because it gives a clear picture of the pattern of the ultimate subjugation of all countries. There are three steps in all revolutionary efforts.

First: Infiltration by the agents of the revolutionary party into the government, civil services, armed forces, and labour organizations in order to be in position to destroy the government from within when the order to revolt is given.

Second: The affiliation of the revolutionary party with the socialist or liberal party left of centre in order to overthrow the established government regardless of whether it is a monarchy or a republic.

Third: Subversive activities to bring about anarchy in order to discredit the Popular Front Government and provide the excuse for forming a proletarian dictatorship. Once this is established, purges turn it into a totalitarian dictatorship as it happened in Russia in 1917.

Karl Marx's agents organized Spain's first General Political Strike in 1865. In 1868, the Directors of the World Revolutionary Movement (WRM) sent Giuseppi Fanelli to Spain to affiliate the Anarchists with the Marxist revolutionaries. Fanelli was a disciple of Bakunin who was a close associate of Marx and Engels. In 1870, Bakunin fell out with Marx over policy. He was expelled from the First International of the WRM[2]

In 1872, Bakunin influenced the Spanish revolutionary leaders into forming the Socialist-Democratic Alliance.[3] The Spanish government decreed Bakunin's extremist organizations illegal, but they continued to exist underground. The Grand Orient Lodges formed convenient headquarters. At a congress held in Zaragoza (Saragossa), the Spanish section of the Marxist International agreed to ally themselves with the Anarchist International. After its affiliation, both groups concentrated in organizing the various Labour Groups into a vast "*Camorra.*" They crowned their combined efforts with a revolution, which produced the first Spanish Republic in 1873.

The effort on the part of the revolutionary leaders was accompanied with the usual Reign of Terror. Anarchy ran wild. All kinds of excesses took place. Finally, General Pavia brought off a 'Coup d'Etat' and the revolutionaries went underground again.

In order to emerge into the open once more, the members of the revolutionary underground supported the *leaders* of a mild "*liberal*" movement to obtain political power. The revolutionary leaders used the quarrel going on between those who claimed the descendants of Don Carlos should occupy the throne, and those who claimed the descendants of Isabella should reign, to start a Civil War. This war ended with the defeat of the Carlist Group in 1876.[4]

The Spanish workers really desired to organize for their own protection, but the majority did not agree with the extreme policy advocated by the Anarchists. The anti-revolutionaries therefore organized the "Workers Association." These moderates were immediately set upon by both revolutionaries and employers of labour alike.[5] This persecution continued until 1888 when, at the suggestion of Pablo Iglesias, the moderate group adopted the name "The Workers General Union," which became known in Spain as the U.G.T. The members of this organization did not get much support until after the government outlawed the Iberian Anarchist Federation.

The syndicalist elements collaborated with the radical Republican party until 1908. They then formed the "Solidaridad Obrera," and two years later, in 1910, they founded the Regional Federation of Labour known in Spain as the C.R.T. Immediately afterwards, they formed the National Federation of Labour (C.N.T.).

In 1913, both the C.R.T. and the C.N.T. were suspended as the result of a series of strikes. The government did not object to the principles of collective bargaining, but it did object to the extremist policy and revolutionary actions of the leaders. So legitimate labour striving for social justice found their organizations barred because the radical element always seemed able to work its way into executive positions within the Unions.

The reaction was what the plotters of world revolution expected it would be. Their revolutionary syndicalist movement greatly increased in power and acted against *all* political parties, and against the State itself. The policy of these extremists was "*direct action,*" advocated with the greatest heat and violence. In 1916, the C.R.T. was reorganized by Angel Pestana and Salvador Segui. In 1918, these two labour leaders were able to form in Barcelona the "Sole Syndicate" generally known as "The One Big Syndicate."

During World War I, Spain, as a neutral country, made a vast amount of money but, generally speaking, the labouring classes did not receive a fair share of the national prosperity. This fact was perhaps the deciding factor which drove the majority of the working classes out of moderate labour organizations into the arms of the revolutionary leaders in the extremist labour groups. However, the more moderate and level-headed labour leaders didn't give up the fight against the radical groups and as a result of their efforts, they brought into being a new labour group known as "The Free Syndicate" in 1920. During the next three years there was continuous strife going on between the *Right* and *Left* labour organizations: local strikes, general strikes, destruction of property, private assassinations to remove labour leaders, wholesale murders to reduce the strength of opposing organizations. All these crimes were committed in the name of *liberty*. By 1923, conditions became chaotic. There was a military coup, and to prevent the Communist Party from bringing about another revolution, the king of Spain appointed the new military dictator General Miguel Primo de Rivera as prime minister.

One of the first results of Primo de Rivera's dictatorship was the successful termination of the Moroccan War. It was during the final stages of this war that General Franco greatly distinguished himself in the field. He turned what looked like a complete military defeat into a brilliant victory. By tempering justice with mercy, he won the admiration and loyalty of many of the Moroccan natives. It was thus he came to the notice of the general public in Spain; Rivera is accused by his enemies of doing everything a man shouldn't do. It is only fair to record that he did restore law and order; he brought about a number of social reforms; he cooperated with Largo Caballero to improve working conditions. He worked so hard that only his breakdown of health in 1929 can explain the errors in judgment he made during 1930.

Tired and worn out, and as if in a hurry to unburden himself of the responsibilities of office, he called in *two socialist* leaders, Besteiro and Saborit. He charged them with the task of re-organizing the electoral machinery of the nation so the people could decide whether they wanted a monarchy or a Republican government. Just why De Rivera appointed Besteiro and Saborit to reorganize the electoral machine of Spain will probably never be known.

The two socialists rigged the election machinery so that a Socialist-Republican Government was assured. In Madrid alone, the number of fictitious voters exceeded 40,000.[6] Similar corruption existed in all the larger centres of population.

To ensure the end of the monarchy in Spain, the Grand Orient Lodges organized a special "Military Brotherly Union," by which they obtained the promise of twenty-one of the twenty-three Spanish generals to support the Republican Cause. General Mola, who was Chief of the Spanish Internal Security, in his book *Tempestad, Calma Intriga y Crisis* informs us that the generals were initiated into the Grand Orient, and had *one and a half million pesetas placed to their credit, to help them escape abroad should the Republican movement fail*. Franco was one of the two generals who refused to join the "Military Brotherly Union." In support of Mola's statement, Cano Lopez said on the floor of the Spanish *Cortes* (parliament):

> Since 1925, Masonry has grouped under the heading 'Military Brotherly Union' most of the high ranking officials of the army. The members include Cabanellas, Sanjurjo, Goded, Mola, Lopez, Ochoa, Queipo de Llana, and others...Of twenty-three divisional generals, twenty-one were Masons...All had taken the oath of the Grand Orient.

(I swear obedience without limitation to the Head of the Council of Thirty-Three...I swear to acknowledge no mortal as above him.)

Lopez added:

> Both in 1929, for the abolition of the dictatorship of de Rivera, and in 1931 for the abolition of the monarchy, the Grand Orient issued the orders most of the other generals obeyed.[7]

General Mola tells how he and most of the other generals broke their oath to the Grand Orient when they became convinced that they were being used to further the secret plans of Stalin to turn Spain into another Communist dictatorship.[8]

The international bankers helped finance the revolutionary effort in Spain without becoming involved themselves. In February 1932, *Le Journal* reports that Stalin promised $200,000 to help finance the Revolutionary Training Schools in Spain.

The financial statements submitted to the 1931 congress of the Communist international disclose the fact that £240,000 (English money) had been received to help the Spanish Revolutionaries.[9]

In addition to the above, two and a half million pesetas were made available for the purchase of arms and ammunition.

General Mola says that by 1938, over two hundred revolutionary leaders had arrived in Spain after being trained in the Lenin Institute in Moscow.

From 1930 to the date of the election, a campaign of *L'Infamie* was carried on against the king of Spain and the royal family exactly as it was against Louis XVI and Marie Antoinette. One of the most ridiculous lies ever invented claimed that one Spanish soldier was bled to death every day to keep the Prince of Asturias alive. He was known to be suffering from haemophilia. Other slanders accused the king of being a libertine, just as the Empress of Russia had falsely been accused of being mistress to Rasputin.

The plugged ballots in the large industrial centres wiped out the strong rural vote in favour of the monarchy. After the election had been declared to favour a republican form of government, King Alfonso XIII of Spain issued his last public proclamation. It read as follows:

> The elections held on Sunday proved to me that I no longer hold the love and affection of my people. My conscience tells me this condition will not be permanent because I have always striven to serve Spain, and my people, with all my devotion. A king may make mistakes. Without doubt I have done so on occasion, but I know our country has always shown herself generous towards the faults of others committed without malice.
>
> I am the king of all Spaniards, and I am a Spaniard. I could find ample means to maintain my *royal prerogatives* in effective resistance to those who assail them, but I prefer to stand resolutely aside rather than to provoke a conflict which might array my countrymen against one another in Civil War and patricidal strife.
>
> I renounce no single one of my rights which, rather than being mine, are an accumulated legacy of history for the guardianship of which I shall one day have to render strict account. I shall wait the true and full expression of the collective conscience and, until the nation speaks, I deliberately suspend the exercise of my *royal powers* and am leaving Spain, thus acknowledging that she is sole mistress of her destinies. Also now I believe that I am fulfilling the duty which the love of my country dictates. I pray God that all other Spaniards may feel and fulfill their duty as sincerely as I do.[10]

Many of the Socialists who formed the Spanish Republican government in 1931 were sincere in their beliefs. They wanted no part of "Red" Communism or "Black" Nazism. But they were proved to be powerless to prevent the Communists and Anarchists from putting the second part of their revolutionary programme into effect.

The tactics the revolutionary leaders employed were to doublecross the Socialists at every opportunity. *Red Cells* within the government caused the government to commit some foolish mistakes. The *Reds* outside then damned the government as a lot of incompetent, corrupt, and inefficient nincompoops. The Communists and Anarchists claimed that only a dictatorship of the proletariat could establish a stable government. The agents of Moscow committed every conceivable kind of crime to bring those responsible for internal security into disrepute also.

General De Rivera had used Largo Caballero a great deal to iron out differences between *labour and employers* during the years he had been dictator. With the advent of the Republican movement, Largo Caballero showed his true colours. By 1935, Caballero openly boasted that he had placed "Tens of thousands of Communist *Cells* throughout Spain."

At the Eleventh Plenum of the Executive of the Communist International, the Spanish delegates were showered with congratulations because "the prerequisites of a revolutionary crisis are being created at a rapid rate in Spain."[11]

At the Twelfth Plenum, the wording of the congratulations to the Spanish delegates was as follows:

> In Spain, in particular, we have been able to observe such revolutionary strike struggles going on uninterruptedly over a period of many months, as the Spanish proletariat has never experienced before. What is happening in these struggles is, above all, the further development of a Spanish Revolution.

There is an old saying, "When thieves disagree the truth will come out." That is exactly what happened in Spain. The three leaders of Moscow's underground in Spain were Joaquin Maurin, Victor Serges, and Andres Ninn. They were all young men. They had all received special training in revolutionary activities in the Lenin Institute in Moscow before being entrusted with the leadership in Spain. Maurin had been mixed up in the Separatist movement in Catalonia since he was sixteen years of age. At the mature age of seventeen this *intellectual thinker* had set out to teach the Spanish people the Soviet solution of the world's economic troubles. At the age of twenty-one, he was elected head of the Anarchists. He preached and practised the religion of hate and violence. In 1914, he was condemned to twenty years' imprisonment but he was not of legal age for such a penalty. Maurin was a delegate to the Third Congress of the Communist International held in Moscow, 1921. He attracted favourable attention.

With the fall of Primo De Rivera, Maurin returned to Spain. He had been hiding out in France and Moscow. He had lived a hectic life. He had been in and out of jail; had escaped from prison; been wounded in 1925; confined in Citadel Montjuich, etc. It is said the only period of peace he enjoyed in his life was the three years he and his young wife spent in Paris, 1927-30.

Maurin wrote a book in 1936. Victor Serges wrote the preface to it. In this book *Hacia la Segunda Revolución,* he exposed the fact that Stalin had departed from the Marxian ideology, and charged that he was using the forces of Communism to forward his own secret totalitarian imperialistic ambitions.[12]

Even after Maurin, Serges, and Ninn broke openly with Stalin in 1936, their power and influence amongst the working classes was so great that Stalin ordered that they should be allowed to live until they had served their purpose. Stalin used them right up to the beginning of the Civil War in Spain. Then he ordered them liquidated. He directed that, "their deaths shall be accomplished in such a manner as to make it appear to the public that all three had died as martyrs to the Communist Cause." Maurin was betrayed to Franco's forces and after trial was executed. Serges is reported to have been shot by Loyalists while fighting, and Ninn was also disposed of. Their deaths were loudly attributed to *acts of violence* by the enemies of communism.

Victor Serges wrote:

The evolution of Soviet Communism was completed in 1936...from revolutionary internationalism to a nationalism of great military power served, in various countries, by parties which it subsidized. After July 1936 the Stalinites formed the unified Socialist Party affiliated with the Third International...and the object of Stalinism is to establish the new power of a Fascist nature to encircle France, the probable ally of Russia, in the war that is being prepared.

Then again Maurin says:

The traditional policy of England is to ruin its adversaries, so as then to pose as the Protector and to render impossible the renaissance of the conquered vassal. Spain is primarily the victim of England and, next in order, of France. When Spain hesitates, England and France attack her strongly. If she inclines towards England, France increases the persecution. So long as France and England are capitalistic countries they will not have to be the natural ally to Spain.[13] The logical line would be the curve through Portugal, Germany, Italy and Russia. A *bloc* of this nature would neutralize France and England.[14]

Serges explained how so much *Loyalist* propaganda found its way into the *universal* press, while so little space was given to Franco's releases. Serges wrote:

Never has there been brought into play, the one against the other, such low and demoralizing methods as those used by Stalin and his instrument, the Third International, in a continuous stream of propaganda at long range and without heed for the truth. The method of repetition and cynicism have become almost mechanical...*The Soviet bureaucracy is plotting this procedure on an international scale*. Every infamy given out by a correspondent of *Izvestia* at Valencia [capital of the Republican government] is at once taken up in a chorus by the special papers in Paris, Stockholm, Oslo, Brussels, London, New York, Melbourne and Buenos Aires... Millions of copies of infamous lies are circulated, they are the only information millions of Soviet workers receive. English, American, Chinese, and New Zealand papers reproduce these lies (by order). Advanced intellectuals, who think they are anti-Fascist, will appear to believe them. One sees that a formidable enterprise of demoralization is functioning in the universe, and I find pitilessly just, the words of Trotsky, that the Stalinite Comintern propaganda is a *Syphilis of the Workers Movement*.[15]

What Maurin and Serges wrote in 1936 only confirms what Pope Pius XI said in his encyclical "Divini Redemptoris" issued in March 1937. One chapter of this famous document reads:

There is another explanation for the rapid diffusion of Communistic ideas... A propaganda truly diabolical that the world has perhaps never witnessed its like before. It is directed from *one common centre*; it is shrewdly adapted to the various conditions of diverse peoples, it has at its disposal *vast financial resources*, innumerable organizations, international congresses, and countless trained workers, it makes use of newspapers, and pamphlets, cinema, theatre, radio, and schools and even universities. Little by little it penetrates into the minds of all classes of the people. Another powerful factor is the suppression and silence on the part of a large section...of the *press of the world...*we say *suppression* because it is impossible otherwise to explain how a press, usually so eager to exploit even the little daily incidents of life, has been able to remain silent for so long about the horrors perpetrated in Russia, in Mexico, and even in a great part of Spain, and that it should have so little to say concerning a world organization as vast as Russian Communism. The silence is due in part to short-sighted political policy and is favoured by various occult forces which for a long time have been working for the overthrow of the Christian social order.

The sorry effects of this propaganda are before our eyes. Communism has striven, as its champions openly boast, to destroy Christian civilization and the Christian religion by banishing every remembrance of them from the hearts of men, especially of the young... In Spain, as far as possible, every church and monastery was destroyed and every vestige of the Christian religion eradicated. The theory has not confined itself to the indiscriminate slaughter of bishops, and thousands of priests and religious of both sexes, it searches out above all those who have been devoting their lives to the working classes and the poor. The majority of victims have been laymen of all conditions and classes...with a hatred and a savage barbarity one would not have believed possible in our age. No man of good sense, nor statesman conscious of his responsibility, can fail to shudder at the thought that what is happening today in Spain may be repeated to-morrow in other civilized countries. For man some restraint is necessary, as an individual or in society... But tear the idea of God from the hearts of men, and they are urged by their passions to commit the most atrocious barbarities.

We will proceed to review the conditions in Spain to which Pope Pius XI tried to draw the attention of the Christian world early in 1937, and failed.

---

1. This refers to the advice sent by the Sanhedrin in Constantinople to Chemor, Rabbi of Arles in Provence in 1489 mentioned previously.

2. For further particulars, see *Michael Bakunin* by Professor E.H. Carr.

3. For details regarding this period of Spanish History, read *La Quiebra Fraudulenta de la Republica* by C. Domi.

4. This is a typical example of how any situation is used to divide the citizens of a nation and get them fighting each other on the principle that all wars pave the way for revolution.

5. This is a typical example of how the agents of the International Bankers are placed in private and responsible enterprise for the purpose of helping their revolutionary leaders to oust moderate leaders they cannot buy or otherwise control.

6. See *The Spanish Arena*, p. 56.

7. See *Jean Dauraya L'Oeuvre Latine* January, 1937.

8. What General Mola said was confirmed by a broadcast over the radio from Moscow on March 13, 1938. The announcer was explaining why the Civil War wasn't going in favour of the Communists (Loyalists). He said: "The great work in Spain was seriously compromised by the wicked generals breaking their plighted word to the Grand Orient."

9. Evidence is given elsewhere to prove the revolutionary leaders were supplying counterfeit English Bank Notes to finance revolutionary efforts in other countries also.

10. This document proves that the International Press lied to their readers when it reported The King of Spain had abdicated. The King of Spain never abdicated. Franco holds control of Government because the International conspirators are still determined to turn Spain into a Totalitarian Dictatorship to serve their ends.

11. See English edition of report of *Eleventh Plenum*, p. 11, and *Twelfth Plenum*, p. 37.

12. Even Maurin and Serges failed to suspect that Lenin and Stalin were only carrying out the orders of the international bankers, who in turn obey the Illuminati.

13. Here again is a typical example of how well the International Bankers kept their secret. Maurin blamed the Governments of England and France for the international crimes perpetrated against humanity by the Bankers, under the direction of the Illuminati.

14. This confirms what has been previously stated, that once the Sphere of Influence was established between the 35th and 45th parallel, the countries within the circle would be subjugated.

15. Victor Serges in *Maurin's Revolution et Contre-Revolution en Espagne*.

CHAPTER TWELVE

The Civil War in Spain

General Mola said:

> Following the election of the Socialist government in Spain, and the king's withdrawal from the country, there was an absolute avalanche of public officials who rushed to the Grand Orient Lodges to request entry. They thought they could thus be free of the persecution which had been practiced by the majority of Masons in the government. Their purpose was to give evidence of their Republicanism and to prevent the certainty of having their careers ruined.

Immediately after the king had left, Franco told the Military Academy, of which he was then in charge, "The republic has been proclaimed in Spain. It is the duty of all at the present time to co-operate with their discipline and allegiance so that peace may reign and the nation be permitted to direct itself through the natural judicial channels. Hitherto, at the Academy, there has always been discipline and exact fulfilment of duty. Today these qualities are even more necessary; the Army needs, serenely, and with a united spirit, to sacrifice every thought of ideology to the good of the nation and the tranquility of the *fatherland*." The wording of this proclamation shows Franco to be anything but a "Black" Nazi which Communist propaganda would have the public believe him to be.

But the Secret Powers were not willing to give the Republican government a chance to operate in an efficient and democratic manner. Churchill wrote: "The Communists helped set it up so they could knock it down again and create more political and economic chaos, until they had the country, and the people, in such a state that the leaders could advocate with reason, that only a proletarian dictatorship could restore law and order and save the day."

Having overthrown the monarchy in Spain, the next logical move was to attack the religion of the people. Secularism was introduced into the schools. A campaign was launched to destroy parental authority and that of the Church. Having created thousands of anti-religious, and anti-social young Bolsheviks, it was only necessary to await the opportunity to turn the masses loose against the forces of law and order in a well-planned revolt.

On May 14th, 1931, a meeting was held in the Ateneo Club, in Madrid, to discuss the new political programme. Its eight points were:

1. Creation of a Republican dictatorship.
2. Immediate punishment of all responsible for illegal acts under the dictatorship.
3. Disbanding the Civil Guard, the Army, and the police, etc., and the substitution of armed Republicans chosen from the labouring classes and Republican Clubs.
4. Confiscation of property of religious orders.
5. Nationalization of land.
6. Suppression of all press agencies hostile to the Republican cause.
7. Utilization of technical schools and other buildings for the public good.
8. Postponement of the *Cortes* until this programme had been carried out.

Azana, an intellectual Liberal; Prieto, a socialist; and Caballero, a Communist, were three of the most prominent political leaders at this time. Azana, with his tongue in his cheek, publicly opposed such radical suggestions, although he secretly approved. When elected to power, he put the programme into effect.

In due course, the Cortes Constituyentes was elected. Under the excuse of "Law for the defence of the Republic," a ruthless dictatorship was set up; the only democratic feature about it was its name "the Republic of the Workers." A Moscow trained revolutionary, Jimenez Asua, drafted the new Constitution.[1] Azana now concentrated his entire efforts on destruction of the churches and persecution of religious orders. In December 1932, he set up the "League of Atheism." He financed its periodical, Sin Dios (Without God) out of public funds. All these moves were made in the name of democracy. The leaders told the people they were being liberated from the control of the religious orders and the clergy who, they said, were allied to feudalism and tyrannical monarchs.

In Catalonia the revolutionary activities which General Primo de Rivera had subdued broke out again. By January 1933, the London *Morning Post* correspondent reported, "Huge stocks of bombs, rifles, and ammunition are being found by the police all over Spain. An enormous amount of money is being spent to foster the revolutionary cause. Many of those arrested, though to all appearances not well-paid, carried note-cases full of bank-notes."[2]

Next an uprising in Asturias was organized, and on September 14th, 1934, a report was issued which implicated war officials and army officers in the sale of arms.

General Franco made a desperate effort to try to reorganize the Spanish Army and put an end to Anarchy, but he obtained little support from government authorities. To indicate how well the Communist underground was organized, over three hundred churches were *set afire at exactly the same time in a hundred different cities and towns*. The assassination of individuals whom the revolutionaries wanted to remove became so common that 'Professional Pistoleros' became competitive. It was possible to have an enemy liquidated for 50 pesetas (a little more than USD $5.00). The Moscow agents used the confused conditions existing in Spain to carry out Lenin's mandate: "The Communist legal Code is to base terrorism on fundamental principles." [3]

Torture, mutilation, rape, burnings, bloodshed and death were the methods by which Communism tried to obtain power. Conditions deteriorated from bad to worse. By the beginning of 1936, the whole country was in a state of turmoil. President Alcala Zamora dissolved the *Cortes*. February 16th was set as the date for a general election. Gil Robles and Calvo Sotelo stamped the country on a straight anti-communist ticket. Bolshevik election propaganda was issued by "*The Friends of Russia.*"

Largo Caballero was in prison at this time for the part he had played in a revolutionary uprising. He was interviewed by Mr. Edward Knoblauch, who afterwards wrote *Correspondent in Spain.*

Caballero said:

> We will win at least 265 seats. The whole existing order will be overturned. Azana will play Kerensky to my Lenin. Within five years the republic will be so organized that it will be easy for my party to use it as a stepping stone to our objective. A union of the Iberian Republics...that is our aim. The Iberian Peninsula will again be one country. Portugal will come in peaceably we hope, but by force if necessary. YOU SEE

BEHIND THESE BARS THE FUTURE RULER OF SPAIN. Lenin declared Spain would be the second Soviet Republic in Europe. Lenin's prophecy will come true. I shall be the second Lenin who shall make it come true.

After the most completely dishonest election Spain ever endured, President Zamora wrote:

> The Popular Front was hoisted into power on the 16th of February, thanks to an electoral system as absurd as it is unfair, which gives an extraordinary advantage to a relative majority though absolutely it may be a minority. Thus in a certain constituency the Popular Front with 30,000 votes *less* than the opposition was nevertheless able to win ten seats out of thirteen, though in no part of the constituency did the number of votes exceed those of its major adversary by more than 2 per cent. Paradoxical cases of this kind were fairly common.

In spite of the illegal means employed, first count only gave the Popular Front 200 seats out of a possible 465. Thus it became the largest *minority* group in the parliament, but did not have enough seats to form a government. The next move was for the Popular Front members to join forces with the Basque, and other minority groups. They elected a Committee to verify the election returns in each constituency. They made sure the final returns were favourable to the Popular Front Party. In several cases Rightist candidates were disqualified and Popular Front candidates were elected as deputies in their place. When the "fixing" was all over, the Popular Front had the 265 seats Caballero predicted they would have... But even after all this had happened, the final breakdown of the votes showed:

For 'Centre' and 'Right' parties	4,910,000
For the 'Popular Front'	4,356,000
'Right Centre' majority	554,000

It must be understood that Popular Front candidates elected to the Spanish *Cortes* represented every kind of individual, from the very mild socialist to the dyed-in-the-wool Bolshevik.

The Stalinites created so much chaos that hellish conditions broke out all over Spain. Previous to the February elections in 1936 the governmental record in Spain was as follows:

From the end of the Prime de Rivera dictatorship in 1931 there had been: one revolution with 2,500 persons killed; seven revolts; 9,000 strikes; five *prorogations of the budget;* two billion pesetas increase in charges; 1,000 municipalities suspended; 114 newspapers forbidden; two and a half years of "States of Exception" (equivalent to our state of martial law). After six weeks of popular front government under Azana, Caballero, and Prieto the record read:

Assaults and robberies:
At Political headquarters, 58;
At public and private establishments, 105;
At churches, 36.
Fires:
At political headquarters, 12;
Public and private establishments, 60;
Churches, 106.

Disturbances:
General strikes, 11;
Risings and revolts, 169;
Persons killed, 76;
Wounded, 346.

Caballero, speaking at Zaragoza, said: "Spain must be destroyed in order to remake it ours. On the day of vengeance we will leave not a stone upon a stone."

Caballero also declared, "Before the elections we ask for what we want. After the elections we will take what we want by any means. 'The Right' must not expect mercy from the workers. We shall not again spare the lives of our enemies."

Azana declared happily, "Spain has ceased to be Catholic."

Communist leader Marguerita Nelken announced, "We demand a revolution. But even the Russian kind will not serve us. We need flames that will be seen throughout the planet, and waves of blood that will redden the seas."

The *Times* correspondent reported conditions in Barcelona. In February 1936, he said, "A vigilance committee warned a number of high officials on February 20th to relinquish their posts. The committee was obeyed."

A month later he wrote, "The Dictatorship of the Proletariat is now the open aim of all the *Reds*." A little later he wrote, "Spanish Socialism had been drifting towards Communism. It is among the younger generation that Marx and Lenin have gained most of their disciples. These young people believe that the conquest of power is the immediate requirement of Spanish Socialism; violence the ultimate means of getting it; and a dictatorship of the proletariat the only way to retain it. The subversive doctrine is preached untiringly." In March 1936 he reported: "Deputies in the Cortes (Spanish Parliament) with clenched fists, in Communist salute, sang the Soviet national anthem, L'Internationale, in the House itself."

Why did the youth of Spain turn in great numbers to Communism? If the technique used by those who direct the WRM is to be understood the answer must be found, because it is from the labouring classes and the youth of the nation that the revolutionary leaders draw their shock troops.

Investigation reveals that Azana represented himself as an intellectual with a sincere belief in Socialism. He was openly anti-religious. He protested, however, that he was not in agreement with the terrorism advocated and carried out by the Anarchists and the Communists. Once he obtained the necessary political power, however, he used it to have the Republican government abolish religious teaching orders from the schools. He engaged Francisco Ferrer to establish secularism in the schools. Instead of opening the school day with a prayer to Almighty God, the new secular teachers opened the classes by having the pupils sing:

We are the sons of the revolution
We are the sons of liberty.
With us comes the dawning
Of a new humanity.

A translation of another "Hymn" sung at the beginning and end of class periods in Barcelona schools is as follows:

Sling the bomb place well the mine; grasp firm the pistol,
Pass on the word of revolution...Help for the Anarchists.
Stand to arms till death; with petrol and dynamite destroy the government.

The news editors of British and American papers refused to publish the truth because it sounded so fantastic. Similar "Hymns" were broadcast in English from Moscow for the instruction of English Communists from 1937 to 1938.

The most damning evidence, proving the systematic method used to subvert, and pervert, youth into becoming revolutionaries, was supplied by Francisco Ferrer himself. In a letter to a revolutionary comrade, he wrote:

In order not to scare people and give the government (Republican) a pretext for closing down my establishments I call them 'Modern Schools', and not schools for Anarchists. My wish is to bring about the revolution. For the time being, however, one must be content to implant the idea of violent upheaval in the minds of the young. They must learn that against the police, and the clergy, there is only one means of action... bombs and poison.[4]

When Ferrer was captured by Franco's forces during the Civil War, he was tried as a traitor to Spain. The above letter was used as evidence. He was found guilty and executed. The High Council of the Grand Orient of Paris protested to Masonic Lodges all over the world claiming that Ferrer had been murdered because of his Anti-Catholic activities.

Investigation into the youth training programme revealed the methods used to corrupt the morals of the youth of a nation also. Lenin had said, "The best revolutionary is a youth devoid of morals." His word being law in Communist organizations, all members work secretly to make young people of both sexes anti-social and immoral.

Children up to teenage are taught to rebel against the discipline of the home. Parents are represented to their children as old-fashioned. Parental authority is scoffed at. The subverters argue that parents have lied to their children since they were old enough to listen, regarding Santa Claus, and where babies come from. The subversives claim that parents are the victims of reactionary teachings and capitalistic exploitation. The child is encouraged to *educate the parents in regard to modern and progressive ideas*. They are warned that, for their own good, they must refuse to be dominated or disciplined by their parents. The purpose of this subversive campaign is to destroy the sanctity, and unity, of the home *which is the foundation upon which our civilization is founded*.

To rob children of their respect for the ministers of religion, the subversives first represent them as being chosen from the less intelligent or physically retarded members of families. They are ridiculed as spineless 'holy joes', 'womanish do-gooders', and servants of the ruling classes. Quoting from Marx, children are told, "Religion is the opium of the people, because it teaches acceptance of poverty, sickness, and hard work as good for the soul."

The Christian child is poisoned against the ministers of his religion by being told the most fantastic slanders against them in connection with their private lives. They are presented as "sheep in wolves clothing," as "black crows" feeding upon the gullibility of their parishioners. If, as often happens, a minister or priest does become involved in a scandal, it is played up for all it is worth.

The Christian religion is ridiculed in a most nauseating manner. Christ is represented as the illegitimate son of Mary, a young Jewess, who, in order to save her face, hoaxed

Joseph into believing she had been conceived by the Holy Ghost. Christ as an adult is depicted as a faker. His miracles are said to be illusions cleverly performed as magicians perform them today. The twelve Apostles are said to have been his accomplices. The so-called comic "Mandrake The Magician" is often used to illustrate how a hypnotist and magician can fool the public.

One favourite story told to Christian children is that Christ was a bootlegger at a very early age. Subversives claim that he pretended to work a miracle at the marriage feast of Cana in order to sell his bootleg wine. They even accused Christ, and *all* Roman Catholics, of being cannibals. They support their arguments with the biblical quotation that Christ admonished his followers that unless they ate his flesh and drank his blood, they could not have eternal life.

Teen-aged youths are introduced to companions who teach them liberalism which is soon turned to licentiousness. They are taught the Anarchist conception of life: the less laws, the better; do as you like. According to subversive teachers, there is only *one* sin and that is disobedience to orders given by authorized leaders. There are only two crimes: neglect of duty and betrayal of *party* secrets.

The next step is to lead anti-social youth into actual conflict with the police. They start them off by linking them up with some "gang." Young Communist leaders *egg* the other members on. They dare them to do things outside the law. They force them into fights to prove their physical courage. They inveigle them into petty crimes and then lead them deeper into the jungle of the Communist-organized underworld.[5]

The publication of Crime and Sex Comics is part of the Communist psychological warfare. These Comics are calculated to awaken in children hidden and suppressed sadistic tendencies and to weaken the moral armour of children who are otherwise normal. Any "professor" who claims that Crime and Sex Comics do not influence children in the way the Illuminati wants them to go is either a fool or a knave.

Toy guns, soldiers, revolvers, movies with plenty of crime and shooting—all are calculated to break down the finer feelings of normal Christian children and acclimatize them to the use of weapons, scenes of violence, and sudden death.

Pornographic books and magazines are circulated profusely at low prices, because such literature is calculated to destroy the thin veneer of virtue and respectability which civilized Christian moral codes have caused us to develop.

Few people realize the important part that modern movies play in subverting youths away from their homes, their country, and their religion. Many movies show an *hour* of film in which the criminals and *bad* men and women do everything that is forbidden by our laws and moral code and devote *one minute* during which the law catches up with them, or they die because of their sins. Films taken of actual fighting during the Mexican revolution in 1913 were shown in Galveston, Texas. The sight of seeing men killed in battle, or being dragged from their homes and slaughtered by revolutionaries caused women to scream and faint, and men to vomit. Public opinion caused the showings to be prohibited. Today these scenes are shown on films advertised as "Children's Special" for Saturday afternoon performances. That is just one illustration of how the general public, and particularly the children, have been systematically hardened to accept the sight of violence and bloody death as normal. It supports the revolutionary motto that "Much needed reforms can only be brought about speedily by revolutionary action."

In every country not subjugated to date, the directors of the World Revolutionary Movement have set up private Film Agencies which supply the most obscene pictures imaginable for presentation to private parties. These films illustrate every form of sexual depravity known to man. They are used for the purpose of demoralizing youth so they can be recruited into revolutionary organizations. This statement is proved by the fact that the laws barring them in the USSR are strictly enforced.

Youths who prove themselves as anti-social, anti-religious, hardened, and brutal, are sent to Moscow and taught "Revolutionary Warfare, and the Art of Street Fighting." This is a different course from that given to prospective labour leaders and intellectuals.

Revolutionary psychological warfare is accomplishing its purpose in the Western World as it did in Spain. This is proved by the fact that no person loses any sleep nowadays when the last thing they hear before going to bed is a recital of the details of air disasters, automobile accidents, crimes, and brutal slayings. A nightcap of that kind would have been too strong to induce sleep fifty years ago.

Public opinion is no longer aroused to action when the newspapers blandly report that several thousand Jews were systematically exterminated in gas chambers by anti-Semitics, or that ten thousand Christians were martyred because of their anti-Communist convictions by Béla Kun or Chinese sadists. Such horrors are now accepted as everyday occurrences. We are being rendered immune to the reactions we once experienced when violence of any kind came to our attention. We no longer are disturbed by the overthrow of established governments by force. If we were, we would have done something to stop what has been going on. People listen to those who continually cry, as they did in Spain, "Communism can never cause a revolution here." They listen to those who give them a sense of false security. The majority of citizens are like children, who hide their heads under the blankets when they fear danger. Pulling the bedclothes over one's head never saved a person from an assassin, a rapist, or an exploding bomb.

A few illustrations will show how psychological warfare worked in Spain. We must remember always that Lenin said, "Part of the training of all revolutionary youths must consist of robbing a bank, blowing up a police station and the liquidating of a traitor or a spy." Not until a youth has been drained dry of the milk of human kindness and all feelings of sympathy is he considered qualified for *party membership*. This is a vastly different status from that of a "Fellow Traveler."

As the day chosen for the revolt drew near in Spain, the purveyors of pornographic literature and obscene pictures became so bold hat they took their stand at the entrances to churches and offered their wares to the congregations going in and coming out. The outside covers of these publications usually showed a picture of priests and nuns engaged in sexual high-jinks. Mr. Edward Knoblauch,[6] who is recognized as an authority on the Civil War in Spain, was so struck by this anti-clerical campaign that he wrote:

> Occasionally, delegates of Protestant clergymen came to Loyalist Spain to investigate stories they had read of anticlerical activities. These delegations were warmly received. Great pains were taken to convince them they had been badly misled. Special guides were detailed to show them around. They saw only what the Communist authorities wanted them to see. After a day or two they were hustled home, suitably impressed.

But one day there was a slip-up. A delegation of clergymen stopped at a book-stall to admire some rare old volumes. Before the guide could prevent it, they saw copies of *La*

Traca and *Bicharracos Clericales*. The covers portrayed priestly orgies with semi-naked nuns. Both magazines were profusely illustrated with obscene pictures. Mr. Knoblauch commented, "The delegates left in a huff."

The situation in Spain between 1923 and 1936 was very similar to that which exists in Canada between the French and English speaking population today. The Basque people have their own language, culture, and traditions, which date back into antiquity. They are deeply religious and very proud. Like many French Canadians they believed they deserved National Independence. To achieve this objective, they organized a separatist movement to liberate the Basque people from the rest of Spain. As was only natural, the plotters of the revolutionary movement in Spain didn't overlook such a situation. The Basque people were devout Roman Catholics. They believed they were justified in fighting for political independence if necessary, although the vast majority would never have *knowingly* affiliated with the Communist Party to achieve their goal. Yet that is exactly what happened. Marxist "cells" infiltrated into Basque society. They hid their real identity so well that they became the leaders of the "Separatists." Then, like the Judas Goat, they led the Basques to slaughter. Operating under the banners of intense patriotism and religious fervour, the Basque leaders—President Aguirre, Gird, and Negrin—blended and beat into an unbelievable mass, Christ's cross, the *pistol* of Anarquism, and the *sickle* and *hammer* of Communism. Then, when the revolt started, the masses were abandoned to their fate. Aguirre was *head* of the Basque State and *generalissimo* of the Basque armies. He sat in his office in Bilbao, while hundreds of Catholic priests and other leaders of Basque society were systematically murdered. Their martyrdom naturally increased the hatred existing between the Basques and Spain.

F.J. Olondriz wrote the foreword to the book *The Red Persecution in the Basque Country*, written by José Echeandia. He said:

> When the day arrived the Basque separatists, blind with passion, many of them forgetting their faith, and their Catholic sentiments, felt closely and firmly united to the Communists, to the Atheists, and to the Anarchists...and they launched into a war, and made themselves responsible for slaughter, and believed all means were licit, rebelliously ignoring the peremptory words of their religious leader, Pope Pius XI, as contained in his encyclical *Divini Redemptoris*—"Communism is intrinsically perverse, and it cannot be admitted that those who wish to serve the Christian civilization may in any way co-operate with it."

It would have done some of our top-level statesmen well if they had remembered those words of wisdom when they tried to cooperate with Stalin during World War II. Another truth that Government leaders must never forget is the fact that Communists, and all other international groups, are used by the Illuminati to further their own secret plans and ambitions.

[1.] Exactly as agents of the WRM drafted the Federal Reserve Banking legislation in the U.S.A. 1910 and 1913 and the "Palestine Mandate" in England in 1916.

[2.] Police seized 90,000 rifles, 33,000 revolvers, 500,000 rounds of ammunition and a tremendous amount of counterfeit money.

[3.] See *The Bolshevik*, October issue, 1930.

4. It was to finance Ferrer's "Training Schools" for youth that Moscow subscribed the $200,000 previously mentioned. In Toronto in 1954 there were seventeen such "Training Schools." There were several in Sudbury. All big cities of population have them.

5. The sex orgy that took place in the Ford Hotel in Toronto, October 23, 1954, after the Red Feather Football game, involved dozens of teenagers of both sexes. It was a typical example of what Communist influence, secretly exerted, can have on the youth of any nation.

6. Mr. Knoblauch was a "Correspondent in Spain." He published a book with that title.

CHAPTER THIRTEEN

Franco

To understand what happened in Spain in 1936, one must have at least a general idea of the type of man Franco really is. Franco entered the Spanish army seriously intending to make it his career. His life in the army reads like a romance. He distinguished himself after he was appointed to the Spanish Legion. He turned the defeat inflicted on General Sylvestre by the Moors, into final victory. Not only did he lead his troops fearlessly, but he inspired in them great confidence because of his genius regarding strategy. He also earned the respect of his foes because of his military progress and his sound administrative policies in Morocco. The Moors finally looked upon him as almost divine. They came to call him "The Victorious," "Chief of Chiefs," and "Brave as a Lion." The above facts explain why they rallied around him when he asked for their loyalty in July of 1936.

Franco is not spoken of as being "popular" with his brother generals. He did, however, have the respect of most of them. It was this fact that prevented the Popular Front Government from being turned into a totalitarian dictatorship.

Azana, Caballero and Carlos Prieto dominated the Popular Front Government. Senor Gil Robles and Calvo Sotelo led the Rightist opposition.

When Sotelo revealed in the *Cortes* that between February and June 1936 there had been 113 general strikes and 218 partial strikes, that 284 buildings, 171 churches, 69 clubs and 10 newspaper offices had been burned, and over 3,300 assassinations committed, Casares Quiroga, Premier at the time, jumped to his feet and angrily retorted, "You will be held personally responsible for the emotion your speech will cause."

Dolores Ibarruri, a Communist, named "Pasionaria" because of her inflammatory speeches and fanatical actions, was a member of the Spanish *Cortes*. She jumped to her feet and, pointing her finger at Sotelo, literally screamed, "That man has made his last speech." She proved to be right. On July 13th, 1936, Senor Calvo Sotelo was dragged from his home by fifteen Assault Guards under command of Captain Don Angel Moreno. He was taken to a nearby churchyard and murdered. It was this event that caused many of the Spanish generals to break their oath to the Grand Orient and ask Franco to take over leadership in Spain. Dolores Ibarruri was a Stalinist agent in Spain. She had been entrusted with the task of corrupting army officials, organizing and directing raids on government armouries, and arming the revolutionary forces in Spain. She performed her various tasks most efficiently.

Assault Guards raided the houses of many other prominent anti-communists following Sotelo's murder, but most of them had been warned and made their escape.

On the day of the elections in February 1936, General Franco telephoned General Pozas, who was then in charge of the Civil Guard. He warned him that the Communists elected to the *Cortes* planned to stir up mob violence, in the hope that they could develop a revolutionary effort for the purpose of overthrowing the Republican government. General Pozas informed General Franco that he thought his fears were exaggerated. General Franco next telephoned General Molero, the Minister for War. He informed him of the threatening danger. Franco suggested that he be allowed to declare Martial Law,

Franco drew up the necessary orders which would give him the authority to prevent excesses and mob violence. Only the signatures of the Council of Ministers were necessary to enable him to preserve law and order, and protect the Republican government from revolutionary action. But Portela, who was then acting as premier, pleaded that he was too old to put the Cabinet's decision into practice. Franco retorted, "You have brought Spain to this sorry pass. It is your duty now to try and save her."

General Franco was given orders to proceed to the Canary Islands. The order actually meant his virtual exile from Spain.

Before he left, General Franco had a conference with Generals Mola and Varela. They assured him, they felt certain that once the other generals who had joined the Grand Orient Military Lodges knew the truth, most of them would break with the Grand Orient and accept his leadership. Before the meeting broke up, a secret means of communication between Mola and Franco had been arranged. Immediately after Franco departed for the Canary Islands, Stalin's agents renewed their activities.

On June 23rd, 1936, Franco wrote a long letter to the Minister for War in which he once again pointed out specific dangers.[1] But these warnings were ignored as the others had been. It was obvious that the Communist members of the Republican government were able to dominate its policy and actions.

The murder of Calvo Sotelo on July 13th decided Franco. He sent a coded message to the generals who were sworn to fight to save Spain from becoming a Russian satellite state.

Among those Franco contacted were Mola, Goded, Fanjul, Sanjurjo, Saliquet, some officers of the Spanish Navy, and Queipo de Llano. After the message was sent, Franco flew from the Canaries to Tetuan, where he knew he could rely upon the loyalty of the Moroccan troops.

On July 21st, 1936, Franco issued his proclamation which defined the issue at stake in the least possible number of words. It read: *"It is the duty of every man to enter this definite struggle between Russia and Spain."* Thus started the civil war. Professor Unamuno explained the issue in even fewer words. He said: *"It is a struggle of Christianity against barbarism."* He should have said "Against Illuminism."

Other evidence was obtained to prove that Stalin's Comintern plotted to subjugate Spain to bring about a total war between Britain and her allies, on the one side, and Germany and her allies on the other. There is the report of the meeting of the Political Secretariat of the Comintern which took place January 25, 1938. The purpose of the meeting was *to discuss ways and means to develop the revolutionary effort in Spain and North Africa.* Attending the meeting were representatives of the Profintern (The Red International of Labour Unions), and the foreign branches of the G.P.U. (The Secret Police). All of Moscow's most experienced revolutionary leaders were present; Iejov, head of the secret section of the Comintern; Georges Dimitrov of the Reichstag Fire infamy; head of the League of the Godless, and the Free Thinkers League; the then Secretary of the Communist International; Schick, Manuilsky, and Lozovsky of the Profintern; Popescu, Weintrauben, Gourovitch, Liemann, Turrini, Adami, and Valdez, who represented the Soviet of Foreign Affairs in the political bureau of the Comintern (these are the names of men who all took an active part in spreading the sphere of Communist influence around the world in later years). After the meeting opened,

Dimitrov gave a fiery speech. He denounced the lack of missionary vigour among the special military envoys that had been sent to Spain to help corrupt the Popular Front Government and direct the military operation of the Loyalist armies. He said their action:

> Has not had sufficient stimulus, and revolutionary elan, on the general European masses. The results obtained have not justified the heavy risks taken. THE PRINCIPAL STRUGGLE, WHICH IS TO BRING ABOUT AN ARMED CONFLICT BETWEEN TWO GROUPS OF CAPITALISTIC STATES, HAS NOT BEEN REACHED.

Then he went on to advocate:

> The Soviet military commandant in Spain should pass under the control of the Comintern emissaries, like the ambassadors, who know how to impregnate him with the necessary revolutionary feeling.[2]

In the Civil War in Spain, the propaganda issued at the time convinced the average person that a small group of generals in Spain had organized a revolt to overthrow the Republican Popular Front Government and establish a military dictatorship. The Popular Front Forces named themselves *Loyalists*. Franco Forces called themselves *Nationalists*. The *Loyalists* were comprised of all political factions *Left* of centre. The *Nationalists* contained all political factions *Right* of Centre.

The Communists were divided into two groups—those who intended to turn the Proletarian Dictatorship into a Stalinist Totalitarian State, and those who wished to make the Spanish Soviet a unit in the International of Soviet Republics as advocated by the Marxism theory. The Nationalist Forces included men who had sponsored the Carlist movement which, ever since 1837, held as its cause the restoration of the Spanish Throne to the descendants of Don Carlos. The Carlists were located in the Navarre province, and they supported Franco's Nationalist Army simply because they didn't intend to tolerate Communism in Spain.

On the *Right* also were the Falangists, the extreme *Rightists* among whom there was undoubtedly quite a number of the German type of Nazi who believed in using Total War to subdue their Leftist enemies. With a situation of this kind, it is understandable that those on the *Right* accused all those on the *Left* of being Communists, while all those on the *Left* accused all those *Right* of centre of being *Fascist*. Most horrible atrocities, including torture, mutilation, rape, and the execution of thousands of innocent victims, were committed by the Communists as part of the accepted pattern of the Reign of Terror. A few extremists on the Franco side committed atrocities also. All civil wars seem to turn a great number of men into inhuman brutes, who descend below the level of brute beasts once the blood lust has been aroused in them. Civil War cannot be justified. Those who advocate revolutionary wars should be executed. The evidence goes to show that the king of Spain in 1931, and General Franco in 1936, did everything in their power to avoid fighting a civil war.

Franco did not call upon the citizens of Spain to rally around him until he had exhausted every other means of preventing the Communist coup taking place on July 26th, 1936. The professional Army in Spain had been reduced greatly in numbers. It had been replaced by a National Police Force controlled by the *Leftist* government. It is extraordinary that Franco's bid to defeat the Communist plot did not fail, because post-war investigations revealed that in 1936 the armed forces were riddled with traitors, both officers and men, who had been placed in key positions by the agents of Moscow working within the Popular Front Government in Spain. On July 21st, 1936, the Moscow-directed organization for taking over the government in Spain was complete.

Franco knew that in one day Julio Alvarez del Vayo, Foreign Minister in the Republican government and Commissar-General, appointed hundreds of political commissars to the Republican army. The majority of these men were Communists. Vayo did this without consulting the Premier. The commissars compelled soldiers to join the Communist Party, offering advantages and promotion if they did; they also threatened persecution by every means in their power if they did not. Luis Araqistain, ex-ambassador of the Spanish Republic in Paris, published this fact in the *New York Times* May 19th, 1939. It was proved to be true.

Indalecio Prieto was Spanish Socialist deputy and minister of National Defence during the Spanish Civil War. He helped direct the war against Franco. In a report published in Paris in 1939 entitled, "How and Why I left the Ministry of National Defence," he said, "It is difficult to be on guard because there are Communists occupying confidential positions who, so as to avoid suspicion, are ordered to hide their affiliation, and sometimes ordered to conceal it by joining other parties. Dr. Juan Negrin was one of these. He was one of the most powerful men in Spain during the Civil War." Prieto wrote of him: "Because I refused to obey orders from Moscow, Juan Negrin expelled me from the government over which he presided on April 5th, 1938. I occupied the post of Minister of National Defence in his government. Two simultaneous actions were initiated against me; one was entrusted to the Russian secret police, and military men who operated in our country, and the other to the Spanish Communists...The Russians ordered and the Spanish Communists obeyed."

Dr. Juan Negrin claims he was, and is, not a Communist, but it was he who ordered that 7,000 boxes of Spanish gold be delivered to Stalin. The boxes were loaded in the ships *Kine*, *Neve*, and *Volgiles*. All three displayed the Soviet flag. Jose Velasco and Arturo Candela accompanied the shipments as persons of trust to Odessa. Everything was done under cover and other members of the Popular Front government were not cognizant of the situation. During Negrin's term of office, three Communists were appointed as under-secretaries of defence, and thus were the true masters of the Republican army, navy, and air force.[3]

Largo Caballero was a Communist, but when he refused to obey the order given him by Moscow's emissaries, they overruled his orders *even when he was serving his presidential term*. When he tried to rectify his own mistakes, he found it was too late. How Moscow's agents in foreign lands obtain such an absolute control of *Leftist* leaders is explained by Prieto. He wrote:

> The majority of the military commands of the Popular Front government were finally occupied by Communists, and in their hands were the most important reins of *power*. How could that phenomenon happen? Through a system of coercion graduated between personal advancement for those who bowed their heads, and the murder of those who rebelled.

Theo Rogers in his *Spain, a Tragic Journey* makes reference to the capture of documents which proved beyond doubt that a full-scale revolution had been planned to break out in July 1936. Rogers wrote:

Discovery amongst militant Communists, and Anarchists, of documents and plans, showed that a carefully schemed plot had been matured for an outbreak which would upset even the central government in Madrid and establish a Soviet Dictatorship. [The Work of the Illuminati.]

Roger's statement was proved to be true. Evidence was produced to prove that both General Franco and General Mola knew as early as April 1936 that a Communist coup was planned first for May 1st, then set back to June 29th, and then set back again to July 22nd. The delays were ordered to give those who were entrusted with putting the plan of revolt into effect more time to complete the final necessary details.

The whole world should have known of the Moscow-directed plot against Spain, because the final orders were intercepted while being passed by the Comintern to the leaders of the revolutionary movement in Spain. The documents were given to the *Echo de Paris*, which published them in April 1936. The *Echo de Paris* article reads:

TEXT OF INSTRUCTIONS FOR THE RED MILITIA

These instructions to the heads of the Spanish Red Militia...do not emanate from a Spanish Central Organization, but from the Technical Services in Paris, which sent them to Spain at that date. These Technical Services are those of the French Communist party, working in close cooperation with the Comintern, and its delegates in France. The document which we are publishing is in the hands of the government, we were not the parties who communicated it to them. We are convinced that M. Daladier, Minister of War and Defence, has given orders for preventive measures of defence and protection to be taken.

The abbreviated text is as follows:

1. Reinforce shock troops and guards in barracks, and supply them with automatic pistols. These shock troops and guards are members of the Communist party serving in the permanent forces and reserves.

2. These troops will be placed in communication with the Groups who are to break into the barracks. The latter will be in uniform, and under the orders of our officers in whom we have complete confidence.

3. When the fight starts our officers will be given admittance with their groups secretly. They will contact the respective committees and carry out the pre-arranged plan of attack inside the barracks.

4. The provisional committees in the barracks shall renew every two days their lists of enemies, neutrals, sympathizers, and experts. When the barracks have been taken over, those classed as enemies, including in particular all commanders and officers, shall be rapidly eliminated, and without hesitation.

5. Each member of the committees shall be provided with a list of the names of individuals who are to be murdered by himself personally.

6. After the enemies have been disposed of, neutrals shall be subjected to severe tests in order to kill in them any hesitation habitual in such undecided characters.

7. The committees handling the neutrals will make the necessary arrangements for the vigilance groups outside to enter the barracks on the pretext of assisting to put down the rebellion.

8. [This has little importance.]

9. Those detailed to liquidate generals on the active list shall consist of ten men with revolvers. The generals have two adjutants, and a secretary, who must be murdered in their own homes. Those detailed to perform these killings shall not withdraw in face of any obstacle or opposition, and they shall eliminate anyone who opposes them regardless of sex or age.

10. Those detailed to eliminate generals not holding command shall consist of three-man groups and shall carry out their duties as outlined in preceding paragraph.

11. and 12. Details how houses and sites, in strategic positions, must be procured by Communist militants, and secretly armed and fortified in order to ambush troops who may succeed in escaping from barracks. The instructions read: "As military officers have protected cars, groups of our militants must proceed to strategic points such as cross-roads, in cars and trucks; armed with machine guns so as to prevent help reaching those inside the cities. Lorries shall carry supplies of grenades."

13. Our militants shall quickly put on the uniform previously obtained and they shall be served with rifles.

14. When the rebellion breaks out our militant groups, wearing uniforms of the Civil Guards, and of the Assault Guard, and equipment already prepared for them, shall arrest all heads of all political parties under pretext of the necessity of doing so for their personal protection. Once in custody the procedure for the elimination of generals not holding command shall be carried out. Uniformed groups shall also arrest and detain important capitalists whose names appear in appendix B of Circular No. 32.

15. Violence shall not be used against these capitalists except if they resist, they shall however be forced to hand over the balance of the current accounts at the banks, and their securities. In the event of concealment they shall he completely eliminated, including their families, without exception. It is desirable that Cells shall be worked in on their staffs as domestics, or mechanics, as they can be very useful.[4]

16. [Can be skipped.]

17. With regard to members of the armed forces who claim to be sympathizers the same tactics shall be followed as was done in Russia. First use their services and then eliminate them as enemies. For our effort to be successful, and permanent, a neutral officer or man is better than one who has betrayed his uniform because his life was in danger. It is likely he would betray us also if provided with the opportunity.

18. Instructions to our militia regarding mobilization, movements of transportation, use of arms, and marksmanship, must be intensified.[5]

19. Militia posted at cross roads must eliminate all defeated troops trying to escape.

20. Machine gun posts shall be located in premises which cover the front and rear of all armouries, police stations, and fire halls and all approaches to, and exits from, the cities, and if, in spite of this, the enemy is able to get out, they shall be attacked with hand-grenades.

21. Other militia shall be placed in armoured lorries in strategic positions within the cities not more than one kilometer apart, they also shall be armed with machine guns.

22. Liaison shall be by light cars, and cyclists, who shall be armed with revolvers.

23. [Is of no special importance.]

24. The most intimate details concerning the lives and characters of all neutrals and sympathizers must be obtained and carefully recorded, including their family requirements, and the influence that love of their children, and desire for these necessary requirements, may exercise over them. If any of our militia, or any of the neutrals, and sympathizers, shows any kind of weakness or resistance to orders, they must be denounced to the highest committee of the organization as being guilty of complicity and/or reaction.

25. Our militia must be organized to work away from their own homes and localities because experience has taught us that at the last moment, through sentimentalism, men working in their own localities, and amongst their families and friends, have failed to carry out our plan with proper enthusiasm.

26. All owners of depots of goods and merchandise shall be regarded as important capitalists. These depots must be organized to serve the proletariat through the administrative groups.[6]

27. Deals with the question of using starvation as a means of reducing opposition quickly, and confirms what has been said regarding the use of this weapon in national disputes, and international warfare. It reads: "During the first week, and until the constitution becomes normal the supply of food and drink to the bourgeois is prohibited."

28. Stock of foods in barracks and in the hands of our enemies, which cannot be captured, must be rendered useless by mixing paraffin or other substances with them.

Since these orders were issued the revolutionary leaders in all countries have been given special instruction to make careful plans to deal with the members of the police and fire-departments, because experience has shown that the majority of these *civic employees* "remain loyal to their bourgeois bosses." The action recommended is to:

1. Infiltrate into the two forces.

2. Corrupt the rank and file.

3. Party members are urged to purchase or rent properties covering the approaches to both back and front of police stations and firehouses, so the member can be eliminated as they change shifts. The hour to revolt is to coincide with the time the police change shifts.

The orders which were given to the leaders of the Communist party in Spain detailed how they were to take over all public utilities and public services as well as civic administration. The objective was to obtain, in the shortest possible time, full and absolute control of all food supplies and communication systems.

Revolutionary Orders seized at Majorca in October 1936 were translated by Jacques Bardoux, who afterward wrote *Chaos in Spain*. They were on their way to revolutionary leaders in Spain.

SPANISH DOCUMENT

With the object of being able to control the smallest details of the movement, from the 8th of May, only the link agents will be able to give orders and they will communicate with each other by means of the Cypher E.L.M. 54-22. The local leaders must give verbal instructions to the committee with the help of the following code:

1.2.1. Order to begin mobilization.

2.1.1. Order to begin the revolt.

2.2.1.1.1. Order to attack at pre-determined points.

3.3.3. Provide for counter-revolutionaries.

2.4.3. Mobilization of trade unions.

2.5.5. General strike.

2.6.5. Acts of sabotage, *i.e.* blowing up railway lines, etc.

1.3.2. Signal to put off the revolt.

1.1.0. Order to provision.

1.0.0. Reorganization is ready.

0.0. Close frontiers and ports.

1.1. Execution of those whose names are on the black list.

All these orders will be given on the day before the revolt, 1st May or 29th, at midnight,[7] from the transmitter installed in the Casa del Pueblo at Madrid, the wave-length of which is nearly the same as that of the Madrid Union Radio. *Organization of Madrid:*

To be divided into the following sections:

A.B. Chamartin de la Rosa, H.Q. at the *Casa del Pueblo* of this district.

C.D. Cuatro Caminos, H.Q. at Socialist Club of the district.

E.F. Palace District, H.Q. at the printing works of *Mundo Obrero*.

G.H. University District, H.Q. at editorial offices of *El Socialista*.

I.J. Latina District, H.Q. at *Casa del Pueblo.*

M.N. Inclusa District, H.Q. at Socialist centre.

N.O. Pardinas District, H.Q. at Garage, at Castello 19.

P.Q. Southern District, H.Q. at Socialist Centre of Vallecas.

R.S. Carabanchel District, H.Q. at Socialist Club.

T.U.V. Centre of Madrid, H.Q. at *Casa del Pueblo,* Secretary's.

X.Y.Z. Offices Nos. 2, 3, 4, 6, 8, 10, 12 (balcony room).

Plan of Campaign in Madrid:

The revolt will be announced by five bombs let off at dusk. Immediately a Fascist attack on one of the C.N.T. (labour) centres will be faked; then a general strike will be declared and the soldiers and chiefs who support us will rise in revolt. The groups will come into action.

Those designated in T.U.V. will take over the Bureau of Communications, the Presidency, and the Ministry of War. Those belonging to the district will attack the Commissariats, and those belonging to the X.Y.Z. Section will take the Bureau of Public Safety.

A special group composed exclusively of machine-gunners with hand-grenades will go to the headquarters of the government and attack it by the following routes: Carretas, Montera, Mayor, Correos, Paz, Alcala, Arenal, Preciados, Carmen and San Jeronimo. The groups, composed of fifty cells of ten men each, will act in streets of the second and third order, and of two cells only in those of the first order and in the avenues.

The orders are for the immediate execution of all the counter-revolutionaries who have been detained.

The Republicans of the Popular Front will be asked to support the movement, and in case of refusal they will be expelled from Spain.

FRENCH DOCUMENT

Secret.

To the Leaders of Groups and Sections:

Cell of St. George du Bois, Look-out Station.

FIRST GROUP: H.Q. Town Hall. Leader of Group, A. President.

First Section: B. volunteers rifles, 1 revolver, 70 rounds of ammunition for rifle, 20 for revolver, 15 grenades.

Second Section: C. volunteers 4 rifles, 3 revolvers, 70 rounds of ammunition for rifle, 20 for revolver.

Third Section: D. Leader, C. 4 volunteers for distributing arms and ammunition and for making ammunition. 6 revolvers, 15 cans petrol, 25 cans (5 litres each) reserve, issued to Comrade C.

SECOND GROUP: H.Q. Railway Station. Leader, D.E.P.7 volunteers, 8 rifles, 80 rounds of ammunition, 20 sticks of dynamite issued to comrade E.

THIRD GROUP: At the Station. Leader, F.E. 5 volunteers (2 experts), 6 rifles, 1 revolver, 60 rounds of ammunition for rifle, 20 for revolver, 1,500 metres of insulated telephone wire issued to Comrade F.

FOURTH GROUP: (attacking party) H.Q. Basement of Town Hall, Leader G. *First Section:* H. 4 volunteers, 4 rifles, 50 rounds of ammunition, 10 knives, 12 ropes.

Second Section: I. 4 volunteers, 4 rifles, 50 rounds of ammunition, 10 knives, 10 ropes.

Special instructions.

SECOND GROUP: Blow up Railway and Fascist convoys.

THIRD GROUP: Link immediately Telephone Exchange P.O., Railway Station and Town Hall.

To ALL GROUPS: Save ammunition pending arrival of arms and ammunition from the cell at Rochefort.

First Group to commander all provisions, animals and fodder pending arrival of instructions from Rochefort for distribution.[8]

COMRADE PRESIDENT

Author's Comment

Recent history has proved that the instructions given by the Illuminati through Moscow for the subjugation of Spain have since been brought up to date, and carried out in all countries in Europe which have been subjugated since 1936. There is no reason to believe that the Fifth Column in Canada, and the U.S.A., is less thoroughly organized. The Fifth Column is ready to carry out the Illuminati's orders when those who direct the World Revolutionary movement consider the time opportune. There is ample evidence to prove that the members of the Communist party in Canada and the U.S.A., have, since 1948, been practising speedy evacuation from large cities and industrial areas so they could be in the country on picnics, and other reasonable excuses, during the initial stages of a Soviet bombing raid. They plan to return and take over while conditions are chaotic and the inhabitants are still in a state of panic.

While it is necessary to check Illuminism in Europe and Asia, it will be a tremendous, and costly, error if we fail to realize the full extent of the danger of their Fifth Column. We must remove our internal danger or all our plans for civic emergency defence will be useless. We must deal with the enemy within first; then our defence plans, and other matters, will fit smoothly into gear unhampered by traitors and saboteurs. The fact to remember is that Communists are used to start the revolt. Those who lead the Communists then form a dictatorship of the Proletariat, which in turn is taken over by the agentur of the Illuminati.

---

1. The details can be obtained by reading Arrara's *Franco*.

2. Reported in *Gringoire* issue February 11th, 1938.

3. The theft of this gold is still an international problem in 1955. Franco demands that the Soviets return the gold.

4. This order protected the bankers and capitalists who were working as agents of the Illuminati in exactly the same way in which similar order protected the Rothschilds in the French revolution.

5. In 1946 the author reported to the proper authorities that .303 rifles had been imported into Canada as scrap; in the same manner Canada's Cabinet Ministers permitted arms to be shipped to the Middle East as scrap in 1956.

6. This order also goes to show the Illuminati are the real leaders of a revolutionary effort. They are always in the top-levels of Governments, Society, Industry and the Armed Forces. The workers, the Mob, are simply the "Pawns in the Game." They are used and then subdued. Prove this to them and the Communist plot will fail. —Author.

7. It was after these orders had been issued that the date to revolt was changed to July 22nd.

8. The above information was made available to the *Free Press of the World* by freelance writers and accredited correspondents as soon as it became available, but it was never published. Why? —Author.

CHAPTER FOURTEEN

The Revolutionary Reign of Terror

Study of the methods employed by the Illuminati's agents in Spain is of great value to those who would protect their country from the danger of similar tribulations. Revolutionary leaders have *Cells* occupy key positions in jails, prisons, and asylums. Their purpose is to control these institutions so they can release the anti-social elements under detention, and use them as shock troops during the revolt. *In every revolution to date the anti-social prisoners, and the criminally insane,* have been used to arouse the blood-lust in the mob and thus introduce the "Reign of Terror" which, the revolutionary leaders calculate, will cause the general public to surrender in the quickest possible time.[1]

The prison policy in Madrid was influenced greatly by the advice given the authorities in the Popular Front government by "General" Kleber, the Canadian-Russian, who, after taking theoretical training in the Lenin Institute in Moscow, was sent to Spain to serve Stalin and obtain practical experience in revolutionary warfare.

As soon as the Popular Front government took office in March 1936, the extreme Leftist members insisted that an Amnesty Bill be passed, granting liberty to all those who had taken part in the Asturian rebellion. In addition to this small army of revolutionaries, 30,000 others, who had been arrested as Communists, were given their liberty. After July 17th, another 40,000 common criminals were released on the condition that they would bear arms in the Loyalist army. Revolutionary leaders liquidate most of the common criminals after they have served their purpose. By doing so, they convince a great many people that the atrocities committed during the revolution were the crimes of irresponsibles acting on their own initiative, and not in accordance with a preconceived plan of terrorism.

These were the conditions existing when General Franco decided he would try to save Spain from Communistic tyranny. Many books have been written telling how Franco, and a mere handful of Spanish generals, finally managed to defeat the Communist plot. It is an exciting story of courage, fortitude, and great faith in their Christian Crusade. As soon as Franco issued his proclamation, the *Red* undersecretaries for army, navy, and air ordered the communist *cells* to liquidate all officers listed as enemies. This task was carried out with great thoroughness. Communist *cells* had been placed in the mechanical, communications, and signals branches of the services. This proved that the organizers were sticking to the pattern laid down for the English, French, Russian, and German revolts.

Taken by surprise, nearly two-thirds of the officers were murdered cold-bloodedly during the initial stages of the attack. The mutineers tried to convince other ranks and ratings that they were carrying out the government's orders, and executing officers who had been convicted as enemies of the Popular Front government.

Many men would not believe what they were told. Before long it was not uncommon for one warship to be seen firing at a range of only a few yards into another. In one case, the foreturret was manned by Reds and the after turret of the same ship manned by anti-Reds. The massacres which started aboard the ships spread to the dockyards and the cities in which they were located.

There might have been some excuse for the drastic action taken against the officers who could be expected to take sides with Franco, but it is impossible to excuse the terrorism which the Communists, acting as soldiers and police of the Popular Front government, inflicted upon the unarmed and unsuspecting populace. The imposition of terrorism proved, at the cost of hundreds of thousands of innocent lives, that Lenin's policy had been accepted. He ruled that terrorism had to accompany every violent effort to overthrow a government, because terrorism was the most economical method of subjugating the masses quickly and thoroughly.

It must be remembered that the leaders of a revolution don't consider the effort entirely wasted if it doesn't end in a proletarian dictatorship. Every revolt against constituted government and lawful authority is considered by those who plot and plan revolutionary efforts as a step in the right direction. If the effort falls short of success, it is bad, but not hopeless. It doesn't matter how many people are killed. They are just pawns in the game. They are expendable. It is extraordinary how few of the top-level revolutionary leaders get killed during a rebellion.[2] It is accepted as good revolutionary technique to sacrifice the masses and preserve the members of the Illuminati, for they are to govern the new order. Even in ordinary strikes, the *Reds* usually stir up the trouble and then sneak away. They leave the other workers to do the actual fighting with the police or militia.

The following facts are given to prove that during a revolution everyone who is *not* a *party member* or a *fellow traveler* may expect no mercy of any kind. Even fellow travelers are liquidated *after* they have been used to advantage.

Prior to July 1936, the directors of the WRM had literally flooded Madrid with agents. Moses Rosenberg arrived as Moscow's ambassador to Madrid. Anteneff Avseenko arrived in Barcelona. Dimitrov arrived to personally conduct the religious persecutions planned to follow the Communist Coup. During the Civil War, Rosenberg ruled as tzar of Madrid. Avseenko assumed command of the Catalan Red Army. Rosenberg organized the Chekas in Spain and saw that they carried out their work of spying out more and more victims.

Moscow's agents organized "Purification Squads." Officially their duty was to seek out Fascists, but secretly they *liquidated* all those who had been previously listed as reactionaries against the Illuminati's plan for subjugation of Spain. These lists had been compiled by Communist spies who had been worked into the Union of Concierges (house and apartment janitors), the tax departments, the Postal Services, and other public offices. The lists of those to be liquidated were very complete because Moscow's spies, some disguised as scissors and knife grinders, had covered every district, street by street and house by house. All citizens were listed according to their political, labour, social, and religious standing and affiliations. When the order for the Reign of Terror to start was given, the Communists worked with the sureness, the ferocity and the thoroughness of starved brutes. Stalin had once stated, "It is better that a hundred innocent people die than one reactionary should escape." They obeyed this order with devilish persistency.

So others who live in countries not yet subjugated may understand what happens during a reign of terror, some actual atrocities will be described.

On July 17th, 1936, a group of Communists wearing the uniforms of government troops called at the Dominican Convent in Barcelona. The leader informed the Mother Superior that because mob violence was feared he had orders to escort the sisters to a place of safety. The sisters gathered together their few belongings and, unsuspectingly, accompanied the soldiers who took them to the suburbs where they murdered them all. The leader callously remarked afterwards, "We needed the building. We didn't want to muss it up before we occupied it."[3]

Señor Salvans was a known anti-Communist. Three times, purification squads visited his home in Barcelona. When the third visit produced no information regarding his whereabouts, the *Reds* murdered the whole family of eight. That vile deed was performed in accordance with paragraphs 15 and 16 of the instructions already referred to.

One of the most senseless acts of violence ever committed in the name of "Liberty...Equality...Fraternity" was the murder of sixteen lay-brothers who worked voluntarily as male nurses in the largest hospital in Barcelona. Their only crime was that they belonged to a religious order. The fact that they nursed all who were sick, regardless of class, colour, or creed, made no difference to those who ordered their "liquidation." E.M. Godden, who published *Conflict in Spain*, on page 72 reported, "The slaughter of the living was accompanied by derision for the dead. During the last week of July, 1936, the bodies of nuns were exhumed from their graves and propped up outside the walls of their convents. Obscene, and offensive, placards were attached to their bodies."

My cousin, Tom Carr, was a Mining Engineer in Spain from 1919 till 1938. He was married to the daughter of Mr. Allcock, the American Consul of Huelva. One of Caballero's Fifth Columnists had been elected mayor of Huelva. When Moscow gave the word, he turned over the civic administration to the Communists. Their first act was to torture and then murder all the priests. The nuns were stripped naked and driven from the convents into the streets to provide sport for the revolutionaries.[4]

Godden also states that he interviewed two English women who only escaped molestation because they were foreigners. These two women told Godden they had been forced to witness a mob of men and women act like fanatical dervishes. In the first instance the *Reds* tortured and mocked a priest before they finally hung his dismembered body and limbs from a statue of the Blessed Virgin. In the second instance the mob drilled a hole through the body of a young priest and then, while he was still living, transfixed him with a crucifix.

In September 1936, Pere Van Rooy, famous French author, reported Dimitrov as saying, "We are reproached with destroying the churches and convents of Spain. What does the destruction of a few convents and churches matter? We are out to create a new world."[5]

A Committee, which officially investigated Communist atrocities in Spain in 1939, agreed that a conservative estimate placed 50,000 as the number of citizens "liquidated" in Barcelona as "reactionaries" between July 1936, and December 1937. In Valencia, the number was set at 30,000. In Madrid, they estimated that fully one tenth of the whole population was systematically murdered to make Spain into another totalitarian state.[6]

To illustrate what happened when the Reds took over control in Spain, I will quote some other independent witnesses. Marcel M. Dutrey, the famous French author, stated:

> At Castre Urdiales the Communist Military commandant was an ex-municipal policeman who had been dismissed for theft. The new Chief of Police had previously made his living making and selling obscene postcards. The public prosecutor was the

illegitimate son of a woman who had previously been a well-known streetwalker. He was nicknamed "Son-of-his-mother." The Red Tribunal was presided over by a miner who was assisted by two "Assessors"...All these men were sadists. They glorified in carrying out the sentences they themselves imposed on their victims. They opened the stomach of Vincent Mura; they martyred Julie Yanko publicly in the market square; they dismembered Varez, the famous Spanish racing motorist, on the grounds that he refused to betray his friends into their hands.

Mr. Arthur Bryant, who wrote the preface to the fully evidenced, and authenticated, report on "Communist Atrocities in Spain" remarked on several occasions: "Soviet agents obtained such a control of the communications systems that only reports favourable to their cause got into the majority of the world's newspapers, but, on the other hand, the most outrageous lies against the Franco forces were conjured up and given to the press of the world without let or hindrance."

Bryant was so disgusted with what he saw that he wrote:

No university lecturer, or anonymous B.B.C. commentator has told the just, and compassionate, British people the truth about the women of San Martin de Valdeiglesias.[7] For no greater crime than that they were found to possess some religious emblem, the women in San Martin de Valdeiglesias were condemned to be violated, and to satiate every vile passion, of twenty-five Red Militia men each. The fact that the fathers of some of the women had been imprisoned, and were under sentence of death, and that their mothers were forced to be present to witness the degradation of their daughters, was not sufficient to dissuade the Red Militia men from carrying out the sentence. The horrors of the hours suffered by these women had terrible effects on some of their minds. The survivors related how, again and again, they implored their executioners to kill them rather than submit them to such dreadful dishonour. The appalling cruelty of such atrocities can be realized by the fact that many of the condemned women were married, and when they were conducted between militiamen, before this pitiless tribunal, they carried children in their arms, and these children were witnesses of this culmination of the horror in the dishonour of their mothers.[8]

It is little wonder that the secret power directing the WRM said, "Communists should not be required to carry out their plan of Terrorism in the localities in which they had lived with their families, but had to be used elsewhere."

Every Communist will declare that these atrocities were committed by "Uncontrollables" who were punished when they were caught. So that no person may be deceived by such lies I will again quote Lenin, the first canonized saint of the Illuminati totalitarian creed. Lenin said on various occasions, "There are no morals in politics, there is only expediency. A scoundrel may be of use to us just because he is a scoundrel."

On another occasion he said, "Young revolutionaries should start training for war immediately, by means of practical operations such as liquidating a traitor, killing a spy, blowing up a police station, or robbing a bank to provide funds for the uprising, etc... Do not shirk from these experimental attacks. They may of course degenerate into excesses, but that is a worry of the future."[9]

The Communist Krassikov was a libertine who squandered party funds on riotous living. Lenin, when ordering his *liquidation* said, "It does not matter that Comrade

Krassikov has squandered party funds in a brothel, but it is scandalous that this should have disorganized the transportation of illegal literature."[10]

Communist training is designed to squeeze the last drop of human kindness out of the hearts of men and women who aspire to become high priests of the religion. Anna Pauker rose to dizzy heights in the Soviet hierarchy. She became Foreign Minister of Rumania. She proved she was loyal to Stalin when she rendered herself a widow by denouncing the father of her three children as a Trotskyite.

Communist terrorists encourage mere boys to become executioners of the enemies of the proletariat in order to harden them, and remove from their hearts every last vestige of human sentiment and sympathy. One such youth told how he had had a lot of fun with a priest. He said:

> Night after night we took him out with the groups we had to kill, but always we put him last in the line. We made him wait while we killed all the others and then we took him back to the Bellas Artes again. (The Bellas Artes was the Building of Fine Arts which the Communists used as a prison). Each night he thought he was to die, but a quick death was too good for him. That *Fraile* (priest) died seven deaths before we finally finished him.

Mr. Knoblauch, on page 87 of his book *Correspondent in Spain*, tells of a horrible incident which confirms the contentions that the planners of World Revolution select potential leaders while they are very young, and then train them until they are devoid of every trace of human sentiment and pity. Knoblauch tells how two Communist youths boasted to a doctor, in his presence, that they had mutilated and murdered two young priests. They penetrated the disguise of these two religious men who, to escape detection and death, were working as coal-heavers. The two youths told how they made the two priests dig their graves with their coal shovels, then, in accordance with the Communist-designed Reign of Terror, they emasculated their two victims and forced the organs into their mouths. They stood by jeering while the priests died slow lingering deaths.

De Fonteriz, in *Red Terror in Madrid,* pages 19-20, tells how the Chekas, organized by Dimitrov and Rosenberg, tried to make a certain lady tell where her husband was hiding. The woman probably didn't know his whereabouts, but to make sure she didn't, the members of the Chekas made her sit and watch while they amused themselves piercing the breasts of eight women members of her household with long hat-pins.

To prove a previous statement, that those who design the pattern of the Reign of Terror used criminals and lunatics to stir up the blood-lust, I report what happened at Alcala on July 20th, 1936: The *Reds* released all the prisoners, both male and female, on condition that they would bear arms for the Communist Cause. They numbered one thousand men and two hundred women. They were formed into the Battalion of Alcala. They excelled themselves in the victorious attack on Madrid. As a reward they were sent to Sigüenza. After taking over the town, they murdered two hundred citizens *to break down the resistance of the others*. This battalion of criminals occupied Sigüenza for sixteen weeks. When they were driven out by Franco's forces, it was found that every female, from ten to fifty, had been violated. Many of them were pregnant and many diseased. Some were both. One girl, a waitress in a hotel, told how *lucky* she had been. She told how the criminals had murdered the bishop of Sigüenza in a most horrible, barbarous, and unprintable manner. At a banquet held in the hotel that night, one of the battalion took a fancy to her and demanded that one of his comrades dress himself in the murdered bishop's vestments and marry them. The others thought this a great joke and carried out the mock ceremony. After the wedding the "Militiennes" performed the *"Danse en Ventre"* using the dining tables as a stage. After the orgy ended, the man claimed the girl as his own personal property. Relating this happening she remarked, "I was lucky. My man was an assassin, but it was better to belong to him than to be the plaything of all. I at least escaped disease."

Marcel M. Dutrey published the fact that in Ciempozuelos over one hundred religious brothers were bound to lunatics who were then furnished with knives. One can imagine the horror which followed. Moscow's army of trained propagandists told the world how Franco's troops had murdered the mayors of many small towns, but they didn't mention the fact that they had been tried by a properly constituted military court and proved to have been Communist agents of Largo Caballero who had plotted to turn Spain into a dictatorship.

If further proof is needed to substantiate the statement that the Secret Powers behind the World Revolutionary Movement use Communists throughout the world to further their totalitarian plans, the numerous desertions from the Communist party, all over the world, should provide that proof. Douglas Hyde, who for the preceding five years was news editor of the *Daily Worker*, Britain's leading Communist newspaper, in March 1948, announced his resignation from the Communist party. In a press release he stated, "I believe that the new 'line' of the Communist party, introduced after the formation of the Cominform last year (1947), if successful, will bring nothing but misery to the common people." Mr. Hyde went on to explain that since the end of World War II he had been worried regarding Moscow's foreign policy. He said he had finally become convinced that the Party Line, as now determined by the Moscow Clique, was no longer in keeping with the ideals for which he had worked so long, and that the ultimate result would be to destroy the very freedoms and decencies for which Communists had been fighting for so long a time. He concluded with these words: "My growing disillusionment led me to seek some other answer to the problem of our day, and another way out of the world chaos."

Right on top of Mr. Hyde's resignation in London, England, came that of Mrs. Justina Krusenstern-Peters, a staff member of Soviet publications for the preceding twelve years. She announced her resignation in Shanghai, China. She said, "The strain of writing according to orders from Moscow became more than I could bear...I am still a Soviet citizen. I am sure my feelings are shared by many of my colleagues in Russia, the only difference is that they are not able to protest against their enslavement."

Most Communists work to bring about an International of Soviet Socialist Republics. In other words, they feel that only by using revolutionary methods can they speedily destroy the stranglehold of selfish capitalism and place political power in the hands of the *workers*. Few party members realize they are working themselves into a state of slavery from which there is no hope of escape.[11]

[1.] Investigation of outbreaks in many prisons in both the U.S.A. and Canada indicate these revolt, were Communistically inspired. It took nearly twenty-three years to prove that some of the officials in Kingston Penitentiary, at the time Tim Buck was confined in the institution, were Communists. Evidence would indicate they helped him organize the Kingston Prison Riots. I was a freelance writer at the time. I wrote that the whole thing smelt to high heaven as a plot to make a martyr of Tim Buck, in order to arouse public sympathy, in order to obtain his release. I declared it my opinion that guards, and other prison officials, were implicated. My story never appeared in print. In 1953, one of the officials I suspected in 1932 of having "Red" affiliations contested the Federal election in British Columbia as the Labour Progressive Candidate. Between 1939 and 1944 this same man had charge of the training of personnel in the engineering branch of the Royal Canadian Navy. This information was given to the proper authorities. —Author.

2. It is a historical fact that ten times as many revolutionary leaders have died during Party Purges than died during the actual revolutionary war.

3. Recorded in the official reports "Communist Atrocities in Spain," parts one, two and three. The investigations were conducted by a committee composed of men of different nationalities. The editing was done by Arthur Bryant, internationally known journalist and author.

4. This statement of my cousin's was confirmed an page 238 of the *Spanish Arena*, written by William Fees and Cecil Gerahty, and also by Arthur Bryant who investigated the Communist Atrocities in Spain.

5. See *Catholic Herald*, February 11th, 1938.

6. In case some people think that Communists hate only Roman Catholics, it is well to remember that the Secret Powers behind the world Revolutionary Movement are determined to ultimately turn this world into the despotism of Satan. That is the essence of Illuminism. In order to lull people in countries not yet Sovietized into a sense of false security, they will try to convince them of their tolerance to religions other than Roman Catholic, but investigation shows that they are determined, when they have sufficient power, to wipe out all religions.

7. Note: Red agents had infiltrated onto the Staff of Britain's B.B.C. in 1938, and for nearly two years the policy was Pro-loyalist, i.e. Communistic. The present trend of the C.B.C. is much the same. The majority of programs are slanted sharply to the "left."

8. The details are on page six of the second report "Communist Atrocities in Spain."

9. Communist agents teach children in all Free Nations the inversion of the Ten Commandments. Communism is therefore responsible for the increase in juvenile delinquency more than any other single cause. While professed atheists, they serve the purpose of Illuminati and Satanism.

10. The magazine *Time* made reference to these views expressed by Lenin; November 17th, 1948.

11. Mr. Hyde, and others who broke away from the communist party, don't seem even yet to realize that they were only tools used to further the plans of the Illuminati.

CHAPTER FIFTEEN

The Events Leading up to World War Two

It has been told how the international bankers enabled Germany to secretly re-arm, with the aid of Stalin, in spite of the restrictions imposed by the Treaty of Versailles. In order to understand what happened in Germany to bring Hitler into power, it is necessary to be familiar with the political intrigue which went on between 1924 and 1934. "The Secret Powers" always have had their agents divide the population of countries they plan to subjugate into many religious, economic, political, social, and labour groups. Their agents then divide the various groups into as many factions as possible. Their motto is: "United we stand. Divided they fall."

Most German citizens, only with the exception of Communists, were in agreement upon the following issues: That Germany had been winning the war when had she had first been betrayed and afterwards victimized. That the national moneylenders had used the so-called democracies of Britain, France, and the United States, to defeat Germany's armed forces. That the Jewish-led Communist Party assisted the international bankers by bringing about the chaotic conditions preceding the signing of the Armistice and the revolution that followed. That every patriotic German, male and female, should do his or her utmost to build up post-war Germany, and break the economic and military stranglehold placed on their nation by the Treaty of Versailles.

Most political leaders, except Communists, were in agreement that in order to free themselves of the economic sanctions imposed upon the nation, it was necessary to break away from their dependence on the international bankers for financial assistance in the form of interest-bearing loans. In other words, most German politicians, except Communists, were in agreement that Germany should depart from the practice of financing the nation's business by incurring debts, a practice which had been imposed upon England in 1694, France in 1790, and the United States in 1791, by the International bankers. They realized that this system had resulted in astronomical National Debts, *the principal and interest payments of which were guaranteed and secured by Direct Taxation of the people.*

The Fascist leaders in Germany decided they were going to create their own money and use their national assets—such as the value of their real estate, their industrial potentials, their agricultural production, natural resources, and the nation's capacity to produce—as collateral.

The people of Germany found that, generally speaking, their views regarding future political and economic policy were shared by the people of Italy, Spain, and Japan; thus came into being *the axis powers* and the Fascist Movement. Because of their dynamic personalities, Hitler, Mussolini and Franco became the chosen leaders. History proves that these three men did a great deal to help their countries recover from the effects of the preceding revolutions and wars. The industrial and agricultural developments were little short of miraculous. Their military re-armament was made possible by the secret assistance given by the agentur of the Illuminati, who planned to bring the Fascist and Capitalistic countries into another World War.

When Hitler and Mussolini first rose to power, they advocated the moderate Fascist policy which demanded that the wrongs done their countries be rectified; that they contain communism; and curb the powers of the Illuminati who controlled finance and industry. But as time went on, both Hitler and Mussolini came under the influence of the leaders of the hard core of Nazi War Lords, who claimed that the only way to establish a permanent peace in the world was by military conquest. The Nazi leaders sold the top military leaders in Italy and Japan solidly on the theories and plans advocated by Karl Ritter in 1849. Franco in Spain refused to go along with their totalitarian plans. His religious beliefs convinced him that promoting an ideology which denied the existence of an Almighty God was doing the work of the Devil.

The Totalitarian-minded leaders in Germany, Italy, and Japan were determined to use Fascism to further their secret Long-Range Plans in exactly the same way as their opponents—the international bankers—used Communism. The immediate plans of the War Lords were: first, to defeat the Stalin-controlled Empire; second, wipe out Communism in Europe; third, consolidate the control of the Axis Powers on Continental Europe; fourth, invade Britain and France and subjugate the people; fifth, to invade and conquer the United States by using two vast pincer movements. Japan was to land invading forces on the west coast of Mexico in the south and in the Northwest Territories in the north. Germany was to invade Canada by air in the North; the German-Italian forces were to jump the Atlantic from Africa, and attack the U.S.A. from South America and the Gulf of Mexico.

The Northern invading forces were scheduled to join together at a point in the vicinity of Chicago and push on down the Mississippi while the South-West and South-East invasion forces were to meet at New Orleans and push north up the Mississippi, thus dividing the country into two halves.[1]

Following the conquest of Britain and the United States, the Nazis planned to exterminate the Jews living in these two countries as they had exterminated those they located in Europe. The international bankers—and big capitalists controlled by them—were listed for immediate liquidation, along with confiscation of all their assets and estates.

While Hitler suffered imprisonment prior to 1934, because he was considered the personal enemy of the Nazi War Lords and the international bankers, he wrote Mein Kampf. On the very last page he stated, "The party (National-Socialist) as such stands for positive Christianity but does not bind itself in the matter of creed to any profession. It combats the Jewish materialistic spirit within and without us."

In 1933, Hitler also announced his policy in regard to Britain. He pointed out that Marx, Lenin and Stalin had all repeatedly reiterated that before International communism could reach its final objectives, Britain and her Empire had to be destroyed. Under these circumstances, Hitler said: "I am willing to help defend the British Empire by force if called upon."

Of the Treaty of Versailles, Hitler wrote, "It was not a British interest (intention) but, in the first place, a Jewish one to destroy Germany." He also wrote, "Even in England there is a continual struggle going on between the representatives of British State interests and the Jewish World dictatorship. Whilst England is exhausting herself in maintaining her position in the world, the Jew today is a rebel in England and the struggle against the Jewish world menace will be started there also."

Hitler never wavered from his personal opinion that the survival of Germany as a great power depended upon an alliance with the British Empire. In 1936, he instituted proceedings to try to bring about this alliance. He arranged for unofficial conversations to take place between German and British diplomats, and after the meetings failed to produce the alliance he so greatly desired, he said:

> No sacrifice would have been too great in order to gain England's alliance. It would have meant renunciation of our colonies; and importance as a sea power; and refraining from interference with British industry by competition."[2] He considered that all these German concessions would have been worthwhile if only he had been able to bring about the German-British alliance. His failure to bring about the British Alliance caused him to weaken in his opposition to the totalitarian ideology as advocated by the extreme Nazi War Lords. The failure of the conference convinced Hitler that no moderate policy would ever break the control that the international bankers had over British Foreign policy. He reluctantly began to concede that Karl Ritter had been right when he said, "The power the Jewish financiers hold over Communism must be destroyed, as well as of those who are members of the world revolutionary movement, before peace and economic freedom can be restored to the world."

The purpose of this book is to record the events in history which provided the "Causes" which produced the "Effects" we experience today. We are not concerned with the "Rights" or "Wrongs" of the decisions made by individuals, except to judge for ourselves whether the decisions furthered the Devil's Plan or were in accordance with the Plan of God. The only value of historical research is to obtain knowledge of how, and why, mistakes were made in the past so we can try to avoid making similar mistakes in the future.

The momentous meeting regarding the possibility of an alliance between Great Britain and Germany took place in January of 1936. Lord Londonderry represented the British government and Goering, Herr Ribbentrop, and Hitler, Germany.

An authority on this phase of history informed me that Herr Goering and Herr Von Ribbentrop outlined the history of the World Revolutionary Movement to Lord Londonderry, explaining the detailed research work done by Professor Karl Ritter and others. They reasoned that the only successful way to fight a totalitarian-minded conspiracy was to use Total War. They explained to Lord Londonderry their plan was to attack all Communist-controlled countries, liberate the people, and execute all Communist traitors. They claimed the only way to wipe out Communism was the extermination of the whole Jewish Race.[3] They produced masses of documented evidence which they claimed was authentic, to prove Communism was organized, financed, and directed by powerful, wealthy and influential Jews, who also organized, financed and directed secret ambitions to bring about the Messianic Age.[4]

Hitler is said to have promised that he would continue to oppose the extreme totalitarian plans of the Nazi War Lords and confine his activities against Communism to Europe, providing the British government would enter into an alliance with Germany. When Lord Londonderry said he doubted if the British government would take part in a plan to abolish Communism, which called for "Genocide," Hitler compromised. He said Germany would undertake the task alone provided England would enter into an agreement that the two countries would under no circumstances war against each other for ten years. *Hitler argued that the only way Britain, France, and Russia could shake off the unbearable and ruinous burden of ever-increasing national debts was to repudiate them and restore the issuing of money to the government where it originally and rightfully belonged.*

Hitler is said to have pointed out that the purpose of his National-Socialist party—call it Fascism—was to put an end, for once and for all, to the power and influence that the international moneylenders exerted on national and international affairs by forcing every nation that still claimed to be independent, further and further into their debt. He is said to have quoted what Benjamin Disraeli made one of his characters say in his famous book *Coningsby*, "So you see, dear Coningsby, the world is governed by very different personages from what is imagined by those who are not behind the scenes."[5]

Goering is said to have backed up the Führer by pointing out that history had proved that the wealthy and influential Jews had obtained economic and political control of every country into which they had infiltrated by using illegal methods and corrupt practices.

Herr Von Ribbentrop is reported to have supported Goering's arguments by reminding Lord Londonderry that as recently as 1927-28 when he was in Canada, the Stevens Royal Commission into the Canadian Customs Service proved that the country was being robbed annually of over ONE HUNDRED MILLION DOLLARS by smuggling and other kinds of illegal traffic and trade organized and directed from an International Headquarters. He pointed out that evidence placed before the Royal Commissioner had proved that in order to get away with gangsterism and licentiousness they "fixed" thousands of public servants and hundreds of government officials, even as high as cabinet level. He pointed out that what had been absolutely proved to exist in Canada was ten times worse in the United States of America. Ribbentrop reasoned that the only way to clean up the mess was to "get" the three hundred men at the top who were "The Secret Power" master-minding the negative forces whose various evil influences and criminal activities all furthered the Long-Range Plan of those who directed the World Revolutionary Movement.[6]

Goering is said to have reviewed once more the part the international bankers had played in bringing about, directing, and financing the Russian revolution in 1917, which had enabled them to bring into existence the adverse conditions being experienced throughout the world at that time.[7]

Hitler reminded Lord Londonderry of the millions of Christians who had been ruthlessly slaughtered in the Communized countries since October 1917, and argued that the men responsible could not be considered as anything other than international gangsters.

The final item of discussion was the manner in which Stalin had been instructed to turn Spain into a Communist dictatorship. The whole pattern of international intrigue was laid bare. The manner in which Germany had been enabled to secretly re-arm, the way French politics were controlled by Grand Orient Freemasonry,[8] the manner in which Britain had been persuaded to disarm while her potential enemies were being re-armed.

According to the Germans, it would be impossible for the world to enjoy peace and prosperity as long as those who directed the World Revolutionary Movement insisted on fomenting wars to create conditions favourable for revolutionary action. They argued that both international Communism and political Zionism had to be stopped and the movements ended at once, or another war was inevitable, because the Secret Powers pulling the strings were determined to reach their ultimate objectives.

Hitler was a great orator, and my informant claimed that he ended the discussions with a plea that Lord Londonderry return to England and persuade the British government to join in the suggested alliance with Germany, "because I am convinced that the British Empire and the Roman Catholic Church are both universal institutions, the continuance of which is absolutely essential as bulwarks for the preservation of law and order throughout the world in the future."

What has been said here of Hitler is so absolutely foreign to the general idea that the following historical facts and documents are quoted to support what has been said:

Lord Londonderry returned to London following the conference and made his report to the British cabinet. On February 21st, 1936, he wrote Herr Von Ribbentrop. He referred to the conversations he had had. The letter reads in part:

> They (Hitler and Goering) forget that here (in England) we have not experienced the devastation of a revolution for several centuries... In relation to the Jews...we do not like persecution, but in addition to this, there is the material feeling that you are taking on a tremendous force which is capable of having repercussions all over the world...it is possible to trace their participation in most of these international disturbances which have created so much havoc in different countries, but on the other hand, one can find many Jews strongly ranged on the other side who have done their best, with the wealth at their disposal, and also by their influence, to counteract those malevolent and mischievous activities of fellow Jews.[9]

After Hitler realized his efforts to bring about an alliance between Germany and Britain were hopeless, he leaned further and further to the "Right." He became convinced that it was impossible for an individual, groups of individuals, or even a single nation to break the power and influence the international bankers exercised over the so-called democratic nations by reason of their financial control and the encumbrance of their national debts.

In July 1936, the Spanish Civil War broke out; Hitler, Mussolini and Franco were drawn closer together. It was the fact that Franco had to start a Civil War in Spain to prevent Spain being Communized without a struggle, that caused Hitler to round out his boundaries and concentrate military power on his borders. He was determined to make sure that Stalin, who he knew was only the agent of the international bankers appointed to rule over Russia, would not extend his dictatorship over other European countries. Every step Hitler took in the direction was termed "acts of aggression" by the anti-Fascist press. Hitler explained such moves as "preventive" wars or occupations. He stated that he was primarily concerned in "preventing" Stalin establishing his sphere of influence on or about the 40th parallel of latitude in Europe. If he was allowed to, Germany, Britain, and other northern European countries would be entrapped like flies in a spider's web.

Hitler had not only failed to bring about the British alliance, but he had earned the enmity of the Nazi War Lords who advocated totalitarian methods for solving the very complicated and dangerous problem. They did not want an alliance with England. They did not want to see Christianity flourish. They did not agree with Hitler's "preventive" measures. They didn't agree with anything Hitler did to hinder their plans to wage "Total

War," first against Russia, then against Britain and France. The "hard core" of the pagan Nazi War Lords demanded that Hitler take offensive action, as the best defence against gradual encroachment by the Communist underground and Stalin's armed forces. When Hitler refused to go all the way with them, they decided to get rid of him. The first attempt was made on his life. The Nazi War Lords next tried to weaken the control he had gained over the German people.

They launched a campaign to sell their Aryan Pagan ideology to the German people. They taught the superiority of the Aryan Race. They advocated war to establish the undisputed supremacy of the Aryan State. They made it a fundamental principle that all men and women of Aryan blood should give unlimited obedience to the Head of the Aryan State and acknowledge no mortal as above him. This campaign was attributed to Hitler, and the anti-Fascist press throughout the world cried to high heaven that Hitler was a pagan, and a Black-shirted totalitarian-minded Nazi War Lord. Thus started the clashes between both Catholic and Protestant clergy with the state. The clergy condemned the Nazi ideology on the grounds that those who preached it were preaching the deification of men.

The Nazi leaders charged that both Catholic and Protestant clergy were breaking the laws and defying the authority of the state. The Roman Catholic and Protestant bishops replied by stating that the extreme Nazi doctrines were antagonistic and contrary to the Divine Plan of Creation. The Nazi leaders countered with the argument that the Church had no right to interfere in matters of state.

Hitler tried to pacify the clergy by banning the Grand Orient Lodges, which were known to be the headquarters of the Aryan extremists throughout Germany. The Nazi leaders rendered this step abortive by changing them over to "Orders of German Chivalry."

Hitler, in order to maintain a united front against Communism, tried to pacify the Nazis by issuing an edict that any clergyman preaching against the laws of the state, or questioning its supremacy, would be subjected to the full process of the law and, if found guilty, would suffer the penalties provided for such "crimes." This situation provides another example of how the forces of evil divided two powerful forces which were both combating a common enemy.

The anti-Fascist propaganda made the most of the disagreement between Hitler and the Pope. It is true that Pope Pius XI denounced Naziism in no uncertain terms in the Encyclical of March 14th, 1937 "on the condition of the Church in Germany." He told Roman Catholics that he had weighed every word of the encyclical in the scales of truth and clarity. In reference to the Nazi conception of the superiority of the Aryan race and the supremacy of the state, he said:

> While it is true that the *race* or the *people*; the state or a form of government; the representatives of a civil power, or other fundamental elements of human society have an essential and honourable place in the natural order, nevertheless, if anyone detaches them from this scale of earthly values and exalts them as the supreme form and standard of all things, even of religious values, deifying them with idolatrous worship, he perverts and falsifies the order of things created and constituted by God, and is far from true faith in God, and from a conception of life in conformity therewith... Our

God is a personal God, transcendent, Almighty, Infinite, Perfect. One in the Trinity of Persons and three in the unity of the Divine Essence; creator of the universe; Lord; King; and ultimate purpose of the history of the world; who does not suffer and can never suffer any other divinity besides Him...Only superficial minds can fall into the error of speaking of a National God, of a National Religion, of foolishly attempting to restrict within the narrow confines of a single race that God, who is the Creator of the world, the King and Law-Giver of all peoples, before Whose greatness the nations are as small as drops of water in a bucket (Isaiah XL-15).

In a pastoral letter dated August 19th, 1938, the bishops of Germany struck out boldly against Nazi ideology. The letter says that the attitude of the Nazi towards the Christian religion in Germany is in *open contradiction with the Fuehrer's* assertions:[10] "What is aimed at is not merely the checking of the growth of the Catholic Church but the wiping out of Christianity and the setting up in its place of a religion which is utterly alien to the Christian belief in One True God." The letter goes on to point out that the Nazi attack on Dr. Sproll, the Protestant bishop of Rottenburg, clearly proved that the "persecution" is directed not only against the Catholic Church but against the whole Christian idea as such: "An attempt is being made to get rid of the Christian God in order to replace Him with a 'German God.' " What does "a German God" mean? Is He different from the God of other peoples? If so, then there must be a special God for each nation and for each people... This is the same as saying "There is no God."[11]

What happened in Germany in 1936 has happened in other countries since. The leaders of "Black" Naziism joined forces with the leaders of "Red" Communism in an attack on both the Christian religion and the British Empire. The totalitarian-minded Nazi War Lords initiated their followers into the German Grand Orient Lodges, using the ancient pagan rites and rituals handed down from the time the barbaric Aryan tribes and the Huns swept over Europe. The totalitarian-minded men who direct international Communism initiate their leaders into the Grand Orient Lodges of other countries using the ancient Cabalistic Rites of Illuminism. To understand this situation, it is necessary to recall that Jews have never, under any circumstances, been admitted into the German Grand Orient Lodges since 1785, when the papers found on the body of the Courier of the Illuminati, who was killed by lightning at Ratisbon, were handed over by the police to the Bavarian authorities, and proved that the Grand Orient Lodges in France were being used as the secret headquarters of the Jewish-inspired revolutionary movement.

When complicated situations such as these develop, it can be understood why the Roman Catholic Church has taken such a definite stand against "Black" Naziism, while tolerating the less extreme forms of Fascism (i.e. anti-Communism) as practiced by Franco in Spain. It also explains why Cardinal Mindszenty collaborated with allegedly Fascist leaders who attempted to overthrow Communist domination in his country.

Franco has consistently refused to go off the deep end. He refused to support German Naziism in World War Two simply because the extreme Nazi Pagan War Lords had become all powerful in Germany. In Germany, Italy, France, Spain, and Japan, millions of citizens, peaceful by inclination and charitable at heart, found themselves in the position of having to decide whether they became actively Pro-Fascist or Pro-Communist. They were given Hobson's Choice. They usually picked what they considered the lesser of two evils. They were immediately labeled accordingly.

By diabolical intrigue, the nations of the world were being lined up for World War Two. The Russian dictatorship was secretly re-arming the German armies. The Italian dictatorship, under Mussolini, was secretly building a huge navy of submarines to German specification and design. These submarines were tested out under conditions of actual warfare during the Spanish Civil War. These tests proved the German designed submarines were, in 1936, practically immune to British anti-submarine weapons including *Asdic*. The British government was informed in regard to this matter. Captain Max Morton, R.N., had emphasized the warnings being given by evading all the anti-submarine devices used for the protection of the British Mediterranean fleet while it was at anchor. He actually got into the guarded harbour and, in theory, sank half a dozen capital ships as they rode to their anchors. This act of Captain Max Morton brought him condemnation from the British Civil Sea Lords instead of praise and recognition. His promotion was held up, and he was silenced. He was not allowed to take a very active part in British naval affairs until 1940. When German U-boats threatened to starve Britain into submission, he was asked to take over direction of the anti-submarine Battle of the Atlantic.

The British government was warned as early as 1930 that German-designed submarines had dived deeper than 500 feet, thus rendering obsolete all depth-charges then in use. They were warned that Asdic gear then in use was also obsolete. But they refused to heed the warnings. The *Secret Powers* were using their agents within the British government to weaken the British war potential, while they were secretly strengthening that of Germany. When the war broke out, Britain did not have one single modern anti-submarine ocean escort vessel in service. As a result she lost 75 percent of her merchant ships and over 40,000 seamen before the tide turned in her favour in April of 1943.[12]

Hitler antagonized the international bankers when he announced his financial policy and monetary reform programme. He persuaded Italy, Spain, and Japan to back him in his determination to challenge the power of the Cartels and Monopolies financed and controlled by the international bankers, particularly their "Brain-child"—the Bank of International Settlements. The German Reich abrogated the clause in the constitution which made Dr. Hans Luther, the president of the Reichsbank, a permanent fixture. Until the change was made, the president of the Reichsbank could not be removed without his own consent and a majority vote of the board of the Bank of International Settlements.

Since the Great War, the international bankers had set up twenty-six central banks. They were modeled after the Federal Reserve Banks in the United States, which had been established in 1913 according to the theories of Mr. Paul Warburg, the German who had gone to America in 1907 and become a partner in Kuhn-Loeb & Co. of New York.

Mr. Paul Warburg's creation of 1913 had been steadily attempting to set up a "Central Banking Organization" which would acknowledge no authority on this planet as above it. Hitler knew that if Warburg and associates had their way, the Bank of International Settlements would become as autocratic as the Bank of England is in regard to British National Affairs and Foreign Policy. Politicians and statesmen were being asked to believe that this banker's dream would stabilize the banking system of the world. In this contention they were absolutely correct. The catch is that with the realization of this dream, all hope of freedom and plenty for the individual and private industry would automatically disappear. The citizens of the world would have the same financial security as the criminal who enjoys social security behind bars. Hitler decided to take a definite stand against this process of reducing the people of the world to financial slavery, and he refused to allow Germany to be merged into the league of Monopolist States, secretly controlled by agents of the Illuminati.

After Paul Warburg's Federal Reserve System had been in operation three years (1913 to 1916) President Woodrow Wilson [Rosicrucian, bought and paid for by the money power, who signed the Federal Reserve Act, who by hook and crook and lies dragged the US into WWI, after four years of his own presidency, during his electioneering] summed up the economic situation in the United States of America as follows:

> A great industrial nation is controlled by its system of credits. Our system of credit is concentrated. The growth of the nation, therefore, and all our activities are in the hands of a few men... We have come to be one of the worst ruled, one of the most completely controlled and dominated governments, in the civilized world... no longer a government by conviction and the free vote of the majority, but a government by the opinion and duress of small groups of dominant men.

That is actually what modern so-called democracy really means.[13]

When the countries of the Western World were plunged into the economic depression of the 1930s, out of which only another war could lift them, President Franklin D. Roosevelt [Marxist, fomenter of WWII] said, "Sixty families in America control the wealth of the nation... One-third of the nation's population is ill-housed, ill-fed, and ill-clad... Twenty per cent of the men working on W.P.A. projects are in such an advanced state of malnutrition that they cannot do a day's work... I intend to drive the money changers from the Temple." [He did not drive any of them anywhere, but introduced the new deal.] Roosevelt knew that unless he could drive the international bankers out of the modern *temple of international finance,* only a full-scale World War could relieve the chronic condition of financial constipation they had brought about on an international scale by withdrawing currency, restricting credits, and other financial manipulations. *They grew richer while everyone outside their select circle grew steadily poorer.* But soon Roosevelt was docile.

President Roosevelt found he couldn't break, or even curb, the power of the Illuminati. He was forced to lead his country into war against the only countries that held firmly to the very policy he had so rashly announced soon after he was elected to office. And, after he had grown haggard and grey doing the bidding of the men whose money and influence had placed him in the office of president of the United States, he allegedly died in the home of the richest and most powerful man in the United States, Bernard Baruch—a man above all others who, for the past forty years at least, has sat quietly in the background, but was acknowledged the "king" over all American bankers, and undoubtedly one of the select few who has been "The Secret Power" behind the scenes of international affairs in our time. If this were not so, why do Winston Churchill and his son visit him so often? Why did Winston Churchill make his momentous announcements regarding his attitude towards political Zionism and peaceful coexistence immediately after his visit to Bernard Baruch in 1954?

It is unfortunate, but true, that today "democracy" is a very deceptive word. It is used to describe all countries which are in fact a *moneylender's heaven.* Today, countries which are termed "democratic" follow a monetary system devised by the international bankers, under which currency originates in debt to groups of private individuals who manipulate the price levels of different countries and use money as a stable value facilitating the exchange of *real wealth*. Britain, France, and the United States are termed "democratic" countries only because they are linked together in debt to the international moneylenders. The Communist countries also call themselves "democratic" republics and they are entitled to do so as long as they also are controlled by the same international financial groups.

When the Axis Powers in Europe refused to place themselves in usury to the international bankers, they placed themselves in exactly the same category as the small independent store keeper is in relation to the big chain-store organizations and business combines and monopolies. They were given the option of joining the big "Happy Family"...or else. In the case of an independent store keeper, if he refuses to "see the light," he is put out of business by systematically applied pressure of unfair competition. In the case of nations who refuse to "play-ball," they are doomed to suffer war or revolution. There is no mercy shown to the nations whose leaders refuse to bow down and worship at the feet of Mammon. There is no consideration given to nations which refuse to place themselves in usury to the High Priests of the God of Mammon. All must pay the tribute demanded of them...or else.

World War Two was started in order to enable the Illuminati *to finally rid themselves of the barriers of caste and creed and prejudice. Their ideas regarding a new civilization had to be built through a world at war*. In proof of the above statement, a portion of the broadcast Sir Anthony Eden addressed to America on September 11th, 1939, is quoted. He said, "Can we finally rid Europe of the barriers of caste and creed and prejudice? ... Our new civilization must be built through a world at war. But our new civilization will be built just the same." What utter rot. Wars are destructive, not constructive."

From 1930 onwards, informed and influential Britishers had been doing everything within their power to try to prevent England and her allies from being inveigled into another war with Germany. As was to be expected, every one of these people was attacked by the anti-Fascist agencies as being "black" totalitarian-minded Nazis.

Some of the British who opposed Communism—and also the continued subservience of the British government to the international bankers—openly declared themselves in favour of the Fascist principles as expounded by Franco and Hitler. This group was led by Sir Oswald Mosley. Others, mostly statesmen, retired admirals, and generals, worked quietly trying to inform politicians and members of the government regarding the purpose behind the international intrigue.

The anti-Semitic movement started in England early in 1921, after Mr. Victor E. Marsden returned from Russia where he had been imprisoned by the Bolsheviks. Mr. Marsden had been correspondent in Russia for the London *Morning Post* since before 1914. When Mr. Marsden returned to England, he was in possession of the document which Professor Sergei Nilus had published in Russian in 1905 under the title *Jewish Peril*. Professor Nilus claimed the original documents had been obtained from a woman who had stolen them from a wealthy international Jew when he returned to her apartments, after addressing top-level executives of the Grand Orient Lodges in Paris in 1901.

While Mr. Marsden was translating the documents, he received a warning that if he persisted in publishing the book he would die. Mr. Marsden published his translation of the documents under the title *Protocols of the Learned Elders of Zion* and he did die under suspicious circumstances a few years afterwards.

Following the publication of the book by the Britons Publishing Society, Mr. Marsden was denounced internationally as a bare-faced, anti-Semitic liar. The book caused one of the greatest controversies the world has ever known. My own research has caused me to believe that the documents published by professor Nilus in Russia in 1905 as *Jewish Peril* and by Mr. Marsden in England in 1921 as *Protocols of the Learned Elders of Zion* are the long-range plans of the Illuminati which were explained by Amschel Rothschild to his associates in Frankfurt in 1773. Rothschild was not addressing rabbis and elders. He was addressing bankers, industrialists, scientists, economists, etc. *Therefore to charge this diabolical conspiracy as a crime against the whole Jewish people and their religious leaders is unjust.* I am supported in this opinion by one of the highest-ranking intelligence Officers in the British Service. He studied the matter in Russia, Germany, and England.

That the document which fell into the hands of Professor Nilus had been used as material for lectures to instruct leaders of the WRM cannot be doubted, because in addition to the original outline of the conspiracy there are additional remarks which explain how the plot had been put into effect, and how Darwinism, Marxism, and Nietzche-ism had been used since 1773. Mention is also made saying how it was intended to use political Zionism to serve the purpose of the WRM in the future.

The term *Agentur* contained in the document would seem to indicate an individual, a group, a race, a nation, a creed, or any other agency that could be used as a *tool* or an *instrument* to further the Long Range Plan of the Illuminati for ultimate world domination.

Regardless of its origin, no person who has read it can deny that the trend of world events has followed the programme suggested in the document from 1773 to date. No one can be other than amazed at the deadly accuracy of the forecast made in the document.

To give only one glaring instance of many: The document outlines how Zionism shall be aided in reaching its objectives. Theodore Herzl was the founder of the Zionist Movement. He is recorded as saying, "From the first moment I entered the Zionist movement my eyes were directed towards England, because I saw by reason of the general conditions there the Archimedean point where the lever could be applied." Then again, "When we sink [*we* referring to Zionists] we become a revolutionary proletariat; the subordinate officers of the revolutionary party; when we rise, there rises also our terrible power of the purse."[14]

More amazing still, and getting back to near the time the document came into professor Nilus's possession, Max Nordeu, addressing the Zionist Congress held in Basel, Switzerland, August 1903, is quoted as saying: "Let me tell you the following words as if I were showing you the rungs of a ladder leading upward and upward... The Zionist Congress; The English Uganda proposition; The future World War; The Peace Conference where, with the help of England, a free and Jewish Palestine will be created." The fact to remember is this: these men who were outstanding leaders of the Zionist Movement probably spoke in all sincerity. History proves, however, that the small select group who have in the past, and still do, comprise "The Secret Power" behind the World

Revolutionary Movement, have used both Communism and Zionism to further their own selfish totalitarian ambitions.

The contents of the document translated by Mr. Marsden detail the "Party Line" as followed by the Bolshevik revolutionary leaders under the leadership of Lenin and Stalin, just as it details the policy followed by the leaders of the Zionist movement. Lord Sydenham read the document and then remarked, "The most striking characteristic...is knowledge of a rare kind, embracing the widest field...knowledge upon which prophesies now fulfilled are based."

Henry Ford studied this document. He had many outstanding and learned men study it also. He published a book of amazing disclosures, all of which add up to the sum total that the document details the plan by which a small group of international financiers have used—and still use—Communism, Zionism, and all other agencies they can control, regardless of whether they be Jewish or Gentile, to further their own secret totalitarian ambitions.

Mr. Henry Ford was interviewed in regard to the document by a reporter of the *New York World*. His comments were published February 17th, 1921. He said, "The only statement I care to make about the *Protocols* is that they fit in with what is going on. They are sixteen years old, and they have fitted the world situation up to this time. They fit it now."

Mr. Ford made his statement thirty-four years ago and what he said then is equally applicable today. This should prove to any unbiased person that the document is a genuine copy of the originally conceived plan which has been put into practice. It has almost achieved the purpose for which it was intended.

One may well ask, "How long are the people going to stand for such a state of affairs?" Revolution is not the answer. Revolution only plays into the hands of the powers of evil. Only the indignant voice of the masses of all free nations can insist that their elected representatives end the totalitarian plans of the moneylenders before they reach their goal.

From 1921 to 1927, Mr. Marsden remained in the employ of the *Morning Post*. He had many friends, but he had made powerful enemies. In 1927, he was chosen to accompany the Prince of Wales on his "Tour of the Empire." It is very unlikely that Mr. Marsden failed to avail himself of this opportunity to inform His Royal Highness in regard to the document and the manner in which international financiers were involved in international intrigue and the Communist and Zionist movements. When the Prince of Wales returned from his tour of the Empire he was a very changed man. He was no longer "a gay young blade." He was much more mature, and had assumed the serious role of "Good Will Ambassador of the British Empire." It may be pure coincidence, but Mr. Marsden, whose health had improved greatly during his travels abroad, took suddenly ill *the day after he arrived back in England and died a few days later*. It reminds one of what Mr. E. Scudder wrote regarding the death of Mirabeau in his book *The Diamond Necklace*. "King Louis of France was not ignorant of the fact that Mirabeau had been poisoned." Mirabeau died because he had told the king of France who the real instigators of the French Revolution were.

Everyone who has had the privilege of knowing the present Duke of Windsor knows how deeply he was affected by his experiences at "The Front" during the 1914-1918 war.

He insisted on spending a great deal of time in the Front Lines cheering and encouraging the troops. He won their admiration and loyalty, and in return he loved and respected his future subjects who fought so well and died so bravely.

After the tour of the Empire, His Royal Highness took a great interest in social and economic problems. He visited the coal-mining districts and entered the miners' homes. He chatted with miners and their families regarding their problems. He wanted to dispense with many of the frills which encumber royal ceremonial proceedings. He had the audacity to disagree when statesmen and politicians tendered him advice he knew was unsound. He dared to express his opinions in regard to Foreign Affairs. He was alert and opposed to any proposed government policy which might play into the hands of "The Secret Powers," and lead the country into another war.

After he was proclaimed King on January 20th, 1936, he took his responsibilities even more seriously. He didn't intend to be just *"another king"* on the international chessboard, to be moved here and there at the will of the Powers-behind-the-throne, until he had been manoeuvred into a position of stalemate or checkmate. It became quite evident that he had a mind and a will of his own. A *king* with his knowledge and characteristics can be a serious obstacle to the men who are determined to have affairs of State managed according to their plans. He had to be got rid of.

From the time he became associated with Mr. Marsden be had been subjected to a modern version of *L'Infamie*. A whispering campaign of slander hinted that he was "wild" and inclined to licentious conduct. He was accused of leaning to the *"Right"* and being associated with Sir Oswald Mosley's Fascist movement.[15]

When his friendship with Mrs. Wally Simpson was discovered, the full power of the "leftist" press was turned loose on them and, regardless of his position, the vilest insinuations were made, and the worst possible construction placed on their relationship. This was exactly the kind of situation his enemies could use to further their own unscrupulous plans. The Prime Minister of Great Britain was given his orders. In 1936, Mr. Baldwin carried out the mandate in regard to King Edward VIII's abdication in exactly the same way Messrs Lloyd George, Churchill and Balfour had done in regard to the Palestine Mandate in 1919.

King Edward was manoeuvred into a position in which he either had to make Mrs. Simpson his "Morganatic" wife, and lose the love and affection of his subjects, or he had to abdicate and marry her. He took the only course a gentleman could take under the circumstances.

The reader may wonder why the document over which there is so much controversy cropped up in 1901. The answer is to be found in the fact that the artificially created depression in 1893 brought about conditions favourable to war. The international bankers met in London to consolidate their position, and work out the details for the Boer War. They considered this war necessary in order to obtain control of the African gold fields and diamond mines. The Jameson Raid took place as scheduled January 1st, 1896. This led to the most unjustifiable war the British have ever fought. Winston Churchill hot-footed it to Africa to act as observer; officially he was a war correspondent. A great deal regarding this period of history remains to be written.

The details leading to the Spanish-American War had to be worked out. This war gave the American bankers control over sugar production in Cuba. More important still was the business that had to be transacted in regard to the war scheduled to take place between Russia and Japan in 1904. This business was very complicated. Matters had to be so arranged that while the Rothschilds financed the Russians, Kuhn-Loeb and Co. of New York financed the Japanese. An understanding had to be reached by which both groups made money while the Russian Empire was weakened and made ready for the Menshevist revolution scheduled to take place in 1905.

While the international bankers met in the financial district of London, the leaders of the World Revolutionary Movement met in the slum-district of the same city. Lenin received his orders. He was told how he should manage the various revolutionary groups so that *independent* action on their part would not seriously interfere with the overall plans of those who directed the WRM. It has been proved that the Directors of the WRM used the heads of the Grand Orient Lodges in France, and other countries, to further their revolutionary plans. So it is reasonable to suppose that an agent was sent from London to Paris in 1900 or 1901 to instruct the top-level executives of the Grand Orient Lodges in regard to the part they were to play to bring about the programme of wars and revolutions agreed upon, in exactly the same way they had sent the agent who was killed in Ratisbon, from Frankfurt to Paris in 1785. It is just another illustration of how and why history repeats itself.

---

[1] This military plan had been in existence since before 1914 and was reported to the Allied Governments fighting World War One by intelligence officers of both the British and American armed forces. The plan is explained in detail in *Hell's Angels of the Deep* and *Check Mate in the North* by W.G. Carr.

[2] This statement and others of a similar nature prove that Hitler never had accepted or agreed with the extreme Nazi War-Lords' Long-Range Plan for World domination by Military conquest.

[3] Once again, rabid anti-Semitism shows itself, and yet history proves that the International conspirators have used every race and creed to serve their own secret and selfish ambitions.

[4] Most of this evidence is reproduced in *The Palestine Plot* by B. Jensen, printed by John McKinley, 11-15 King Street, Perth, Scotland.

[5] The book *Coningsby* was published in 1844 just before Karl Marx published *The Communist Manifesto*. At that time several revolutions were being planned and took place immediately after Karl Marx's book appeared in print.

[6] Ribbentrop was evidently quoting from an article in the *Wiener Freie Presse*, published December 14th, 1912 by the late Walter Rathenau in which he said, "Three hundred men, each of whom is known to all the others, govern the fate of the European Continent and they elect their successors from their own entourage." These are the Illuminati.

[7] Most countries of the world were mired deep in economic depression.

[8] Hitler closed all Grand Orient Lodges in Germany.

[9] Quoted from the *Evening Standard*, London; dated April 28, 1936. For further particulars regarding Lord Londonderry's conversations with Hitler, Goering, and Von Ribbentrop, read *Ourselves and Germany* published by Lord Londonderry.

[10] For the full text of these letters read, *The Rulers of Russia* by Rev. Fr. Fahey, pp. 64-70.

11. The opening paragraph of this letter confirmed the opinion reached by the author: the extreme Nazi plan was at variance with Hitler's plan.

12. The author personally informed both the Canadian Chief of Naval Staff, the First Lord of the Admiralty and other government officials regarding this sorry state of affairs.

13. For further particulars regarding international finance read Wealth, Virtual Wealth and Debt by Professor Soddy, pp. 290 and onward.

14. Theodore Herzl in *A Jewish State* (*Judenstaat*) re-quoted from p. 45 of *The Palestine Plot* by B. Jensen.

15. As recently as November 1954, this old slander regarding the Duke of Window's connection with Fascism was revived. He was accused in the Press of having given secret information to German officials regarding allied defences and plans in 1936. This he vigorously denied.

CHAPTER SIXTEEN

World War Two Breaks Out

After King Edward *VIII* abdicated, many well-educated Britishers, including members of parliament and retired naval and military officers of high rank, carried on a strenuous campaign to try to convince the leaders of the British government of the truth regarding "The International Bankers' Conspiracy." Amongst these were Capt. *A.H.M.* Ramsay and Admiral Sir Barry Domvile, K.B.E., C.B., C.M.G. Captain Ramsay was educated at Eton College and Sandhurst Military College. He served with His Majesty's Guards in France from 1914 to 1916, when he was seriously wounded. He was appointed to Regimental H.Q. after recovering from his wounds. Later he was transferred to the British War Office. He served with the British War Mission in Paris until the war ended. He was elected to parliament in 1931 as member for Midlothian-Peeblesshire and served in that capacity until 1945.

Admiral Sir Barry Domvile had a brilliant naval career. He earned the reputation of being one of Britain's better Gunnery Officers.

He started his naval service 1894 as a midshipman in sail and steam driven warships. Because of his ability, he received accelerated promotion and was made lieutenant in 1898. In 1906, he was awarded the gold medal of the Royal United Services Institution. He was placed in command of destroyers in 1910. When World War I appeared unavoidable, he was appointed assistant secretary to the Committee of Imperial Defence. After hostilities started, he was appointed to the Harwich Striking Force, consisting of light cruisers and destroyers under Admiral Sir Reginald Tyrwhitt. He commanded seven destroyers and light cruisers, all of which earned enviable reputations as Fighting Ships. He was made Flag Captain to Admiral Tyrwhitt in 1917 and served in that capacity until the end of the war.[1] His postwar service included Director of Naval Intelligence; president of the Royal Naval College, Greenwich; and vice-admiral commanding the War College. He retired in 1936 with the rank of full Admiral. During the years 1920-1923, because of his special ability and varied war experience, he was first assistant director and then director of the Plan (Policy) Division of the Admiralty Naval Staff. In this capacity he attended a number of conferences at Paris, Brussels, Spa, San Remo, and the Washington Naval Conference.

Both these ex-officers—one army, the other navy—suspected the Bolshevik revolution in Russia had been plotted and planned, financed and directed, by men who considered that the liquidation of the British Empire was essential before they could achieve undisputed control of the wealth, natural resources, and manpower of the entire world.

Both these gentlemen have been frank to admit that until 1935 they had failed to identify those who constituted the "Secret Power" behind the world revolutionary movement and international affairs.

In 1933, by reason of their studies and research, they reached a decision that the leaders of World Jewry, headed by the international Jewish bankers, were the "Secret Power" behind the World Revolutionary Movement. They became convinced that these men used the wealth they possessed to purchase sufficient power to influence international affairs in such a manner as to bring nations into conflict with each other. They also reached the conclusion that the motive behind the Long-Range Plan was to establish the Messianic Age, so that International Jewry, with a central government in Palestine, could enforce their totalitarian ideology upon the peoples of the entire world. With this latter conclusion I agree. As the reader knows, I admit going through the same period *i.e.*, 1907 to 1933, in doubt and uncertainty, but in 1939 I became convinced, after the way the Jews had been "purged" by Stalin in Russia, and used to start abortive revolutions in other countries, and then abandoned to their fate, that the men who constitute the "Secret Power" behind national and international affairs were the Illuminati who used Zionism and anti-Semitism, Communism and Fascism, Socialism and selfish Capitalism to further their secret plans to bring about a One-World Government which they intended to control in exactly the same way as they had controlled Russia, in the person of Lenin, after October 1917. A worldwide dictatorship is the only type of government which could, by police rule, enforce their edicts upon the people, and thus assure peace. If there is only ONE STATE governed by ONE DICTATOR, there can't be any wars. This is pure logic, because to have a dispute—a quarrel, a fight, a revolution, or a war—there must of necessity be two parties, holding opposing ideas and opinions, which they intend to make the other accept by force of arms, if argument and negotiation fail. Furthermore, my studies and research convinced me that from the time of Christ right down to the present day, the men who have been the "Secret Power" behind national and international intrigue have always used their wealth *illegally* to obtain the *power* and influence to put their secret plots and plans into effect. They have used usury, bribery, corruption, graft, illegal methods of traffic and trade, slavery, assassinations, wars, revolutions, prostitution, drugs, liquor, and any and every other form of licentiousness and vice to bribe, blackmail, or in other ways force unwilling humans to do their bidding. These "tools," be they Jew or Gentile, Freemason or otherwise, have been, without exception, liquidated by one method or another if, after serving their purpose, they were considered to know too much.

Considering these facts, I became convinced that the top conspirators did not belong to any one race or nation; they were "Agents of Satan," doing his will, and serving his purpose, here on earth. The one and only purpose of the Devil is to win the souls of men away from the Almighty God. The men who plot and plan wars and revolutions have done a great deal to bring about a Godless world. This reasoning enabled me to understand the evil genius of these men. They could not move nearer to their totalitarian-materialistic goal without fomenting wars and revolutions. They must of necessity destroy the civilization founded in accordance with the Divine Plan of Creation before they could impose their evil totalitarian ideology upon the peoples of the world.

Both Captain Ramsay and Admiral Domvile tried from 1936 to 1939 to prevent Britain becoming engaged in war with Germany, because they considered "international Jewry" intended to arrange a war in which the German and British Empires would destroy each other. The people who survived could be easily subjugated by Communism afterwards in exactly the same way Russia had been communized.

I agree that World War II was engineered by the Illuminati who used anti-Communism, anti-Fascism, anti-Semitism and anti-everything else to further their evil Long Range Plans and secret totalitarian ambitions. I arrived at the conclusion that it was a fatal mistake to be anti anything but anti-evil. I believe the only way to defeat the diabolical international conspiracy is to educate as many people as possible in regard to the truth, and convince them that they have been used as "Pawns in the Game" by these evil men.

Captain Ramsay tried hard to convince Mr. Neville Chamberlain that it was against the best interests of the British Empire to allow the international conspirators to involve Britain in war with Germany. He was right. He did not *convince* the British Prime Minister, but he at least impressed him sufficiently so that when he went to Munich he compromised with Hitler and returned to England waving exuberantly his famous umbrella, and a paper which he said was an agreement "guaranteeing peace in our time."

Immediately after this announcement was made, the Press, controlled by the international bankers, started an anti-Fascist campaign of hate. The controlled Press damned Chamberlain as "an old woman willing to buy peace at any price." They lampooned him with his umbrella. They accused him of being pro-Fascist. Their agents in Moscow burned Chamberlain in effigy in the public squares. The British public was never allowed to know the difference between Pagan Aryan Naziism, and Christian Anti-Communistic Fascism. According to the Press, German and Italian Fascism are both black-pagan atheistic ideologies and totalitarian in purpose. Few people understand the difference between Naziism and Fascism or Communism and Socialism.

Space does not permit recording all the details of the intrigue put into effect by the evil group who were determined to bring about war between Britain and Germany. In my opinion, Hitler's anti-Semitic policy was wrong, but throwing Britain and Germany at each other's throats wasn't going to save the Jews residing in Germany, Poland, and other countries from persecution and death. Forcing the countries into a war enabled the anti-Semitic hatreds of the Nazis to be vented on the Jews by direct action on a tremendous scale, with a hideous ferocity only witnessed previously during a *revolutionary* "Reign of Terror." If those who claim the way was brought about by the international Jews, and not the Illuminati, (who don't give a damn for the Jews or anybody else for that matter) would stop and think, they will realize that by fomenting World War II, those responsible condemned a great many innocent Jewish people to death, while most of the Jewish revolutionary Communists escaped death by going "underground," and later obtained illegal entrance into Palestine, the U.S.A., Canada, and other countries. If peace had continued, the German anti-Semitic feelings could never have reached the extremes they reached during the war. A peaceful solution could have been found for the problem. But NO! The Long-Range Plan of the International Illuminati called for the destruction of the British, the German Empires, and the *Jews who were not actively Communistic and therefore not their "Tools."*

Captain Ramsay had promised Mr. Neville Chamberlain that he would produce documentary evidence to prove a conspiracy existed to force Britain into declaring war on Germany. This evidence consisted of secret coded cables which had passed between Mr. Winston Churchill and President Roosevelt, unknown to Mr. Chamberlain, at that time the Prime Minister. Captain Ramsay offered to obtain copies of these documents to prove that the International Bankers were determined to bring about World War II for the purpose of bringing the rest of the European nations under Communist control. The Illuminati control both.

Tyler Kent was the coding officer who had coded and decoded these secret documents in the American Embassy in London. Anna Wolkoff was his assistant. Like Gouzenko they felt sick at the thought of the world being plunged into another Global War to further the ambitions of a few totalitarian-minded men, whose wealth compelled even presidents and top-level statesmen to do their will. The same conditions existed in 1938 as existed in Paris in 1919, prior to the signing of the Treaty of Versailles.

Tyler Kent, like many other people, knew Captain Ramsay was suspicious of "an international Jewish conspiracy." He knew Captain Ramsay was trying to prevent the war. When Captain Ramsay told him Mr. Chamberlain would prevent such a conspiracy from being put into effect if he was given authentic documentary evidence to prove such an international conspiracy did actually exist, Tyler Kent offered to show Captain Ramsay the damning documents in his flat at 47 Gloucester Place, London.

The international conspirators had, however, been busy. In March of 1939 they had tricked Mr. Chamberlain *into signing a guarantee to protect Poland from German aggression by presenting him with a false report to the effect that a 48-hour ultimatum had been delivered by Germany to the Poles.* The facts are that the German government *did not issue any 48-hour ultimatum.* The German note set forth reasonable suggestions for a "peaceful" solution of the problems created by the Treaty of Versailles in regard to the Polish Corridor and Danzig.

History will prove that the only reason the Polish government ignored the German note was because agents of the international conspirators advised its leading statesmen *that the British guarantee assured them against German aggression.*

Month after month went by and still Poland ignored the German note completely. Meanwhile the anti-German Press speeded up its torrents of abuse against Hitler because he had dared to defy the power of the international Money-Barons. Hitler had earned their hatred by his independent financial policy and monetary reforms. The public was made to believe that Hitler's word couldn't be trusted. The public was told after his *"Putsch"* into Sudetenland, that Hitler had said he "intended to make no further demands." It was made to appear by the press that the German note to Poland suggesting a "peaceful" solution to the problems created by the Treaty of Versailles was "another demand," and therefore, "a broken promise."

History proves it was no such thing. What Hitler had said was that *he would make no further demands AFTER he had rectified the injustices inflicted upon the German people by those who had dictated the terms and conditions incorporated into the Treaty of Versailles.* That is a horse of a very different colour. It is a typical example of how a half-truth is far more dangerous than a direct lie.

Hitler's promise was qualified. He promised he would make no further demands after the problems involving Sudetenland, part of Czechoslovakia, the Polish Corridor and Danzig, had been solved.

The German grievances were real and justified. By the Treaty of Versailles, the Polish Corridor had separated East Prussia from the rest of Germany. Danzig, a purely German city, had been isolated. The Germans who had remained in the territory which became known as Czechoslovakia, had been persecuted, the expressed wish of the Austrian people to unite with Germany, for their own protection against Communist aggression, had been denied. Generally speaking, public opinion in the Western World has been moulded to blame France and the nations which formed the "Little Entente" for insisting on this policy towards Germany. It cannot be denied that the post-war policy of the Allied

Powers towards Germany was in direct contradiction to the principles of "Self-Determination" which had been accepted by the governments involved on behalf of the people who had elected them to manage their affairs.

Each succeeding German democratic chancellor had tried by diplomatic negotiation to obtain redress and had failed. It was their failure to obtain justice by peaceful means that influenced the German people when they swept Hitler to power. Winston Churchill labeled Hitler "that monstrous abortion of lies and deceits," but it cannot truthfully be denied that in 1939 Hitler was trying once again to arrange a peaceful solution of the problems created by the Polish Corridor and Danzig, when the agents of the international conspirators deceived Prime Minister Chamberlain into believing that Hitler had issued an "Ultimatum" to the Polish government, and had moved in his armies to back up his demands. It was this act of deception that caused Mr. Chamberlain to reluctantly advise His Majesty's government to declare war on Germany.

This is a grave accusation to make, but its truth and justification is proved by the fact that exactly the same thing happened all over again towards the end of, and immediately after the end of, World War II.

It would be ridiculous to suppose that sincere Christian statesmen could repeat, and compound, such injustices as those perpetrated by the Treaty of Versailles. But these injustices were repeated by the Allied Powers by the adoption of the policy of *unconditional surrender*, by the adoption of the Stalin-White-Morgenthau Economic Plan, by the partitioning of Germany, by the evil motives behind the German rearmament plan, by the post-war crisis with France, and (as will be explained in another chapter) by the dangerous game that has been played between the international financial interests, and the Soviet and Chinese dictators, since the war with Japan ended. Any unbiased person must admit that it is not the common people of the democracies who demand that their governments carry out such a policy of hatred and injustice against the German people. It is not the elected representatives of the people who conceive these diabolical programmes of persecution and irritation. It is *the evil powers* behind the scenes of government who are responsible. Their evil policy is based on devilish cunning. They know that a house divided against itself must surely fall; that nations divided against each other must surely be subjugated also. *The more human beings are forced to fight each other, the stronger grow those who sit back and push them into the wars.* By allowing this secret scheming, plotting, and planning to continue, we are allowing the forces of evil to make us commit national and racial suicide.

When Hitler tired of waiting for Poland's reply, and of being insulted by the Allied Press, he moved his armies into Poland. Britain then declared war in accordance with her agreement. The criminal nature of the advice given Poland can be realized by the fact that although Britain declared war on Germany, she was powerless to give Poland any direct aid, either naval, military, or with air power.

No less an authority than Lord Lothian, who was in recent years British Ambassador to the United States, stated in the last speech he made at Chatham House, "If the principles of self-determination had been applied in Germany's favour, as it was applied against her, it would have meant the return of Sudetenland, Czechoslovakia, parts of Poland, the Polish Corridor, and Danzig to the Reich."

It is safe to assume that had the British people been permitted to be correctly informed regarding these matters, they would never have permitted war to be declared. But it was "War," not Truth or Justice, upon which the international conspirators were determined.

Even though Britain had declared war, Hitler refused to depart from the policy he had set forth in *Mein Kampf* regarding Britain and her Empire. He ordered the generals, in command of the famous Panzer Corps, to halt on May 22nd, 1940, when they could easily have driven the British armies into the sea or made them surrender. Captain Liddell Hart in his book *The Other Side of the Hill* quotes Hitler's telegram to General Von Kleist:

> The armoured divisions are to remain at medium artillery range from Dunkirk. Permission is only granted for reconnaissance and protective movements.

General Von Kleist was one of the Germans who didn't agree with Hitler's policy towards Britain. He decided to ignore the order. Captain Hart quotes Von Kleist as telling him after the event. "Then came a more emphatic order. I was ordered to withdraw behind the canal. My tanks were kept halted there *for three days.*"[2]

Captain Hart next quotes a conversation which took place between Hitler, Marshall Von Runstedt, and two members of his staff. According to Marshal Von Runstedt:

> Hitler then astonished us by speaking with admiration of the British Empire; of the necessity of its existence, and of the civilization that Britain had brought into the world ... He compared the British Empire with the Catholic Church — saying they were both essential elements of stability in the world. He said all he wanted from Britain was that she should acknowledge Germany's position on the continent; the return of Germany's lost colonies would be desirable but not essential; and he would even support Britain with troops if she should be involved in difficulties anywhere. He concluded by saying that his aim was to make peace with Britain on a basis that she would regard compatible with her honour.

Thus it was that Britain was given time to organize her evacuation forces and get her soldiers home from Dunkirk.

It will be recalled that for the first few months of the Second World War, Hitler did not bomb Britain. While Neville Chamberlain remained Prime Minister, Britain did not bomb Germany. The controlled press called it "A Phony War."

It is quite obvious that two great empires cannot destroy each other if they will not fight. Chamberlain would not initiate the offensive because he was almost convinced that he had been the victim of international intrigue. Mr. Winston Churchill had been given full powers and responsibilities regarding all *naval, military, and air operations.* He decided he would take the initiative.

Churchill conceived the idea of "The Norway Gamble." This poorly planned and executed "combined operation" involved Britain's army, navy, and air force. It was doomed to failure before those involved ever got into action. Even a person with only an elementary knowledge of military strategy would have realized that such an operation could not possibly succeed *unless the invading forces had control of the Kattegat and Skagerrack.* Churchill had this fact pointed out to him by competent naval authorities. Churchill is not a fool, but he went ahead with his project in opposition to his naval and military advisers, exactly as he had done when he sent the Naval Divisions to save Antwerp in 1914, and when he insisted upon the invasion of Gallipoli in 1915. The results in all three of "Churchill's Gambles" were the same. No gains, severe reverses, exceptionally heavy casualties, and loss of valuable equipment and materials. The fiasco of "The Norway Gamble" was not blamed on Churchill, however. His friends, "The international Money-Barons" used their controlled press to release their full powers of hatred, criticism, invective, censure, sarcasm, and satire against the Prime Minister, Mr. Chamberlain. They wanted Chamberlain out of the way so they could put Winston Churchill in his place and turn the "Phony War" into a "Shooting War."

This propaganda campaign forced Chamberlain to resign, exactly as Mr. Asquith had been forced to resign in 1915. Thus, once again, history repeats itself. In May 1940, Churchill again joined hands with the Socialists to form a new government.

Mr. J.M. Spaight, C.B., C.B.E., was the principal assistant secretary to the British Air Ministry during World War II. In his book *Bombing Vindicated*, published in 1944, he reveals that the ruthless bombing of German cities started on May 11th, 1940, the *evening of the day Winston Churchill became Prime Minister*. Britain started the bombing and, as was to be expected, Germany *retaliated*. Thus the war was placed on a destructive basis.

Mr. Spaight also reveals that on September 2nd, 1939, when Mr. Chamberlain was still in office, a declaration had been made by the British and French governments that, "*Only strictly Military objectives, in the narrowest sense of the word, would be bombarded.*" Churchill's policy to bomb open towns and cities has been defended but it can never be justified.

There is another point, not generally known, that needs to be mentioned. It has been recorded that many German generals did not agree with Hitler's policies. The Nazi War Lords knew they had to get Hitler out of the way, and subjugate the Communist Dictatorships controlled by Stalin, before they could carry out their Long-Range Plan for world domination. The all-out war against Britain was not in keeping with their programme. Russian Communism and the Jews had to be subjugated and destroyed before they could launch their attack westward and subjugate Britain and the United States. This was the Nazi Plan, *not* the Fascist policy. The Nazi plan was international in scope. The Fascist cause was national.

A secret meeting of Nazi War Lords was held in May, 1941. They decided they would use Herr Hitler's friendly policy towards Britain to try to get Britain to call off the war against Germany. Rudolf Hess was instructed to fly to Scotland and contact Lord Hamilton and Churchill, so he could try to influence the British government to sign a Peace Treaty.

Hess was instructed to tell the British government that if they would sign a Peace Treaty the German generals would get rid of Hitler and then concentrate all their military power on the destruction of Communism in Russia and other European countries. *Hitler knew nothing of this plan.*

Hess flew to Scotland, but Churchill refused his offer. The German generals then persuaded Hitler to undertake an all-out offensive against Russia, pointing out that until Russia was defeated, they could not extend their military operations outside of Germany without undertaking the serious risk of being stabbed in the back by Stalin when he considered the moment to be opportune.

On June 22nd, 1941, German Forces invaded Russia. Once they took action to crush the Communist menace, Britain and the United States of America immediately pooled their resources to aid Stalin in defeating the German armed forces. Convoys of ships were organized to carry munitions of war to Russia via Murmansk and the Persian Gulf.[3]

During the Irish Rebellion, a security regulation 18-B had been passed by Order in Council to enable the English police to detain and interrogate people they "suspected" might be members of the Irish Republican Army intent on committing acts of annoyance or sabotage. By 1940, the practice had been discontinued for many years.

On May 23rd, 1940, *during the first two weeks of Mr. Churchill's Premiership, he used this obsolete regulation* to arrest all the prominent people who had tried to prevent Britain from being dragged into a war with Germany prior to September 1939, and those who had opposed his policy to turn the Phony War into a Fighting War.

Many hundreds of British subjects were arrested without *any charge* being made against them. They were thrown into prison without *trial* under Regulation 18-B *which deprived them of the rights and privileges of the Habeas Corpus Act.* The Magna Carta was ignored and ridiculed.

These wholesale arrests were made by the police on the unsupported statement of Mr. Herbert Morrison that he, as Secretary of State, "had reasonable cause to believe the said persons had been recently concerned in acts prejudicial to the public safety, in defence of the realm, or in the preparation or instigation of such acts, and that by reason thereof, it was necessary to exercise control over them."

Captain Ramsay, Admiral Sir Barry Domvile, their wives and friends, and hundreds of other citizens were thrown into Brixton prison. Some of them were detained until September 1944.[4] They were treated like criminals, and far worse than prisoners on remand.

Just prior to this outrageous action on the part of those who did the bidding of the international bankers, the press controlled by the Money-Barons had conducted an hysterical propaganda campaign, claiming that Germany had a strong and well-organized Fifth Column in Great Britain, ready to give aid to invading German troops the moment they landed.

Subsequent investigation proved that the very competent British Intelligence Service never produced *at the time, or since, even the flimsiest evidence that any of those arrested were ever engaged in any conspiracy.*

There is plenty of evidence to prove that the newly formed British government, under Churchill, was ordered to take this unjust action against all prominent and influential people in Britain who had voiced their opinion that "International Jewry" had promoted the war between Britain and Germany.

Just before the wholesale arrests were made, Mrs. Nicholson, the wife of Admiral Nicholson, another very distinguished British naval officer, had been arrested as a result of a "smear" campaign. She had stated publicly she thought the plot to involve Britain in war with Germany was the work of the international Jewish bankers. Four charges were actually "framed" against Mrs. Nicholson. She was tried by a judge and jury. She was acquitted on all counts. This action on the part of the judge and jury did not suit those who were determined to persecute people who objected to the international bankers in Britain,

France, and America running the affairs of the nation so as to inveigle them into another Global War. So the antiquated Regulation 18-B was used to put them out of the way. The Phony War became a fighting war. The British and German Empires weakened, as those who started the wars strengthened their positions. The Illuminati laughed up their sleeve.

Notwithstanding the fact that Mrs. Nicholson had been exonerated of all guilt and blame regarding the charges laid against her, *she was among those arrested and imprisoned under Regulation in 18-B in May of 1940.*

Captain Ramsay tells the whole story of the events that led up to his arrest and imprisonment in his book *The Nameless War*. Admiral Sir Barry Domvile tells of his experiences in his book *From Admiral to Cabin Boy*. These are books which should be read by every person interested in the continuance of freedom.[5]

Mr. Neville Chamberlain died in 1940. He was worn out in body and soul fighting "The Secret Powers" who govern from behind the scenes. So also had died Mr. William Pitt. But those who swim with the tide of Illuminism, and do as they are told, usually live to a "Ripe Old Age". They are showered with earthly honour and worldly wealth. One thing is certain: They can't take wealth and honours with them when they die—and after death will come the judgment.

---

[1] The author published the story of the Harwich Striking Force in 1934, under the title *Brass Hats and Bell-Bottomed Trousers*.

[2] The review of *The Manstein Memoirs* in the Globe and Mail, Toronto in 1955 confirms this statement.

[3] I was one of Canada's Naval Control Officers at this time. I felt it my duty to protest the policy which diverted ships that were sorely needed to take supplies to England, and send them to Murmansk. My protest was ignored. The battle to save International Communism had started.

[4] Mr. Herbert Morrison visited Canada in November 1954. He was Chief Speaker at a meeting held in Toronto to raise funds for the support of "Political Zionism." The author is informed that the U.S.A. Government agreed that the British authorities arrest and detain Tyler Kent. This action was against all the accepted principles governing personnel attached to Embassies in foreign countries. This matter was brought up again in the U.S.A. as recently as 1954 but nothing seems to have come of it.

[5] While revising and editing this MS in October 1954, I received a letter from the head of the publishing firm in England who had dared publish Admiral Domviles' book. The letter said in part: "The 'Evil Powers,' regarding which you are so well informed, made things so difficult that I was 'forced' to go out of business after more than 50 years."

CHAPTER SEVENTEEN

The Present Dangers

By studying history it is possible to predict future trends with a certain degree of assurance. History repeats itself because those who direct the WRM do not *change* their Long Range Plans; they simply adapt their policies to suit modern conditions and adjust their plans to take full advantage of the advancement of modern science.

In order to understand the international situation as it is today, we must recall what has happened since Lenin established the totalitarian dictatorship in Russia in 1918. It has been proved that the dictatorship was established to provide the Western Internationalists with the opportunity to put their totalitarian ideas and theories for a universal dictatorship into effect. They wished to iron out any wrinkles by the process of trial and error.

When Lenin died, Stalin took over. At first he was ruthlessly obedient to the dictates of the international bankers. He appointed Béla Kun to put their ideas for the collectivization of farms into effect in the Ukraine. When the farmers refused to obey the edict, five million were systematically starved to death when their grain was taken from them forcibly. This grain was dumped on the markets of the world to aggravate the artificially created depression. Another five million farmers and peasants were sent to forced labour to teach the rest of the subjugated people that the *state* was supreme and the Head of the state their God, whose edicts must be obeyed.

It was not until Stalin began to purge a great number of Jewish Communist leaders, who were undoubtedly Marxists, that Trotsky and other revolutionary leaders knew for certain that he had abandoned the Illuminati and developed imperialistic ambitions.

Stalin's conduct of the revolution in Spain perturbed the Western Internationalists still more, particularly when Serges and Maurin *proved* Stalin was using international Communism to further his own secret plans and imperialistic ambitions.

After Franco won the Civil War, Stalin's conduct was very difficult to understand. Revolutionary leaders in Canada and America just couldn't follow the drastic changes in the Party Line as they had been taught it during their indoctrination into the Marxian theories. When Stalin signed the non-aggression pact with Hitler, after the British and German Empires had been plunged into World War Two, it appeared as if Stalin wanted to do everything within his power to aid Hitler in overrunning Western Europe and destroying the power of the international bankers.

The situation looked so grave from the international bankers' point of view that they decided they had to try to persuade Stalin to abandon his imperialistic ambitions and go along with them in a spirit of peaceful coexistence. They tried to persuade Stalin that it was quite feasible that he should rule the Eastern World by Communism, while they ruled the Western World under a super-government. Stalin asked for proof of their sincerity. This was the beginning of the now much talked-about theory of peaceful coexistence. But peaceful coexistence between two internationalistic groups, or between people who believe in God and those who believe in the devil, is impossible.

By secret communications between Churchill and Roosevelt, which Tyler Kent exposed, it was agreed that Chamberlain should be removed as Prime Minister so that

Churchill could assume office and turn the "Phony" war into a "Hot," and shooting war. They considered this act would convince Stalin of the sincerity of their intentions.

History reveals that Mr. Chamberlain was ousted as Prime Minister in May 1940 in much the same way Asquith was ousted in 1913. Churchill assumed office as Prime Minister on May 11th, 1940. He ordered the R.A.F. to start bombing German cities and towns that same night. Mr. J. M. Spaight, C.B., C.B.E., was principal assistant secretary at the Air Ministry at that time. After the war he wrote a book, *Bombing Vindicated.* In it he justifies Churchill's policy to bomb German cities and towns on the grounds that it was done to "save civilization." The author admits however that Churchill's order was a breach of the agreement entered into by Britain and France on September 2nd, 1939. On that day the Prime Minister of Britain and the President of the French Republic agreed that war must be declared on Germany because of Hitler's invasion of Poland; they also agreed they would NOT bomb German cities and towns and make the German people suffer for the sins of one man. The leaders of the two governments solemnly agreed that bombing should be restricted to strictly military objectives in the narrowest sense of the word.

Since the war, it has been proved that the real reason Churchill bombed German cities, contrary to the agreement, was because the Western international bankers wished to give Stalin a definite assurance that they were sincere in their desire to carry out their suggested policy of peaceful co-existence between Eastern Communism and Western Illuminism.

The bombing of Germany brought about immediate retaliation, and the people of Britain were subjected to an ordeal the like of which had never been experienced since the dawn of creation.

It is difficult for the average citizen to appreciate the depths to which those involved in international intrigue can sink. It will be proved that the Illuminati had no intention of keeping faith with Stalin. It will be proved that Stalin had no intention to keep faith with them. It will also be proved that the Nazi War Lords, while secretly determined to crush both international Communism and international capitalism, actually tried to deceive Churchill into believing they did not have secret plans for world domination by military conquest.

In the spring of 1941, the Nazi War Lords, unknown to Hitler, ordered Hess to fly to Britain and tell Churchill that if he would agree to end the war against Germany, they would guarantee to get rid of Hitler and then destroy Stalin and international Communism. After consultation with Roosevelt, Churchill turned down the offer made by Hess.

The Nazi War Lords then tried to convince the Western internationalists of the sincerity of their intentions by ordering Hitler's assassination. The plot failed and Hitler escaped with his life.

When this act failed to change the minds of those who were secretly instructing Churchill and Roosevelt, the Nazi War Lords decided they must *first* attack Russia and defeat Stalin, and then turn their military forces against Britain and the Americas. They launched their attack against Russia on June 22nd, 1941. Immediately after this happened, both Churchill and Roosevelt announced publicly that they pledged their respective governments to support Stalin to the limit of their resources. Churchill, ever dramatic, said he would shake hands with the Devil himself if he promised to help him destroy German Fascism. He referred to Hitler as "that monstrous abortion of lies and deceits," and yet Churchill must have known that Hitler, for all his faults, was not an internationalist.

This action was calculated to remove from Stalin's mind any doubt he might still have regarding the honesty of the intentions of the Western internationalists, to divide the world into two halves and then live in peaceful coexistence. Roosevelt and Churchill then proceeded to provide Stalin with unlimited aid. They borrowed astronomical sums from the international bankers and paid them interest on the loans. They then charged the principal and interest to the national debts of their two countries so that the tax payers paid for and fought the war fomented by the Illuminati, while the bankers sat back and made hundreds of millions of dollars out of the deal. This extraordinary generosity with the people's blood and money paved the way for the meetings which "The Big Three" subsequently held in Tehran, Yalta, and Potsdam.

Stalin played a very cunning game at Tehran. He made it clear that he still suspected the Western internationalists might be deceptive rather than sincere. He played at being difficult to persuade, and very hard to get. He made outrageous demands. He demanded unreasonable concessions. He implied that in making these demands he was only testing out the sincerity of the men that he knew from long experience were the directors of the international conspiracy. Roosevelt had been well briefed. He gave Stalin everything he asked for. Churchill had to go along or lose the financial backing of the international moneylenders and the military support of the United States.

Then came Yalta. Stalin changed his attitude. He pretended he had been won over. He became the perfect host. Churchill and Roosevelt were wined and dined. Stalin dissolved the Comintern. The Comintern was the executive body which had plotted and planned revolutions in every country. Stalin, Roosevelt, and Churchill drank damnation to the Germans. Roosevelt assured Stalin that after they were through, there wouldn't be enough Germans left to worry about; he is reported to have advocated shooting 50,000 German officers without trial. The controlled press has never stopped harping upon the Nazi policy of genocide against the Jews, but it has been singularly silent in regard to Roosevelt's policy of genocide against the Germans. In return for the dissolution of the Comintern, Roosevelt gave Stalin more concessions. Six hundred million human beings east of Berlin were handed over into Communist bondage.

Churchill acquiesced in everything that Roosevelt and Stalin did. History will prove that at the Yalta meeting, Stalin and Roosevelt had several secret meetings after Churchill had been wined and dined too well to allow him to keep his wits alert. Roosevelt pretended to be friendly with Churchill but, on the evidence of his own son, he often said things, and suggested policies, which showed that secretly he looked upon him with contempt.

Only Churchill can explain *why* he had to sit and listen to Roosevelt's suggestions that Hong Kong be given to Communist China to bribe Mao Tse-Tung to play along with the Western internationalists. How could Churchill profess publicly such a close and sincere friendship for Roosevelt when Roosevelt was constantly repeating that he considered the dissolution of the British Commonwealth necessary to the future welfare of the human race? After all, Hitler thought just the opposite.

But Stalin was nobody's fool. He had been associated with the agents of the international bankers so long that he could read their most secret thoughts like an open book. He knew better than any man alive that they had used Communism to further their totalitarian ideas, so he played them at their own game. During the final stages of the war he forced the Allied Armies to halt and wait until his armies occupied Berlin.

The above statements are proved by the existence of a secret order issued by Stalin to the General Officers of the Soviet Armies to explain his policy. The order is dated February 16th, 1943. It reads:

> The Bourgeois Governments of the Western Democracies, with whom we have entered into an alliance, may believe that we consider it our sole task to throw the Fascists out of our land. We Bolsheviks, *and with us the Bolsheviks of the whole world*, know that our real task will only begin after the second phase of the war is ended. Then will begin for us the Third phase which for us is the last and the decisive one ... the phase of the destruction of world capitalism. OUR SOLE GOAL IS, AND IT REMAINS, THE WORLD REVOLUTION: THE DICTATORSHIP OF THE PROLETARIAT. We have engaged in alliances because this was necessary, to reach the third phase, *but our ways part where our present allies will stand in our way in the achievement of our ultimate aim.*

Stalin did not show his true colours until after he had captured Berlin and occupied Eastern Germany. Then he broke every promise he had made. This turn in events was kept out of the Press because neither Roosevelt nor Churchill wished the public to know how Stalin, the bank robber, murderer and international counterfeiter had put it over them like a blanket.

The Western internationalists just had to bide their time. They realised that if Stalin and Mao TseTung joined forces, the Communist hordes could sweep over the western world like a plague of locusts. They reasoned that Stalin was getting old. They knew he hadn't too long to live. It was better to curry favour with him rather than have him spill the beans and expose the whole diabolical conspiracy.

The Western capitalists considered Stalin's open defiance a serious matter, but they had a trump card up their sleeves. Before playing this card, they instructed Roosevelt to make one more effort to bring Stalin back into line again. Roosevelt offered to grant anything Stalin demanded, as far as the Far East was concerned, if only he would play along with the Western capitalists. The controlled press has persistently reported that Roosevelt gave Stalin the concessions he did in the Far East because his military advisers had told him that it would require two full years of heavy fighting, *after* the collapse of Germany, before Japan could be brought to her knees. This lie is so apparent that it was really unnecessary for General MacArthur to give Roosevelt the lie directly. The American generals knew that Japan had been trying to negotiate peace for a considerable time before Roosevelt made the concessions he did to Stalin.

Once again, Stalin took all he could grab in Manchuria. He again reneged on his promises and renewed his defiant attitude. This time the powers behind the White House administration were really angry. They must have made some suggestion of such a diabolical nature that it even shocked Roosevelt, for he sickened and died. It has been said that he died in the house of Bernard Baruch. The Advisers of the United States government then decided to play their trump card: the atomic bomb. The atomic bombs were dropped on Hiroshima and Nagasaki to indicate to Stalin what was in store for Russia unless he toed the line. The fact that America had atomic bombs had been kept secret. *Japan was already defeated when they were dropped. Surrender was only a few days off.* Over one hundred thousand human beings were sacrificed, and twice that number injured, in Japan, to demonstrate to Stalin that the United States actually did have atomic bombs. Thus it is seen that Churchill ordered the unrestricted bombing of Germany to try to fool Stalin into believing the international capitalists wanted to be friends, and then the U.S.A. bombed Japan with atomic bombs to warn him that he better play along and do as he was told...or else.

Molotov was the one man best able to judge what was going on in Stalin's brain. During the post-war period Molotov was the Soviet's Foreign Minister. He represented the Kremlin at the United Nations for many years. Molotov married the sister of a Russian Jewish émigré, businessman Sam Karp of Bridgeport, Connecticut. Thus Molotov became the connecting link between the Kremlin and the international financiers of the Western World. It has been reliably reported that immediately after Stalin withdrew Molotov from the United Nations, he sent Molotov's wife into exile in Siberia. These acts alone strongly indicate that Stalin had broken with the Western capitalists who had helped put him in power in Russia.

The fact that Tito broke with Stalin after the war ended is further proof that Stalin had determined to go ahead with his imperialistic programme. Tito had always been subservient to the western Financiers who supplied him with all the money he required to establish himself in his present position in central Europe. Churchill's son risked his life on more than one occasion during World War Two by parachuting into Tito's territories to confer with him on behalf of the western powers.

Finally Stalin died or was disposed of. He left this world with his lips sealed like any other gangster. The agents of the Western internationalists, located in Moscow, struck as soon as Stalin died. Beria and Stalin's other trusted lieutenants were done away with. Stalin's son disappeared without a trace.

In order that what was happening in Russia would not appear too obvious, it was arranged that Malenkov should take over temporarily after Stalin's death. He was ordered to decry the Great Stalin and, for a time, he did deflate him in the eyes of the people. Then he changed his tactics. He renewed friendly relations with the Chinese Dictator; he started to make friends with the Russian people; he sponsored the development of a spirit of national pride. By doing so he sealed his own fate.

The Western internationalists countered with a demand that Western Germany be immediately re-armed. France was the stumbling block. Mendes-France was placed in power long enough to have France ratify the agreement to re-arm Germany. Having served his purpose, he was placed amongst the discards as so many others have been.

The situation in the Far East has deliberately been confused but it is not difficult to explain. The Western internationalists had friends in China, just as they had in Russia, but Mao Tse-Tung cannot be considered one of them. He and Stalin had very similar ideas in regard to the Western internationalists. But both the Eastern and Western totalitarian-minded groups had one thing in common: They wished to get rid of Chiang Kai-Shek.

The Western capitalists started a propaganda campaign against Chiang Kai-Shek just as soon as the Japanese war ended. This action had a two-fold purpose. They wanted to prove to Mao Tse-Tung that coexistence with them was feasible and, at the same time, they wished to eliminate the nationalist leader. The press charged that the nationalist government was corrupt; that the nationalist generals were lax, and did not maintain discipline amongst their troops; that the nationalist troops committed pillage and publicly performed rapes. It is only right to admit that many of the charges made against the nationalists were true.

The fact that many officials in the nationalist government in China were proved to be corrupt was used to justify Great Britain's policy to recognize the Communist regime. It was also used by certain United States advisers as the grounds on which they advocated that America withdraw support from Chiang Kai-Shek. What the general public has *not* been told is the fact that, *after* the Communists took over in China, it was proved that most of the high officials who had brought Chiang Kai-Shek and his nationalist government into disrepute were Communist cells who had infiltrated the nationalist government for the purpose of *wrecking it from within*. This statement is substantiated by the fact that many of the nationalist government officials, who came under criticism for corrupt practices, were absorbed into the Communist regime and given favoured positions and accelerated promotions. The Rev. Leslie Millin of Toronto, who was a missionary in China during this period, will vouch for the truth of the above statements.

The way international affairs developed after 1946 would indicate that Stalin did not have atomic weapons at the time of his death. Had he possessed atomic weapons he could have knocked the principal cities of Canada and the United States into a cocked hat.

Churchill has served their purpose as far as the international bankers are concerned. He is growing old and a bit troublesome. He has to be relegated into the discard also. But Churchill has been built up by the propaganda of the western Capitalists as a GREAT man. He is the people's national hero. He couldn't very well be disposed of by a campaign of *L'Infamie*. He couldn't be ridiculed out of office. With rare cunning the Western internationalists disguised their intentions by ordering the Press to organize the greatest tribute a man ever had. On Churchill's eightieth birthday they showered him with gifts and honour. They convinced the vast majority of people that Churchill didn't have an enemy in the world.

Events indicate that both the Communist dictators and the Western internationalists were agreed that Churchill could be an obstacle to the furtherance of their plans. The Communist dictators decided they would use Aneurin Bevan to grease the skids under Churchill. They indicated this to Communists throughout the entire world when the Chinese dictator Mao Tse-Tung entertained Attlee and Bevan at a banquet on their visit to China in 1954. The international press published pictures taken at this banquet.

It is unlikely that one person in a million, other than a Communist, understands the significance of that picture. Attlee was shown as sitting at the head table. Bevan was shown as having been placed at the bottom nearest the door. The general impression was that Attlee was the guest of honour, and that Bevan was considered of very little significance as far as the Communist regime in China, and the Soviets, were concerned. But this is how the public is confused and deceived. In China it is customary to seat *the guest of honour nearest to the door.*

In view of the events recorded, it is reasonably safe to predict that in the near future the following events will take place.

One: With or without his knowledge, the Communist dictators will use Aneurin Bevan to help oust Churchill by attacking his foreign policy in the House of Commons.

Two: The Western internationalists will use Bevan's attacks on Churchill as a lever to get Bevan out of the British Labour party and parliament. At the same time they will get rid of Churchill by casting doubts into the minds of the people regarding his ability to carry on top-level secret negotiations now that he is past eighty. It is possible that the Western internationalists may lift the screen from secret diplomacy just sufficiently to justify those chosen to lead the attack. By doing so, the threat would be implied that if he didn't step down gracefully they would make known *all* that went on behind the scenes at Tehran, Yalta, Potsdam, etc.

Three: It is safe to predict that Churchill will step down immediately after pressure is brought to bear on him. It is equally safe to predict that Bevan will *not* step down. The chances are a hundred to one that Attlee and Deakin will leave, or be removed, from the Labour party in Britain and that Bevan will lead the party against Sir Anthony Eden when he decides to contest a general election after taking over from Churchill.[1]

Four: Roosevelt's son has given a glimpse of the fact that Churchill *had* to play along with his father, had to do as he was told, and even had to profess publicly his friendship with the president after the president had so rudely told him that he favoured the dissolution of the British Commonwealth of nations. This clearly indicates the line of attack the Western internationalists will take to get rid of "The Grand Old Man of British Politics."

The point to remember is this. The Nazi internationalists have, for all intents and purposes, been eliminated from the game. Two totalitarian-minded groups of men remain: the Communist dictators of Russia and China; and the Western capitalists, or internationalists—however one wishes to name them.

Just as long as both groups are satisfied to live in peaceful coexistence, with the world practically divided between them, there will be an uneasy peace. But if the leaders of either side decide that coexistence is too frail a structure upon which to build their respective New Orders, there will be war.

If started by the Eastern Communist dictators, World War Three will begin without any preliminary warning. An international general strike will be called in all capitalistic countries. This action is calculated to produce the paralysis previously referred to. The Communist planes will bomb all industrial centres to knock out the war potential of the United States and Canada and kill as many of the population as possible in order to bring about speedy surrender and subjugation. Britain will likely get the same treatment. Nerve gas may be used on any industrial areas the enemy does not wish to destroy. Soviet forces will occupy the mining districts of northern Canada from coast to coast. The occupied areas will be used as bases of operation against the southern objectives. The international general strike will tie up shipping in every port in the world, making it impossible for supplies to reach the people of Great Britain. A blockade of the British Isles by Soviet submarines will stop any leaks. The people of Britain will be starved into submission four weeks after the outbreak of hostilities. The members of the Communist underground in all cities in the western world will evacuate target areas immediately before the attacks. The underground armies will return and take over the devastated areas as soon as the "All-Clear" has been given. The Communist Fifth Column will round up and liquidate all people whose names are on the black list. Thus will the directors of the Western internationalists be got rid of in much quicker time than they got rid of their Nazi opponents by means of the Nuremberg Trials.

On the other hand, if the Western internationalists become convinced that an attack is to be made upon them by the Communist dictators, then they will force the western democracies into another World War, in order that they may get in the first blow. As a prelude to their attack, the public will be made aware of the dangers of international Communism. The danger to Christian democracy will be emphasized. The atheistic-materialists, who have the western world in economic bondage, will call for a Christian Crusade. They will justify their atomic attacks upon Russia and China as Churchill justified his attack on Germany. They will say it was necessary to save our civilization. But let's not fool ourselves. Regardless of how the case may be presented to the public, the fact will remain that if World War Three is allowed to take place, it will be fought to decide whether Eastern Communism takes over the entire world or whether the Western capitalists will continue to rule the international roost.

If World War Three is permitted to take place, the devastation will be so extensive that internationalists will continue to justify their contentions that ONLY a world government, backed up by an international police force, can solve the various national and international problems without resorting to further wars. This argument will appear very logical to many people who overlook the fact that both the Eastern Communist leaders, and the Western capitalist leaders, intend to ultimately bring into effect THEIR ideas for an atheistic-totalitarian dictatorship.

People who wish to remain FREE can follow only one plan of action. They must support Christianity against ALL forms of atheism and secularism. They must support private responsible enterprise against cartels and combines. They must support those who advocate "The New Economy" against those who would continue with the old.

When a person is in doubt regarding the right and wrong of anything, all he or she needs to do to solve his or her uncertainty is recite the first half of the Lord's Prayer SLOWLY and contemplate on the meaning of those wonderful words of wisdom. "*Our Father...Who art in heaven... hallowed be Thy name...Thy kingdom come...Thy will be done...on earth as it is in heaven.*" It doesn't require more than a few minutes to decide if any act to be performed individually or collectively is in accordance with the Will of God, or furtherance of the machinations of the Devil.

If we intend to save the future generations, from the fate being prepared for them by the forces of evil, we must take IMMEDIATE ACTION...THERE IS NO TIME TO LOSE. The reader may well ask: "But what action must we take?"

That is a very good question. If the answer wasn't provided, there would be no justification for the publication of this book. Far too many men spend a great deal of time damning this and damning that. They are anti this and anti that. But very few speakers or writers who condemn an idea, an organization, or a movement, offer practical solutions to the problems, or make suggestions to bring to an end the evils exposed.

First: We must as individuals recognize the spiritual issues involved. Once again the Scriptures advise us how to accomplish this purpose. Ephesians chapter 6, verses 10 to 17, tells us:

> Brethren be strengthened in the Lord and in the whole of His power. Put on the whole armour of God, that you may be able to stand against the wiles of the devil. *For our wrestling is not against flesh and blood, but against Principalities, against Powers, against the rulers of the darkness of this world, against the spiritual forces of wickedness on high.* Therefore take up the armour of God that you may be able to resist in the evil day, and having done all, to stand. Stand therefore, having girded your loins with TRUTH, and having put on the breast-plate of righteousness, and your feet shod with the preparation of the Gospel of peace. Above all taking up the shield of *Faith*, with which you may be able to quench all the fiery darts of the *wicked*. And take the helmet of salvation, and the sword of the spirit, which is, THE WORD OF GOD.

Second: We must take *practical* steps and use constitutional means to counteract the threat of both international Communism and international capitalism, and any other subversive ideologies which may try to destroy TRUE Christian democracy. In order to carry out the mandate in the above Gospel we must do the following things:

A.   *Demand monetary reforms:* Because selfishness, greed and the desire for power are the roots from which all evil grows, it is only logical that constitutional means be instituted to take away the wealth, and curb the powers, of the leader, of all atheistic-materialistic groups who usurped it from the governments of the people in the first place. This being the TRUTH, the tax-payers have a legal right to demand that their elected governments redress the wrongs committed against them, put an end to all forms of usury, and reimburse their treasury departments to the extent of the loans floated during the last century to fight wars fomented to further the interests of those who loaned the money and charged interest on these loans. If this advice is followed, the proletariat will have restored true democracy and the Soviet and Chinese dictators would have no excuse to disguise their imperialistic ambitions under the cloak of anti-capitalism.

B.   *Monetary controls:* The electors must insist that the issue of money, and the control thereof, be placed back in the hands of the government where it rightfully belongs. By government is meant the top-level executive body chosen from the elected representatives because of their qualifications to conduct the affairs of the nation in an efficient and business-like manner, basing their decisions on democratic justice and Christian charity.

C.   *Punitive action:* The electorate can justifiably demand that heavy penalties be imposed on all those found guilty of corruption and graft, because these two evil practices are the principal means used by the agents of *all* revolutionary organizations to subvert, or force, others into doing their will. All subversive organizations must be outlawed and all people proved to be members must be made liable to punishment provided by the law.

Those who advocate the violent overthrow of constitutional government do so in order that they may usurp wealth and power without having to work for it. Their punishment should therefore consist of performing manual labour and/or public services. Their hours should be extended 25 percent beyond the union limits, and their pay should be 25 percent below the union rates. The period of their detention should be decided by the way they improve from their negative attitude towards society and religion.

D.   *Diplomatic negotiations:* Because the agents of the international conspiracy always work behind the scenes of government, and always use SECRET meetings and diplomacy to further their own plans and ambitions, secret negotiation should not be allowed under any circumstances. If government is to be "Of the people; by the people; for the people;" then the people have every right to know every detail of what is going on.

E.   *Christian Crusade:* Laymen of all Christian denominations should unite in the Name of God to put an end to the bigotry and misunderstanding that enables anti-Christian ideologies to keep Christians divided and at logger-heads. The house divided within itself will fall. The Crusade should be organized for the purpose of educating the public in regard to the methods used by those who direct atheistic-materialistic ideologies. Special attention should be given to interesting the youth of our nations in the movement, in order that they may be protected from the subversive actions of the agents of the conspirators. The Crusaders should be trained to take a POSITIVE approach when dealing with those who have joined subversive organizations, either willingly or because of ignorance. Abusing, knocking, or condemning a person will only increase their resistance, making them more anti-social.

By first gaining their confidence, the Crusader is in position to prove to them that the heads of all atheistic-materialistic ideologies only use others as "Pawns in the Game" to further their secret plans and ambitions. Once a person is convinced that he or she will be thrown into the discard just as soon as the directors of their movement consider they have outgrown their usefulness, this will hurt their pride and cause them to reflect upon the wisdom of their behaviour. Having once created doubt in their minds, it is then possible to convince them by supplying them with suitable literature on the subject. It was to supply this need that *Pawns In The Game* was published. A religious revival amongst the members of all Christian denominations is essential in order to change men's thinking in regard to the values and importance they place on worldly possessions. The hearts of men must be turned towards love of the Almighty God. We must learn once again to take a real delight in rendering Him service and in performing His Holy Will. The National Federation of Christian Laymen has been organized to put this idea into action.

F.   *United Nations:* Because the constitution of the United Nations comes up for revision this year, possible changes may be recommended. It is important, therefore, that all those who oppose internationalism in any form organize political pressure groups in all parties to urge that the delegates of the Christian-democratic nations do not lend themselves in any way to suggestions favouring the trial of a World Government, regardless of whether it is called a super-nationalist government or disguised in any other way. Churchill's suggestion for a United States of Europe was only a move in the direction of internationalism. Only he can say whether it was intended to help the Eastern Communists or the Western capitalists.

G.   *Illegal traffic and trade:* Because the subversive Fifth Columns and undergrounds are organized, hidden, and subsist in the underworlds of large cities, and because no revolutionary effort can hope to succeed without the full cooperation of a well organized, properly trained, fully equipped, and well disciplined Fifth Column, or *underground* organization, it is necessary that public opinion be organized to demand that all those engaged in illegal traffic and trade, or criminally connected with the underworld, shall be arrested and brought to trial regardless of what their political affiliations may be, or what position they hold in society. The public must be organized to give support to all honest police officers and law administrators. Public opinion expressed on the floor of the Houses of Parliament must insist that the underworld be CLEANED up, and not just raided and scattered. The policy of raiding and scattering underworld characters has only resulted in creating a hundred dens of iniquity where only one existed before. Those convicted should be treated as recommended in subsection 'C'.

H.   *Publicity:* Christian laymen must be organized to counteract the propaganda of those who advocate internationalism and the atheistic-materialistic ideologies. Local branches should be organized to insist that subversive propaganda be eliminated from the press, the air, and T.V. programmes. They should demand that time and space be made available so the Christian democratic way of life may be presented to the people. It is unfortunately TRUE that it is several centuries since Christian democracy functioned properly.

I.   *Defeatism:* Every effort must be made to counteract the efforts of those who preach defeatism. They usually argue that there is nothing that can be done to correct the existing conditions. They suggest that since the pending fate is inevitable, it is no use worrying. The attitude of the Defeatist is like that of the professional rapist who advises his intended victim that, because her fate is inevitable, she might as well relax and enjoy it. Those who claim that there is nothing we can do to escape totalitarianism ignore the fact that God exists and is interested only in the destiny of man. People who get discouraged must be reminded that the only way they can save their immortal souls is to keep on fighting against the Forces of Evil, thus giving service to God. They must be made to realize that they won't be judged according to their achievements and victories, but solely on the merits of the effort they put into the Crusade.

J.   *Brotherly Love:* Because God has provided mankind with all he requires for this earthly existence, there is no logical reason why some of his creatures should live in opulence while others starve to death. The theories of the new economists should be tried out to devise better methods for the more equitable distribution of the necessities of life. Once these have been assured to all human beings, it will be a comparatively simple matter to persuade those who have too much to share it with those who have decidedly less and a greater need. To share what we have with others in need provides the greatest happiness it is possible to enjoy on this earth. By living in accordance with the plan of God, economic conditions would improve to such an extent that the establishment of homes, and the raising of families, could be undertaken in reasonable security. Conditions of "fear" and "uncertainty" would be abolished.

K.   *Military Preparedness:* Military preparedness is absolutely necessary just as long as the conditions exposed in this book are allowed to continue. Everyone who accepts the hospitality of a country, and enjoys the privileges of citizenship, should be prepared to defend that country from aggressors, be they external foes or the enemy within. The only justification for fighting a war is to prevent subjugation by the enemy, on the rational argument that as long as we have some semblance of freedom left, there is still hope that we can overcome the forces of evil and re-establish true Christian democracy.

L.   *Internal Security:* The best way to strengthen the internal security of any nation is to build up a strong and efficient Civil Defence organization. To permit of rapid development, Civil Defence should be made part and parcel of the national internal security system. As such, it should be a Federal project and responsibility. This suggestion is particularly applicable to Canada because the Minister of Justice, supported by the Royal Canadian Mounted Police, is charged with the responsibility for the nation's internal security.

Civil Defence is the organizing and training of the civilian population into auxiliary units to augment the regular departments which render public service during normal conditions. Civil Defence workers are trained how to protect themselves and the communities in which they live in the event of attack by an enemy. Because our only potential enemies use their Fifth Column and underground organizations to overthrow the constituted government by revolutionary action, and subjugate the population by means of terrorism, it stands to common sense that Civil Defence should be organized as a counter-revolutionary organization. The Civil Defence special police and intelligence units should therefore be trained under the supervision of the R.C.M.P., so they could cooperate with them to ensure our internal security during any emergency.

M.   *Action. There is no time to lose:* In reading this book you have faced the challenge; your response to the action outlined, undertaken with a strong faith in God, will determine the future of humanity, and bring about the overthrow of the forces of *evil* which plot to destroy our Christian democratic way of life. The task is not beyond our capabilities. We must remember that the Devil's important nucleus of evil in this world at the present time is centred in no more than about three hundred masterminds.

N.   *Faith, Hope and Charity:* We must never forget that the Christian religion is based on Faith, Hope and Charity, while all atheistic ideologies are based on doubt, hatred, and despair. Almighty God has permitted us to GRADUALLY solve many of the mysteries of NATURE in order that we would use rather than abuse these extraordinary benefits. We can now use or misuse atomic energy. If we allow it to be misused, the powers of evil will undoubtedly kill off one-half the human race and cripple most of the others. We can rest assured that amongst those who survive will be the agents of the *powers of evil.*

Almighty God has provided the human race with all we need to live. He has provided for our comfort and reasonable pleasures. It is our duty to see that all members of the human race share equally in the bounties and blessing provided by Almighty God. There should never be a time when the granaries of the western world are bursting at the seams, while the people of the Far East are dying by the millions from starvation. We must share freely and generously with others what we have above our own requirements, because it is certain that *we cannot take anything with us when we die.*

Our Policy

1. We advocate Christianity and oppose illuminism and atheistic-materialism. We hold out the hand of friendship to ALL who worship God and oppose Satanism.

2. We support Nationalism and oppose Internationalism of any kind.

3. We advocate responsible private industry and oppose cartels and combines.

4. We advocate Loyalty to the Constitution and oppose all kinds of subversive activities.

5. We support lawful authority and oppose organized crime.

6. We advocate the practice of ethics in trade and commerce and oppose all forms of illegal traffic and trade.

7. We recommend brotherly love amongst all God-fearing people and oppose bigotry in any form.

8. We stand for Liberty and oppose licentiousness.

9. We stand for Freedom as opposed to Dictatorships and tyranny.

10. We advocate justice for all and favours for none.

11. We recommend that punishment should be made to fit the crime.

12. We advocate National Preparedness against internal and external foes.

13. We advocate active interest and participation in political, economic, health and educational matters as opposed to apathy, indifference, and despair.

14. We work so that Almighty God's plan for creation may be put into practice in this earth.

Glossary

Agentur: Well-bred, exceptionally clever-minded individuals whom the Illuminati select in early youth, educate, and then indoctrinate into the ideology of secular materialism. They are then trained and made capable to act as experts and specialists behind the scenes of ALL governments. The Illuminati thus obtain control AT THE TOP of all legitimate and subversive movements, as well as all levels of politics, economics, finance, industry, the social sciences, and religion. By exercising this control they can persuade, or force, executives to adopt policies which further their own secret plans to bring about a One-World Government whose powers they are organized and ready to usurp.

Anarchists: People who believe a person has the "Right" to do as he or she pleases without restraint. They claim there should be no government, police force, or code of law. Their motto is, "The less government, the better."

"Apparatus": Code name for the National organization of the Communist Party.

ASDIC: All manner and types of anti-submarine detection devices and weapons.

Auto-da-fe: The extreme torture of the Inquisition.

Black Book: A book in which the directors of the international conspiracy kept a record of the private lives of influential people, together with a detailed report of their characteristics, faults, and failings. The information is used to "persuade" people into doing the bidding of the Conspirators either because of fear of exposure or for the sake of obtaining more luxury and material rewards.

Black Markets: The markets in the underground and underworld organizations in all large centers of population where smuggled and stolen goods are disposed of. The "Black Markets" are the biggest single cause of bankruptcy and business failures.

Black Nazism: The hard core of Aryan War Lords who believe in the Deity of Man. They don't believe in God or a Supreme Being. They believe the State should be all-powerful; that only men of Aryan blood should rule; and that all others should be forced to serve the State.

Blood-Lust: The last degree of fanaticism when only blood will satisfy the sadistic desires of men and women who have already satiated their animal passions. It is a condition deliberately aroused in "The Mob" by revolutionary leaders as a prelude to introducing their "Reign of Terror."

Bolsheviks: Followers of Lenin; the revolutionary party which overthrew the Soviet formed by the Mensheviks, and the republican government formed by Kerensky, in Russia in the early half of 1917. The Bolsheviks brought about the Dictatorship of the Proletariat, which Lenin promptly turned into a Luciferian dictatorship. Most of the Mensheviks and Bolsheviks were liquidated after they had served their purpose.

Brainwashing: A combination of scientifically applied mental anguish and physical torture used in conjunction with hypnotism, drugs, and psychiatric treatments to induce a person to give up certain beliefs and accept others. It is the exact opposite of God's gift of a "Free Will" to human beings. A common term for psychopolitics as developed into a science by Sigmund Freud.

Cabala: Originates back in antiquity and has to do with Black Magic and Devil Worship. A modern version was announced in the 10th century as a mysterious Hebrew or Jewish theosophy. It was carried to great excesses as Cabalists among the Rabbis claimed they could explain the hidden meanings of the 'Sacred Scriptures pretending to read signs, letters, forms, and numbers. It is still practiced today in a combination of pagan and heathen rituals used in "The Black Mass" by those who practice Satanism. It is used in the ritual of Illuminism also.

Capitalism: The word is generally used to indicate or identify the system by which selfish and greedy men use ruthless means to obtain more wealth and greater power regardless of whom they crush or brush aside. Capitalism is one half of the international conspiracy, the other half being international Communism. International Capitalism destroys private responsible enterprise. The international Capitalists use combines and cartels and finance the illegal traffic trade (used by Communists and other subversives) to put legitimate business and private enterprise into bankruptcy.

Cartels: International agreements between those who produce certain commodities which ensure a profit for the participants, regardless of circumstances or world conditions.

Classicism: Old-fashioned ideas "whereof the memory of man runneth not to the contrary." Ancient and antiquated ideas. Wrong ideas generally accepted as sound.

Combines: National and international agreements entered into by industrialists and financiers by which they control the production, distribution, and price of commodities, and restrict trade to their own benefit and to the detriment of the public welfare and interest.

Cominform: Top-level officials organized to take over the duties of plotting and planning popular world revolution after Stalin dissolved the Comintern in 1944, a pretended gesture of good-will towards the Western Powers.

Comintern: The Communist Executive Committee which, prior to 1944, was charged with the responsibility of plotting, planning, and directing world revolution.

Communist "Cells": Groups of three to five people who put into effect the subversive orders issued by the Central Committee of the Communist Party in the country in which they reside.

Council of Thirteen: The supreme executive of the Illuminati.

Darwinism: The theory that man evolved from the ape species and was not created by God in his own image and likeness, i.e., with a soul, intellect, and free will.

Fascism: The original organization was formed in 1919 in Italy to counteract International and Atheistic Communism. It did a tremendous amount of good for the Italian people until the Agentur of the Illuminati obtained control AT THE TOP, and gradually changed the policies of the leaders, until they were led into the various conspiracies which enabled the Illuminati to throw the British and French, German and Italian peoples at each others throats again in 1939.

Forces of Evil: Every person who thinks and acts contrary to the Commandments of God and the teachings of His Divine Son Jesus Christ. As Christ said: "He who is not with me, is against me." There can be no compromise between "Good" and "Evil" forces.

Genocide: The practice of destroying a whole race of people to obtain control over their domains. The U-boat blockade of Britain was an act of genocide which just failed in its purpose.

Gestapo: A secret police force controlled by Dictators who have usurped the powers of government.

Glass Club: A luxurious den of iniquity used as an espionage centre controlled by agentur of the Illuminati in London, England, 1914-1918.

God: The Supreme Being—Creator of Heaven and earth.

Goyim: A contemptuous term meaning "human cattle." Some claim it is the term used by Jewish internationalists to refer to Gentiles. The author believes it is the term used by the Illuminati to refer to all those who are marked down for subjection, regardless of Race or Creed.

Heaven: Wherever the Rule of Almighty God prevails. There could be heaven on earth as well as in heaven if we so desire.

Hell: Wherever the Rule of Satan prevails. There is Hell on earth everywhere the powers of Satan have been permitted to prevail.

Illegal Traffic and Trade: All business transactions, and professional practices, which are outside the law. People who engage in unlawful practices constitute the subversive "Underground" and are members of the "Underworld."

Illuminati: Members of Grand Orient Lodges who have been initiated into "The Order and Sect of the Illuminati." They are a small but powerful group which includes international-minded bankers, industrialists, scientist, military and political leaders, educators, economists, etc. They are men who have accepted the Luciferian plan for the rule of Creation as being preferable to that of Almighty God. They worship Lucifer as required by Weishaupt in his book *Morals and Dogmas*. They acknowledge the authority of no mortal except their leader. They give loyalty to no nation. They direct the CONTINUING LUCIFERIAN CONSPIRACY to prevent God's plan for the rule of Creation being put into practice; they plot to obtain absolute control of this world and everything in it. They use ALL subversive movements to divide masses of the people into opposing camps on political, social, racial, economic, and religious issues, then arm them, and make them fight and destroy each other. They hope to make humanity follow this process of self-destruction until all existing political and religious institutions have been eliminated. They then plan to crown THEIR leader King-despot of the entire world and enforce the Luciferian dictatorship with Satanic despotism.

Illuminism: The name given the special rites as written by Professor Adam Weishaupt of Frankfort, Germany, at the instigation of the men who in 1773 constituted the High Priests of Satanism. The ritual of the Illuminati was introduced into the Bavarian Grand Lodge in 1776 as a preliminary step towards infiltrating the Grand Orient Lodges into French Freemasonry for the purpose of furthering the plans for "The Great French Revolution" which was scheduled to take place in 1789.[1] A modern version of "The Black Mass" was introduced by General Albert Pike in 1871.

[1] While this book was in galley proof stage Mr. Ron Gostick, editor of Canadian Intelligence Service, was so impressed by the fact that my independent research reached

the same conclusions as Mrs. Nesta Webster in Secret Societies and Subversive Movements, a book I had not read, that he made arrangements to obtain some copies from England. He gave me a copy, and turning to Weishaupt on pages 285-7, I find that this modern historian agrees with what I say in this regard.

Internationalists: All who advocate doing away with National Sovereignty and favor a One-World Government. They include "world federalists."

International Moneylenders: The Illuminati and their agentur who by reason of their cartels and combines, and the use of usury have obtained control of the monetary systems and economy of the so-called "Free Nations." They lead the people of those Nations slowly into economic bondage, so they can ultimately enslave them body, mind, and soul.

Jews: The word is used in its generally accepted sense. The majority of those who control the wealth and power in this world use Jews and Gentiles alike to further their evil secret plans and ambitions.

"Joint Stock Company principle": An organization in which the identity of the real directors is never made known to the public. It means "Secret government."

Junkers: Young German nobles who followed military careers out of a sense of National pride and duty. They are not to be confused with the "Black Nazis."

Lesser Brethren: All Jews who are under the Evil control of the False Priests and Elders in their communities. They differ in no way from the masses of the Gentiles who have been led into revolutions and wars by the same "Evil Experts" and "Advisers" who usurped control of our governments.

L' Infamie: The practice of character assassination. The use of calumny, detraction, lies, and slanders to ruin those who try to make God's will and the TRUTH known. Commonly known as "The Smear."

Luxury: Comfort, belongings, extravagances, and possessions purchased beyond a person's ordinary needs. Things bought with money which should be used to benefit others less fortunate than themselves. Luxury is the opposite of Charity.

Mammon: The God of Gold and Evil Power: Materialism.

Marijuana: A drug derived from Indian Flax, generally used in cigarettes to bring about artificial stimulation of the animal instincts in human beings and to deaden the finer susceptibilities in young people and remove restraints and inhibitions.

May Laws: Severe laws passed by the Russian Government restricting the lives and activities of the Jews in retaliation for terrorism practiced by Jewish revolutionaries.

Materialism: Consideration only for this world's goods and pleasures. The disbelief in all spiritual values.

Miscegenation: Calculated results of indiscriminate intermarriage between white and colored people.

Modern Schools: Those in which Secularism is taught; it teaches that our human interests should be limited to the concerns of the present life.

National Debt: The accumulation of principal and interest on loans forced on nations to fight wars which were fomented by the people who had the money to lend. National debt was instituted by the International Bankers for the purpose of leading masses of the people into economic bondage in order that they—could then tell them how they must live, what they must think and do, and when they must die.

National Socialist: The opposite to International Socialists.

Nationalist: A person who believes in National autonomy and the right of the people to elect and direct the policy of their government.

Nazi: The extreme "Right" of the Nationalist Party, the same as the Illuminati are the extreme "Left" of the Internationalist group.

Nihilists: The executioners used by all conspirators who aspire to control of a world dictatorship. History reveals these assassins are to be found in all classes of society. They try if possible to make the murders they commit look like accidents, suicides, or natural deaths.

Obscene Movies: These are "Black Market" films. They illustrate the acts described in the very worst of pornographic literature in full-length films showing every type of subversion and perversion. They are owned and controlled in Canada by the agentur of the Illuminati rather than by Communist "Cells." Two distributors are top-level business executives.

Premier-Dictators: The Prime Ministers and Presidents of so-called democratic Nations who rule by "Orders-in-Council" and decide their government policies in accordance with the "advice" (orders) given them by "The Illuminati" through their "Experts," "Specialists," and "Advisers" with whom they have been surrounded. They do not ask for plebiscites.

Protocols: The original written record of the conspiracy by which the Illuminati intend to use internationalists of all kinds to further their secret ambitions to form a World Dictatorship.

Psychological Warfare: The war for the minds of men. Those who put it into practice try to make others believe what they tell them to believe regardless of whether it is true or false, good or evil. It is hooked up with propaganda. Every negative thing we see or hear is propaganda for the forces of Evil.

Racketeers: All those who engage in illegal tragic and trade and prostitute their professional knowledge and skills regardless of their race or creed or standing in society

Reign of Terror: The period in every revolution when the directors stir up blood-lust in "The Mob" and turn them loose on the public so that vast majority will be reduced to one common level by degradation, physical suffering, and mental anguish. The Illuminati consider it the quickest and cheapest way to subjugate the people and make them obedient to their edicts.

Satan: Lucifer's Prime Minister, an actual supernatural being with great powers for everything Evil. He is determined to win the souls of men away from Almighty God. Satanists claim he is the elder son of God the Father, and that Christ was the younger son of God. Satanism teaches that Satan was in the RIGHT when he quarreled with Christ.

Secularism: Teaches that we should only concern ourselves with the matters of this life.

Subversion: Every act, every word, and every deed which is against the Commandments of God and subversive to our lawfully constituted government. Every book and picture, every spoken word, which leads persons to believe they are entitled to use force to achieve any desired goal.

Theism: Belief in a personal Deity.

Underground: The revolutionary Fifth Column and subversive organizations planned to overthrow the existing government.

Underworld: The milieu where anti-social people live and where illegal traffic and trade flourishes. A secret subversive empire within the State.

WHAT READERS HAVE SAID

The Very Rev. Monsgr. **W.C. McGrath**, Mamaronack, N.Y.

Pawns In the Game is the most profound study of the International Conspiracy I have ever seen. Such a book has never before been written. I pray it may be read by millions of the hapless Pawns while there is still time to avert disaster.

Admiral Sir **Barry Domvile**, KBE., C.B., C.M.G., R.N. Ret'd.

I am sure the book will do much good and make people use their idle brains. The general effect of your books is bound to help in the fight against evil providing you can get circulation.

[Admiral Domvile was one of Britain's greatest fighting men. He was at one time Director of the Naval Intelligence Service.]

Rev. **Leslie Millin**, Chinese Missionary

I went through the Chinese revolution but failed to realize what it was all about until I read your book. Now the "Causes" which produced such "Effects" are perfectly clear. I use material in your books in my lectures.

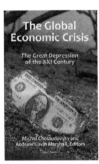
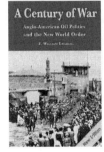

Seeds of Destruction: The Hidden Agenda of Genetic Manipulation. A corporate gang is out to control of the world by patenting our food. Inside the boardrooms and science labs, a world of greed, intrigue, corruption and coercion. 340 pp. $~~$25.95~~ **$19.95**.

Six by Webster Griffin Tarpley

9/11 Synthetic Terror: Made in USA — by a network of moles, patsies, killers, corrupt politicians and media. The authoritative account of 9/11. "Strongest of the 770+ books I have reviewed" – R. Steele. 5th ed., 569 pp., $~~$19.95~~ **$14**.

George Bush: The Unauthorized Biography Vivid X-ray of the oligarchy dominating U.S. politics, with a full narrative of GWHB's long list of crimes. How Skull-and-Bonesmen Bush and Brown Bros. Harriman made fortunes building up Hitler's war machine. Bush Sr. linked to Iran-Contra, Watergate, and war crimes like luring Iraq to attack Kuwait. 700 pp, $~~$19.95~~ **$11**.

Barack H. Obama: the Unauthorized Biography The abject corruption of a Wall Street lackey, with a richly detailed profile of the finance oligarchy. 595 pp, $~~$19.95~~ **$18**.

Obama – The Postmodern Coup: Making of a Manchurian Candidate. The Obama puppet's advisors are radical reactionaries. This work distills decades of astute political insight and analysis. 320 pp, $~~$15.95~~ **$6**.

Surviving the Cataclysm**, **Your Guide through the Greatest Financial Crisis in Human History, by W.G. Tarpley. Detailed history of the financier oligarchy who plunder our nation. How to cope with the crisis. 668 pp, $~~$25~~ **$16**.

Just Too Weird: Bishop Romney and the Mormon Putsch against America; Polygamy, Theocracy, and Subversion, by Webster Tarpley. 284 pp., $~~$14.95~~ **$10**.

History

Two by George Seldes: *1,000 Americans Who Rule the USA* (1947, 324 pp, $~~$18.95~~ **$13**) and *Facts and Fascism* (1943, 292 pp., $~~$15.95~~ **$12**) by the great journalist, whistleblower on the plutocrats who keep the media in lockstep, and finance fascism.

Propaganda for War: How the US was Conditioned to Fight the Great War Propaganda by Britain and her agents like Teddy Roosevelt sucked the USA into the war to smash the old world order. 350 pp and $~~$18.95~~ **$15**.

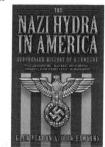

Inside the Gestapo: Hitler's Shadow over the World. Intimate, fascinating tale of ruthless intrigue, and geopolitics. 287 pp, $~~$17.95~~ **$14**.

The Nazi Hydra in America: Suppressed History of a Century. US plutocrats launched Hitler, then recouped Nazi assets to erect today's police state. Fascists won WWII -- they ran both sides. "Shocking and sobering... deserves to be widely read." – Howard Zinn. 700 pp, $~~$19.95~~ **$12**.

Sunk: The Story of the Japanese Submarine Fleet, 1941-1945. The bravery of doomed men in a lost cause, against impossible odds. 300 pp, $~~$15.95~~ **$13**.

Terrorism and the Illuminati: A 3000-Year History. "Islamic" terrorists are tentacles of the Illuminati. 332 pp, $~~$16.95~~ **$13**.

Psychology: Brainwashing

What is brainwashing? What traits help us resist? Self-directedness, sense of purpose, loved ones...

The Rape of the Mind: The Psychology of Thought Control, Menticide and Brainwashing. Tools for self-defense against torture or social pressure and conditioning. 320 pp, $16.95 $12.

The Telescreen: An Empirical Study of the Destruction of Consciousness. Mass media brainwash us with consumerism and war propaganda. Fake history, news, issues. 199 pp, $14.95 $10.

Conspiracy, NWO

Corporatism: the Secret Government of the New World Order by Prof. Jeffrey Grupp. Corporations control all world resources, media, information and institutions. Their New World Order is the "prison planet." 408 pp, $16.95. 408 pp, $16.95 $12.

Descent into Slavery? How the banksters took over America and the world. 310 pp, $16 $11.

Dope Inc.: Britain's Opium War against the United States. "The Book that Drove Kissinger Crazy." Underground Classic, new edition. 320 pp, $19.95 $15.

Final Warning: A History of the New World Order. Classic, in-depth research into the Great Conspiracy: the Fed, the CFR, Trilateral Commission, Illuminati. 360 pp, $14.95 $15.

How the World Really Works by A.B. Jones. Crash course in conspiracy offers digests of 11 classics like *Tragedy and Hope, Creature from Jekyll Island*. 336 pp, $15 $9.00.

Conspiracy: False Flag Operations

Conspiracies, Conspiracy Theories and the Secrets of 9/11, German best-seller explores conspiracy in history, before tackling 9/11. 274 pp, $14.95 $9.00.

Gladio, NATO's Dagger at the Heart of Europe: *The Pentagon-Mafia-Nazi Terror Axis.* The blood-red thread of terror by NATO death squads across Europe, 1945 to 2012. 488 pp, $29.95 $17.

Terror on the Tube: Behind the Veil of 7/7, an Investigation. The only book with the glaring evidence that all four Muslim scapegoats were completely innocent. 322 pp, $17.77 $15.

Truth Jihad*: My Epic Struggle Against the 9/11 Big Lie.* Kevin Barrett's seriously funny story. 224 pp, $9.95 $5.00.

E-Books:

9/11 Synthetic Terror; Barack Obama Unauth. Biography; Fall of the Arab Spring; Gladio; Iraq Lie; ISIS IS US; JFK-911; Just Too Weird; Kennedy Assassination Cover-up; Killing Us Softly; Nazi Hydra; NWOIA in Action; Numbers of the Gods; Obama the Postmodern Coup; Rape of the Mind; Subverting Syria; Surviving the Cataclysm; Target: China; Unmasking ISIS

~ **PROGRESSIVEPRESS.COM** ~
San Diego, California

ProgRESSive

Contacts -2.25- Rain Barrell
Liquid Bleach
Cat Food Cans

Printed in Great Britain
by Amazon